Robert F.
KENNEDY:
Apostle of Change

ROBERT F. KENNEDY:

APOSTLE OF CHANGE

by
Douglas Ross

TRIDENT PRESS   NEW YORK

ACKNOWLEDGMENTS

Reprinted by permission of Harper & Row, Publishers, from *The Enemy Within* by Robert F. Kennedy. Copyright, ©, 1960, by Robert F. Kennedy.

Reprinted by permission of Harper & Row, Publishers, from *Just Friends and Brave Enemies* by Robert F. Kennedy. Copyright, ©, 1962, by Harper & Row, Publishers.

Reprinted by permission of Harper & Row, Publishers, from *The Pursuit of Justice* by Robert F. Kennedy. Copyright, ©, 1964, by Harper & Row, Publishers.

Reprinted with permission of The Macmillan Company from *The Heir Apparent* by William Shannon. Copyright, ©, 1967, by William V. Shannon.

Reprinted with permission of The Macmillan Company from *Robert F. Kennedy: The Brother Within* by Thompson & Meyers. Copyright, ©, 1962, by The Macmillan Company.

Reprinted from *Robert Kennedy at 40* by Nick Thommesch and William Johnson. By permission of W. W. Norton & Company, Inc. Copyright, ©, 1965, by W. W. Norton & Company, Inc.

I would like to extend my thanks to the following people for their invaluable assistance in this undertaking: Peter Workman, Margot Cates, Harold Wolman, Victor Navasky, Laura Ross Pitler, Savannah Gant, Kazetta Robinson, and Nancy Feikens. Special thanks must go to Kathleen McGhee for her able help in researching this book.

This book is dedicated to Burnette and Neil Staebler and Patricia and William Thornton, who have disproved by their actions the charge of the cynic and the opportunist that ethical standards and political success are mutually exclusive in America.

And, in the same spirit, to the memory of Robert F. Kennedy who said, quoting George Bernard Shaw, "Some men see things as they are and say, why? I dream things that never were and say, why not?"

Contents

Introduction

Throughout most of Robert Kennedy's career, Americans had little difficulty placing him in their political scheme of things. To his ardent supporters he was the "heir apparent," the young hero, slightly stooped by the tragic burden of his family's misfortunes, to whom the fallen President had passed the torch. Combining the toughmindedness and embarrassed compassion of Bogart with the irreverence and studied shagginess of the Beatles, he ignited the imagination of a generation growing bored with the social-work mentality and plodding commitment of aging New Dealers.

His actions as Attorney General and his Senate speeches on fiscal policy, civil rights, and foreign aid meant little to these enthusiasts. Their bonds of fidelity were symbolic and cathartic, not programmatic. As a near-delirious matron at a Kennedy rally in Marion, Iowa, burbled, "I can't hear what he said, but whatever it was, was right." She was speaking for millions of Bobby fans.

Similarly, those who hated or distrusted Robert Kennedy felt freed from the inconvenience of listening to him. The fact that he was an abrasive rich kid, his father's son ("Bobby is like me; he hates the way I do"), a former aide of Joseph McCarthy, and the crusading inquisitor for the McClellan "Rackets Committee" was enough to make him anathema to anyone who valued civil liberties and a liberal philosophy of government. Kennedy's words and actions no longer counted because his character and motives were suspect.

As author-politician Gore Vidal inveighed in a piece for *Esquire* in 1963, "His obvious characteristics are . . . vindictiveness and a simplemindedness about human motives . . . . To Bobby the world is black or white. Them and Us. He has none of his brother's ease; or charity . . . .

dangerously authoritarian-minded Presi-

...obert Kennedy polarize American public
... n extent unmatched by any "mainstream"
... ...re in this century, with the exception of
... ...oosevelt. And the "Bobby phenomenon," as it
... tagged by *Newsweek*, was without precedent
in ou... ...litical tradition. For the love-hate dichotomy of
opinion that marked Roosevelt's reign did not develop
until FDR was perceived as the harbinger of a new
political order. Kennedy accomplished the same thing
almost completely by dint of parentage and personality
alone.

Then in early 1966 the emotion-laden caricatures of
Robert Kennedy as hero and villain began to crumble—at
least around the edges. On February 19 Kennedy broke
unmistakably with the Johnson Administration on Vietnam, calling publicly for a negotiated peace based upon
granting the Viet Cong a voice in the government of
South Vietnam. For liberals who had long derided Bobby
as the "Irish Roy Cohn" this was a transparent act of
opportunism aimed at outflanking Lyndon Johnson for
control of the left wing of the Democratic Party. Even
many Kennedy supporters saw the breach with LBJ in
those terms.

Yet Robert Kennedy seemed determined to become the
accepted spokesman for the growing discontent in America. In March he flew to Delano, California, to demonstrate
his support for the striking grape pickers. In June, before
an overflow audience at Cape Town University in South
Africa, he attacked that nation's apartheid policies, pro-
claiming that "government must answer—not just to those
of a particular religion, or a particular race—but to all its
people." Later he joined a crowd in singing the civil rights
anthem, "We Shall Overcome."

Seeking to wed the Kennedy name to the new spirit of
dissent on American college campuses, he journeyed that
fall to Berkeley, California, the mecca of student activism
in this country. He instructed his youthful listeners that
"it is not enough to allow dissent. We must demand it.
For there is much to dissent from." This was what his
audience had come to hear. Kennedy began to demon-

strate a remarkable sensitivity to the concerns and style of student audiences. Not only had his liberal support on campuses far exceeded that of any other prominent politician, but increasing numbers of New Left partisans regarded him as one of the few "establishment" figures worthy of consideration and communications.

The year 1967 recorded more of the same. Kennedy renewed his call for the cessation of bombing over North Vietnam. His office deluged the Senate and the mass media with speeches and statements on our China policy, rebuilding the cities, the Negro revolution, poverty, air pollution, understanding the new generation, foreign aid, juvenile delinquency, and even the evils of smoking. Most were controversial, some were daring and imaginative, a few were radical. Nearly all contained an undercurrent of criticism of the Johnson Administration's failure to solve America's problems.

The result of the Senator's effective efforts to identify himself with a broad range of programs and policy proposals was a massive public case of cognitive dissonance. The incessant injection of program and policy into public view by a political figure whose "image" had been largely the product of his personality—real and imagined—had begun to cause unsettling conflicts of attitude among many Americans. Shrieking suburban housewives who flocked to see Bobby were sobered by his proposals to end de facto segregation in housing and education. Veterans who cheered him as a committed anti-Communist were confused by his condoning blood donations to the Viet Cong. The rebellious young and intellectual middle-aged, many of whom still didn't trust him, could not deny that Robert Kennedy had become the national spokesman for their campaigns to end the war and confront the crises in our cities.

Everywhere ambivalence toward Kennedy grew. Voters of all hues were being forced to ask themselves questions about his political philosophy and his suggestions for solving the nation's ills; questions they previously were able to ignore in assessing him. "For" and "against"—such suitable categories for measuring the prevailing attitudes toward him two years before were progressively less useful to the pollsters.

Add to the ambivalence the fact that Robert Kennedy had become an authentic contender for the White House and Democratic party leadership, and the reason for the escalating interest in him and the torrent of books pouring off the presses about him become clear. He was no longer merely the brash little brother of John F. Kennedy to be either loved, hated, or ignored. He was a man who might be President of the United States.

At last the traditional questions of substance and motive reserved for public figures of serious stature were being asked of Robert Kennedy. Did his definition of the proper spirit and role of government characterize him as a liberal, a conservative, or something beyond the bounds of these labels? What were his positions on the important international and domestic issues of the day such as Vietnam, the Negro revolution, and management of the economy? Did his speeches and statements reveal a superficial or insightful understanding of the problems to which they were addressed? Was he consistent before different audiences, or did he give the American Legion one version of the cold war and the Americans for Democratic Action another? Were the changes in his outlook over the past few years the result of honest growth or of alert opportunism? Was he bright? Was he mature?

The most direct and objective approach to these questions is a careful review of Kennedy's public record. By studying his speeches, campaign statements, press releases, published interviews, Senate votes, Congressional testimony, and his own books and articles, we can discover what Robert Kennedy said, and failed to say, at different times and before different audiences about government, politics, and the principal issues of our times—all in his own words.

Robert F. Kennedy: Apostle of Change has sought to embody this approach. Fashioned from direct quotations, this volume is a documented presentation of Kennedy's political philosophy and policy positions. Its purpose is to provide a lucid and logical arrangement of what would otherwise be a discursive and unwieldy collection of public papers and pronouncements. Its mode is descriptive. Evaluation is left to the reader's own sensibilities and political predilections.

However, as the reader will quickly discover, any attempt to uncover a political figure's beliefs and motives by exploring his public record raises certain problems. Should all statements be accepted at face value? Should they all be given equal weight? What are reasonable standards of consistency and candor to apply to a national politician? Are addresses and other public statements the product of the politician's time and imagination or simply the work of an unsupervised speech writer? Some sophistication is necessary if our evaluations are to be realistic.

Probably the most important fact to remember when interpreting public statements is that every major elected officeholder operates under a great number of political pressures, many of which conflict. Winning office probably requires that he induce into coalition a diversity of interest groups and individuals. Re-election hinges on his ability to keep as many elements of that winning coalition as possible satisfied and in his camp.

Since the spokesmen for these various groups—labor unions, corporations, civil rights groups, home owners' associations, farmers, conservationists, students' organizations, local and state political parties, important campaign contributors, and so on—frequently approach the officeholder with contradictory and divergent demands, political survival requires much diplomacy and often a bit of duplicity. Certain supporters will have to be turned down, one hopes without irrevocably alienating them. Some need to be "strung along" until the "right time" for either granting or rejecting their demands. Still others will have to be educated to a change of view if the coalition is to be preserved.

It might be comforting to believe that a courageous and conscientious officeholder need only consult his convictions to act. But this is no more realistic than expecting a Ford executive committed to auto safety to pursue that cause without regard to his obligation to sell automobiles. He would soon be removed from his position of power and denied any voice in the future design of his product. So it would be with the politician who failed to recognize and cultivate the sources of his influence.

In short, every major politician's public record is going to reflect the accommodation—compromise, if you like—

inherent in our political system. Speeches and press statements are used as more than a vehicle for expressing the politician's specific views on official affairs of state. They are often devices for flattering certain groups, forestalling the criticism of others, creating a congenial climate of opinion for a planned future action, threatening and intimidating opponents, or sometimes just convincing certain people that the politician is really not a bad fellow. Clearly, many of these are situations in which a frank, serious presentation is neither advantageous nor necessary, so we must be careful not to erect standards of political behavior which no man can hope to meet and still survive the struggle for power.

The relevant issue concerns the nature of the accommodation involved. Is it the minimum required to retain an influential voice in the decision-making process and further the politician's ideals and programs without sacrificing his principles in the process? Or has the man compromised himself to advance his own career at the expense of his professed reasons for wanting to hold political office? This is the distinction between unavoidable accommodation to political realities and opportunism.

Unfortunately, it is a distinction which is not always easy to draw, given the confusion and furtiveness of the American political arena. Furthermore, no simple a priori criteria exist. Each case must be judged in its own context, with the reader attempting to weigh the relative costs and benefits of a public statement to the politician's programs and personal position.

These general comments ought to make it obvious that accepting all portions of a politician's public record at face value is simply naive. No senator, congressman, mayor, or state legislator believes everything he says or writes. Nor does he even intend all his words to be taken literally.

Ethnic groups in our large cities, for example, traditionally have insisted that politicians courting their favor shamelessly flatter them. This gives occasion to such outlandish hyperbole as "Hamtramck is the Democratic capital of the world" (as heard in that Polish section of Detroit, from a normally restrained Democratic candidate for governor). And what Columbus has in common with

Cleveland's present-day Italo-Americans or St. Patrick with Brooklyn's sons of Eire is far from clear. But these generous associations are political protocol that must be observed.

Many political speeches include praise of government programs, civic projects, community groups, and prominent citizens, which the speaker may feel obliged to extend even if he believes the contrary. It is a good rule of thumb to ignore all gratuitous political remarks unless they are couched in very specific terms. In fact, any subject treated in a vague, general fashion is suspect as an accurate reflection of a politician's own convictions.

The context in which a speech or statement is offered is another clue to the weight it ought to be afforded as a serious effort to express the politician's philosophies and programs. Although there are no hard and fast rules, speeches delivered personally before large heterogeneous audiences (campaign speeches in particular) tend to be the shortest on meaningful content. Such statements are often aimed at creating a "feel" or tone which will strike a positive note with as wide a variety of voters as possible. They are helpful indicators of the type of "image" the politician is attempting to project, but tell us little else.

Kennedy, like many of his colleagues, saved his most serious and thoughtful expositions for major Senate addresses, lengthy statements to the mass media, speeches before academics and students (with the notable exception of graduation exercises), and for remarks to relatively sophisticated interest groups on subjects within their purview. The four books and numerous magazine articles he wrote also tend to reflect his considered views of national problems and the policies needed to alleviate them.

The topic a politician chooses to discuss with a given audience can also be an aid in weighing the speech. If a topic confronts an audience's prejudices and challenges it to redefine its interests to include the welfare of other segments of the community—like urging Mississippi whites to accept integrated schools or a midwestern Chamber of Commerce to recognize the benefits of a vigorous war on poverty—the politician is undertaking the laudable and courageous task of trying to educate his constituents. Knowing the risks of antagonizing supporters that this kind of speech entails, we can assume that such bold efforts are not taken lightly by their makers, and therefore should be taken seriously by us.

"Clever" politicians will steer clear of subjects likely to antagonize their listeners. Daring opportunists—for there are dangers involved—will tell each audience what it wishes to hear, throwing constraints of consistency and intellectual honesty to the winds. Once discovered, this tends to undermine the credibility of the man's entire public record, Richard Nixon being a case in point.

One question that occurs to many people trying to evaluate a speech or press statement is whether the ideas and eloquence belong to the public figure or some anonymous wordsmith. As a former congressional speechwriter, I believe this is an irrelevant concern. For practical purposes, speechwriters should be regarded as an extension in time and talent of the man they serve. No writer-researcher in a congressional office will hold his job long if he is unable to adopt the perspectives and style of his boss.

The Kennedy staff contends that the Senator played an active role in the drafting of every speech he delivered and every statement issued by his office. Whether this is true or not really doesn't matter. A major politician hires the men who do the writing and who help develop his themes and proposals. He also receives the full weight of the public praise and castigation their work evokes. Therefore, in every meaningful way, the finished product that his office turns out is his own.

Along with these few bits of cracker-barrel political science, it might be well to keep in mind several factors peculiar to Robert Kennedy's career as we examine his public record. Unlike most American politicians, he always addressed himself to a national audience. Catching the public's attention first as a staff member of the McCarthy committee, he was denied the security of a small constituency in rural Kansas or east Detroit isolated from the ears and eyes of the mass media. Thus he was deprived of the opportunity given most political newcomers of indulging the mores and biases of a particular locale or region of the country. This deference to local color, which found Lyndon Johnson a segregationist, George Wallace a New Dealer, and John F. Kennedy a fervent anti-Communist in the dawn of their careers, is absent in Bobby's background.

The nature of Robert Kennedy's early views is further obscured by the fact that his first years of public service were spent almost exclusively on the issue of crime, and were followed by three years in his brother's administration during which he had only limited opportunity to voice publicly his opinions on matters outside the Justice Department's jurisdiction. This means that most of his policy positions must be learned from his record as a Senator since 1965, a period rather short for a confident measure of the man. However, it is all we have.

This volume was undertaken with no firm preconceptions about Kennedy and with much of the ambivalence and uncertainty so many Americans seem to share about this man. It is arranged topically, so that it can be read either sequentially or by jumping from one subject to another as the reader's interests dictate. Not intended as a polemic, this book will, I hope, inject a bit more reason into a political scene increasingly beclouded by glamor, "image-makers," and the cult of personality.

PART I

Robert F. Kennedy:
What Manner of Man?

Chapter 1

Foundations of Action

The free way of life proposes ends, but it does not prescribe means. It assumes that people—and nations—will often think differently, have the full right to do so, and that diversity is the source of progress. It believes that men advance by discussion, by debate, by trial, and by error.

It believes that the best ideas come not from edict and ideology, but from free inquiry and free experiment; and it regards dissent, not as treason to the state, but as the tested mechanism of social progress. And it knows that diverse nations will find diverse roads to the general goal of political independence and economic growth. It regards the free individual as the source of creativity, and believes that it is the role of the state to serve him, and not his role to serve the state.[1]

Like Marx, the American politician has turned Hegel upside down (or "right side up" as Marx would have it), relegating ideology to an ex post facto role. Thus it was in keeping with the traditions of modern American politics that Robert Kennedy entered public life without a considered, coherent set of political and social principles. Preferring to focus on specific problems and their solution, he never outlined the beliefs that constituted the philosophic foundation of his actions.

Yet implicit in the decisions and proposals of most political figures is at least a rudimentary point of view toward such fundamentals as the nature of the good life, the proper organization of society, the responsibilities of

[1] Robert F. Kennedy, *The Pursuit of Justice* (New York: Harper & Row, 1965), pp. 108-109.

3

the state, and the role of the individual in history. On many occasions Robert Kennedy spoke of these fundamentals. Although they hardly constitute a political philosophy, these sporadic remarks are a sensible starting point in our search to discover what manner of man Robert Kennedy was.

On Freedom

He spoke of freedom several times, often in conjunction with Communist alternatives:

We know that freedom has many dimensions. It is the right of the man who tills the land to own the land; the right of the workers to join together to seek better conditions of labor; the right of businessmen to use ingenuity and foresight to produce and distribute without arbitrary interference in a truly competitive economy. It is the right of government to protect the weak; it is the right of the weak to find in their courts fair treatment before the law. It is the right of all our citizens to engage without fear or constraint in the discussion and debate of the great issues which confront us all. We understand this regardless of the extent to which we may differ in our political views. We know that argument in the open is one of the sources of our national strength.[2]

Social progress and social justice, in my judgment, are not something apart from freedom; they are the fulfillment of freedom. The obligation of free men is to use their opportunities to improve the welfare of their fellow human beings. This, at least, has been the tradition of democratic freedom in America.[3]

There are hazards in debating American policy in the face of a stern and dangerous enemy. But that hazard is the essence of our democracy. Democracy is no easy form of government. Few nations have been able to sustain it. For it requires that we take the chances of freedom that the liberating

[2] Speech, Seattle World's Fair, Seattle, Wash., August 7, 1962.
[3] Kennedy, *op. cit.*, p. 108.

play of reason be brought to bear on events filled with passion; that dissent be allowed to make its appeal for acceptance; that men chance error in their search for the truth.

"The best test of truth is the power of a thought to get itself accepted in the competition of the marketplace," said Justice Holmes. That at any rate is the theory of our Constitution. It is an experiment, as all life is an experiment. Every year, if not every day, we have to wager our salvation upon some prophecy based on imperfect knowledge. While that experiment is part of our system, I think that we should be eternally vigilant against attempts to check the expression of opinions that we loathe and believe to be fought with depth.[4]

Communism everywhere has paid the price of rigidity and dogmatism. Freedom has the strength of compassion and flexibility. It has, above all, the strength of intellectual honesty. We do not claim to know all the answers; we make no pretense of infallibility. And we know this to be a sign, not of weakness, but of power.[5]

As for the relationship of religion to freedom, he explained to a convention of Jewish young people in 1964:

The principles of religion remain to this day our greatest safeguard against tyranny over the mind of man. The most dangerous dictatorship, we know now, is not that which imposes itself by force of arms.

It is the dictatorship which raises children to conform to its ideology. Against that dictatorship, traditions handed down from father to son, from generation to generation, are the surest safeguard.

That is why I regard religious persecution in the Soviet Union as one of the ominous developments of our day.

For where religion dies, tradition dies; and where tradition dies, freedom and sanity die as well.[6]

[4] Speech, U.S. Senate, February 19, 1966.

[5] Kennedy, *op. cit.*, p. 110.

[6] Campaign speech, President's Convention for United Synagogue Youth, Laurelton, L.I., N.Y., October 26, 1964.

Political Power in an Open Society

On the question of political power in an open society, Bobby rejected conservative fears of concentration per se.

The case [of James Hoffa] heightens the awareness of the dangers of power without purpose, of power sought and used merely for the sake of power, of power as pure self-indulgence. But one can go too far in reaction and conclude that all power is evil and that no human can be so entrusted. If we really believed this, we would have to abandon social life altogether.

The real problem of power, of the concentration of power, is not its existence, because we cannot wish it away. The problem of power is how to achieve its responsible use rather than its irresponsible and self-indulgent use—of how to get men of power to live *for* the public rather than *off* the public.[7]

He went on to mention two approaches to the problem of political power in a democracy.

First, it is necessary to mistrust personal power enough to provide for some restraints upon its use. This is the idea of political competition that underlies everything else in the American political system and the Constitution. Do not deprive a man of his capacity to act. Just be sure that he in turn is willing to obey the rules. Nobody ever enunciated the rule of competition as well as James Madison, justly credited as the Father of the Constitution. To Madison, the solution of the problem of power could be found in the natural diversity of faculties and interests among men. If these were allowed to flourish, no one set of interests and no one person could go too far in pursuit of a goal without bringing on a counteraction by some combination of interests adversely affected.

Second, it is the essence of responsibility to put the public good ahead of personal gain. This still leaves room for individual goals and for the pursuit of them with energy and intelligence. This of course applies to daily life—to the family—as it does to politics. It simply requires that when men take on positions of high responsibility and enjoy the

[7] Kennedy, *op. cit.*, p. 6.

honors of high office they must be willing to relinquish something in return—their narrow self-interests.

Thus, we have nothing to fear from cooperative organization and authority lodged in government unless we fear individualism itself.[8]

Most importantly, by unnecessarily diffusing authority, it will obscure the responsibility for decision which is the necessary condition to the sound judgment of the people on their leaders. Legislatures and executives must have ample scope to organize themselves and meet their general responsibilities. Their inadequacies and abuses can be corrected at the voting booth.[9]

Once, in exasperation over government inefficiency, Bobby suggested half-jokingly:

What is really needed is a minor dictator who listens to everybody involved, weighs all the factors, then decides and says, well, this is what has to be done now, and this is what you are going to do.[10]

Government and the Law

More seriously, he wrote about government:

There should be no question about the power or responsibility of government in our lives, but only the question of how it should be employed and what commitment each of us individually will make to maintain it. The challenge of politics and public service is to discover what is interfering with justice and dignity for the individual here and now, and then to decide swiftly upon the appropriate remedies. . . .

Government belongs wherever evil needs an adversary and there are people in distress who cannot help themselves. . . .

I believe that, as long as a single man may try, any un-

[8] *Ibid.*, pp. 6-8.
[9] Address, New York State Constitutional Convention, Albany, N.Y., April 4, 1967.
[10] *Newsweek,* March 18, 1963.

8   ROBERT F. KENNEDY: APOSTLE OF CHANGE

justifiable barrier against his efforts is a barrier against mankind. A government that can destroy such a barrier without
erecting any others in the process is a good force. A government too weak for that is not only a waste but an evil because
it holds out false hope. . . .

. . . I would add to the oath to support the Constitution
an additional oath to be faithful to Madison's belief in the
"diversity of the faculties of men" and that the "protection
of those faculties is the first object of government." With that
in our hearts how can we go wrong? [11]

And about the proper nature of a constitution in a
democracy:

A constitution is not a law or an action, not the resolution
of a dispute or the instrument of a particular program. It is
a guiding charter, designed to liberate the abilities of succeeding generations in their distinct and personal search for an
enlarged existence. Its achievement is gauged by the extent
to which, in George Washington's words, it unites "security
with energy"; security of private liberty and public order,
with the energy of imagination and action necessary to the
beneficent conduct of public affairs.[12]

In this context Kennedy was fond of quoting Lord
Acton's famous remarks on the design of a society's laws:
"Laws should be adapted to those who have the heaviest
stake in the country, for whom misgovernment means not
mortified pride or stinted luxuries but want and pain, and
degradation and risk to their own lives and to their children's souls."

The Individual in History

Like most men who devote themselves to the affairs of
state, Robert Kennedy had great faith in the potential of
the individual to affect the course of history.

[11] Kennedy, *op. cit.*, pp. 8, 9, 10, 11.
[12] Address, New York State Constitutional Convention, Albany,
N.Y., April 4, 1967.

If John F. Kennedy's life stood for anything, it was for the fact that an individual can make a difference—that an individual has an obligation and a responsibility to try to make a difference. I think that whether in the field of civil rights or in the field of housing, the problems that are facing us in Latin America or Asia or Berlin or any of these places, all of us must make some kind of sacrifice—make some kind of effort—on behalf of our country, and on behalf of our own fellow citizens, and on behalf of the citizens of the world—it is absolutely essential.[13]

If I saw anything in the last four years, it was that an individual can make an important contribution to the country whether in the Peace Corps or in some government office or in a community far removed from the center of power.

Jacqueline Kennedy said not long ago that "John Kennedy believed so strongly that one's aim should not just be the most comfortable life possible—but that we should all do something to right the wrongs we see and not just complain about them. He believed that one man can make a difference and that every man should try." [14]

When things are done on too vast a scale, the human imagination bogs down. It can no longer visualize such fantastic things and thus loses its grip on their essential reality. Killing one man is murder; killing millions is a statistic. The disclosures of the Eichmann trial remind us all how quickly the world has forgotten the massive horrors which one set of human beings perpetrated against another a short twenty years ago.

Our problems, having grown to the size of the world, if not of the solar system, no longer seem our own. Each day we are required to respond to new crises created by people whose names we cannot pronounce in lands of which we have never heard. After a time, the capacity to respond begins to flag; and we turn, not cheerfully, but almost in despair, to the sports pages and the comics.

And yet I would say to you that the stake is just as

[13] Statement following speech, University of Rochester, Rochester, N.Y., September 29, 1964.

[14] Kennedy, *op. cit.*, p. 9.

personal today as it was a century ago, the obligation just as personal, the capacity to affect the course of history just as great. What we require is not the self-indulgence of resignation from the world but the hard effort to work out new ways of fulfilling our personal concern and our personal responsibility.[15]

We still wait for the prophet who will discover for us the full meaning of the Warsaw Ghetto. The mystery of the Ghetto is not clarified or deepened by knowledge. I have stood twice in that place. The first time, it was as it was in 1943—rubble, not one stone straight upon another; the marks of the flames still plain. The second time, only a monument marked the spot. Warsaw was rebuilding. But nothing could change the air of the Ghetto. It is still a place of tragedy.

It is in one respect like the death camps to which so many of its people were taken—a never-to-be-forgotten reminder of man's inhumanity to man. We share that tragedy because we are all men. We share the responsibility because we permitted it to happen. We cannot forget it.[16]

Of the rights and responsibilities of the individual:

When we talk about birthright we talk about *the right of opportunity, the right of opportunity to succeed or fail on individual talents developed unfettered by manmade barriers.* That is what gives a man his dignity.[17]

Let no man think he fights his battle for others. He fights for himself and so do we all. The golden rule is not sentimentality, but the deepest practical wisdom. For the teaching of our time is that cruelty is contagious and its disease knows no bounds of race or nation.[18]

[15] Speech, Joint Defense Appeal of the American Jewish Committee and the Anti-Defamation League of B'nai B'rith, Chicago, Ill., June 21, 1961.

[16] Address, Anniversary of the Warsaw Ghetto Uprising, New York, N.Y., April 29, 1965.

[17] Kennedy, *op. cit.,* p. 15.

[18] *Look,* August 23, 1966.

We who are educated, we who are healthy and well-fed, would remember the justice of the Incas—who punished nobles more severely than peasants for identical crimes.

For the failing of inaction—in the face of poverty and ignorance and injustice—we will deserve greater punishment as well. For to us is put the great question of our time: whether our heritage of freedom can survive in an era of sweeping technological change—whether revolution can succeed without destroying the very humanity in whose name it is carried on.[19]

We have not solved our problems; but we are committed to find solutions. And most important, the country has turned away, I hope forever, from those whose hearts are dry as summer dust, those who feel that the poor are evil, that security is weakening, and that every man should fend for himself.[20]

". . . But What You Can Do for Your Country"

John Kennedy's challenge to the nation to 'ask not what your country can do for you, but what you can do for your country" was echoed by his brother on numerous occasions. These are particularly interesting statements because they yield insights into his convictions about the state of the world and the obstacles opposing those who seek to reform it. In addition, they are among his most eloquent remarks.

Everywhere, new technology and communications bring men and nations closer together, the concerns of one inevitably becoming the concerns of all. But our new closeness has not yet stripped away the false masks, the illusions of difference which are the root of injustice and hate and war. Earthbound man still clings to the dark and poisoning superstition that his world is bounded by the nearest hill, his universe ended at river shore, his common humanity enclosed in the tight circle of those who share his views and

[19] Address, Peruvian students, Lima, Peru, November 1965.
[20] Address, testimonial dinner for Lieutenant Governor Patrick Lucey, Milwaukee, Wis., August 15, 1965.

his town and the color of his skin. And therefore the survival of the human species itself depends on our ability to strip the last remnants of that ancient, cruel belief from the civilization of man.[21]

Thus the great challenge to all Americans—indeed to all free men and women—is to maintain loyalty to truth; to maintain loyalty to free institutions; to maintain loyalty to freedom as a basic human value and above all else to keep in our hearts and minds the tolerance and mutual trust that have been the genius of American life throughout our history. . . .

Upon you and me, and our fellow countrymen, falls the challenge of protecting, not only our country, but the free people of the world in this hour of maximum need—of greatest danger.

With confidence born and nurtured by knowledge and truth, and with the courage of free men, we shall prevail.[22]

The challenge and obstacles of this nation, the cruelties and dangers of this swiftly changing planet, will not yield to obsolete dogmas and outworn slogans. The world cannot be moved by those who cling to a present which is already dying, who prefer the illusion of security to the excitement and danger of even the most peaceful progress. This world demands the qualities of youth, not a time of life but a state of mind, a temper of the will, a quality of the imagination, a predominance of courage over timidity, of the appetite for adventure over the love of ease. It is a revolutionary world we live in—and revolutions are young men's work. Thus you, and your young compatriots everywhere, have had thrust upon you a greater burden of responsibility than any generation which has ever lived.

"There is," said an Italian philosopher, "nothing more difficult to take in hand, more perilous to conduct, or more uncertain in its success than to take the lead in the introduction of a new order of things." [23]

[21] Address, Fordham University, New York, N.Y., June 10, 1967.
[22] Speech, National Conference of Christians and Jews, Cleveland, Ohio, December 3, 1961.
[23] Address, Fordham University, New York, N.Y., June 10, 1967.

Devoted and intelligent men have worked for generations to improve the well-being of the American people, diminish poverty and injustice, and protect freedom. Yet even as we honor their accomplishments we know that our own problems will not yield to the ideas and programs on which past achievement has been built. Ideas are often more confining, more difficult to discard, in their success than in their failure. Yet we must now cast aside many tested concepts in the face of challenges whose nature and dimensions are more complex and towering than any before. For this we must look to your generation, a generation which feels most intensely the agony and bewilderment of the modern age, and which is not bound to old ways of thought.[24]

Progress is a nice word. But change is its motivator. And change has its enemies.[25]

Yet this is the measure of the task of your generation and the road is strewn with many dangers.

First is the danger of futility; the belief there is nothing one man or one woman can do against the enormous array of the world's ills—against misery and ignorance, injustice and violence. Yet many of the world's great movements, of thought and action, have flowed from the work of a single man. A young Italian explorer discovered the new world, a young general extended an empire from Macedonia to the borders of the earth, and a young woman reclaimed the territory of France. It was the thirty-two-year-old Thomas Jefferson who proclaimed that all men are created equal. "Give me a place to stand," said Archimedes, "and I will move the world." These men moved the world, and so can we all. Few will have the greatness to bend history itself; but each of us can work to change a small portion of events, and in the total of all those acts will be written the history of this generation. Thousands of Peace Corps volunteers are making a difference in isolated villages and city slums in dozens of countries. Thousands of unknown men and women in Europe resisted the occupation of the Nazis and many

[24] Speech, University of California at Berkeley, Calif., October 22, 1966.
[25] Kennedy, *op. cit.*, p. 12.

died, but all added to the ultimate strength and freedom of their countries. It is from numberless diverse acts of courage and belief that human history is shaped. Each time a man stands up for an ideal, or acts to improve the lot of others, or strikes out against injustice, he sends forth a tiny ripple of hope, and crossing each other from a million different centers of energy and daring those ripples build a current which can sweep down the mightiest walls of oppression and resistance.

The second danger is that of expediency; of those who say that hopes and beliefs must bend before immediate necessities. Of course, if we would act effectively we must deal with the world as it is. We must get things done. But if there was one thing President Kennedy stood for that touched the most profound feelings of young people across the world, it was the belief that idealism, high aspirations and deep convictions are not incompatible with the most practical and efficient of programs—that there is no basic inconsistency between ideals and realistic possibilities—no separation between the deepest desires of heart and mind and the rational application of human effort to human problems. It is not realistic or hardheaded to solve problems and take action unguided by ultimate moral aims and values. It is thoughtless folly. For it ignores the realities of human faith and passion and belief; forces ultimately more powerful than all the calculation of economists or generals. Of course to adhere to standards, to idealism, to vision, in the face of immediate dangers takes courage and self-confidence. But we also know that only those who dare to fail greatly, can ever achieve greatly.

A third danger is timidity. Few men are willing to brave the disapproval of their fellows, the censure of their colleagues, the wrath of their society. Moral courage is a rarer commodity than bravery in battle or great intelligence. Yet it is the one essential, vital quality for those who seek to change a world which yields most painfully to change.

For the fortunate among us, the fourth danger is comfort: the temptation to follow the easy and familiar paths of personal ambition and financial success so grandly spread before those who have the privilege of education. But that is not the road history has marked out for us. There is a Chinese curse which says, "May he live in interesting times."

Like it or not we live in interesting times. They are times of danger and uncertainty; but they are also more open to the creative energy of men than any other time in history. Everyone here will ultimately be judged—will ultimately judge himself—on the effort he has contributed to building a new world society and the extent to which his ideals and goals have shaped that effort.[26]

There is discrimination in New York, apartheid in South Africa, and serfdom in the mountains of Peru. People starve in the streets of India; intellectuals go to jail in Russia; thousands are slaughtered in Indonesia; wealth is lavished on adornment everywhere. These are differing evils. But they are common works of man.[27]

No government—and no people—can foresee all that is to happen; nor can any society escape its share of crises. But too many of the issues we now confront are the harvests of indifference—and, still, we seem, in our confrontation with the future, not to have learned the cost of this indifference.[28]

Philosophy of Action

When it came to his own actions, Robert Kennedy consistently denied any ideological underpinnings for them and preferred a problem-solving approach. He told an overflow audience at Nihon University in Tokyo early in 1962:

We in my country are by disposition and inheritance a people mistrustful of absolute doctrines and ideologies, persuaded that reason and experiment are the means by which free people fulfill their purposes. Yet we live in a century obsessed with ideology—a century that has been filled with leaders persuaded that they knew the secrets

[26] Address, Fordham University, New York, N.Y., June 10, 1967.
[27] *Newsweek*, June 20, 1966.
[28] Address, Ninth Constitutional Convention of Oil, Chemical and Atomic Workers, New York, N.Y., August 23, 1967.

of history, that they were the possessors of absolute truth, and that all must do as they say—or perish.

One of the great creative statesmen of our age was Franklin Roosevelt. He was creative precisely because he preferred experiment to ideology. He and the men of his time insisted that the resources of the democratic system were greater than many believed—that it was possible to work for economic security within a framework of freedom. . . .[29]

Therefore it was not surprising that Kennedy sought assiduously to avoid association with labels like "liberal" and "conservative." "I don't believe in labels," he said. "They're somewhat phony."

Shortly after he was elected President, John Kennedy was quoted in *Look* as saying, "Bobby is caught in a cross current of labels we pin on people. We tend to check off an arbitrary list, add up the results and come up with a liberal or conservative. Bobby doesn't fit this. I could say that he is essentially conservative, but not on a matter like the minimum wage or a number of other issues. He acts pragmatically. I think he might once have been intolerant of liberals as such because his early experience was with the high-minded, high-speaking kind who never get anything done. That all changed the moment he met a liberal like Walter Reuther."

Whatever his intolerance for liberals, Kennedy had overcome it sufficiently by the time of his campaign for the Senate in liberal New York to announce:

And I am a candidate for the United States Senate because I want to serve the people of this state, in the tradition of American liberalism which men like Senators Robert Wagner and Herbert Lehman established.[30]

Regardless of what he or others chose to label it, Bobby's dominant political precept was the need for determined and tireless action to right the wrongs of America and the world—action unfettered by considerations of

[29] Robert F. Kennedy, *Just Friends and Brave Enemies* (New York: Harper & Row, 1962), p. 54.
[30] Campaign speech, New York, N.Y., October 19, 1964.

dogma or ideology. His statements leave the impression that he believed no manmade problem can long resist earnest assaults by men of reason and resourcefulness. He could make no more devastating indictment of a group or a society than that it failed to act in the face of challenge. Using a passage from Eliot's "The Love Song of J. Alfred Prufrock," he summed up this feeling:

If we fail to dare, if we do not try, the next generation will harvest the fruit of our indifference; a world we did not want—a world we did not choose—but a world we could have made better, by caring more for the results of our labors. And we shall be left only with the hollow apology of T. S. Eliot:

> "That is not what I meant at all.
> That is not it, at all." [31]

[31] Address, Ninth Constitutional Convention of Oil, Chemical and Atomic Workers, New York, N.Y., August 23, 1967.

Chapter 2

Personalities and Politics

Johnson isn't as afraid of me as he was. He's not so worried that I am going to rise up and run against him. As he has gone along in his job, he has developed more confidence in himself. He is more experienced. I'm not so sure either that he thinks Hubert Humphrey is going to be the man to succeed him.[1]

I am so well aware of being disliked by many that it no longer surprises or disturbs me. I no longer care. On the contrary, I do understand the reason. I have been too closely involved in too many struggles, in too many battles. But there are people who do like me: They elected me, did they not? The poorer people like me. Negroes and Puerto Ricans, for instance. The deprived, if you like. They are for me, I know. . . . So let the others say whatever they like.[2]

The present patronage system corrupts politics in [New York] state, by providing an immoral but widely used method of supporting political organizations and paying off political debts. This financing in turn enables political organizations to survive which are totally unresponsive to the voters and the community.[3]

Robert Kennedy understood politicians and politics long before he began to grasp the subtleties of affairs of state. By the time he was twenty-seven, his stewardship of his brother's upset senatorial victory over Henry Cabot

[1] Nick Thimmisch and William Johnson, *R. F. K. at 40* (Boston: W. W. Norton, 1965), p. 288.

[2] *Ibid.*, p. 22.

[3] Statement, Joint Legislative Committee on Court Reorganization, Brooklyn, N.Y., November 29, 1966.

18

Lodge in 1952 and the *Realpolitik* nature of Massachusetts politics (a polite way of characterizing them) had combined to give him a solid grounding in the strategies and mechanics of managing political campaigns and parties. His skillful direction of John Kennedy's bid for the White House—a presidential campaign which has been praised as the best conceived and executed in our history—merely reconfirmed his place among the top practitioners of professional electoral politics.

Unfortunately, like most American professional politicians who prefer active participation to academic analysis, Kennedy made little effort to present publicly his views on the practice of politics. Scattered throughout his public record, however, are incidental remarks and casual references to the political parties, to his colleagues, and to his own career and public personality. Discursive as they are, any attempt to categorize these excerpts precisely would probably impose meanings and associations where none were intended. Therefore, I offer a loosely structured collage of these quotations in the hope that a rough representation of Bobby's attitudes toward his work and himself will result.

Commitment to Public Service

I don't think any of us thought of public service as a sacrifice or as a means strictly of repaying a beneficent country. We looked to it as an opportunity for an exciting and fulfilling way of life. Since public affairs had dominated so much of our actions and discussions, public life seemed really an extension of family life. . . . By the time I became chief counsel of the Senate Rackets Investigating Committee in 1957, I knew that I would want to work for the government as long as I was able. Jimmy Hoffa provided a principal reason, for through him I discovered for myself the consequences of irresponsible use of power, how it threatened the freedom of all of us and what was required of each of us to stand against it.[4]

[4] Robert F. Kennedy, *The Pursuit of Justice* (New York: Harper & Row, 1965), p. 5.

A year after the Committee had exposed Bushkin's operations [illegally fixing contracts with unions] and he had pleaded the Fifth Amendment before us, we found some of the most reputable firms in Detroit—Federal Department Stores, Cunningham Drug Stores, the ACF Wrigley Grocery chain—still had him on their payrolls as a consultant and they had no intention of getting rid of him. While this would have been disillusioning for me in 1957, by 1959 it no longer seemed surprising.[5]

The will to win is so important to us as individuals, and as a nation, that without it we are lost. Without doubt, we learn it best as individuals in athletic competition. We have seen it in games that we have played ourselves. I know for I have seen it at home. I am ashamed to report that my father who is seventy-three has never been beaten by any of his four sons in golf. We have all become resigned to the fact that he has determined that he won't be beaten.[6]

Robert Kennedy's attitude about very social events was: "Nobody who goes to those things all the time makes any real contribution." [7]

The Kennedy Campaign—1960

The 1956 Democratic Convention and Adlai Stevenson's presidential campaign provided Kennedy with an opportunity to observe the intricacies of national politics. Managing his brother's unsuccessful attempt at the vice-presidential nomination, which Estes Kefauver finally won after Stevenson threw the selection open to the convention, he learned the value of personal ties.

I remember a wonderful Maryland delegate and his wife.

[5] Robert F. Kennedy, *The Enemy Within* (New York: Harper & Brothers, 1960) p. 221.

[6] Speech, "Dinner of Champions," New York, N.Y., October 17, 1961.

[7] R. E. Thompson and H. Meyers, *Robert F. Kennedy: The Brother Within* (New York: Macmillan, 1962).

They were entirely friendly. They liked us. But Kefauver had visited them in their home. He had sent them Christmas cards. We couldn't shake them. Believe me, we've sent out lots of Christmas cards since.[8]

During the campaign he was assigned as liaison to Stevenson's campaign staff by the Democratic National Committee.

Nobody asked me anything, nobody wanted me to do anything, nobody consulted me. So I had time to watch everything—I filled complete notebooks with notes on how a presidential campaign should be run.[9]

John Kennedy's run for the presidency four years later gave his brother the chance to apply what he had learned. Recapitulating the Kennedys' successful strategy, he remarked:

We simply had to run and fight and scramble for ten weeks all the way, and then we would win. We got on top with the [Kennedy-Nixon television] debates, we fought to stay on top, and we did win. And if we'd done one bit less of anything, then we might have lost.[10]

What Made Bobby Run?

With obvious delight, journalists have applied their analytic arts to the personality of a man as apparently driven and compulsively competitive as Robert Kennedy. To some he was a slightly simple-minded New England Puritan, a kind of Boston Batman, defending decency and right against the forces of evil. Others thought that having two bigger older brothers, Joe, Jr. (who was killed in World War II), and John, caused him to develop into an aggressive, competitive type (Bobby reputedly cheated

[8] Theodore H. White, *The Making of the President, 1960* (New York: Atheneum, 1961), p. 137.

[9] *Ibid.*, p. 246.

[10] *Ibid.*, p. 320.

in family touch football games to avoid losing). And numerous other theories of personality were proffered by the press to explain Bobby's behavior.

At times Kennedy seemed to lend support to one or another of these theories with his own utterances. On one widely reported occasion when he was chief counsel for the McClellan "Rackets Committee," he greeted hoodlum Joey Gallo, who had just walked into Kennedy's office for the first time, with:

You think you are tough, but you are not, and I would like to show you up in a fight.[11]

As his brother's political manager he did not bother to hide what amounted to habitual rudeness. When politicians complained in the 1960 campaign, he hit back:

I'm not running a popularity contest. It doesn't matter if they like me or not. Jack can be nice to them. I don't try to antagonize people but somebody has to be able to say no. If people are not getting off their behinds and working enough, how do you say that nicely? Every time you make a decision in this business you make somebody mad.[12]

Meeting with a group of United States attorneys in 1961, he explained:

It doesn't matter if you hurt my feelings. The important thing is to get the job done.[13]

The New Frontier

Bobby was enthusiastic when speaking about his brother's new administration. Barely two weeks after John Kennedy's election, he exclaimed:

[11] *Look*, March 9, 1965.
[12] William V. Shannon, *The Heir Apparent* (New York: Macmillan, 1967), p. 42.
[13] Thompson and Meyers, *op. cit.*, p. 49.

We're going to do what we thought Eisenhower was going to do in 1952 and never did—bring a new spirit to the government. Not necessarily young men, but new men, who believe in a cause, who believe their jobs go on forever, not just from nine to five; who believe they have a responsibility to the United States, not just to an administration, and who can really get things done. It really makes a hell of a difference. Our campaign was made up of new faces, to a large extent, and this Administration will be made up of new faces, to a large extent.[14]

On his appointment as Attorney General:

Q: Mr. Attorney General, to go back to the beginning—why did you hesitate . . . or at least seem to—before accepting the President-elect's offer to become Attorney General?
RFK: Well, I had a feeling that I wanted to move perhaps in a different direction than this area. I had been involved in matters of law enforcement for eight or nine years, and I felt that I might want to get away from it. I also felt that it posed some difficult problems for the President, appointing his brother as Attorney General, and all of those things made me hesitate about it.
Q: Could you tell us what finally tipped the scales?
RFK: Well, I think the President felt that it would be helpful—and I felt it would be an honor.
Q: How does being a brother of a President affect your role as a member of the Cabinet? Do you find that it gives you extra built-in authority, or does it perhaps occasionally inhibit you?
RFK: Well, I think it probably makes things easier. I think having the same last name as the President of the United States helps, probably.[15]

At times, Kennedy was not above poking fun at himself and the circumstances under which he had accepted a Cabinet position. In a series of introductory meetings with Justice Department lawyers in 1960, he could not resist:

[14] *Newsweek*, November 21, 1960.
[15] Press conference, U.S. Department of Justice, June 20, 1961.

Don't forget, I came to this department ten years ago as an assistant attorney at a salary of $4,200 a year. But I had ability. I had integrity. I had an interest in my job. I stayed late at night. My brother became President. And now I'm Attorney General. ["After a pause," the authors write, "his face would break into a smile."] Of course, those qualifications were not necessarily listed in the order of their importance.[16]

After Dallas

Then came the bewildered and searching year following his brother's assassination.

HUGH DOWNS: What do you consider was your brother's greatest accomplishment during his three years in office as President?

RFK: Well, I think—I think, really it's re-establishing in the American people their confidence in themselves, the confidence in our ideals, and confidence that we could really accomplish what was needed of us. I think that many years, I suppose based on some of the progress that the Soviet Union was making in outer space particularly, and also with the people continuously saying that really communism is the wave of the future, I think he reversed that and we really came to realize that we are the wave of the future, and that what we believe in is what is correct and what is in fact. We have the courage and the tenacity that is going to finally prevail, and I think we've re-established that, I think it was in the back of all of our minds always, but I think it was re-established, and I think also, which is tremendously important, re-established in peoples in other countries confidence in the United States, and that we deserved to be the leaders of the free world and that we would stay, and that we had the courage, and that in the last analysis that this struggle would be won by those who believed in the same principles as we did and do. So I think that was of tremendous importance.

HUGH DOWNS: What do you think was his biggest disappointment, in those three years?

[16] Thimmisch and Johnson, *op. cit.*, p. 26.

RFK: Well, I suppose if you took a specific event it would have to be the Bay of Pigs. . . . I think if you took general terms, perhaps the fact that we weren't able to do more for the field of unemployment and the field of the—those—that fight, really, was just beginning for those who were less well-off in the United States. . . ."[17]

I'd like to harness all the energy and effort and incentive and imagination that was attracted to the government by President Kennedy. I don't want any of that to die. It's important that the striving for excellence continue, that there be an end to mediocrity. The torch has passed to a new generation. People are still looking for all that idealism. It permeated young people all over the globe. And I became sort of a symbol, not just as an individual. If I could figure out some course for me that would keep all that alive and utilize it for the country, that's what I'd do.[18]

LBJ Reviewed

Rumors circulated that Bobby was eying the second spot on the Johnson ticket in the upcoming 1964 elections.

Actually I should think I'd be the last man in the world he [Johnson] would want, because my name is Kennedy, because he wants a Johnson Administration, because we travel different paths, because I suppose some businessmen would object, and because I'd cost them a few votes in the South . . . I don't think as many as some say, but some. Most of the political leaders in the North want me. All of them really. And that's about all I've got going for me.[19]

There isn't anything you can do in the Vice-Presidency . . . not one damn thing . . . that you are not told to do.[20]

I'd just say that, first, there was no disagreement between

[17] "Today" (NBC-TV), February 6, 1964.
[18] *U.S. News & World Report*, March 16, 1964.
[19] *Newsweek*, as reported in *U.S. News & World Report*, July 13, 1964.
[20] Shannon, *op. cit.*, p. 9.

President Kennedy and myself as to the advisability of having Lyndon Johnson as the Vice-President. I'm not going to go into all the details as to what happened that day, but I will say that there was no disagreement between President Kennedy and myself as to Vice-President Johnson.[21]

There was no disagreement between my brother and me on this. We did, however, have our supporters to consider. Our primary aim at the convention had been to put over John Kennedy on the first ballot. We had had little time to think about the vice-presidential slot. We'd finally narrowed the field down to [Washington Senator] "Scoop" Jackson, [Minnesota Governor] Orville Freeman and Lyndon. When Johnson's name was selected, I pointed out to my brother that this was going to be very hard to explain to many of our supporters. Johnson had tried to block us, to fight us all the way, and the fight had unfortunately gotten personal in the final stages. I was afraid the news of Johnson's selection to be vice-president would cause the Walter Reuthers, John Baileys and others to collapse. And some of them did fall on the floor when they got the word. We were afraid there would be a floor fight to prevent Johnson's nomination. We didn't know whether he would be willing to go through a floor fight and all the acrimony again. I was sent as emissary to ask him this. He said he was willing to risk a floor fight to accept the nomination. I went back to my brother with the news.[22]

The Senate Campaign

On July 30, 1964, Lyndon Johnson resolutely slammed the door on any such speculations, ruling out all members of his Cabinet as vice-presidential possibilities (Kennedy was still Attorney General). Less than a month later Kennedy resigned and threw his hat into the New York senatorial race.

I have made that decision because I think our country faces a fundamental political choice. Our traditional aspirations for peace and prosperity, justice and decency, are being

[21] *U.S. News & World Report,* September 6, 1965.
[22] Thimmisch and Johnson, *op. cit.,* pp. 119-120.

questioned. All that President Kennedy stood for and all that President Johnson is trying to accomplish, all the progress that has been made, is threatened by a new and dangerous Republican assault. No one associated with President Kennedy and with President Johnson—no one committed to participating in public life—can sit on the sidelines with so much at stake.[23]

Q: If elected to the Senate, do you plan to serve a full term?
A: I have heard that before my term is up I am going to use the Senate as a steppingstone. I'd like to know where I'm going to go.

Assume that I was using it as a "power base"—that's the other expression that is used. Let's just assume the worst —that I am using it as a power base and I am really just trying to get someplace so that I can go somewhere else, which is the Presidency of the United States. In the first place, truthfully now, I can't go any place in 1968. We've President Johnson and I know he's going to be a good President. I think he's going to be re-elected in 1968 and he'll have my support and my efforts on his behalf.

Now we get to 1972. That's eight years. Assume that I am still using it as a "power base." I'm going to have to be re-elected in six years. If I am re-elected—if I have done such an outstanding job and I really want to be President of the United States, I'm going to have to do a tremendous job for the State of New York, and for the people of New York. People are going to have confidence in me. Then if I have done such an outstanding job in eight years that people just demand all over the country that I be a presidential candidate, I don't see how New York suffers.[24]

If I'm elected this time [1964], I'm going to run again in 1970.[25]

To the cry of "carpetbagger" from Republicans and Democrats alike, he replied:

I would not have entered this campaign unless my candi-

---

[23] Statement, Gracie Mansion, New York, N.Y., August 25, 1964.
[24] Question and answer following speech, University of Rochester, Rochester, N.Y., September 29, 1964.
[25] News conference (WINS), October 25, 1964.

dacy had conformed to the laws of the State of New York and the Constitution of the United States.

And despite what has been written and said my candidacy establishes no precedent. There have been many similar cases around the country and even here in New York.

The first Senator for the State of New York was from Massachusetts. And he served this state well.

Further, for every citizen who is a New Yorker by birth there is one who is a New Yorker by choice, or whose parents were.

I am in the second category, but so was Thomas E. Dewey.

I am confident, therefore, that the voters of New York will judge me fairly, on my record of thirteen years of public service, the record that has been made over the last three and a half years by the national government, and by my commitment to carry on this effort in the future. I ask for no more.[26]

But he retained his sense of humor. In *The Heir Apparent*, William Shannon writes that during an early meeting to organize the 1964 campaign in New York, Fred Papert, who planned the television advertising, said, "The basic aim of all our commercials, Bob, will be to present you as a warm, sincere individual." Deadpan, Kennedy asked: "You going to use a double?"

Questioned by an interviewer about the generous support he received from Democratic party bosses, Charles Buckley in particular, during his New York campaign, Kennedy replied:

Well, let me say this—that Congressman Buckley was a help to President Kennedy when President Kennedy and I needed help and Charlie Buckley has been friendly to my brother and has been friendly to me. And he's still that way.
INTERVIEWER: In effect, then, you are refusing to repudiate him, as some people have demanded that you do, because he has been a good friend and has been helpful.
RFK.: Well, Charlie Buckley is having a much more difficult time now than he had in 1960—Buckley was on top of the wave in 1960 and he was the same Charlie Buckley as he is

[26] Address, New York State Democratic Convention, August 12, 1964.

in 1964. And Charlie Buckley was good enough for us to ask help in 1960 . . . it's the same man.

I wouldn't be able to look at myself in the mirror in the morning if I thought that now that he's down and has a difficult time if I turned on him, and in that fashion. Now there are matters which we disagree . . . I run based on my record. I've never been told by anybody, I don't think anybody's ever accused me of being controlled by anybody and as I've explained our relationship with Congressman Buckley—Mr. Buckley has been beaten and I'm supporting his opponent who beat him in the primary. I think he'll make an outstanding congressman.[27]

About the campaign itself, he commented when it was over:

There were some surprises . . . I didn't expect the personal attacks. I didn't expect the Nazi stuff. I didn't think Keating [the Republican incumbent] would do that. I was also surprised by the degree of bitterness from the liberals. But I think they actually helped me. Those people are impossible. We went through the 1960 stuff all over again—my father, Senator McCarthy and so on. *The New York Times* gave us trouble. Jack Javits was plenty tough. He gave me hell.[28]

There's still a deep scar for what the church did to the Jews; it goes back to the Middle Ages. My brother was up against the same thing, but Jack's advantage in New York was that his opponent was Nixon, and the Jews could not take Nixon. My opponent, on the other hand, is a man greatly admired and, from what I have seen, greatly beloved by the Jewish people. Furthermore, the Jews, since the days of the Cossacks, look with suspicion on the investigator and that's all I have really been so far, an investigator and a cop.[29]

As for the Senate:

To me, the role of a senator is to look for the problems and the opportunities ahead. It is to seek out the counsel of the

[27] News conference (WINS), October 25, 1964.
[28] Thimmisch and Johnson, *op. cit.*, p. 220.
[29] *Esquire*, June 1965.

best and wisest on how to meet those problems and seize those opportunities. It is the job of a senator to then put these challenges before the people—to alert them, and to urge action. And it is the job of a senator, having developed a consensus on the problem and the approach to its solution, to lead the necessary action.[30]

But two years later he was grumbling:

They only take about one vote a week here, and they never can tell you in advance when it is going to be so you can schedule other things. If I am not going to be working here, I want to go somewhere I can do something.[31]

Foes Beware

He had advice and warnings for others whose ambitions clashed with his:

It worries me a little when I read these stories about how much the President [Johnson] is thinking about Roosevelt and how he lost his popularity in 1936, because he did too much. But you can lose popularity by doing something, or you lose it by doing nothing. You lose it anyway. It's there to be spent.[32]

The convention system for selecting candidates for public office in New York State deprives them of an opportunity to take their case and cause directly to the voters of their parties. Because it wanted the people of New York to choose their nominees, the Legislature, while under Democratic control, passed a bill establishing a direct primary system. Governor Rockefeller vetoed it, thereby guaranteeing that no one in his party could challenge him for renomination. Thus the democratic processes of government paid once more the price of the Governor's personal ambition.[33]

[30] Campaign speech, University of Syracuse, Syracuse, N.Y., October 20, 1964.
[31] Shannon, *op. cit.*, p. 89.
[32] *The New Republic,* January 2, 1965.
[33] Press release, August 16, 1966.

Political Parties

As de facto leader of New York's Democrats, he was forced to pay increasing attention to matters of party, elections and campaign finances.

I conceive of a political party not as a mechanism for re-election but as a vital instrument of government. The political party can be a collection of office seekers and those who live off their bounty—or it can be an association of those concerned and active citizens. It can operate in every second or fourth year—or throughout the year, bringing the ongoing concerns of people to the attention of officialdom. It can halt and reverse the trend toward impersonal government, detached from those it serves.[34]

Grover Cleveland, who was Mayor of this City, once asked, "What good is a party unless it stands for something?" The reason the Democratic party has won elections, despite our difficulties—and can win this year, despite our difficulties—is because the people knew we stand for something. But a party is and must be more than a roster of illustrious names. In the final telling, the character of a party is what every individual, standing alone with his conscience, makes of it. Our party has achieved what it has, because each of its leaders—whether from Hyde Park, Franklin Roosevelt, or from the sidewalks of New York, like Al Smith—was confident and unafraid, ready to take the lead, to dare, to share in the excitement and danger of innovation and change.[35]

"It is not yesterday, tradition, the past which is the decisive, the determining force in a nation," said Ortega. "Nations are made, and go on living, by having a program for the future."

That is also true for political parties. The Democratic party stands at one of the most critical moments in history. It must now begin to shape a fresh set of goals and programs for the American nation—or be discarded as an instrument of na-

[34] Campaign speech, University of Syracuse, Syracuse, N.Y., October 20, 1964.

[35] Speech introducing gubernatorial candidate Frank D. O'Connor, New York State Democratic Convention, Buffalo, N.Y., September 7, 1966.

tional leadership. For parties do not triumph out of gratitude or remembrance. Leadership is not an award for years of faithful service. The people will only extend their trust and support to that party and those men who offer goals and programs fitted to the most urgent needs of the future. Our old programs were effective and just—but they cannot meet new needs. Our old battles were well and generously waged —but they are over.

We cannot run on our record—on social security or rural electrification, collective bargaining or aid to colleges—for the nation asks, how we propose to meet new problems.

We cannot run on a platform of more of the same—for that is not enough to conquer the conditions which now scar and cripple our national life.

Everywhere I go in this country I find people groping for answers to problems they barely understand; searching for purpose in the midst of baffling change, confusions and danger. We are losing the young, to extreme movements or to public indifference—for their fears and expectations have no answers in the politics of the past. We are losing members of the older generation who lack confidence in their ability to protect the future—and thus turn to conservative movements, hoping at least to protect what they already have. Radicalism and reaction, the New Right and the New Left, reflect a common theme—the desire of individuals to find some sense of inner significance by sharing in a larger common purpose. And they reveal what danger there is in feelings of impotence and lack of direction—polarizing groups and individuals, creating a nation of strangers; until even those with whom we sympathize glare at us across an impassable barrier of hostility.[36]

If there is one thing for which the Democratic party has always stood, it is commitment: to political democracy; to social justice; to a society in which we are judged not by birth, or wealth, or beauty, but by the importance of the contribution we make to our fellow citizens, our country, our world.[37]

[36] Address, Jefferson-Jackson Day Dinner, Detroit, Mich., May 5, 1967.
[37] Address, Annual Political Conference, Women's Division, New York State Democratic Committee, Albany, N.Y., March 1, 1965.

In my view, these two principles are the base upon which the Democratic party of New York State must be built:

First, we must engage in a great educational effort. I see the Democratic party—this collection of fabulously talented men and women—as the vehicle by which the skills we take for granted are taught to the poor—how to buy, how to organize, how to ask, how to complain.

I think the Democratic party can be a nongovernmental community action program; working not just at election time, but all year round; working not just for success within the present political system—but for the creation of a politics more true to the ideals of its founders and our dreams of its future.

As we help those who are now helpless, we can only strengthen ourselves and our world.

Second, we must increase our day-to-day concern with government—to not be satisfied with setting out programs once every four years, but to take active part in the way those programs are implemented—in the schools, in the welfare department, in law-enforcement and housing repair. Only if we do these things can we truly secure rights to the poor. Only if we help them—and teach them to help themselves— will our statute books and our constitutions come alive. Only if we build a party that can and does represent these people, in the review of the law as well as in the grand sweep of its design, will we have a party that truly represents ourselves and our children.[38]

Campaign Finances

When Marshall McLuhan told us that in this century "the medium is the message," he was doing more than merely giving us a phrase to go with "Keep the faith, baby." He was, in my judgment, giving us an insight into modern politics, and a disturbing one, at that.

For more and more, as our population increases, as the problems of our society become more complex, and as the

[38] Address, Lexington Democratic Club, New York, N.Y., February 4, 1965.

cost of political campaigns continues to mount—it becomes more and more clear that the package is often more important than the product; that the perceived "image" of a candidate is often more important than what he says. . . .

This situation [exorbitant campaign costs] is rapidly becoming intolerable for a democratic society, where the right to vote—and to be a candidate—is the ultimate political protection. For we are in danger of creating a situation in which our candidates must be chosen only from among the rich, the famous, or those willing to be beholden to others who will pay the bills.

Heavy dependence on the relatively few who can meet these enormous costs is not only demeaning and degrading to the candidate, it also engenders immense cynicism about the political process itself. We must begin to find solutions.[39]

There is wide agreement, I think, that some form of public support for election campaigns is needed. Holders of public office should not have to be obligated, or even appear to be obligated, to large contributors who made it possible for them to stand for office. Able young people should not be deterred from entering politics by the fear of having to compromise their values and their independence in order to obtain financing. . . .

And large-scale giving in small amounts would free candidates from having to solicit and rely upon a small number of large gifts.

I believe we can best accomplish these objectives by some form of tax incentive—by which each citizen can contribute to the party or candidates, the committees or organizations of his choice, and receive partial forgiveness of his contribution on his income tax. . . .

A tax incentive for individual donations does not raise the most serious objection to direct subsidies—its potential for centralization of political power, for a major realignment of our traditional political system. Our political parties have always been collections of separate state and local organizations. But a subsidy fund, controlled by a central authority, could all too easily be used to build a party to the liking of the National

[39] Address, Skidmore College, Saratoga, N.Y., February 22, 1967.

Committee or the presidential candidate—to enforce party discipline and party ideology by advancing particular local candidates, and starving others.[40]

The Long Act must be repealed. It places funds where they are least needed and, more important, it does so by giving massive amounts of funds in a dangerous and unrestricted way to the national leadership of the two major political parties. The Long Act has the potential of changing our whole political system. Our national political parties have always been coalitions of state parties, which in turn are coalitions of local parties. Our ideal and our working rule have been that political decisions and policies will be made from the bottom up, not from the top down. Unrestricted public financing of national political campaigns is a revolutionary overturn of principles which have served our Republic for 175 years. The national parties would be divorced to a large extent from local control, and given immense power to reward or punish local candidates. By this power to decide where to concentrate, and where to refrain from, presidential campaign efforts, the national chairman would wield enormous leverage over the prospects and policies and, indeed, over the very process of selection of local candidates all over the country. The national leadership of the two parties could thereby dominate state and local elections all over the country.[41]

First of all, it was suggested that contributions of both individuals and groups, including unions and corporations, be encouraged with respect to *bipartisan* or nonpartisan activity. Thus, funds contributed to registration drives, to bipartisan campaigns of whatever kind, or for forums or debates, would be encouraged to be declared deductible for income-tax purposes.

As a further tax incentive to widespread political contribution, that Commission proposed a tax credit of up to $10 per taxpayer, amounting to 50 percent of any contribution to a political campaign, and alternatively a deduction for the first $100 contributed.

[40] Testimony, Senate Finance Committee, June 6, 1967.
[41] Press release, April 4, 1966.

Finally, it was strongly urged that present limitations—now widely ignored—be enforced, and that full disclosure of all political gifts or expenditures of more than a minor nature be required. As we have seen in other fields, the light of publicity is often a more effective regulator than written limitations. In any event, today's situation, with a proliferation of committees at all levels, serves only to mock the dollar limits in theory imposed by law. . . .[42]

In the midst of this serious and concerned speech, he was still able to add:

The cost of campaigning has become so high that to make a candidate and his views well enough known in a state like California or New York is impossible without either a well-known personality or enormous sums of money. As an unknown virtually without funds, I was of course an exception.[43]

Kennedy several times proposed that the voting age be lowered:

I urge that New York's constitution be amended to lower the voting age to eighteen. I believe our young people have shown that they are mature enough at that age to participate in the process of government. Their record of concern and action for civil rights and in public affairs generally is one of which we can all be proud, and has proven—if proof was needed—that they would contribute significantly to the quality of American government if they had the franchise. And rewarding their interest and participation in the vote might well have useful effects in encouraging their continued participation later in life. An eighteen-year-old voting age would in my judgment be a useful and desirable reform.[44]

Kennedy for President

In the fall of 1967, with the public opinion polls recording a dramatic decline in Lyndon Johnson's popularity,

[42] Address, Skidmore College, Saratoga, N.Y., February 22, 1967.
[43] *Ibid.*
[44] Campaign speech, fall 1964.

speculation about Robert Kennedy's political plans grew. However, denying an incumbent President who wishes to run for re-election and who seeks his own party's renomination without fatally splitting the party is regarded by professional politicians as virtually impossible. There is every reason to believe that Kennedy accepted this verdict and was setting his sights on 1972 or beyond.

Yet many Democrats who were against the war in Vietnam, or who felt our national priorities must be reordered to make available more resources for our ailing cities, or who simply did not like Lyndon Johnson for reasons of personality and style, persisted in the hope that Kennedy could be persuaded to lead their crusade to unseat the President. For over two years, Bobby had wished to win the support and affection of the discontented in the Democratic party. He had succeeded to a remarkable degree, and now they were demanding he validate his credentials as their spokesman with an active program.

Kennedy, however, offered them little encouragement. As late as November 1, 1967, he was quoted as stating unequivocally:

I support President Johnson in 1968 and I support Vice President Humphrey.[45]

But a few weeks later, the first of a series of events which would mark 1968 as one of the most unusual and unpredictable political years in American history forced Kennedy to seriously re-evaluate his plans. Quite unexpectedly, Minnesota Senator Eugene McCarthy started talking about seizing the liberal banner and leading the fight against President Johnson's renomination. Because McCarthy would be running on many of the same planks Kennedy advocated, such as the need to extricate ourselves from Vietnam and devote more attention to our troubled urban areas, Kennedy was confronted with a difficult dilemma. If he supported McCarthy, as the issues would dictate, he would tie himself to a fringe candidate who was given little chance by the experts to win, while running the risk of alienating party regulars around the

[45] *The New Republic*, November 1, 1967.

country whom he would need in his own possible campaign for the presidency four years later. On the other hand, if he did not support McCarthy, he would be vulnerable to attacks from the liberals he had so determinedly wooed, on the grounds that he was simply an opportunist unwilling to fight for what he believed in if it entailed a possible danger to his own political career.

At first, Kennedy attempted to buy more time before making a commitment regarding McCarthy in the hope that outside events would make a decision unnecessary or, at least, easier. In late November, when McCarthy's candidacy was still in the rumor stage, Kennedy declared:

I'm going to wait until McCarthy announces before I do anything. . . . I expect Lyndon Johnson to be the candidate of the Democratic party and I will support the Democratic party.[46]

That same month, he was questioned about his intentions on the television program, "Face the Nation."

MR. AGRONSKY: Senator Kennedy, if President Johnson were to feel next year that he could only win re-election by asking you to replace Vice President Humphrey, would you accept the Democratic Vice Presidential nomination in 1968?

SENATOR KENNEDY: No, I would not. But I think there is no indication that he would ask me, and I think he has made his alliance in association with Vice President Humphrey, and I think Vice President Humphrey should continue as the nominee of the Democratic party. And I would support President Johnson and Vice President Humphrey if they receive the nomination of the Democratic party.

MR. WICKER: Senator Kennedy, does that mean, then, that you think given all the circumstances that exist today, unfortunate though some may be, given all the circumstances, that you think that the nomination and re-election of President Johnson is the best thing for the country because in all the circumstances he would be the best man?

SENATOR KENNEDY: Well, I expect that he is going to receive the nomination and I will support him. I think that one of

[46] *Newsweek*, December 27, 1967.

the great problems that we are having at the moment is the fact that we are not really having much of a dialogue about some of these matters. That is why I said a week ago that it is possible that if Eugene McCarthy declares and decides to enter some of the primaries, there will at least be a discussion. I think one of the problems in the country at the moment is the fact that there is no communication between races and between various groups in the country, that there is no real dialogue about Vietnam, really, any more. We have taken to the streets, there is violence, there is lawlessness; we frequently will not let those who disagree with us speak. I think that not only the Democratic party suffers but the whole country suffers, and our society suffers. And I think that it is possible that if Senator McCarthy decided to run, as it has been suggested, that there could be a healthy element in that. We could then get around to beginning to discuss these matters and exchanging views. I do not think, as I said earlier to Mr. Agronsky, that it is possible for me to do it, because I do not think that I would be accepted on that basis. But I think that if he performs that function, and we get it out of the streets, we get it out of marching into the Pentagon, as we did several weeks ago, and we have a debate, that it could be healthy for the country. I think that we can expect at the end of it, looking at tradition and looking at history, that President Johnson will be nominated. But I think that this kind of exchange can be very healthy. And we are not getting it from the Republican party, certainly. They have not offered any program, either in the domestic field or in the international field, or about Vietnam that really is very helpful or very different from the Democratic party, and I think that has been harmful.

MR. MUDD: Senator, are you saying that your support of President Johnson and Vice President Humphrey applies after they receive the nomination?

SENATOR KENNEDY: Well, I think it really depends on, assuming that Senator McCarthy goes into the race, as I gather from the newspaper reports he will, I think that I would remain out of it until the time of the nomination, purely because I think it would be hypocritical for me, on one hand, to support many of these issues and many of the questions that I have heard Senator McCarthy speak about before, to support his position and have some opposition to the present administration, and yet support President Johnson against him. On the other hand, I could not support Senator McCarthy against President Johnson because there are many of the things that President Johnson stands for in the domestic field that I also support. So I think that I would remain out of it.

MR. AGRONSKY: Well, Senator, leaving hypocrisy aside, this business of dealing yourself out of the campaign until after the nomination perhaps might seem excessively timid, even self-serving for your own political future. Don't you feel that the issue of Vietnam is so important that you should participate in this debate?

SENATOR KENNEDY: Yes, I am going to continue to, and I am going to continue to talk, and I have just finished a book, which was mentioned at the beginning of this program, about my feelings about Vietnam. And I am going to continue to talk about these issues. But I am not talking about these issues, as a competitor to anyone, I am talking about these issues as issues which I think are important to the American people. And I would like to have them examined on that basis. I think that what we are doing at the present time in Vietnam is a mistake. I think that the course that we are following is an error. But I am saying that as a United States Senator, and I want to have what I say analyzed on that basis, and that is what I have tried to make clear for some period of time. I am not doing it on the basis of trying to build up a political following so that I can grab the nomination from President Johnson, but I am going to discuss the issues. I am going to discuss what I think should be done domestically, and I am going— and I think it is within the Democratic party that we should have dissent. I do not think that to dissent here in the United States or those who disagree should be confined to those who are young. I think that when we sign up for the Democratic party we don't say that we are never going to disagree. I think that there is much to disagree about. I mean we have done a great deal within this country but that there also is much more that we can do, in my judgment, not only in Vietnam but in other parts of the world that we are not doing, and I am going to continue to talk about those things.[47]

When McCarthy finally did announce a few days later,

[47] "Face the Nation" (CBS-TV), November 26, 1967.

Kennedy simply labeled the Minnesotan's candidacy as a "healthy element" for the party, and said little else. On at least one occasion, however, he was able to joke about his dilemma. At a Democratic fund-raising dinner in New York, with Senator McCarthy in attendance, there was great suspense when Bobby rose to announce

. . . my support for a man of Minnesota who because of his deep feeling over Vietnam has decided to run for the Presidency despite heavy odds against him. [Kennedy paused, then added:] I speak for Harold Stassen.[48]

Then, on March 12, 1968, the second bombshell of the political year was exploded: Eugene McCarthy defeated Lyndon Johnson in the New Hampshire primary. Possibly believing that Johnson could now be denied the nomination, or at least that the McCarthy campaign posed a real threat to his claim to liberal leadership in the party which had to be met, Robert Kennedy decided to run for the Presidency. On Saturday, March 16, at a press conference in the Senate Office Building, he made his announcement.

KENNEDY'S ANNOUNCEMENT TO RUN
FOR THE PRESIDENCY
New York Times, March 17, 1968

I am announcing today my candidacy for the Presidency of the United States.

I do not run for the Presidency merely to oppose any man but to propose new policies. I run because I am convinced that this country is on a perilous course and because I have such strong feelings about what must be done, and I feel that I'm obliged to do all that I can.

I run to seek new policies—policies to end the bloodshed in Vietnam and in our cities, policies to close the gap that now exists between black and white, between rich and poor, between young and old in this country and around the rest of the world.

I run for the Presidency because I want the Democratic party and the United States of America to stand for hope instead of despair, for reconciliation of men instead of the growing risk of world war.

[48] *Newsweek,* December 27, 1967.

I run because it is now unmistakably clear that we can change these disastrous divisive policies only by changing the men who are now making them. For the reality of recent events in Vietnam has been glossed over with illusions.

The report of the riot commission has been largely ignored.

The crisis in gold, the crisis in our cities, the crisis in our farms and in our ghettos have all been met with too little and too late.

No one who knows what I know about the extraordinary demands of the Presidency can be certain that any mortal can adequately fill that position.

But my service on the National Security Council during the Cuban missile crisis, the Berlin crisis of 1961 and 1962 and later, the negotiations on Laos and on the nuclear test ban treaty have taught me something about both the uses and the limitations of military power, about the value of negotiations with allies and with enemies, about the opportunities and dangers which await our nation in many corners of the globe in which I have traveled.

As a member of the Cabinet and a member of the Senate I have seen the inexcusable and ugly deprivations which cause children to starve in Mississippi, black citizens to riot in Watts, young Indians to commit suicide on their reservations because they've lacked all hope and they feel they have no future, and proud and able-bodied families to wait out their lives in empty idleness in eastern Kentucky.

I have traveled and I have listened to the young people of our nation and felt their anger about the war that they are sent to fight and about the world that they are about to inherit.

In private talks and in public I have tried in vain to alter our course in Vietnam before it further saps our spirit and our manpower, further raises the risk of wider war and further destroys the country and the people it was meant to save.

I cannot stand aside from the contest that will decide our nation's future and our children's future.

The remarkable New Hampshire campaign of Senator Eugene McCarthy has proven how deep are the present divisions within our party and within our country. Until that was publicly clear my presence in the race would have been seen as a clash of personalities rather than issues.

But now that that fight is won and over policies which I have long been challenging I must enter that race. The fight is just beginning and I believe that I can win.

I have previously communicated this decision to President Johnson and late last night my brother, Senator Edward Kennedy, traveled to Wisconsin to communicate my decision to Senator McCarthy.

I made clear through my brother to Senator McCarthy that my candidacy would not be in opposition to his but in harmony. My aim is to both support and expand his valiant campaign in the spirit of his November 30 statement, taking one month at a time.

It is important now that he achieve the largest possible majority next month in Wisconsin, in Pennsylvania and in the Massachusetts primaries.

I strongly support his effort in those states and I urge all my friends to give him their help and their votes.

Both of us will be encouraging like-minded delegates to the national convention, for both of us want above all else an open Democratic convention in Chicago, free to choose a new course for our party and for our country.

To make certain that this effort will still be effective in June, I am required now to permit the entry of my name into the California primaries to be held in that month. And I do so in the belief, which I will strive to implement, that Senator McCarthy's forces and mine will be able to work together in one form or another.

My desire is not to divide the strength of those forces seeking a change, but rather to increase it.

Under the laws of Oregon and Nebraska this decision requires the Secretary of State in each of these states to place my name on the ballot, but in no state will my efforts be directed against Senator McCarthy.

Both of us are campaigning to give our forces and

our party an opportunity to select the strongest possible standard bearer for the November elections.

To insure that my candidacy must be tested beginning now, five months before the convention and not after the primaries are over. I think that is the least that I can do to meet my responsibilities to the Democratic party and to the people of the United States.

Finally, my decision reflects no personal animosity or disrespect toward President Johnson. He served President Kennedy with the utmost loyalty and was extremely kind to me and members of my family in the difficult months which followed the events of November of 1963.

I have often commended his efforts in health, in education, and in many areas, and I have the deepest sympathy for the burden that he carries today.

But the issue is not personal. It is our profound differences over where we are heading and what we want to accomplish.

I do not lightly dismiss the dangers and the difficulties of challenging an incumbent President. But these are not ordinary times and this is not an ordinary election.

At stake is not simply the leadership of our party and even our country. It is our right to the moral leadership of this planet.

I thank you. I appreciate the members of my family and my office showing up.[49]

While circumstances forced him into the race at a time and in a manner hardly of his own choosing, there can be little doubt that Kennedy was a man who wanted to be President. In late 1966, in an interview in *Newsweek*, he had spoken of the Presidency and his own popularity rather philosophically:

Obviously I feel strongly about certain things, and the Presidency is the place where you can do most to get things done. Existence is so fickle. Not only can this feeling [of Kennedy fever] pass but also your own existence can pass. . . . Robert

[49] Announcement for the Presidency, Senate Office Building, Washington, D.C., March 16, 1968.

Frost once said that you go on the tennis court to play tennis, not to see if the lines are straight. So you do what you can while you're here and the future will take care of itself.[50]

But in the Kennedy home in Virginia there is a cigarette box presented to Bobby after his brother captured the Democratic presidential nomination in 1960. It has this message inscribed across the top:

Robert F. Kennedy
When I'm through, How about you?
Democratic National Convention
Los Angeles, 1960

Beneath the inscription is the scrawled signature of the donor, John F. Kennedy.

[50] *Newsweek,* October 24, 1966.

PART II

America At Home

Chapter 3

Civil Rights and the Black Revolution

I won't say I stayed awake nights worrying about civil rights before I became Attorney General.[1]

But suppose God is black? What if we go to heaven and we, all our lives, have treated the Negro as an inferior, and God is there and we look up and He is not white? What then is our response?[2]

We meet at a time our nation is on the brink of its greatest domestic crisis since the Civil War. This summer we have seen violence erupt in our cities, taking dozens of lives, destroying billions of dollars in property. Hopefully the worst has passed. Surely we cannot tolerate this wanton killing and burning. Clearly those who destroy must feel the full force of the law. But just as surely, just as clearly, it is fruitless simply to quell the explosions without attacking the roots. This violence is not simply an aimless burst of savagery, nor the product of outside agitators. It is brutal evidence of our failure to deal with the crisis in urban America and of our failure to bridge the widening gap between the affluent and poor, black and white Americans.[3]

Until very recently most "New Deal" liberals—i.e., those who share the Rooseveltian faith that social change can

[1] William V. Shannon, *The Heir Apparent* (New York: Macmillan, 1967), p. 63.
[2] *Look*, August 23, 1966.
[3] Testimony, National Commission on Urban Problems, New York, N.Y., September 6, 1967.

be induced gradually and peacefully in a democratic society through the limited intervention of the federal government—believed that the second-class status of the black man in America could be rectified through a combination of enforceable civil rights laws, an improved welfare system, and increased understanding and communication between blacks and whites. Throughout the 1940s and into the 1950s these liberals defended their approach with an avalanche of statistics showing average Negro income, educational attainment, and social acceptance steadily on the rise.

Then unexpectedly, in the late 1950s, this liberal optimism was threatened by the "rediscovery" of widespread poverty in this country. A series of federal manpower studies, popularized by muckrakers like Michael Harrington and Ben Badikian, revealed that, although a large minority of Negroes had entered a growing and increasingly affluent black middle class during the decade and a half since Pearl Harbor, their real economic advances appeared more than offset by a complete lack of improvement in the condition of the majority. Millions of Negroes continued to live in the grinding poverty and deepening despair of our urban ghettos. Nothing the government had done since World War II had materially affected the stagnating lot of these neglected and alienated people. Indeed, there was evidence that the gap between the haves and the have-nots was widening, not decreasing.

Liberals, their confidence in their approach to the "Negro problem" somewhat shaken by these findings, and also by the first stirrings of an activist civil rights movement in the South, hastened to accelerate their tactics. During the Eisenhower, Kennedy, and Johnson administrations, Congress passed legislation to strengthen Negro voting rights, economic opportunities, and access to public accommodations. It was hoped that these sincere signs of good will, along with the new federal war on poverty and the unprecedented economic boom of the first five years of the 1960s, would release much of the mounting tension threatening to detonate the ghettos.

The racial insurrections in Watts, Harlem, Newark, Detroit, and other northern cities during the summers of

1965-1967 unceremoniously exploded the credibility of this lingering New Deal faith in a gradual, piecemeal solution to Negro grievances. The civil rights laws had not eliminated the de facto economic and social segregation in the North. By the admission of its own creators, the poverty war had been a flop, lacking both the design and resources necessary for success. And the prosperity of the sixties, spurred by tax cuts rather than increased federal domestic spending, had failed to reach those in the lower economic strata, with the result that average Negro family income had decreased in the past few years relative to average white income.

Thus, in the late 1960s, the United States is entering a period of intellectual confusion in which concerned politicians and social scientists are casting about for a new conceptual framework within which to understand black-white relations in America. To make the situation even more complex, the rules under which new policies and programs will be tested have changed dramatically. New demands for political and economic self-determination, along with pride and reverse racism—all the currents generated in the ghettos by the mixed bag of beliefs called "black power"—must be considered in any attempts by the white community to bring about change. Furthermore, the growing tendency by members of both races to view solutions in terms of violence—black revolution and the reinforcement of urban police forces to crush these uprisings—merely exacerbates the destructive racism which lies at the core of the difficulties.

Time, contrary to liberal expectations, has served to deepen the crisis and move quick, simple solutions beyond our grasp. We are clearly confronted with the most serious and dangerous domestic situation since the Civil War. Either we must find a way to open our society to all, or the growing violence and fear may unleash political and social forces which will close it to everyone.

Robert Kennedy's career coincided with this period of shaken confidence in America's ability to reconcile the two races. Though it now seems a little difficult to believe, Kennedy still appeared unaware of the desperate plight of many Negroes in this country when he became Attorney General in 1961. Like his brother, who was genuinely shocked by the terrible poverty he saw in rural West Virginia during the presidential primary there in 1960, he had been ignorant of the conditions in which much of the nation was forced to exist. Perhaps, as William Shannon says, "This slowness is understandable in a youth who grew up in the sheltered, privileged world of Hyannis Port and Palm Beach."

To a remarkable extent the evolution of Robert Kennedy's thoughts on the racial problem from those innocent beginnings in 1961 was a speeded-up parallel to the shifts in liberal thinking outlined above. Within a five-year span he passed through successive stages of virtual unawareness, unquestioning faith in the efficacy of time and understanding, confidence that new federal programs and prosperity would ease the black man's burden, disillusionment with New Deal strategies, and finally the proposal of new approaches to the economic and social difficulties of the ghettos based on cooperation between the black community and private enterprise, with the federal government reduced to the role of providing fiscal incentives.

Robert Kennedy made more statements about civil rights than any other topic, with the possible exceptions of crime and Vietnam. The large number of quotes that follow are designed to help the reader trace the Senator's intellectual development in this area. In the process there will come some useful insights into his mode of thought.

Early Views

Let us begin with his early remarks as Attorney General. Upon his appointment to the post in December, 1960, he was asked what his approach to new civil rights legislation would be. Replying with candor, if not quite the zeal of a rights crusader, he said:

I have not had a chance to study the situation, the laws, in this whole field. My general philosophy is that we have to move strongly and vigorously in the field of civil rights. I do not think that this is a subject or matter that can be solved overnight, however. . . . I would wait for my instructions and guidance from President-elect Kennedy on this matter. He is the one that is going to make the decision, not me.[4]

Later, speaking of the racial problem in general terms and of his reaction to it when he first took office:

I think if there was anything that shocked me when I became Attorney General it was the fact that there are large numbers of our population, hundreds and hundreds of thousands of individuals, who cannot vote because of the fact that they are Negroes.[5]

Our responsibility as a nation is most plain. We must remove the injustices.[6]

Well, what I said—and I have said it in all sections of the country—that I think that first the vast majority of people in the United States, and that includes the people in the South, are law-abiding people who wish to live by the law. They might not fully approve of Supreme Court decisions, might not fully approve of legislation that has been passed, but they want to abide and live by the law and do not want to circumvent court decisions which can bring about violence. I think this is particularly true in the southern states, and I have said as much.[7]

But as long as inequities exist in the South, North, East, and West, we have a task to perform. The Negro was called the White Man's Burden in the nineteenth century. Our treatment of the Negro is the White Man's Burden in this half of the twentieth century. We have to move ahead because our freedom, our strength, depend upon the maintenance of these ideals. We must advance if we want to fulfill our destiny and remain leader of the Free World.[8]

[4] Nick Thimmisch and William Johnson, *R. F. K. at 40* (Boston: W. W. Norton, 1965), p. 89.

[5] "Washington Report" (CBS-TV), March 3, 1963.

[6] Robert F. Kennedy, *The Pursuit of Justice* (New York: Harper & Row, 1965), p. 77.

[7] Press conference, Columbia, S.C., December 12, 1961.

[8] Robert F. Kennedy, *Just Friends and Brave Enemies* (New York: Harper & Row, 1962), p. 192.

From the Congo to Cuba, from South Vietnam to Algiers, in India, Brazil and Iran, men and women and children are straightening their backs and listening—to the evil promises of Communist tyranny and the honorable promises of Anglo-American liberty. And those people will decide not only their future but how the cause of freedom fares in the world. . . . In the world-wide struggle, the graduation at the University of Charlayne Hunter and Hamilton Holmes will without question aid and assist the fight against Communist political infiltration and guerrilla warfare. . . . When parents send their children to school this fall in Atlanta, peaceably and in accordance with the rule of law, barefoot Burmese and Congolese will see before their eyes Americans living by the rule of law.[9]

My grandfather came to this country many years ago. He was brought up in Boston and when he went out to look for a job there were signs on many stores that no Irish were wanted. Now after some forty or fifty years, an Irish Catholic is President of the United States. That progress has been made over the last fifty years. And we feel that the same kind of progress will be made by the Negroes. There is no question about it. In the foreseeable future a Negro can achieve the same position that my brother has.[10]

Northern Hypocrisy

He recognized that the Negro had many legitimate grievances in the North, not just in the South as many have assumed.

Many millions of white people, especially in the North—people who until recently assumed that the Negro was satisfied with the great social progress of the past twenty years—are faced now with the startling discovery that it is not true, that whatever progress Negroes have made is inadequate to their need for equality. And none of us can deny that their need is real, that their frustration is genuine. We have been

[9] R. E. Thompson and H. Meyers, *Robert F. Kennedy: The Brother Within* (New York: Macmillan, 1962), pp. 140-141.

[10] Voice of America broadcast, May 26, 1961.

unreasonable about it, or ignorant of it, far too long. We are only now paying the price. . . . Military and police law have been needed to replace normal local rule in countless cities in the North as well as the South.

This is what happens when long-standing legitimate grievances are not remedied under law. Great moral damage is done to individuals, to communities, to states and to the very fabric of the nation.[11]

There is no question that segregation in the South is socially, politically and morally wrong. But there is deep-seated segregation in the North, also, and it is just as wrong. Racial discrimination is a national, not a regional problem, and it cannot be solved simply by individual instances of federal action on behalf of Freedom Riders or a single college student.[12]

People in the North—pointing to the South—go to their private clubs, go to their all-white housing developments and send their children to all-white schools and say: "Those damned southerners!" They don't understand they can start with themselves.[13]

Financial leaders from the East who deplore discrimination in the South belong to institutions where no Negroes or Jews are allowed and their children attend private schools where no Negro students are enrolled. . . . Union officials criticize Southern leaders and yet practice discrimination with their unions. Government officials belong to private clubs in Washington where Negroes including ambassadors are not welcomed even at mealtime.[14]

QUESTION: Is the danger of an explosion as great in the North as in the South?
RFK: It can be more difficult, because the problems in the South, at least temporarily, are more easily resolved. The

[11] Kennedy, *The Pursuit of Justice,* p. 76.
[12] Speech, Civil Rights Committee, New York City Central Labor Council, AFL-CIO, March 9, 1963.
[13] Interview, Washington, D.C., June 5, 1963.
[14] Speech, Law Day exercises, University of Georgia Law School, Athens, Ga., May 6, 1961.

Negroes are concerned in Birmingham about being able to sit at a lunch counter, employment, taking the signs off the drinking fountains and taking the signs off the rest rooms. Well, you can do that and you release a valve and people are at least happy—

QUESTION: But for how long?

RFK: Well, for some time. . . . But in the North, in Chicago or Los Angeles or San Francisco. . . . What steps could you take to release that valve? What you have to do is make over some of these cities and really take some drastic action, so you *could* have a more serious situation in the Northern cities than you do in the South.[15]

The South Is Warned

While showing an understanding of the special problems faced by the South in granting Negroes full equality, Kennedy's remarks to Southern white audiences were similar in tone and content to those delivered in the North. After describing the discrimination and humiliation heaped upon Negroes in the South in a speech to Georgia College students, he declared,

I don't think it makes much sense. I don't think you're going to get people to accept that system. I don't think you and I would accept that system, that educated people would accept that system. . . . So Mississippi is not going to do it, Alabama is not going to do it themselves; they make quite clear that they're not going to do it. And I think the individual Negro is a citizen of the United States as well as a citizen of Massachusetts—ah, of Mississippi, therefore they're entitled to have the Federal Government afford them some protection.

I think it's unfortunate it has to be done, but I don't see any alternative to it at the present time.[16] [Long applause]

At the Law Day exercises of the University of Georgia, three years previously, Kennedy had said:

[15] Interview, Washington, D.C., June 5, 1963.
[16] Speech, West Georgia College, Carrollton, Ga., May 26, 1964.

I happen to believe that the 1954 decision was right. But my belief does not matter—it is the law. Some of you may believe the decision was wrong. That does not matter. It is the law. And we both respect the law. By facing this problem honorably, you have shown to all the world that we Americans are moving forward together—solving this problem—under the rule of law. . . .

To the South, perhaps more than any other section of the country, has been given the opportunity and the challenge and the responsibility of demonstrating America at its greatest—at its full potential of liberty under law. You may ask, will we enforce the Civil Rights statutes? The answer is: "Yes, we will. . . ."

The hardest problems of all in law enforcement are those involving a conflict of law and local customs. History has recorded many occasions when the moral sense of a nation produced judicial decisions, such as the 1954 decision in *Brown v. Board of Education,* which required difficult local adjustments.[17]

He moved early to discredit the notion that Negroes might somehow deserve their inferior status for reasons of heredity.

Recent intelligence and aptitude tests clearly indicate that any margin that exists between the scores of white and Negro students is related directly to their social and economic environment.[18]

Responsibilities: White and Black

On occasion he spoke of what he expected from black and white leaders in this country.

The lesson of Prince Edward County is the lesson of the entire country. Where were we after the 1954 school decision? Where were the pulpit, the press, the public officials? The an-

[17] Speech, Law Day exercises, University of Georgia Law School, Athens, Ga., May 6, 1961.
[18] Kennedy, *op. cit.,* p. 85.

swer is that there was a vacuum of leadership—until it was filled, finally, by demagogues with strident slogans of "segregation forever" and "massive resistance."

When a whole generation and a whole region is told by its leaders that a Supreme Court decision is an unconstitutional nullity, how can it be expected that the mortar of public respect will be added to the bricks of law? [19]

MR. SPIVAK: You have spoken pretty forcefully on the rights of the American Negro today. What do you see as his responsibility today?

RFK: I have also spoken frequently on that. I think that they have a responsibility not only to Negroes but to white people and to the United States. I think we can make great progress in this field. I think that the progress that is required and necessary will be made only if whites and Negroes join together to make that progress. If Negroes under pressure get the idea that the only way to have steps taken is to act the role of the bully and that as at least one Negro leader has said, "We have the white man on the run now, let's keep him on the run," I don't think that kind of attitude will remedy the situation. I think whites and Negroes working together is what is needed at the present time, so I think that Negro leaders have a major responsibility. [20]

Those who achieve Negro leadership understand it can't be done immediately, but if I were in their place, I'd be saying: "We've been waiting a long time, we want to get it now," and making that kind of an effort. [21]

New Frontier Gradualism

Yet despite the fine words and calls to action, the federal government exhibited little initiative in the field of civil rights during the Kennedy Administration's first

[19] Speech, Herbert H. Lehman Human Relations Award Dinner, American Jewish Committee Appeal for Human Relations, New York, N.Y., April 16, 1964.

[20] "Meet the Press" (NBC-TV), June 23, 1963.

[21] Interview, Washington, D.C., June 5, 1963.

two years in power. Robert Kennedy was frequently called upon to come to the Administration's defense.

. . . It's not a field in which I think a great deal is going to be accomplished just by talking about, by continuously introducing legislation which has no possibility of enactment and is not really going to accomplish the purpose. And the President isn't interested in that. This Administration is not interested.

Maybe the papers will write up that the Kennedy Administration is a real advocate of civil rights legislation or civil rights action, even though they don't do anything, just because they keep pushing legislation that has no chance of being enacted.

What we want to do is actually accomplish something, actually get something done. We're not interested in pushing anything down people's throats, but we're trying to work these matters out, easily, realizing the whole time that we have to make progress and that we won't accept the status quo. That has been our philosophy.[22]

QUESTION: As a candidate, President Kennedy said in Los Angeles in early September, 1960, that with a stroke of a pen the Executive could wipe out discrimination in the federally subsidized housing and that this order was already long overdue. Nearly two years later nothing has been done about it. Why?
RFK: Well, it is a question of the timing of it and he has responsibilities in many other areas at the same time, so it is just a question of his making a judgment as to when would be the best time to sign such an executive order. It would be easy just to go ahead and do it and certain other pieces of legislation which could be very helpful. . . . Certain other steps that he has taken and which he plans to take would be seriously jeopardized, but he could go ahead and sign the executive order and it would be acclaimed. He has his overall responsibilities and this is just a question of timing.[23]

MR. SPIVAK: It has been estimated that about 6,000 Negro children have been integrated in the public schools this year, making a total of about 220,000 out of some three million in

[22] "Today" (NBC-TV), January 30, 1962.
[23] "Issues and Answers" (ABC-TV), June 17, 1962.

the Southern and border states. Would you say at the present rate of school desegregation we are meeting the Supreme Court's injunction of "with all deliberate speed"?

RFK: This is not in the hands of the Executive Branch of the government. . . .

MR. SPIVAK: Is there any way in which the federal government is going to be able to speed up the desegregation of the schools? There are still, I believe, some three million Negro children who are not integrated.

RFK: I don't know whether all of those three million want to be integrated.

MR. SPIVAK: But there are many millions who aren't. Is there anything more the federal government can do? Do you think the evasive action of the localities now is almost at an end?

RFK: Of course, there has been so much criticism of certain localities in trying to deal with this problem, but there should also be recognition of what they have been able to do and under very difficult circumstances. Maybe it is not as quick and as fast as some of us would like, but there has been a great deal of progress that has been made over a period of the last year or so. I think they will continue to make progress. But this situation is not just going to go away; it is not going to disappear. I think there will continue to be affirmative gains. Maybe, as I say, not as quickly as we might hope, but I think we will continue to make them.[24]

The Kennedy philosophy at the time seemed to counsel much caution and maximum reliance on local government as the primary enforcer of the law. As late as 1963, Robert Kennedy still opposed withholding federal funds to states that discriminated in the administration of welfare and education programs.

Well, I personally wouldn't support that kind of an effort. I think that this is difficult. Whether it was Oxford or Greenwood, we have problems. But in my judgment, although it is perhaps slow, we are making progress. . . . I don't think that we should treat Mississippi, however much some of us might disagree with some of the policies of some of their leaders, as

[24] "Meet the Press" (NBC-TV), September 24, 1961.

a foreign state that we are going to whip because we don't happen to agree with what they are doing.[25]

When asked what legal steps the Justice Department was considering in regard to the Prince Edward County school closure in Virginia to avoid integration, he answered:

We had some conversations and discussions with the Attorney General of the State of Virginia, because I think, as in Dallas, that these matters should be decided and determined by the local authorities, not by the Federal Government, and that the Federal Government should come in only at a time when either the local authorities refuse to take action or have indicated that it is impossible to take action.[26]

Busing Students

And in discussing the related problem of de facto school segregation in the North, RFK was against federal pressure on local school boards to bus Negro children into white schools.

QUESTION: . . . Do you think that the neighborhood school system policy where children have to go to the nearest school, do you think this is breeding segregation? Do you think it should be abandoned altogether?
RFK: No, I think again these are matters that should be determined at the local level.[27]

I do not believe that any federal official or any United States senator should tell local school boards or school superintendents how to manage their affairs provided there is no conflict with the Constitution of the United States.
My personal opinion is that compulsory transportation of children over long distances, away from the schools in their neighborhoods, doesn't make much sense and I am against it.

[25] "Issues and Answers" (ABC-TV), April 21, 1963.
[26] Statement, Associated Press Luncheon, Dallas, Tex., November 15, 1961.
[27] Press conference, Newark, N.J., February 28, 1963.

I opposed any federal support for it when I testified on the Civil Rights Act over a year ago and when I testified before the Platform Committee of the Democratic National Convention last month.

. . . Finally, the attainment of human rights goes far deeper than the transportation of students from one place to another. I don't think we can put the entire burden of resolving de facto racial segregation upon the schools when the problem is really much broader and involves so many aspects of our society.[28]

The Vote

Throughout the period of 1961-1963, Kennedy emphasized the franchise as the key to black progress.

I think that once the Negro obtains the franchise, that the situation will be far different in the United States in many areas.[29]

The long-range solution for Negroes is voting rights. I think all other rights for which they are fighting will flow from that. Political power comes from votes and rights come from political power.[30]

I think probably the most important area, in my judgment at least—and I don't know that there are others who feel differently, but in my judgment the most important area is the field of voting. That all of our citizens can exercise their franchise. I think if they can exercise their franchise, if they can register and vote in elections that they can frequently remedy their problems themselves in their own areas.[31]

Well, I think as Negroes gain more and more political power, exercise their franchise, vote in elections and partici-

[28] Campaign statement, Binghamton, N.Y., September 9, 1964.
[29] Press conference, U.S. Department of Justice, April 6, 1961.
[30] R. E. Thompson and H. Meyers, *Robert F. Kennedy: The Brother Within* (New York: Macmillan, 1962), p. 142.
[31] "Issues and Answers" (ABC-TV), April 21, 1963.

pate in politics, that they can then use that political power to achieve within a state or within a community their rights.[32]

Demonstrations

Yet during this same span of 1961-1963, forces were gaining momentum that challenged Kennedy's easy optimism and eventually drove him to adopt a more assertive civil rights strategy. The South was alive with the sound of civil rights songs and chants, mingled with the vicious taunts and jeers of angry white bigots. Freedom rides, sit-ins, mass marches, university riots, and racial violence in unknown hamlets like Greenwood and Selma flooded the headlines. The quietude and time the President and his brother had banked on were to be denied them.

Bobby's initial public reaction to the civil rights demonstrations was polite, though sometimes less than enthusiastic.

QUESTION: What is your opinion of the freedom rides with regards to solving this particular problem [desegregation of interstate facilities]? Do you think it is an aid, or do you feel it is a deterrent?

RFK: I think that they have a right to travel, as I have said, in Interstate Commerce, and to bring matters to the attention of the public. I think there is always a question of judgment, as to when a particular action or activity might be so provocative as to lead to bloodshed or violence. Judgment has to be used in all of those cases, and I have seen nothing here yet on Route 40 [U.S. highway in Maryland, with segregated facilities] which would lead me to believe that violence was imminent.

That was different, I might say, than was the situation I found on occasion in the states of Alabama and Mississippi.[33]

The freedom riders and the trouble encountered in Alabama, Mississippi and now Florida highlight a problem which exists far beyond the South. The freedom riders are a product

[32] "Press Conference, USA" (Voice of America), June 3, 1963, in response to a question by a Japanese correspondent.

[33] Press conference, Baltimore, Md., December 15, 1961.

of a quickening desire on the part of many Americans to break down discrimination and bigotry. The first groups of freedom riders traveled to call attention to segregation laws. It took considerable courage on their part as their injuries demonstrated. But they succeeded in moving the nation's conscience. Perhaps 'even more important they also succeeded in calling attention to a fundamental truth of our society:

If respect for law and order is upheld vigorously by the leaders of the community, the law stands as a bulwark for freedom. But if over a period of time the law is challenged and the responsible officials do not stand for law and order, then order begins to give way to violence. Whenever men take the law into their own hands, the loser is the law—and, when the law loses, freedom languishes.

This by now should be clear to all Americans. It should be clear that the smallest county courthouse in Alabama and the august chambers of the Supreme Court of the United States must be dedicated to the same purpose—to maintain the individual's fundamental rights. It should be clear that, if one man's rights are denied, the rights of all are in danger—that if one man is denied equal protection of the law, we cannot be sure that we will enjoy freedom of speech or any other of our fundamental rights.

This was what was at stake when the freedom riders ventured into Alabama.[34]

We are disturbed about the fact that beatings took place [in Montgomery, Alabama], and about the fact that people's rights were not being protected. Police and police officials of states and cities in this area were not properly guarding the people because of color. We sent 500 representatives of the U.S. Government to help and assist these people.[35]

By 1963 Kennedy had come around to a more openly sympathetic point of view.

MR. KAPLOW: I would like to jump back again and ask you a

[34] Speech, Joint Defense Appeal of the American Jewish Committee and the Anti-Defamation League of B'nai B'rith, Chicago, Ill., June 21, 1961.

[35] Voice of America broadcast, May 26, 1961.

sort of blanket question: What do you think in general of the policy of street demonstrations by Negroes?

RFK: First, I think there have been many injustices that have gone on for a long period of time, and so I can see Negroes who attempt to rectify those injustices and find some remedies. They go to the local authorities, to the local merchants, and they are not able to get anywhere, and so the only way in which they can air their injustices and try to obtain remedies is to picket, to have a parade, to have a demonstration. I think this is in the oldest tradition of the United States, so I have great sympathy for that kind of an effort.

I think that if it can be solved and resolved around the conference table, it is much better to have it done in that fashion. I think also that demonstrations that are going to lead to violence, I would be strongly against those. Demonstrations however that air grievances and try to obtain remedies for injustices that have existed for a long period of time, I would have great sympathy for that kind of a thing.[36]

It has been one hundred years since the slaves were freed. During that time in many places little progress has been made to give full liberty to the descendants of the slaves. Now time is running out fast for this country.

We must recognize, as responsible citizens and as responsible government officials, that the Negroes in this country cannot be expected indefinitely to tolerate the injustices which flow from official and private racial discrimination in the United States.

The troubles we see now, agitation and even bloodshed, will not compare to what we will see a decade from now, unless real progress is made. I am not speaking of the South alone, for these injustices are not a matter of region.

As years pass, resentment increases. The only cure for resentment is progress. The only antidote to agitation is the effort which state, local, and federal officials are making to deal both with discrimination itself and with its deep-seated economic and social effects.[37]

[36] "Meet the Press" (NBC-TV), June 23, 1963.
[37] Speech, American Association of University Professors, University of South Carolina Chapter, Columbia, S.C., April 25, 1963.

QUESTION: Mr. Kennedy, as you said before, if you don't watch out there may be something in the next decade that would make what has already happened look small. Are you referring, in part, to the rise of militancy on the part of some Negro organizations?

RFK: Well, I think it should be expected, and I would be surprised if you didn't have that, if we don't make progress. I don't think you can expect a group of people to live and be treated as inferiors and be subject to injustices and not have remedies for it, and if you don't find remedies along in the course of events and progress being made, I think it is the most natural thing in the world that people would become disillusioned with the system and discouraged, and turn in some different direction, and so, if great progress is not made and continuously made, not that the fact that this problem is going to disappear overnight or you pass a law in Washington, and it is all going to go away, that is not going to be the answer.[38]

MR. SPIVAK: Mr. Kennedy, the country is being told that there is a danger of violence, even of revolution if the Negroes' demands for equality of opportunity are not met. Do you see the situation as serious as that?

RFK: I think that it is serious, Mr. Spivak. I think that the injustices have existed for a long period of time. I think that the Negroes feel that it is unacceptable that the situation should continue. I think this is supported by the vast majority of American people, so I think that the time has come to take some remedial steps—the federal government, the state governments, the local governments and individuals in the relationship with other local individuals—to rectify the situation.

MR. SPIVAK: Do you think then that if the President's civil rights proposals are not enacted that we are headed for a real racial explosion?

RFK: I think we are in for great difficulty. I think that the legislation that the President has suggested will be extremely helpful in alleviating some of these problems. Even if that is enacted, I think that this difficulty and trouble is still going to be with us because we have not met our responsibilities for a long period of time. We are paying for it now, and although

[38] Press conference, Atlanta, Ga., April 26, 1963.

the legislation, I think, will be a major step forward, I think we will still have troubles because of unemployment amongst Negroes, lack of education, lack of skill, and a great deal needs to be done in this field as well as in the field and category of civil rights.[39]

We can reflect as well on the individual responsibility demonstrated by 200,000 Negroes and whites in the March on Washington last summer. There were dire prophecies of angry crowds, of violence and of riot. All of us saw what happened instead. A London newspaper called it the Gentle Flood.[40]

QUESTION: In candor, did Gregory's presence [in the Birmingham protests] help or hinder?

RFK: I think in fairness to Dick Gregory it indicates to the Negroes his interest and his commitment, and his cause and he has been associated with it, so that although you can't say Dick Gregory coming down and getting involved in it made a difference in the result there, it indicated to the Negroes there and the Negroes around the country that there were people who were in important positions in the Negro community that were vitally concerned with the future of the people, so I didn't want it to go out that Dick Gregory means nothing to them.[41]

Kennedy defended the civil rights movement against the charge of Communist infiltration.

QUESTION: What specific action is the federal government contemplating to keep the Communists out of the civil rights movement?

RFK: First, I'd say there has been an effort by the Communist party, a major effort by the Communist party to infiltrate the civil rights movement in various parts of the United States. They really have been remarkably not successful considering the amount of turmoil and distress that's going on in the

---

[39] "Meet the Press" (NBC-TV), June 23, 1963.

[40] Speech, Herbert H. Lehman Human Relations Award Dinner, American Jewish Committee Appeal for Human Relations, New York, N.Y., April 16, 1964.

[41] Press briefing, Washington, D.C., May 10, 1963.

United States among the Negro population. We watch that, as we watch the activities of the Communist party continuously, and we—of course if there's violation of the law we would take action. If we find that there has sometimes been infiltration of the Communist party and it's not known to those who are involved in the movement, then we try to bring it to their attention and see if they, the individuals, were in control. If not, we'd take some action ourselves.[42]

Just Compensation or Something for Nothing?

To those who argued that Negroes were demanding too much too quickly, he retorted,

I think great progress has been made. But I think we have a long, long way to go. And I don't think you can look at the situation, not just in the South, but all over the country, where we hold to believe in certain principles, where we go around the world and tell everybody what a fine democracy we are—and yet we have these practices where in many areas of the country we treat a portion of our population as inferiors—it doesn't seem to me it makes any sense. And talk about the progress we make—considering that it has been now one hundred years since the Civil War, and still these practices are taking place, where an individual cannot even register and vote in an election for the President of the United States because he happens to be a Negro—not just one man, but hundreds and hundreds and hundreds and thousands of individuals—I don't think that is very satisfactory.[43]

The problems that remain are massive. The results of racial discrimination carry on for generation after generation. To face this openly, and to try to meet it squarely, is the challenge of this decade of change.

It is one thing to open the schools to all children regardless of race. It is another to train the teachers, to build the classrooms, and to attempt to eliminate the effects of past educational deficiencies. It is still another to find ways to feed the incentive to learn and keep children in school.

[42] Speech, West Georgia College, Carrollton, Ga., May 26, 1964.
[43] "Washington Report" (CBS-TV), March 3, 1963.

It is one thing to open job opportunities. It is another to train people to fill them, or to persuade American enterprise to seek Negro as well as white applicants.

It is one thing to free new housing for all citizens regardless of race. It is another to enable more Negroes to have the means to take advantage of decent housing.

The federal government, the states, each city, and all organizations which have devoted their energies to the cause of racial justice should recognize clearly that these are the challenges of the future: that meeting them requires a great outpouring of energies of a very different kind than the instruments of government and the private organizations have used in the past.[44]

That same year, on "Meet the Press," Kennedy was asked his opinion of the assertion by some black leaders that Negroes are entitled to special, or compensatory, treatment because of past discrimination.

What I think is that he is entitled to special attention to try to remedy the sins of the past. I think we have to focus a good deal of attention—those of us in positions of responsibility and the individual citizens—on this problem. But I don't think that an individual should be hired just because he is a Negro, but, on the other hand, I think Negroes are not qualified for certain positions of skill because they have been discriminated against in the past, so I think we should make an extra effort to make sure that that problem has been remedied, that we do more for vocational training, that we do more for education, that we see that they then are entitled to the same privileges that the white person is entitled to. . . . I don't think an individual should be given a particular position because he happens to be a Negro, nor do I think he should be discriminated against because he happens to be a Negro. I think you have to look also into the background as to whether Negroes have been discriminated against in years gone by and therefore that the promotions of Negroes to positions of responsibility have not come along as fast as they might otherwise have.[45]

[44] Speech, Kentucky's Centennial of the Emancipation Proclamation, Louisville, Ky., March 18, 1963.
[45] "Meet the Press" (NBC-TV), June 23, 1963.

However, he continued to state clearly that, in his eyes, violence was not an acceptable avenue to change.

We cannot excuse violence from any source or from any group. The responsibility of the Negro leaders who set these demonstrations in motion is very great, as is the responsibility of the white leadership in every community.

I think that if we learned anything in the Department of Justice over the last four years, it is the heartache, the misery, the pain and the suffering that come when community leaders tell their communities that they do not have to obey the law.[46]

MR. KILPATRICK: In Virginia, on Thursday of this week, the President and the Executive Secretary of the NAACP sent a telegram to Governor Harrison saying that they had every intention to make 1963 a year of full emancipation. Then they said in their wire: "This is to be accomplished nonviolently if possible, but violently if necessary."

Would you have any comment on that telegram?

RFK: I am against the use of violence, and the President has come out against the use of violence. I would be strongly against those kinds of procedures.[47]

The Civil Rights Act of 1964

Finally, the increased tempo of rights demonstrations and a growing skepticism about the Kennedys' willingness to act boldly on behalf of Negroes led to the Administration's proposal of major new legislation in this area. The 1964 Civil Rights Act, submitted to Congress in 1963 and enacted over a Senate filibuster in 1964, was the result. It went far beyond previous acts by banning discrimination in public accommodations, requiring full equality in employment, and, in a reversal of Bobby's earlier views on the matter, permitting the withholding of funds from states or localities that administered federal programs in a discriminatory manner.

In *The Pursuit of Justice*, Kennedy wrote at length about this law:

[46] Kennedy, *op. cit.*, p. 77.
[47] "Meet the Press" (NBC-TV), June 23, 1963.

The Civil Rights Act of 1964 is really the first determined effort by the popular branches of government to eliminate second-class citizenship. The "Civil Rights Bill," so long and sorely and famously debated, is now an established fact. It is the law of the land.[48]

This legislation is neither vengeful nor extreme. It is a statement of what should long have been the reality of America. The rights proclaimed by *Brown v. Board of Education* and in countless companion cases must be provided to Negroes at a faster pace, in education, employment, and the enjoyment of those things offered to the public. As the Supreme Court pointed out in *Watson v. City of Memphis* (1963), these rights are "present rights; they are not merely hopes to some *future* enjoyment of some formalistic constitutional promise. The basic guarantees of our Constitution are warrants for the here and now. . . ." The Court made it clear that the Brown decision meant "deliberate speed," not indefinite delay.[49]

Now that we have the Act, one still hears the questions asked: "Is it needed?" and "Does the national government have the constitutional power to pursue such goals?"

Clearly, it is needed. No American can condone the injustices under which many American Negroes and other of our fellow citizens are forced to live, injustices that vary in kind and in cause from place to place, injustices that are sometimes so intense that in one of our states, with a nonwhite population of more than one million, of which 442,000 are of voting age, less than 25,000 of those Negroes are registered to vote.

Consider, also, the innumerable difficulties that face a Negro just traveling from state to state in our country, something the rest of us take for granted. If he makes reservations in advance, they may not be honored. If he seeks accommodations along the way, he is likely to be rejected time after time, until, just to obtain lodging and food, he must detour widely from his route; and if he does find accommodations available to him, they are likely to be inferior.

An ironic note here is provided by two of the available tourist guidebooks. One lists only one establishment with over-

[48] Kennedy, *loc. cit.*
[49] *Ibid.*, pp. 87-88.

night accommodations where a Negro can find lodging in Montgomery, Alabama. None is listed for Danville, Virginia. But a dog, provided he is traveling with a white man, is welcome to spend the night in at least five establishments in Montgomery and in four in Danville.

Everywhere we look, we find irrefutable evidence, too, that they are no longer willing to tolerate the burdens we have imposed on them.[50]

Defending Title I of the Act, which calls for the introduction of federal registrars in localities where Negroes are being denied an equal opportunity to register to vote, he wrote:

In these cases [forty-two suits filed by the Justice Department in 1963 dealing with voting discrimination] we found shocking instances of discrimination against Negroes. Under the guise of literacy tests or constitutional interpretation tests, barely literate whites have been registered while Negro teachers, graduate students and pharmacists have been rejected for the most technical or imperceptible errors.[51]

And on the controversial Title II section:

All titles of the bill are important, but none is of more vital and immediate significance than the public accommodations title [Title II].

For an American man, woman or child to be turned away from a public place for no reason other than the color of his skin is an intolerable insult, an insult that is in no way eased by the bland explanation that it has been allowed to go on for a hundred years or more. It is plainly a wrong and must be corrected.

Moreover, this is the wrong that has caused most of the recent demonstrations. If we can remove this cause, we will be giving the Negroes legal redress, taking the demonstrations off the streets and into the courts, averting the bitterness that will almost surely ensue if we fail. . . .

It has been suggested that somehow a public accommoda-

[50] *Ibid.*, pp. 75-76.
[51] *Ibid.*, p. 82.

tions statute might interfere improperly with private property rights. However, this is really not a valid argument. Thirty-two states already have laws banning discrimination in business establishments, and most of those laws are far more encompassing and far more stringent than the legislation we have suggested.

Moreover, federal action in this field involves no novel constitutional concept. Congress often has regulated private business enterprises to remove burdens from the national commerce. The National Labor Relations Act, the Taft-Hartley Act, the Fair Labor Standards Act and the Agricultural Adjustment Act—these are only a few that come readily to mind, and there are countless others.

These old and revered Acts of Congress suggest that Congressional power, therefore national power, to secure civil rights for all is clear beyond question under the commerce clause. And the suggestion that Congress should not exercise the commerce power because there is an overriding moral issue makes no legal or historical sense. It is because of the importance of the moral issue that Congress should act if it has power to act. Child labor, minimum wages, prostitution, gambling—all these raise moral issues, too, and all have been dealt with by Congress under the commerce clause. . . .

This title does not infringe on private property rights. It does not apply to private facilities or clubs, to private homes or apartments, or, in general, to service or professional facilities. Its aim is to end racial discrimination in public accommodations—in short, to help restore the word "public" to its true meaning.[52]

Before southern audiences, his explanations of this section lost none of their forceful candor.

I'd just like to say a few words about that, because it's the most controversial area, part, really of the Civil Rights Bill. It just seems to me that here it is 1964 and a motel or a hotel will serve somebody who is a Communist or a bank robber or somebody who pushes narcotics. Yet a Negro who comes in who might be a college professor or college graduate, just because he happens to have a different color skin than the rest

[52] *Ibid.*, pp. 76, 77, 78-79.

of us, service is refused to him. Yet we ask the Negro to perform many of the services for the United States—he has to
serve in the Army, he has to serve in the military forces; if
he's called upon he has to go to Vietnam, he has to serve in
South Korea, he has to serve in Berlin. He risks his life therefore for the white people in the United States, as well as the
Negro. I read just a short time ago about the fact that there
were six Negroes that were killed in Vietnam, over the period
of the last few months. Most of them came from southern
states, but they've been killed there and they've been killed
there for all of us and for the United States. And they were
called on and they went over to Vietnam and they fought and
they were killed, fighting against communism.

And yet, if one of their families comes from Alabama, for
instance, and if she wants to bury her husband in Arlington,
and he's entitled to be buried in Arlington, and she has her
husband's body flown back from Vietnam and placed in
Arlington and if she starts to travel home and she has a couple
of children, and she gets in the car and in the first place she
doesn't know what hotel she can stay at. She doesn't know
whether they'll be permitted to stay at any motel. She doesn't
know what restaurant she can possibly stop at in order to feed
herself or her children. She doesn't know what rest rooms; for
instance if the children want to stop, she stops by the side of
the road. And yet her husband, in 1964, was killed for all of
us, and she's denied this very basic right which is a continuous
insult. Not because they have bad character, but just because
they happen to be a different color, therefore Negroes aren't
invited.

So I think that's—I think that part of the legislation, to
speak quite frank [sic], I think that part of the legislation is
long, long overdue.[53]

He pointed out what Title IV, designed to hasten the
desegregation of public education, did and did not do.

These large numbers of Negroes who were given virtually
no education, whom the community denied any real chance of
earning a high school diploma, all these people are seriously
hampered in their search for employment today.

[53] Speech, West Georgia College, Carrollton, Ga., May 26, 1964.

These are the people whose unskilled jobs are being eliminated by automation, and for whom industrial retraining will
be of very little help. The situation can be seen as nothing less
than tragic when we realize that the undereducation of
Negroes is a clear and direct result of racial oppression—
nothing else.

Education is basic to the future of this nation. When thousands of our citizens are afforded only inferior educational opportunities, they suffer a loss which can never be compensated
and the whole country is subjected to unnecessary social and
economic waste. . . .

The law makes it clear that the Federal Government is *not*
authorized to deal with racial imbalance or to establish racial
quotas in schools. No Federal official or court is empowered
by this law to issue any order seeking to achieve racial balance
in any school by requiring the transportation of pupils from
one school to another or from one school district to another.[54]

He recognized, however, that this historic legislation
was no cure-all for the discrimination and disabilities
America's Negroes faced.

We are today in the midst of a great debate, whether or not
this nation, the champion of freedom throughout the world,
can now extend full freedom to twenty million of our own
citizens who have yet to achieve it. Passage of the Civil Rights
Act does not end the debate. It only shifts the arena and form
of the debate.[55]

. . . national power, however broad in reach and however
responsible in use, is severely limited in grasp. In the fight for
social justice national power can create and encourage but
local power is determinative.

National action is also not enough because the law is not
enough. The right defined by law is not enough whether it
concerns education or civil rights. We have a new Civil Rights
Law, and many of us live in states that have additional public
accommodation and fair employment laws. But a decade of

[54] Kennedy, *op. cit.*, pp. 85-86.
[55] *Ibid.*, p. 75.

painful struggle for compliance must make us all wonder whether mere submission to the process of law is enough.

The mere presence of machinery—for civil rights or for idle youth and their impoverished parents—does not insure service. The fact that the structure exists has not insured its full use, and particularly its use to best advantage.[56]

Kennedy hoped the Act would at least serve to strengthen the black man's faith in the efficacy of working within the framework of our legal system in his drive for full equality.

Right now, all over the nation, the struggle for Negro equality is expressing itself in marches, demonstrations and sit-ins. It seems very clear to me that these people are protesting against something more than the privations and humiliations they have endured for so long.

They are protesting the failure of our legal system to be responsive to the legitimate grievances of our citizens. They are protesting because the very procedures supposed to make the law work justly have been perverted into obstructions that keep it from working at all.[57]

Only if we are able to instill that understanding [of our legal system] will people with grievances begin to realize that there is a practical and realistic alternative to street demonstrations and sit-ins. But we have to make sure both that there *is* an alternative, and that the nature of that alternative is clearly understood.

If we can accomplish this, I believe we will begin to see a new phase in the movement for civil rights: an increased awareness that direct actions outside the law do not in themselves cure social evils. They serve to awaken the public conscience, and they can form a means of protest when no other means are available. But they will not dictate solutions; they can only alert us to the problems.[58]

[56] *Ibid.*, pp. 17-18.
[57] *Ibid.*, p. 93.
[58] *Ibid.*, pp. 93-94.

The Ghetto and "Gut" Reactions

These and other essentially theoretical expositions on the racial problem characterized the end of the first phase of Robert Kennedy's civil rights position. After his brother's death he began almost imperceptibly to assume a stance toward black degradation that was based increasingly on the brutal facts of ghetto life and the "gut" emotions they evoked. Whether it was because his brother's departure had freed him to cast a more critical eye on government policies, or because of the personal contact with the squalid ghettos of Harlem and Bedford-Stuyvesant afforded by his Senate campaign and subsequent senatorial duties, or both, gradually he seemed to feel what formerly he had only intellectualized.

His speeches became bundles of statistics about poverty, unemployment, slum schools, substandard housing, and family disintegration bound together with first-hand recollections of rats scratching under broken floors, the stench of uncollected garbage, and the hopeless looks of black men who had been broken, who had given up. Here is a sample of his statements over the past four years detailing the problems confronting the American Negro:

The Negro baby born in America today, regardless of the section of the nation in which he is born, has about one-half as much chance of completing high school as a white baby born in the same place on the same day, one-third as much chance of completing college, one-third as much chance of becoming a professional man, twice as much chance of becoming unemployed, about one-seventh as much chance of earning $10,000 a year, a life expectancy which is seven years shorter, and the prospects of earning only half as much.[59]

The brutalities of Selma, and its denial of elementary rights of citizenship, were condemned throughout the North; and thousands of white Northerners went there to march to Montgomery.

[59] Statement made by the late President John F. Kennedy, frequently quoted by RFK.

But the many brutalities of the North receive no such attention. I have been in tenements in Harlem in the past several weeks where the smell of rats was so strong that it was difficult to stay there for five minutes, and where children slept with lights turned on their feet to discourage attacks.

In central Harlem, over 50 percent of all housing units are seriously deteriorating or dilapidated, as opposed to about 10 percent of housing units in this condition occupied by whites. Thousands do not flock to Harlem to protest these conditions —much less to change them.[60]

And the 1967 Manpower Report states flatly that "economic and social conditions are getting worse, not better, in slum areas"; the Labor Department has explained that the youth of the slums "just don't have the connections." There are, of course, connections they can make. For a few blocks away, or on a television set, the young man can watch the multiplying marvels of white America: new cars and new homes, air conditioners and outdoor barbecues. Every day television commercials tell him that life is impossible without the latest products of our consumer society. But he cannot buy them. He is told that the Negro is making progress. But what does that mean to him? He cannot experience the progress of others, nor should we seriously expect him to feel grateful because he is no longer a slave, or because he can vote or eat at some lunch counters. For he compares his condition not with the past, but with the life of other Americans. He and his brother, as Daniel O'Connell said of the Irish, "have been made more thirsty for liberty by the drop that has fallen on their parched lips." Now, as ever, it is when submission gives way to expectation, when despair is touched with the awareness of possibility, that the forces of human desire and the passion for justice are unloosed.[61]

The discrimination of which I speak is the discrimination of the urban ghettos of the North. The denial of right is unwritten in law, though it is observed more strictly than most laws; it is the denial of the basic human rights of employment, of

[60] Speech, National Council of Christians and Jews, April 28, 1965.

[61] Address, dinner in honor of ex-Senator Paul Douglas, Chicago, Ill., October 23, 1967.

education, of decent living, the denial of dignity itself. Here is the "Tragic Gap" for more than 50 percent of all American Negroes—those who live in the ghettos of our central cities. For this is the twentieth year since the Employment Act of 1946 proclaimed the right of employment to all Americans willing and able to work. It is the seventeenth year since the Congress committed the nation to provide "a decent home and a suitable living environment" for every American family. It is the twelfth year since the Supreme Court declared that all children have the right to an equal and unsegregated education. Yet this is also a year in which Negro unemployment, overall, continues at over twice the white rate; in which official estimates are that over 10 percent of the labor force in Harlem and Bedford-Stuyvesant is unemployed, and unemployment of young Negroes, seeking to establish their identity and their manhood, is estimated at an even greater percent.[62]

Of all our problems, the most immediate and pressing, the one which threatens to paralyze our very capacity to act, to obliterate our vision of the future, is the plight of the Negro of the center city. For this plight—and the riots which are its product and symptom—threatens to divide Americans for generations to come; to add to the ever-present difficulties of race and class the bitter legacy of violence and destruction and fear.[63]

He described the vicious circle of problems strangling the Negro ghettos of America:

Segregation is becoming the governing rule: Washington is only the most prominent example of a city which has become overwhelmingly Negro as whites move to the suburbs; many other cities are moving along the same road—for example, Chicago, which if present trends continue will be over 50 percent Negro by 1975. The ghettos of Harlem and Southside and Watts are cities in themselves, areas of as much as 350,-000 people.

[62] Address, NAACP Legal Defense Fund Banquet, New York, N.Y., May 18, 1966.
[63] Statement, Subcommittee on Executive Reorganization of the Senate Committee on Government Operations, December 10, 1966.

Poverty and unemployment are endemic: from one-third to one-half of the families in these areas live in poverty; in some male unemployment may be as high as 40 percent; unemployment of Negro youths nationally is over 25 percent.

Welfare and dependency are pervasive: one-fourth of the children in these ghettos, as in Harlem, may receive Federal Aid to Dependent Children; in New York City, ADC alone costs over $20 million a month; in our five largest cities, the ADC bill is over $500 million a year.

Housing is overcrowded, unhealthy and dilapidated: the last housing census found 43 percent of urban Negro housing to be substandard; in many of these ghettos, ten thousand children may be injured or infected by rat bites every year.

Health is poor and care inadequate: infant mortality in the ghettos is more than twice the rate outside; mental retardation caused by inadequate prenatal care is more than seven times the white rate; one-half of all babies born in Manhattan last year will have had no prenatal care at all; deaths from diseases like tuberculosis, influenza, and pneumonia are two to three times as common as elsewhere.[64]

The rate in infant mortality in Bedford-Stuyvesant is twice the rate in more affluent parts of the city; and the city's Health Commissioner says that poverty is the third-leading cause of death in New York.

Thousands marched for James Reeb—but who marches for our own dead children?

Why do our actions so often—and so tragically—belie our words?

Part of the reason, of course, is that it is easier to see the mote in our brother's eye than the beam in our own.

But a larger part, I think, is that action at home requires change in our own way of life. And—in a world already beset by change—to people whose lives are often tragically insecure —further unsettling change is unacceptable.

In the midst of the greatest peacetime economic expansion in our history, 5 percent of our labor force remains unemployed; and competition for the few unskilled and semiskilled jobs that remain is fierce.

It is not enough, in these circumstances, to preach for fair

[64] *Ibid.*

employment, or even to pass a fair employment law. If there are not enough jobs for all, the elimination of Negro unemployment and poverty will be impossible.

Another example: we all know the importance of education for our children, and how severe is the competition for admission to colleges.

It is not enough to tell a worried parent that prejudice against Negroes is undemocratic; if he fears that desegregation will handicap his child's education, he will fight it almost to the death.

If we wish to achieve peaceful desegregation of the schools —if we wish to improve the quality of education afforded Negro children—we must improve the quality of education throughout our schools, and assure every qualified child the chance for higher education.[65]

. . . any attempt to discuss the problems of the cities, and the ghettos which presently threaten their future, cannot ignore the findings of commission after commission, student after student, public official after public official. The McCone Commission looked into the Watts riots—and said that the most serious problem in Watts is unemployment.

The crisis in Negro unemployment . . . is significant far beyond its economic effects—devastating as those are. For it is both measure and cause of the extent to which the Negro lives apart—the extent to which he is alienated from the general community. More than segregation in housing and schools, more than differences in attitudes or life style, it is unemployment which marks the Negro of the urban ghetto off and apart from the rest of us—from Negroes who have jobs (including Negro leaders) almost as much as from whites. Unemployment is having nothing to do—which means having nothing to do with the rest of us. . . .

. . . there are government programs which seem at least to have some promise of ameliorating, if not solving, some of the other problems of the Negro and the city. But no government program now operating gives any substantial promise of meeting the problem of Negro unemployment in the ghetto. The Manpower Development and Training Act, the Vocational

[65] Speech, National Conference of Christians and Jews, New York, N.Y., April 28, 1965.

Education Act, the Elementary and Secondary Education Act, the Economic Development Act—these and similar efforts have been going on for five years. Yet in these same five years, while family income nationwide was increasing 14 percent, and family income of Negroes nationwide was increasing 24 percent, family income in Watts *dropped* 8 percent.[66]

Children whose fathers are without work for months or years on end are not likely to learn the value of work in school or elsewhere. High school seniors who see last year's graduates standing on street corners—or working part-time at menial jobs —are not likely to be impressed with the value of the last year's schooling. And the effects of the shortage of meaningful employment are reinforced by a welfare structure which is frequently destructive both of individuals and of the community in which they live. "Thus," as one economist says, "we penalize old-age pensioners who get jobs, by cutting their social security benefits in correspondence with their pay; we terminate welfare payments when the wage-earner head of a large family gets even a poor-paying job, sometimes at a lower level of income than that provided by his welfare payments; we evict the dweller in a low-rent, public-housing project who succeeds in raising his income even if his rent costs will exceed his income increase. Instead of providing real incentives to self-help efforts, we in effect deter them by the equivalent of 100 percent taxation on the additional income the poor may earn.

And, in the midst of much hand-wringing about the disintegration of Negro families, we compel fathers to leave home so that their families may receive federal assistance; this teaches their sons the lesson that the best way to provide for a family is to abandon it. Neither is the Aid to Dependent Children of Unemployed Parents program an answer; for where jobs are menial and pay too low, a father may still be forced to leave home to bring his family a living income. . . .

And Negro Americans have been told to cast down their buckets to find and adopt the standards of our society. But our "welfare" programs have too often destroyed families and pe-

[66] Statement, Subcommittee on Executive Reorganization of the Senate Committee on Government Operations, December 10, 1966.

nalized thrift; our law-enforcement has too often stopped short of protecting Negroes from those, white and black, who have preyed on them, in their homes and on their jobs and in the streets; and sometimes we have not even helped them remove the garbage from their neighborhoods. The time for all this to change is now, just as it has been time to change since the first Negro stepped off the first slave ship onto American soil.[67]

Serious as they are, these disparities lay bare only part of the problem. The deeper part, the really dangerous part, is in the gulf which separates the Negro from the white power structure that governs him, and in the failure of the establishment to afford him full participation in shaping the governmental services he receives. For three hundred years the Negro has been a nation apart, a people governed by a repression that has been softened to the point where it is now only a massive indifference. The Watts riots were as much a revolt against official indifference, an explosion of frustration at inability to communicate and participate, as they were an uprising about inferior jobs and education and housing. What exploded in Watts is what lies beneath the surface.[68]

We must create a society in which Negroes will be as free as other Americans—free to vote, and to earn their way, and to share in the decisions of government which shape their lives. We know that to accomplish this end will mean great tension and difficulty and strife for all of us, in the North as much as in the South. But we know we must make progress, not because it is economically advantageous; not because the law says so; but because it is right.[69]

Is there anything as important as just the fact that a child

[67] Speech, Second Borough President's Conference of Community Leaders on the Revitalization of Harlem-East Harlem Community, New York, N.Y., January 21, 1966.

[68] Address, luncheon of the Federation of Jewish Philanthropies of New York, New York, N.Y., January 20, 1966.

[69] Address, University of Mississippi Law School Forum, Oxford, Miss., March 18, 1966.

grows up in this country and by the time he is four years old his life is known: he will be unsuccessful and a derelict.[70]

RFK Looks at the Issues

The Senator began dealing with specific problems like education, housing, discrimination in unions and the draft, and police-ghetto relations in more depth, often devoting entire speeches to a single topic.

Clearly, the most important problem in Harlem is education of every kind. Fathers must learn job skills, and mothers how to buy food economically; students must learn to read, and little children how to speak—and teachers must learn how to teach and employers how to hire. But our educational efforts have thus far not been sufficient. For this there have been many reasons, which by now are familiar to all of us: segregation; lack of stimulation or stability in many homes; lack of preschool preparation; lack of adequate resources in the schools themselves; lack of effort in the schools which have not been determined that all children *must* learn. All these shortcomings exist; all are destructive and wasteful; all must be changed. But we will only be deluding ourselves if we look just to improve schools as a solution to the problems of the ghetto. The most ambitious preschool projects we have yet devised, for example, do not reach children before the age of three, and those we have carried out do not reach below the age of four or five; yet even by three, children may be so damaged that any compensatory program can only make up part of the potential that has already been lost. We can improve the schools at every level, yet not reach the parents of even our youngest children—and these parents must be reached if their children are to have a full chance at life. And reliance on integration of schools in the center of our cities would mean the virtual abandonment of those children now in school—for true school integration depends on a desegregation of residential patterns which simply cannot take place overnight. More fundamentally, better schools do not automatically produce better or more dedicated students. For perhaps the greatest

[70] *The New Republic,* January 21, 1965.

barrier to education in Harlem is simply a lack of hope, a lack of belief that education is meaningful to a Negro in the city of New York.[71]

In recent years, education has come to be regarded as the answer; and last year, Congress enacted an historic program of education for the disadvantaged. But past efforts to improve life conditions simply by the expenditure of more money on education have not been notably successful: a recent Brookings Institution study, I am advised, finds that in only 5 percent of all cases is there any observable correlation between increased expenditure on education in the ghetto and better jobs later in life. And the major study prepared for the Office of Education has also found that other factors—family, home, general environment and motivation—determine whether a child can benefit at all from the best schools we provide. Education has failed to motivate many of our young people because of what they could see around them: the sharply restricted opportunities open to the people of the ghetto, whatever their education. The Negro college graduate earns, in his lifetime, no more than a white man whose education ended at the eighth grade.[72]

Twenty-six and a half percent of the Negroes of the state of New York—young Negroes—are out of school and out of work. The basic problem is to provide the best possible education for our young people. Seventy-five percent of the Negroes who came from Mississippi over the age of twenty-one haven't the equivalent of the fifth-grade education. They want to get out of Mississippi. They come up here. They live here, and then they have children. But still they have to educate their children. How do they get their children to read a book? What kind of conversation do they have when the child comes home? For the child whose parents escape from Mississippi or escape from Alabama and come up here, is bringing up a child who cannot keep up with school or in the school system which does not provide any special services for that child. I

[71] Speech, Second Borough President's Conference of Community Leaders on the Revitalization of Harlem-East Harlem Community, New York, N.Y., January 21, 1966.
[72] Statement, Subcommittee on Executive Reorganization of the Senate Committee on Government Operations, December 10, 1966.

think that we have to start facing up to the fact that this is a problem. When the child starts in first grade—a Negro child who moves into this area—he is already behind. When he gets to the eighth grade, he is two years behind. How is he going to survive? How is he going to be able to compete?[73]

First, we must evaluate existing federal housing programs in light of the goal of desegregation. It will turn out, of course, that we have been doing things just about backwards for a long time.

Public housing has been a significant force in perpetuating segregation. It has been built, on the whole, as large projects in ghetto areas, and it is all too clear that this has not been wholly accidental. The result is that in 1962, 80 percent of all public housing projects receiving federal subsidy were occupied by members of only one race. And the approach of building mainly in central cities has been uneconomic. Land and construction costs have brought the cost per unit in New York City to over $21,000. To illustrate the consequences of this policy, we should note, for example, that projects in areas outside the central city could have been built and every tenant have been provided a brand new automobile to commute with, and the cost would still have been far less.[74]

Yet we would be dishonest with ourselves if we did not admit that some discrimination continues to exist within the labor movement—and by no means only in the South. I am thinking, for example, of a particularly ironic situation that exists right now in Washington. Howard University, a distinguished Negro institution, is building a new gymnasium. At least four of the building trades locals involved, however, have no Negroes working on the project. For that matter, these locals have only a handful of Negro members or apprentices.

The fundamental responsibility for solving problems like this is that of labor itself. Your group and others like it do a

[73] Question period after speech, University of Rochester, Rochester, N.Y., September 29, 1964.

[74] Address, luncheon of the Federation of Jewish Philanthropies of New York, New York, N.Y., January 20, 1966.

great deal to help. The government also has a responsibility in this field. . . .[75]

And we have a special responsibility based on the war in Vietnam. The poor man—the Negro, the Puerto Rican, the Spanish-American, the poor white—serves in Vietnam out of all proportion to his place in the population figures. And the casualty lists reflect disproportionate numbers of the poor as well. That Negroes and the poor in general bear the brunt of the fighting must intensify our efforts at home, for we must keep faith with the sacrifice they are making.[76]

It is to say that these other questions can only be properly dealt with in concert with action on the major problem. A police force, for example, can exert every possible effort, and imagination, and will to better relations with the community. But it still must enforce the law. And if the conditions of the ghetto produce stealing—for which people must be arrested—or nonpayment of rent—for which people must be evicted, even if they have no place to go—then the police will inevitably bear the brunt of the ghetto's resentment at the conditions which the police, through no fault of their own, enforce.[77]

At times Kennedy called on the community to take specific actions, though his recommendations up to late 1966 were still along conventional lines.

There are many things that all of us can do in our neighborhoods and in our communities which can make a difference in the lives of our children and in the lives of fellow citizens who need our help. Here are just a few:

1. Start preschool centers, aimed at three- to five-year-olds, to give them a head start if their families cannot.
2. Help stop dropouts—with part-time jobs, or loans for

[75] Speech, Civil Rights Committee, New York City Central Labor Council, AFL-CIO, March 9, 1963.
[76] Address, Third Annual WGHO Human Relations Award Dinner, Ellenville, N.Y., April 19, 1966.
[77] Statement, Subcommittee on Executive Reorganization of the Senate Committee on Government Operations, December 10, 1966.

those who need financial help, and with special vocational and remedial training for those who cannot make the grade.

3. Insist on play areas, or swimming pools, or recreation centers, and get the young people off the streets.

4. Encourage experiments in teaching those who will never go beyond high school.

5. Locate the unfilled jobs, find the unemployed, and bring the two together with training programs at each skill and education level.

6. Devise programs to improve existing housing by using the unemployed for renovation work.[78]

White Backlash

For the unfinished business at hand is the most difficult and dangerous that we have ever faced. Today's problems of intolerance are harder than yesterday's; tomorrow's will be harder still.

One reason for this difficulty is that racial intolerance is harder to combat than religious intolerance. Most people, after all, have to be told whether the man they are talking to is Catholic, or Protestant, or Jewish; none need instruction on which are the Negroes or the Puerto Ricans. Most of us can walk on each other's streets without arousing comment. If our children go to school together, few of us will know what religion their classmates practice.

But if a Negro walks down a quiet suburban street, or Negro children attend a school, all know it immediately. Simply by being more visible, the Negro is more vulnerable to prejudice.

The Negro's heightened visibility makes easier another kind of prejudice and intolerance: prejudice against the poor, intolerance for the unsuccessful. Because Negroes are twice as likely to be unemployed, because their children are three times as likely to be slow in school, even to the point of mental retardation—because of these things, prejudice against Negroes often masquerades as adherence to principles of individual freedom and responsibility. "This is a free country," says

[78] Speech, New York State NAACP Convention, Buffalo, N.Y. October 3, 1964.

the new voice of intolerance. "They have the same chance as anyone else. If they don't take advantage of what we offer that's their responsibility." And these voices then use the continued extent of Negro poverty, Negro unemployment and lack of education, as an excuse for not doing more.

When we see society's failures—dropouts or dope addicts, petty thieves or prostitutes—we do not know whether they are Italian or English, Baptist or Orthodox.

But we know when they are Negro. So every Negro who fails confirms the voice of prejudice.[79]

In recent months we have seen comment on what some have called the "backlash." Opposition to violence and riots and irresponsible action is the justified feeling of most Americans, white and black. But that "backlash" which masks hostility to the swift and complete fulfillment of equal opportunity and treatment, which contains opposition to demands for justice and freedom, which denies the need to destroy slums, provide education and eliminate poverty—that is wrong, shameful, immoral and self-defeating. And any leader who seeks to exploit this feeling for the momentary advantage of office fails his duty to the people of this country.

It would be a national disaster to permit resentment or fear at the actions of a few to drive increasing numbers of white and black Americans into opposing camps of distrust and enmity. Understandable alarm at sporadic turbulence and irresponsibility cannot be allowed to create new barriers of oppression, revive old hatreds, or cause us to falter for a single moment in our drive toward the day when the truths we hold to be self-evident are as clear to black Americans as to whites. Some say that in the last analysis, after all, we need not fear injustice; that if our great common purpose divides into conflict and contest the whites will win. In one sense, that is true. We are far more numerous and more powerful. But it would be a pyrrhic victory. The cost would be decades of agony and civil strife, the sacrifice of our ideal of liberty, and ultimately the loss of the soul of our nation.[80]

[79] Speech, National Conference of Christians and Jews, New York, N.Y., April 28, 1965.

[80] Speech, University of California at Berkeley, Calif., October 22, 1966.

Black Power and Rebellion

He had this to say about "black power":

> In my judgment, the slogan "black power" and what is associated with it has set the civil rights movement back considerably. . . . It would appear that you are turning your back on Negroes and whites working together, and if people can't meet your definition, you read them out.[81]

But when he theorized now, his conclusions were more penetrating and revealed a fuller understanding of the Negro's plight than his earlier efforts had. A series of statements made in late 1966 at the University of California is a good case in point:

> That revolution [of Negro Americans] has now entered a new stage, one that is at once more hopeful and more difficult, more important and more painful. It is the effort to enforce newly won rights and give them content. It is to give every Negro the same opportunity as every white man to educate his children, provide for his family, live in a decent home, and win human acceptance as well as economic achievement in the society of his fellows. And it is to do all this in the face of the ominous growth of renewed hostility among the races.
>
> Some among us say the Negro has made great progress—which is true—and that he should be satisfied and patient—which is neither true nor realistic. In the past twenty years we have witnessed a revolution of rising expectations in almost every continent. That revolution has spread to the Negro nation confined within our own. Men without hope, resigned to despair and oppression, do not make revolutions. It is when expectation replaces submission, when despair is touched with the awareness of possibility, that the forces of human desire and the passion for justice are unloosed.
>
> For the American Negro that time has come. Courts and Congresses and Presidents, in the name of the country, have

[81] Remarks during testimony of Floyd McKissick, Ribicoff Subcommittee on Executive Reorganization of the Senate Committee on Government Operations, December 8, 1966.

said that the color of a man's skin shall no longer be a bar to the right to vote, or learn, or work, or enter a public place. We have unveiled the prospect of full participation in American society, while television, radio and newspapers bring to every Negro home the knowledge of how rewarding such participation can be. With so bountiful a promise how much greater must be the frustration and the fury of the Negro—especially the young Negro—who desperately wanting to believe, and half-believing, finds himself confined in slums, unable to get an education and a job, confronted by the open prejudice and subtle hostilities of a white world, and seemingly powerless to change his condition or shape his future. For him the progress of the past can count for little against the crushing awareness that his hopes for the future are beyond his reach, for reasons which have little to do with justice or his worth as a man. Occasionally, broken hope and a deeply felt futility erupt in violence and extreme statements and doctrines. If we deny a man his place in the larger community then he may turn inward to find his manhood and identity, rejecting those he feels have rejected him. Therefore, far more impressive than the violence of a few is the fact that the overwhelming majority of American Negroes retain their faith in the good will of the nation and the possibilities of peaceful progress within the ordered framework of American politics and life.

But if any man claims the Negro should be content or satisfied, let him say he would willingly change the color of his skin and go to live in the Negro section of a large city. Then, and only then, has he a right to such a claim. . . .[82]

Moreover, we must all understand that the problem will not go away. The twenty million Negro Americans are a reality. The slums and ghettos, unemployment and the denial of education, are all realities. Prejudice, discrimination and segregation are realities, as are frustrated expectations and disappointed hopes. Most importantly the awareness of injustice and the passion to end it are inescapable realities. No force in the world can wish these facts out of existence or abolish them. Thus we have only one choice. We can face our difficulties and strive to overcome them; or we can turn away,

[82] Speech, University of California at Berkeley, Calif., October 22, 1966.

bringing repression, steadily increasing human pain and civil strife, and leaving a problem of far more terrifying and grievous dimensions to our children. Anyone who promises another course, who pledges a solution without cost or effort or difficulty, is deluding himself and the people to whom he speaks. . . .

Like other minority groups, Negroes will bear the major burden of their own progress. They will have to make their own way, as they are doing. But we must remember that other minorities, including my own, also made progress through increasing their political and economic power as well as by individual effort. Nor was that progress completely without violence, fear and hatred. Moreover, earlier immigrants often began their cities by moving to the unsettled West, a door now closed; or finding unskilled labor, a door which is swiftly narrowing. Today to find a job requires increasingly complex skills, denied to those without education. Nor did other minorities suffer under the special handicaps of the Negro heritage —centuries of slavery and a century of oppression, an intricate web of legal disabilities, and the crushing forces of racial feeling from whose poisons few whites have fully liberated themselves.[83]

The Riots

He addressed himself frequently and forthrightly to the riots exploding in the nation's cities, to their causes, and to the spreading exhortations for "black revolution."

The riots which have taken place—and the riots which we know may all too easily take place in the future—are therefore an intolerable threat to the most essential interests of every American, black or white—to the mind's peace and the body's safety and the community's order, to all that makes life worthwhile. None of us should look at this violence as anything but destructive of self, community and nation. But we should not delude ourselves. The riots are not crises which can be resolved as suddenly as they arose. They are a condition

[83] *Ibid.*

which has been with us for one hundred years and will be with us for many years more. We can deal with the crises without dealing with the underlying conditions—just as we can give novocain to a man with a broken arm, without setting that arm in a splint; but the end result will only be more pain, pain beyond temporary relief, and permanent crippling of our urban society.[84]

We cannot rest content because we have tried to help Negroes in Jackson, or Selma, or Montgomery. The problems, last summer, were here. They will be here again, unless we act. For the root causes of the Harlem riots were dissatisfaction and frustration—at the difference between civics classes and civic practices; between America's promise and the other America's poverty; between Hollywood dreams and Harlem nightmares. To solve these problems, to ease this frustration, it is not enough to teach brotherhood in the schools; we must assure that they educate each child to the limit of his capacity. It is not enough, in this technological society, to hire qualified Negroes, nor even to try to raise the number that are qualified; we must create new jobs for all that can work, regardless of their level of skill.

It is not enough to open housing opportunities in the suburbs for a few well-to-do Negroes: we must build housing appropriate for the low- and moderate-income Negro outside the center city. These are not easy things to do. But the fulfillment of American ideals has never been easy, if only because they are so high.[85]

Last August a random argument between a policeman and a drunken driver in a place called Watts set off an explosion which shook the nation. In the aftermath of the ordeal of death and destruction came a period of national discussion which suggested that perhaps the Watts tragedy had at least taught us a lesson—a painful and costly lesson, but a lesson nonetheless. At a terrible price, it appeared that we might now have finally acquired a real awareness of the problem and

[84] Statement, Subcommittee on Executive Reorganization of the Senate Committee on Government Operations, December 10, 1966.
[85] Speech, National Conference of Christians and Jews, New York, N.Y., April 28, 1965.

a real commitment to finding a solution. This is not to say that we had failed to act on behalf of Negro Americans. We had passed two historic pieces of legislation in two years. But that legislation applied for the most part to the Negro in the South, and did little for the Negro in the North. For the problem that is Watts—and Harlem and Bedford-Stuyvesant and South Chicago and North Philadelphia—is not one that yields to laws protecting legal rights. It is the kind of problem that will yield only to other kinds of fundamental change—to the forces created by better education and better housing and better job opportunities. And it will yield only when the people of the ghetto acquire and wisely exercise political power in the community, only when they are able to establish meaningful communication with a society from which they have been excluded.[86]

There is no point in telling Negroes to obey the law, because to many Negroes the law is the enemy.[87]

Yet however much the condition of most Negroes must call forth compassion, the violence of a few demands condemnation and action. In the streets of many of our cities, in recent months, we have seen riots and looting and even occasional murder. Still far more disturbing than the chaotic, self-destructive violence of Watts or Oakland are the statements of a very few Negro spokesmen—those who have called for hatred to fight prejudice, racism, violence to destroy oppression. Here is the seed of tragedy for black and white alike.

To understand the causes is not to permit the result. No man has the right to wantonly menace the safety and well-being of his neighbors. . . .

I know many of you understand the terrible frustration, the feeling of hopelessness, the passion for betterment which, denied to others, has turned to violence and hate. It is difficult to live in the shadow of a multimillion-dollar freeway, to watch the white faces blur as they speed by the problems of the city, returning each evening to the pleasant green lawns of the suburbs. And it must be difficult beyond measure to share in

[86] Address, Third Annual WGHO Human Relations Award Dinner, Ellenville, N.Y., April 19, 1966.

[87] Statement referring to the Watts riot, *U.S. News & World Report*, March 26, 1966.

America's affluence enough to own a television set—and to see on that set the hate and fear and ugliness of little Negro children being beaten and clubbed by hoodlums and thugs in Mississippi.

Some have turned to violence. And the question many Negroes surely ask themselves—the question many of you surely ask yourselves—is, why not?

Why not turn to violence?

After all, even humorous columnists are making jokes about the fact that poverty funds and municipal action seem to follow riots—that a community which wants a swimming pool need only start a riot, while a community which keeps the peace can take its place at the end of the line.

And how many, watching the faces of Grenada, must have asked again, how long—how long turn the other cheek, how long hold to the counsels of nonviolence?

But the course of violence would be terribly, awfully wrong. Not just because hatred and violence are self-defeating—though they are self-defeating, for they strike at the very heart of obedience to law, peaceful process and political cooperation which are man's last best hopes for a decent world.

We must oppose violence not because of what violence does to the possibility of cooperation between whites and blacks; not just because it hampers the passage of civil rights bills, or poverty legislation, or open-occupancy laws.

The central disease of violence is what it does to all of us—to those who engage in it as much as to those who are its victims.

Cruelty and wanton violence may temporarily relieve a feeling of frustration, a sense of impotence. But the damage of those who perpetrate it—these are the negation of reason and the antithesis of humanity, and they are the besetting sins of the twentieth century.

Surely the world has seen enough, in the last forty years, of violence and hatred. Surely we have seen enough of the attempt to justify present injustice by past slights, or to punish the unjust by making the world more unjust.

We know that the color of an executioner's robe matters little.[88]

[88] Speech, University of California at Berkeley, Calif., October 22, 1966.

The deeper part . . . is in the gulf which separates the Negro from the white power structure which governs him, and in the failure of the establishment to afford him full participation in shaping the governmental services he receives. For three hundred years the Negro has been a nation apart, a people governed by a repression that has been softened to the point when it is now only massive indifference. The Watts riots were as much a revolt against official indifference, an explosion of frustration of the inability to communicate and participate, as they were an uprising about inferior jobs, education, and housing.[89]

For it is clear that the riots in Los Angeles were no isolated phenomenon, no unlucky chance. All these places—Harlem, Watts, Southside—are riots waiting to happen. To look at them is to know—why. . . . First these are places of poverty. We know that the rate of Negro unemployment is twice the white rate—that the rate of Negro unemployment since World War II has been about 10 percent, far higher than the white rate has ever been outside of the Great Depression. . . . Our society . . . all our values, our views of each other and our own self-esteem, the contribution we can make to ourselves, our families, and the community around us, all these things are built on the work we do. But too many of the inhabitants of these areas are without purpose, the satisfaction or the dignity that we find in our work. . . . Most important, these are places of slighted hopes and disappointment. . . . Median income of white families reached a record of $6,237 in 1967. But median Negro family income was only $3,330, which means that nearly half of all Negro families are living on incomes under the poverty line.

The damage and destruction caused by this minority should warn us that we must do everything we can to keep more Negroes from becoming so disaffected that they feel they have little to lose from violence. . . . We have a long way to go before law means the same thing to Negroes as it does to us. . . . The law does not fully protect their lives, their dignity or encourage their hope and trust for the future. . . . The first step is to move beyond the thinking that this is "a Negro problem." The second broad step we must take is to bring

[89] *The Nation*, November 14, 1966.

these problems into the political process—to make them the subject of public action. And more leadership will have to come from Negroes themselves.[90]

I do not mean to denigrate the value of protest. Protest for redress of just grievances is the right and the duty of every citizen in a free society. But protest must not be allowed to distract our attention from the job at hand—nor may the need of protest be used as an excuse for our own inaction. So it is you—leaders of the Negro American community—who know what must be done better than white Americans can ever know—you who must take the lead; you who must take the first steps, using what is available, and showing what is needed but not available.

On you is a heavy responsibility. For what is at stake is not just the fate of the Negro in America; at stake is the fate of all America, of the legacy of our past and the promise of our future. The kind of country in which my children will grow depends as much on you as on any men and women in this land.[91]

He feels denied membership in that American society to which by birth and natural allegiance he belongs. And it is precisely among the most vital and determined young men that frustration is greatest. Here, and not in the frantic charade of revolutionary oratory, is the breeding ground of black nationalism and "reverse racism." The violent youth of the ghetto is not simply protesting his condition, but trying to assert his worth and dignity as a human being—to tell us that though we may scorn his contribution, we must still respect his power. But this is the most destructive and self-defeating of attempts. This is not revolution. The word means to seize power, but the advocates of violence are not going to overthrow the American government; when Rap Brown threatens to burn America down, he is not a revolutionary, he is an anarchist. The end is not a better life for Negroes, but a devastated America: as William Pfaff has said, "a program for

[90] Address, New York State Convention of the Independent Order of Odd Fellows, Spring Valley, N.Y., August 18, 1965.
[91] Speech, Second Borough President's Conference of Community Leaders on the Revitalization of Harlem-East Harlem Community, New York, N.Y., January 21, 1966.

death, not life." So it has already proven, all over the face of America.

We cannot abandon the young Negro to this kind of leadership, or let the voice of his protest turn into such despair. We must act—and the fact is that we can.[92]

We know we must have order—we know that those who incite others to loot and burn must feel the full force of the law. But we also know that punishment is not prevention; that force cannot long suppress latent grievance. Without a rapid change in the fate of these other Americans, we will not have the order we seek. Further, we know we must also act, not only because inaction will bring further violence, not only because it is right and we owe it to our fellow citizens, but because we must give encouragement to those who still believe progress is possible within our democratic system. We cannot denounce those extremists who reject it if we do not prove that our society is capable of helping people lead a better life—in our urban ghettos, in our areas of rural poverty, and on our Indian reservations as well.[93]

Of all these divisions, none is more fateful and dangerous than the deepening division between white and black America. This division has bred riot and repression, sending violence and fear across the country, leaving death and devastation behind. The weather now is cool. But we know that if action is not taken in the leisure and calm of winter, the next turning of the seasons may become a grotesque spiral of greater violence and even greater vengeance, threatening the well-being and liberties of every citizen.[94]

The Failure of Government

By early 1966 Kennedy showed signs of responding to his own warnings that only through imaginative action

[92] Address, dinner in honor of ex-Senator Paul Douglas, Chicago, Ill., October 23, 1967.

[93] Remarks, U.S. Chamber of Commerce, Washington, D.C., October 3, 1967.

[94] Address, dinner in honor of ex-Senator Paul Douglas, Chicago, Ill., October 23, 1967.

on an enormous scale could major disaster in our ghettos be averted. Yet he lacked a comprehensive blueprint of reform to champion. Thus his speeches and releases during this period concentrated on the necessary, though essentially negative, task of exposing obstructionist attitudes and ineffectual government programs.

Let us, as a beginning, stop thinking of the people of Harlem—the unemployed, the dropouts, those on welfare and those who work for less than the minimum wage—as liabilities, idle hands for whom some sort of occupation must be found. Let us think of them instead as a valuable resource, as people whose work can make a significant contribution to themselves, their families and the nation. Now ask if there are jobs to be done. In his State of the Union address, President Johnson said that whole areas of our cities must be immediately rebuilt; indeed, it has been national policy since 1949 to provide "a decent home and a suitable living environment for every American family." But there are in New York City at least one and one-half million people living in totally inadequate dwellings—cold, rat-infested, dirty and overcrowded.

The Medicare Bill is already generating pressures for new hospital and nursing-home construction; and even before Medicare, New York's Commissioner of Hospitals stated that the city-owned hospitals alone require $50 million worth of rebuilding in *each* of the next ten years. Our school classrooms are already overcrowded and deteriorating—and in the next ten years, we must build thousands more in the city alone to teach the children now being born. The College of the City of New York is becoming more difficult to enter each year—principally because it is without adequate classroom space. In fact, the inventory is almost infinite—parks and playgrounds to be built, the beaches to be renovated, the subways to be refurbished. If we begin—as the President said we will—to meet these pressing needs, there will be jobs enough for all our people.[95]

We are at a point of crisis: the plight of the Negro, and the intolerable violence which are its product and symptom,

[95] Speech, Second Borough President's Conference of Community Leaders on the Revitalization of Harlem-East Harlem Community, New York, N.Y., January 21, 1966.

threaten to divide Americans for generations to come; to add to the ever-present difficulties of race and class the bitter legacy of violence and destruction and fear. What we Democrats do is at the heart of the matter. We can treat this as just another political question—in which case we will tell both Negroes and whites that their demands will be met—Negroes that they will have full justice and equality now, and whites that the problem of violence and discord will disappear—and all without great sacrifice on the part of any individual or group. We can do this—and we would be deeply, terribly wrong. Or we can assume the burden and responsibility of leadership—which is above all to tell the truth. In this case, we will tell Negroes that there can be no gains through violence, no sudden overturning of the social order. We will tell whites that Negroes must have truly equal opportunities—for jobs and housing and education and a voice in the decisions of government. And we will tell both Negro and white Americans that there are no quick solutions, no easy answers—that the way ahead is full of continued difficulty and danger for all.[96]

It's much easier to pass a law allowing a Negro to eat at Howard Johnson's or to spend a night at the Waldorf, than it is to pass a law to increase opportunities, to get more doctors, to improve schools and hospitals. You aren't going to do a poverty program in this country with a billion seven hundred and fifty million dollars; it's a drop in the bucket. We're the richest country in the world, and we have a responsibility—not only to the effort in Vietnam. A third of the money being spent there could be used here on poverty. A Negro child born in Harlem has twice as much chance of dying as a white child born elsewhere.[97]

Next to these facts, arguments over whether unemployment can best be improved by job training or general prosperity become meaningless. Neither has been adequate, something more is needed. At this point let us make clear what that something more is not. It is not a massive extension of welfare

[96] Speech, Democratic State Committee Dinner, Columbus, Ohio, October 8, 1966.
[97] *The New Yorker,* May 14, 1966.

services or a new profusion of guidance counselors and psychiatrists, whether on a block, neighborhood, or other basis. All these have a role to play. But there are not enough social workers, psychiatrists, or "indigenous workers" in the country to minister to all the broken families and hopeless children on a case-by-case basis. More to the point, welfare workers, or higher welfare payments, cannot confer self-respect or self-confidence on men without work—for in the United States, you *are* what you *do*. Cecil Moore, head of the Philadelphia NAACP, once described welfare as the worst thing that could have happened to the Negro. Even for such an extreme position, there is factual support. . . .

So if we are to break out of this cycle—if our educational programs are to work—we must move immediately to provide jobs for all those willing and able to work. This, of course, we have tried to do. In the last five years we have increased the general level of employment. And we have instituted many training programs to help people qualify for those jobs. But these efforts have not done enough.[98]

Our efforts to remedy this situation would be worthwhile in purely monetary terms. President Johnson's Council of Economic Advisers tells us that if we could suddenly bring Negro unemployment down to the same level as white unemployment and equalize productivity, the result would be the addition of $27 billion—a full 4 percent—to our annual output of goods and services. Fuller participation for the Negro and other disadvantaged groups obviously makes economic sense for us as a nation.[99]

The Senator lent his name and support to several bills aimed at protecting the constitutional rights of Negroes, particularly in the South, and of Spanish-speaking Americans.

I have asked that my name be added as co-sponsor to S. 2923, which Senator Douglas introduced today on behalf

[98] Speech, Second Borough President's Conference of Community Leaders on the Revitalization of Harlem-East Harlem Community, New York, N.Y., January 21, 1966.
[99] Address, Third Annual WGHO Human Relations Award Dinner, Ellenville, N.Y., April 19, 1966.

of a bipartisan group of senators. This bill is an omnibus set of proposals, the main purposes of which are to create a federal assurance of fair selection of jurors, both federal and state, and to bring a better measure of federal protection for the personal security of Negroes and civil rights workers in the South.[100]

The result was that defendants in clearly unconstitutional state prosecutions were forced to wend their way through the state courts up to the United States Supreme Court, and sometimes further yet—to the federal district court on petition for habeas corpus. The path to exoneration was slow and costly indeed. The Bar Association report mentions the Shuttlesworth case and the Jackson Freedom Riders cases, and there are dozens more where the road to dismissal of the changes was traversed successfully, but only at great cost in time and money. And there are, of course, hundreds and hundreds of cases where the defendants lacked either the financial resources or the legal skills or perhaps just the inclination to travel the whole way. The bill which I introduced today broadens the right to removal for immediate federal consideration of the case by spelling out that state proceedings which interfere with constitutional and federal statutory guarantees in the area of civil rights can be removed to federal court.[101]

He addressed himself to the task of open housing in the North.

What, then, are the specific elements of our course of action? Ultimately, we must succeed in wiping out the huge central city ghettos. By this I do not mean that the outcome will be racial balance in every urban and suburban neighborhood. Many Negroes, given a completely free choice, will choose to live in predominantly Negro neighborhoods just as members of other racial and nationality groups have chosen in the past to live predominantly among their own kinsmen.

The important thing is that the Negro must have freedom of choice. What we must achieve is freedom for him to move

---

[100] Press release, February 10, 1966.
[101] Statement, U.S. Senate, April 1, 1966.

if he wants to and where he wants to. And if his desire in the end is for a Negro neighborhood, the choice must not be so narrow that he has to live in a central city neighborhood to live in an urban neighborhood.

Wiping out the ghetto is essential to the future of the Negro and of the city itself. It is essential because the ghetto is *not* a neighborhood. Rather it is a vast, undifferentiated mass. Its very size contributes to its lack of contact with the white community and to the total segregation in schools and everyday life that has been so damaging. And because the present economic characteristics of this population make it a huge pocket of poverty, its location in the center city is a continuing disproportionate burden on city welfare, health, police, and other services. The uneconomic use of land which it represents is a serious loss to the city's tax base as well.

If we can break down the massive housing segregation of the ghetto, we can break down the other forms of segregation which it has caused. The ghetto, for example, makes it practically impossible to achieve meaningful racial balance in the schools. Even if there were enough whites left in the city to make a balance, the physical distances involved in transporting children, particularly in a large city, might be insuperable. The existence of smaller Negro and integrated neighborhoods throughout the metropolitan area would, on the other hand, permit the achievement of improved racial balance in the schools.

Many have said that the goals of improving living conditions in Negro areas and of dispersing the ghetto are mutually exclusive. I disagree most emphatically. In fact, the two goals are interdependent. As G. Franklin Edwards has pointed out:

"There is some resistance on the part of Negroes to moving into areas, especially the suburbs, where few Negroes live. This is particularly characteristic of families with children who must attend school and are dependent on neighbors for play and other social experiences. . . . The forces tying Negroes to the Negro community are the products of fear and isolated living and are likely to discourage any large exodus of Negroes to suburban communities in the immediate future. Upgrading the quality of life in the Negro neighborhoods can break down this pattern of fear. As the Negro engages in better communication with a newly sensitive white community, receives a better education, and improves his economic status, his view of himself in relation to the white community is bound to change. Improving life in the ghetto is necessary, then, to create the seeds for dispersal of the ghetto."

Finally, it would be invaluable to desegregation if we established, with federal assistance, well-publicized advisory agencies to tell new arrivals to the city of available places to live, available jobs, and so on. We might have such agencies both in areas from which people are migrating and in their destination cities. These agencies could be invaluable in preventing the further growth of the ghetto. They would have to be well staffed and sympathetic, and would need wide contacts with local government and industry, with real estate experts and civic groups. And if they were truly national in scope—located in both areas of departure and areas of arrival—they would have to be fully computerized so that full and accurate information is available for any part of the country on a moment's notice. But if they were done well, they would pay for themselves many times over in the savings in welfare expenditures that they would bring.[102]

Indeed, a corporation engaged in rebuilding the urban ghetto could also lead the way toward ending the housing segregation which now pervades our cities. This segregation is the product of two principal causes: most Negroes of the central city cannot afford much suburban housing; more importantly, few suburban developers make positive efforts to attract Negro residents—and many take positive efforts to exclude them. But a private corporation such as I propose would have the resources and the interest to develop neighborhoods and communities open to Negroes outside the ghetto—and it would also give to tens of thousands of Negro families the new employment and education and security they need to enable them to break out of the ghettos, as more fortunate Negroes have been able to do in the past.[103]

[102] Address, luncheon of the Federation of Jewish Philanthropies of New York, New York, N.Y., January 20, 1966.
[103] Address, NAACP Legal Defense Fund Banquet, New York, N.Y., May 18, 1966.

We need funds for the summer of 1967 not as a bribe to the small number of extremists—but to insure that the disadvantaged youth of our cities are not again forced to waste their summers. Time is short, not only in New York City, but in Rochester and Syracuse and Buffalo as well; and not only in the cities of New York State, but in Los Angeles, in Chicago, and Cleveland and every other city which has felt the effects of a century of poverty and discrimination. . . .

Summer programs are not the answer to the problems of the poor, but they are, at least, a constructive part of the continuing effort that must be made at every level of government, and by every citizen, to improve the quality of life in our cities.[104]

Bedford-Stuyvesant—New Approach

In December of 1966, Robert Kennedy unveiled a plan to redevelop, physically and economically, Bedford-Stuyvesant, an area of hard-core Negro poverty in Brooklyn. Combining existing federal programs and the resources of private enterprise with the creation of neighborhood management corporations to involve ghetto residents in the rebuilding effort, his proposal constituted a comprehensive, long-range attack on the area's poverty (see Chapter 5, Poverty, for details of the plan). Though much of the program is currently being implemented, it is still too new for its effectiveness to be assessed realistically.

On July 12 and 13, 1967, Kennedy introduced in the Senate two dramatic new proposals based in part on what he had learned from his Bedford-Stuyvesant endeavor, and designed to provide jobs and decent low-cost housing for the nation's ghetto dwellers. Openly rejecting the New Deal apparatus of "reform by bureaucracy," he called for the direct intervention of private enterprise in the war against poverty, and for the intervention to be spurred by federal tax incentives to make it profitable. (Kennedy's explanations of the purpose and operations of his suggested job opportunities and housing programs

[104] Press release, April 29, 1967.

can be found in Chapter 5, Poverty, and Chapter 4, Cities, Slums, and Suburbs, respectively.)

The important fact to be noted about the Bedford-Stuyvesant program and the Senate bills is that Kennedy had finally committed himself to a specific set of actions for eliminating much of the poverty in which nearly half of America's blacks live. He was making the first efforts to honor the pledge he had made to a group of Harlem community leaders in January of 1966 when he vowed "to turn rhetoric into actions and dreams into fact."

KEY KENNEDY VOTES ON CIVIL RIGHTS

Voting Rights Act of 1965 (S. 1564). Kennedy (D-Mass.) amendment to prohibit the collection of a poll tax as a condition for registration or voting in state or local elections. Rejected 45-49, May 11, 1965. (D 39-24; R 6-25.) Kennedy: FOR.

Voting Rights Act of 1965 (S. 1564). Hart (D-Mich.) motion to invoke cloture on debate on the bill. Cloture agreed to 70-30 (two-thirds vote required), May 25, 1965. (D 47-21; R 23-9.) Kennedy: FOR.

Civil Rights Act of 1966 (HR 14765). Mansfield (D-Mont.) motion to invoke cloture on debate of the bill to ban discrimination in the selection of jurors and in the sale and rental of some housing and to protect Negroes and civil rights workers. Rejected 54-42 (two-thirds vote required), September 14, 1966. (D 42-21; R 12-21.) Kennedy: FOR.

Chapter 4

Cities, Slums, and Suburbs

> For our past efforts to deal with the problems of our cities have not worked; their promise failed, their purpose flagged.[1]

America's metropolitan areas are in trouble. The large central cities, most of whose cores were built at the turn of the century or before, are increasingly characterized by mile after mile of drab slum housing intersected by once-vital commercial avenues now lined with boarded-up buildings, bars, pawnshops, and small, struggling clothing and grocery stores. To make matters worse, these slums, like most of the other areas of the cities, are segregated; they are the involuntary preserves of a majority of the nation's urban blacks.

During the past decade, however, members of the Negro middle class have experienced some success in breaking out of these slum ghettos into the better areas of the cities. This invariably triggers a chain reaction which finds whites fleeing the recently integrated neighborhoods for distant lily-white parts of the cities or the suburbs, and the integrated neighborhoods becoming completely black within a few years.

This seemingly immutable process has made available a large amount of middle- and upper-middle-class housing previously closed to Negro buyers. But on the negative side, the white exodus to the suburbs has robbed the cities of many of their wealthier residents and busi-

[1] Remarks, Buffalo Model City Conference, Buffalo, N.Y., January 20, 1967.

nesses, leaving local governments with shrinking financial resources to support growing lists of services. The result: most cities have entered periods of severe financial crisis with no solution in sight.

The suburbs, too, have paid a price for this rapid immigration into their midst. Lacking even the rudimentary planning some of the cities have undertaken, they have literally "sprawled" in every direction, spawning innumerable social and aesthetic problems. Furthermore, the suburbs tend to be truncated communities, lacking the apex of commercial and cultural centers that traditionally has given the city its appeal. The "solution" has been the widespread practice of commuting to the cities, which has created unnerving, time-wasting traffic jams and forced the cities to construct expensive networks of freeways of little use to inner-city residents (further reducing the cities' tax bases and accelerating the flight to the suburbs).

In addition, the past fifty years have witnessed the introduction into urban life of many new elements that result from our radically changing technology. The cities —most of which assumed their existing dimensions and structure by the late nineteenth and early twentieth centuries—have failed to integrate many of these changes successfully. This lagging of politics and the social sciences behind the physical sciences has reached a point where our "progress," of which we constantly boast, is threatening to strangle us.

Intracity transportation is inefficient and dangerous. The air and water, which in the most basic sense are the life substances of every society, are being poisoned. Lack of foresight, poor zoning regulations and inadequate public transportation have cut off less mobile portions of the urban populace from many job opportunities as well as adequate recreational and cultural facilities. In short, these and other failures have made many of our cities vast concrete wastelands, unpleasant to live in and lacking all sense of community pride and cooperation. To date, almost nothing has been done by government or with private initiative to remedy this untenable situation.

Our Sick Cities

It was not until Robert Kennedy ran for the Senate in the fall of 1964 that he began to explore publicly the problems of our urban areas. On several occasions he discussed the malaise of the American city in broad terms.

One great problem is sheer growth—growth which crowds people into slums, thrusts suburbs out over the countryside, burdens to the breaking point all our old ways of thought and action—our systems of transport and water supply and education, and our means of raising money to finance these vital services.

A second is destruction of the physical environment, stripping people of contact with sun and fresh air, clean rivers, grass and trees—condemning them to a life among stone and concrete, neon lights and an endless flow of automobiles. . . .

A third is the increasing difficulty of transportation—adding concealed, unpaid hours to the workweek; removing men from the social and cultural amenities that are the heart of the city; sending destructive swarms of automobiles across the city, leaving behind them a band of concrete and poisoned atmosphere. And sometimes—as in Watts—our surrender to the automobile has so crippled public transport that thousands literally cannot afford to go to work elsewhere in the city.

A fourth destructive force is the concentrated poverty and racial tension of the urban ghetto—a problem so vast that the barest recital of its symptoms is profoundly shocking. . . .

Fifth is both cause and consequence of all the rest. It is the destruction of the sense, and often the fact, of community, of human dialogue, the thousand invisible strands of common experience and purpose, affection and respect which tie men to their fellows. It is expressed in such words as community, neighborhood, civic pride, friendship. It provides the life-sustaining force of human warmth, or security among others, and a sense of one's own human significance in the accepted association and companionship of others.

We all share things as fellow citizens, fellow members of the American nation.

As important as that sharing is, nations or great cities are too huge to provide the values of community. Community demands a place where people can see and know each other, where children can play and adults work together and join in the pleasures and responsibilities of the place where they live. The whole history of the human race, until today, has been the history of the community. Yet this is disappearing, and disappearing at a time when its sustaining strength is badly needed. For other values which once gave strength for the daily battle of life are also being eroded.[2]

Our cities, for example, are peopled more and more by the poor and unskilled, who came in search of new jobs and a new life, while their more affluent fellow citizens moved to the suburbs. The two Americas are shut apart, and long-smoldering despairs and frustrations have blazed into violence. But did we not shape this crisis when we let FHA concentrate its massive home financing in the suburbs, and when federal aid built the highways to carry the new suburbanites to their work? Did we not shape this crisis when we paid farmers millions of dollars not to produce cotton, but paid nothing to and did nothing for the thousands of workers who were thrown off the land as a result, and came to the city because they had no other choice? Our air is polluted and our water unfit for recreation. But did we not shape those two crises of our environment? Our lives were revolutionized by electricity, but to do this we built unsightly power plants in the heart of our cities, which spew forth clouds of harmful smoke. Automobiles changed our lives, but we heedlessly watched them multiply until one day, almost too late, we discovered that they poison the air we breathe as well. And the expanding industry which has swelled our prosperity also helped turn the Hudson River into a sewer and Lake Erie into a swamp.[3]

And, in recent years, an exploding population and sweep-

[2] Statement, Subcommittee on Executive Reorganization of the Senate Committee on Government Operations, December 10, 1966.
[3] Address, Civil Service Employees Association, New York N.Y., September 7, 1967.

ing changes in the economy have turned the center city into a trap—an "airtight cage," as one writer has called it. The slums spread—the city withers—those with means flee to the suburbs; and jobs follow. The tax base of the city is eroded, just when the physical decay has made it more urgent than ever to find resources now.[4]

Yet even as in the drive toward bigness, concentration, the city has reached heights never before dreamt of in the past, we have come suddenly to realize how heavy a price we have paid: in overcrowding and pollution of the atmosphere, and impersonality; in growth of organizations, particularly government, so large and powerful that individual effort and importance seem lost; and in loss of the values of nature and community and local diversity that found their nurture in the smaller towns and rural areas of America. And we can see, as we enter the last third of the twentieth century, that the price has been too high. Bigness, loss of community, organizations and society grown far past the human scale— these are the besetting sins of the twentieth century, which threaten to paralyze our very capacity to act, or our ability to preserve the traditions and values of our past in a time of swirling, constant change.

To these central dangers, besides, we can trace a hundred others, the signs around us that all is not well in the Republic: spreading violence, unconcern for others, too many seeking escape in noninvolvement or in drugs, debate become acerbic and bad-tempered, and over all a sense that no one is listening.[5]

Lewis Mumford told the Ribicoff Subcommittee [holding hearings on the Federal Role in Urban Affairs] a few days ago that "democracy, in any active sense, begins and ends in communities small enough for their members to meet face to face."

If the massiveness and congestion of the city have damaged us all, the damage and the frustration have been the deepest

[4] Testimony, National Commission on Urban Problems, New York, N.Y., September 6, 1967.

[5] Speech, dedication of community-sponsored junior college, Worthington, Minn., September 17, 1966.

and most debilitating for the child of the ghetto. If we have suffered somewhat the loss of personal identity that comes from the disintegration of the neighborhood as the basic unit of local democracy, the child of the ghetto has suffered most. For he is a prisoner in an area which is not a community or even a series of communities, but a vast, gray, undifferentiated slum, isolated physically and in every other way from the rest of the city and its resources.[6]

Therefore, the time has come to stem the flow to the cities—to prevent their further sprawling over the landscape, their further oppression of men's souls. The time has come when we must actively fight bigness and overconcentration—and seek instead to bring the engines of government, of technology, of the economy, fully under the control of our citizens, to recapture and reinforce the values of a more human time and place.[7]

The cities need help in many forms. By far the most important is in the redevelopment of their economics to bring back jobs and income to the unemployed and poverty-stricken who now are so large a part of the city's population—and so serious a drain on its financial resources. As David Rockefeller has said, we must begin to develop the economics of our cities just as we try to develop poor nations abroad. Nothing can take the place of new jobs, affording dignity and self-sufficiency for those who now languish in idleness, or on the welfare roll.[8]

The city is not just housing and stores. It is not just education and employment, parks and theaters, banks and shops. It is a place where men should be able to live in dignity and security and harmony, where the great achievements of modern civilization and the ageless pleasures afforded by natural beauty should be available to all.

If this is what we want—and this what we must want if men are to be free for the "pursuit of happiness" which

[6] Address, Day Care Council of New York, New York, N.Y., May 8, 1967.

[7] Speech, Worthington, Minn., September 17, 1966.

[8] Speech, U.S. Senate, July 13, 1967.

was the earliest promise of the American nation—we will need more than poverty programs, housing programs, and employment programs, although we will need all of these. We will need an outpouring of imagination, ingenuity, discipline and hard work unmatched since the first adventurers set out to conquer the wilderness. For the problem is the largest we have ever known. And we confront an urban wilderness more formidable and resistant and in some ways more frightening than the wilderness faced by the pilgrims or the pioneers.[9]

Is Washington the Answer?

To those who look primarily to Washington for the direction and resources to attack these problems, Kennedy warned:

. . . to say that we have reached the limits of our action is to say that the federal government itself can provide all the answers to our problems. Nothing could be further from the truth. The federal government is far away in Washington; therefore, it cannot know your local needs as well as you. The federal government must deal with a large and diverse nation; therefore, it cannot adapt its general policy to your local conditions as well as local officials can.

So it is, in my judgment, absurd to think that the federal government can find all the answers or meet our needs in any significant fashion.[10]

The federal government does have a role to play. It can and should assist local communities with their financial burdens, since local taxes have already become so great as to hamper development. The federal government can and should provide local communities with technical assistance,

[9] Statement, Subcommittee on Executive Reorganization of the Senate Committee on Government Operations, December 10, 1966.
[10] Speech, Convention of Editors of the New York State Associated Press Broadcasters Association, Lake George, N.Y., September 20, 1965.

with new techniques and new knowledge developed elsewhere. But the federal government should not administer
programs of action which would do better run by local
officials.[11]

The Medicare Bill, the Hill-Burton Hospital Construction
Program, the Mental Retardation Act, the Higher Education
Bill, the Agricultural Extension Program, the Economic
Opportunity Act, the Appalachia Program—all these will
provide money and materials, techniques and technicians.

But the job of building—the job of putting these programs
to work—and the over-all job of renewing these communities
and their contribution to a better New York and a better
America—that job must be done in detail, town by town
and brick by brick, by you and the people you lead and
energize.[12]

Eliminating Slum Ghettos: The RFK Plan

He saw the elimination of Negro slum ghettos as the
key to the cities' futures.

It [a program for the cities] must attack the fundamental
pathology of the ghetto—for unless the deprivation and
alienation of the ghetto are eliminated, there is no hope for the
city. And it must attack these problems within a framework
that coordinates action on the four central elements: employment, education, housing, and a sense of community.[13]

. . . breaking down the ghetto, together with intelligent re-
use of vacated slum land, will give the cities a new lease on
life—a double inoculation of reduced costs for services and an
improved tax base.

[11] Address, Greater Utica Chamber of Commerce, Utica, N.Y.,
October 24, 1965.

[12] Speech, Western New York Publishers Association, Painted
Post, N.Y., October 9, 1965.

[13] Statement, Subcommittee on Executive Reorganization of the
Senate Committee on Government Operations, December 10, 1966.

Thus, the long-run life of the city itself depends on the Negro's being able to live where he chooses, in any part of the metropolitan area, and, I might add, on stemming the migration of whites out of the city.[14]

However, he pointed out that, if anything, big-city slums have been growing worse, not better, in recent years.

We have known of this disgrace since the cities were born—we have been shocked at the filth amid wealth since Jacob Riis awakened New York at the turn of the century. And government at all levels has mounted program after program to erase this scar on the souls of the people. We have torn slums down—others have risen in their place. We have tried to rehabilitate them—and decay has outstripped repairs. We have built blocks of public housing—and they have become the new slums of the core city, slums which lack even that sense of neighborhood the poor once had.[15]

In his second month as a senator, he supported an experimental program to renovate a block in Harlem.

Senator Robert F. Kennedy today hailed a "bold program" for community renovation of a Harlem block. Under this program, the Housing and Home Finance Agency, in cooperation with the New York City Department of Rent and Rehabilitation and the Office of Economic Opportunity, will renovate an entire city block. The present occupants will remain in the buildings after renovation, at rents which will be only slightly increased. "This illustrates the validity of my position that renovation efforts of the federal government should be sharply increased," said Mr. Kennedy. "I will press for greatly expanded authority for programs of this type in the 1965 Housing Act.

[14] Address, luncheon of the Federation of Jewish Philanthropies of New York, New York, N.Y., January 20, 1966.
[15] Testimony, National Commission on Urban Problems, New York, N.Y., September 6, 1967.

"But renovated buildings, like new buildings, do not by themselves build communities. This block will be a block like any other—unless we improve the education given to its children. The rents will be kept low—but no rent is low enough when there are not enough jobs. This block may be an island of beauty and comfort—but no island is proof against the deprivation and indignity that are too often the lot of the poor." [16]

He also supported a program of rent subsidies.

Rent subsidies, a radical idea never tried in this country, but a way to break up segregation of the poor in slums and public housing programs—Congress agreed to experiment with rent subsidies—and they are already in demand by low-income families in small communities here in Wisconsin. [17]

Less than six months later, before a conference of community leaders called to discuss the revitalization of Harlem and East Harlem in New York, Bobby outlined an eight-point plan for rebuilding the slums of our cities. It was the first time he had offered a comprehensive plan of action to deal with urban problems.

In any program of rebuilding now begun, therefore, I urge the following:

First. Priority in employment on these projects should go to residents of the areas in which they are undertaken. The fathers and young men of Harlem need work—and this is the best kind of work we could possibly offer them. For this is man's work—which is dignified, which is hard and exacting, which is at the same time rewarding to the man who does it and rewarding to the community around him. Much of it is work which can be done by unskilled workers, who now have the most difficult time finding jobs; but in such a program there would be jobs in Harlem which would make a major change in the entire environment in which its young people grow up.

[16] Press release, February 2, 1965.
[17] Address, testimonial dinner for Lieutenant Governor Patrick Lucey, Milwaukee, Wis., August 15, 1965.

Second. Public and private training programs should concentrate their funds and their efforts in on-the-job training on these projects. Not only will job training be needed to make initial employment possible for many of the ghetto's residents; just as important, the availability of jobs will make many of our training programs more meaningful than they have been before. In a very real sense, these projects could be a vast new educational institution—teaching skills, but teaching pride of self and pride of craft as well.

Third. Our conventional educational system should be directly integrated with the rebuilding effort; for many of our most serious educational problems, there is real hope of solution within such a program.

The central problem of motivation, for example, would be directly confronted. Any high school student who so desired—whether for financial or other reasons—could be allowed to leave school to work on such a project. The schools would maintain jurisdiction over these students; and they would, as a condition of employment, be required to continue schooling at least part-time until the requirements for graduation were met. In fact, all jobs on these projects should require part-time study to remedy educational deficiencies, and advancement on the job should be directly related to school credits gained, just as it is in the Armed Forces. Without the need to discipline unmotivated students, the schools would find it far easier to educate students who wish to learn. And the young men who work on these projects will learn that the ability to read a blueprint or a specification is worth returning to school to acquire. Another of our serious educational problems is how to discover and develop aptitudes for managerial and technical work among the great bulk of slum residents: our great universities are eager for qualified Negro students. But on the job, it would be possible for young people to show such aptitudes—just as millions of young men first discovered their potential in the Armed Forces in World War II, and later went on to college and new positions of leadership.

Fourth. The rebuilding should be consciously directed at the creation of communities—the building of neighborhoods in which residents can take pride, neighborhoods in which they have a stake, neighborhoods in which physical surroundings help the residents to create the functioning community which must be our goal. We should, for example, make provision for condominium ownership of low-income apartments. At another level, we should engage in as much rehabilitation as possible, saving all of the old that is economical and sound. We should build in stores and workshops and play space. And the planning of the neighborhoods should, from the outset, involve the people of the areas affected.

Fifth. Present social-service programs, particularly welfare, should be integrated with the rebuilding effort. The program I envision would make it possible for families to turn dependence into self-sufficiency; but we must work to make possibilities into fact—for example, by using a man's new employment as an aid to reuniting him with his family. For another example, the rebuilding program should focus in significant degree on unmet social needs—such as by constructing clinics and physicians' group practice facilities in the ghettos, which are notoriously short of medical services.

Sixth. Using the building program as a base, occupational opportunities and training should be opened up in all related ways. As building takes place, for example, some should learn and then operate building-supplies businesses; small furniture manufacturing establishments; or restaurants in which the workers can eat. As health clinics are established, young people should be trained to work in them as both clerical and medical aides. Buildings should be decorated and embellished by art students; housing should contain facilities in which students of music and drama could put on entertainments.

All of these have been proposed before; many have been attempted. But it is becoming increasingly clear that without a common focus—without the framework of a total effort at regeneration within the entire slum community—these efforts will not fulfill our hopes. For example, present proposals to train "subprofessionals," or "helping aides," as they are sometimes called, all concentrate on training people for jobs which do not yet exist—with the hope that once we have trained the people, someone will find a use for them. But neither instructors nor students can be serious in a program from which students are without a defined place to go when their training is complete—which may explain why most of the proposals have remained on paper. But if the jobs are available—if training has a goal and a reward —and if the helping technicians are given proper opportunities to become full professionals—these programs will be worthwhile.

Seventh. An essential component of any program for regeneration of the ghetto will be the active participation of the business community in every aspect of the program, in a partnership of shared costs and effort with government. Housing, for example, should be constructed by limited-profit corporations, with financing guaranteed and appropriate rent subsidies furnished by the government. Business should be encouraged to create jobs in the ghetto—for example, by establishing branch or franchise operations in which local residents would be trained for ultimate management; this is no more than business now does in foreign countries. The ingenuity of American industry should also be engaged in the job-training programs, just as it now is in certain job corps camps. Commercial and industrial facilities should be erected and leased to both major industry and local merchants. And the business community should be encouraged not only to do better the things we now do—such as, for example, to improve building techniques for lowered cost— but also to show us entirely new things to do, to become a generator of social change and improvement. For example, one of the ghetto's most serious problems is the poor quality of goods sold in local stores—and the ignorance of many housewives that better goods are available at lower cost elsewhere. I would like to see the government encourage private industry to establish demonstration stores in Harlem, stores in which quality goods of all kinds—food, clothing, appliances—would be sold at prices comparable to those in the large discount stores downtown and in the suburbs. Combined with consumer-education programs now under way in the poverty program, such stores could be both schools and yardsticks against which other stores could be measured. The government operates the electric-power plants of the TVA so that buyers will have a standard against which to measure the costs of private power; slum residents should have the same yardsticks against which to measure the cost and quality of their daily needs.

Eighth. Equally essential is the full participation of private groups—especially of labor unions and of universities. Labor unions should furnish training cadres and supervisors on the job, and instructors in the training programs. Unions should also be encouraged to establish and administer neighborhood health and social-service programs similar to those they now operate for their members. And they should also be encouraged to organize the workers in these programs. Universities should be invited not only to establish special education programs, but to lend their expert knowledge in the planning and execution of every part of the process. Medical schools could help to train medical aides, and to instruct the population generally about hygiene and sanitation. Law schools could furnish legal assistance to projects and to individuals. Business schools could have special training classes and consultant services for small businessmen.

What is called for, in short, is a total effort at regeneration—an effort to mobilize the skills and resources of the entire society, including above all the latent skills and resources of the people of the ghetto themselves, in the solution of our urban dilemma.[18]

He then turned to the question of financing his proposal.

This is not to say that all the cost can be met out of the present budget; it cannot. But a start can be made, in some of our great cities—a start which will teach us the techniques of such a massive effort. And in the longer term—over the next five or ten or twenty years—there is no doubt that federal revenue at *current levels of taxation* will be $10 to $14 billion greater than in 1966. By 1970, only four years away, revenues will be $11 to $15 billion greater again than in 1968. By 1975, when children now being born are only nine years old, when students now in junior high school will

[18] Speech, Second Borough President's Conference of Community Leaders on the Revitalization of Harlem-East Harlem Community, New York, N.Y., January 21, 1966.

be forming their families—federal revenues will be greater than 1966 by at least $52 billion. Even allowing for the increase in the population to be served, the federal government will still have over $40 billion in new resources available. Moreover, the pace of building, the most labor-intensive industry in the economy, must rise precipitously in the coming years. So there will be jobs for all—if we now take the action, for skills and self-reliance, homes and hope, which all our people deserve. And any costs of this program will be to a substantial degree offset by lower welfare costs. More than one out of four children in Harlem, for example, now receives money under the Aid to Dependent Children program; the average recipient family gets over $2,500 a year in ADC funds. To give their fathers or young men jobs at $5,000 a year would actually cost us only $2,500 per family—for which we would receive the full value of their labor. The money we now spend on welfare administration we could spend on teachers and administrators for the program; and we must always bear in mind that the cost of keeping a criminal in jail for a year is over $3,000—and that we cannot make up the loss to his victims. But the greatest returns of the program I have outlined would be returns in human spirit—in lessened dependency, in lower delinquency and crime, in more beautified cities and children stronger and healthier in every way; and these returns are beyond our capacity to measure.[19]

Housing: The Kennedy Blueprint

Many of Kennedy's statements and proposals for rebuilding the decaying cores of our cities focused on the provision of low-cost housing for slum residents. In a campaign statement issued just before his election to the Senate in 1964, he first expressed his views on this subject.

Even more critical are the housing problems in urban areas and the need for increased and improved rental housing which serves so many of our city dwellers. What is

[19] *Ibid.*

needed is a large-scale, creative program coordinating existing federal, state and local programs and providing some needed new ones. This effort must be concerned with more than buildings—it must deal with the over-all problem of community and neighborhood development. Decent housing units alone are not to my mind sufficient without supporting facilities such as recreational areas and mass transit facilities. . . .

Buildings do not make a viable neighborhood, but people do. We must be more careful in the future that old-time residents of an improved area are not driven out and the sense of community dissipated. For example, urban renewal should come in stages so that people who are evicted from their homes can move to newly completed housing in the same neighborhood. Relocation allowances must be provided both to individuals and to businessmen to help them adjust to their forced move. Small businesses particularly can be unfairly injured if they are forced to move away from a neighborhood where they have developed a local reputation. If it is not possible to relocate them in the same neighborhood, they should be compensated for their loss of goodwill. Existing federal legislation should be amended to provide relocation benefits in addition to actual moving expenses. Rent assistance should be provided for a maximum period of three years to help residents remain in their old neighborhoods if they cannot afford the higher rents resulting from neighborhood improvements, and to make sure that they aren't simply moved from one slum to another. More limited assistance to commercial tenants should also be provided. . . .

I support an expansion of the public housing program to authorize the construction of at least 100,000 units per year nationwide for the next five years. The present provision which requires that families living in low-income housing be evicted if they increase their earnings should be abolished. This provision has forced many responsible families out of public housing, thereby weakening community leadership and destroying responsible community action. It has also served to penalize incentive and advancement. If the income of a tenant increases, his rent can be increased up to the point of an economical rent for the particular project, but he should be left the option, and indeed encouraged, to stay in the community. And most important, we must make sure that public housing is not built in isolation, but in relation to the neighborhood where it is located and the needs of the people which it serves. The law should be amended to increase the cost per room permitted in construction so as to permit the construction of small vest-pocket projects which would blend more easily into the neighborhood and encourage a community of interest among inhabitants. . . .

Perhaps no government programs are more important in the housing field than those which help our citizens acquire and maintain their own homes. FHA mortgage guarantees have been a great help in this direction and should be continued. But this program is of little help to families earning less than $6,000. I think we should enact new legislation enabling the government to make direct loans at low interest rates to permit these families to finance home purchases. The interest charged should be geared to what families can afford and raised if income increases during the loan period. Such a program would assist young couples to acquire homes when their children are young and grow into them. I would also support new legislation to provide federal insurance of mortgage payments to protect those who undertake major indebtedness to purchase their own homes. A family should not have to give up its home because the wage-earner becomes sick or suffers an accident. Reasonable federal insurance should be provided to homeowners guaranteeing mortgage payments against such contingencies. . . .

The first essential, it seems to me, is to insure that the good neighborhoods of today do not deteriorate into the slums of tomorrow. The federal government should assist local communities to develop comprehensive building codes and to see that they are adequately enforced. It is very much less expensive to prevent the formation of slums in this manner than to tear them down after the fact. And vigorous code enforcement is an immediate way to bring about significant improvement in basic health and safety conditions in areas where improvement is badly needed. The National Conference of Mayors has called for this type of federal assistance, and I support it. . . .

For those neighborhoods which have already deteriorated, urban renewal can be the answer if it is carried out sensitively and in conjunction with other federal programs. Urban renewal is the key to any large-scale program to improve deteriorated neighborhoods, and I think the federal government should appropriate at least $1 billion per year for the next five years for this program. But, the object of urban renewal should not be to bulldoze an entire area and start afresh. It should be to preserve the character of the neighborhood and protect the inhabitants. The object should not be simply to erect steel and concrete. It should not be to envelop people of a single economic and racial background together in tall buildings. It should provide for a balanced and varied community. . . .

I think we must determine to devote the necessary federal resources to fulfill the congressional policy, stated in the 1949 Housing Act, of "a decent home and a suitable living environment for every American family." [20]

By 1966 Senator Kennedy had lost much of his enthusiasm for existing federal housing programs. He began to attack them as economically inefficient and as the deliberate perpetuators of urban segregation.

Public housing has been a significant force in perpetuating segregation. It has been built, on the whole, as large projects in ghetto areas, and it is all too clear that this has not been wholly accidental. The result is that in 1962, 80 percent of all public housing projects receiving federal subsidy were occupied by members of only one race. And the approach of building mainly in central cities has been uneconomic. Land and construction costs have brought the cost per unit in New York City to over $21,000. To illustrate the consequences of this policy, we should note, for example, that projects in areas outside the central city could have been built and every tenant have been provided a brand-new automobile to commute with, and the cost would still have been far less. [21]

Public housing was once thought of as *the* answer to the

[20] Campaign statement, October 6, 1964.
[21] Address, luncheon of the Federation of Jewish Philanthropies of New York, New York, N.Y., January 20, 1966.

problems of slums. Therefore it became another of those programs, addressed to some symptomatic shortcoming, which has ignored the wider problem, the other needed government action. Our housing projects were built largely without either reference or relevance to the underlying problems of poverty, unemployment, social disorganization and alienation which caused people to need assistance in the first place. Too many of the projects, as a result, became jungles—places of despair and danger for their residents, and for the cities they were designed to save. Many of them are preserved from this fate only by screening, such as is practiced in New York City, to keep the "problem" families—who of course are most in need of help—out of public housing projects, while families with incomes as high as $9,000 a year may live there.

And therefore it has been, too often, a failure. For no single program, no attempted solution of any single element of the problem, can be *the* answer.[22]

. . . relocation is another aspect of our federal housing policy that has served to perpetuate segregation. One study showed that two-thirds of those displaced by a large renewal project had relocated within twelve city blocks of their original residence.[23]

In housing, it is a responsibility to realize that programs for low-income housing will not accomplish all they can unless you take the leadership in site dispersal—unless you lead the community to accept the idea that low-income families should be able to live outside the ghetto, the old slum, if they want to do so.[24]

The strategy of desegregation requires us to strike out in new directions. Our major effort, I might say, will have to be in connection with low-income families. The number of

[22] Statement, Subcommittee on Executive Reorganization of the Senate Committee on Government Operations, December 10, 1966.
[23] Address, luncheon of the Federation of Jewish Philanthropies of New York, New York, N.Y., January 20, 1966.
[24] Address, Neighborhood Preservation and Renewal Conference, New York University, New York, N.Y., April 2, 1966.

Negro families who can now afford to buy a home is relatively small at present. One important new direction was President Johnson's proposal last year of federal aid to finance new town developments. The proposal was dropped from the housing bill as enacted. Resubmission of this proposal, together with a requirement that, say, 15 percent of the housing in a new town be set aside for low-income families, would be a major contribution. If the new town builders received the benefits of the rent-supplement provisions of last year's Act, they would not be disadvantaged financially in providing the low-income housing.[25]

On July 13, 1967, Kennedy introduced a proposal for an alternative to existing housing programs, a bill (S. 2100) to induce private investment in urban poverty-area housing. The bill provided private investors with federal tax credits and subsidies for low-interest loans. In return, investors would be expected to put up large equities, hold the housing for a considerable period of time, and reinvest proceeds from sales in additional low-rent housing projects.

The bill also called for participation by tenants in "management corporations," which would undertake management and maintenance as well as educational and cultural functions. Inducements to investors were included, to encourage the eventual sale of these projects to their tenants through the management corporations.

Private enterprise builds nearly all of our housing today. But the one area in which private enterprise has not played a full part has been in the area of greatest present need: the construction of low- and moderate-income housing in the center city, and the rehabilitation of the slums which scar its face. It is in these areas also that government programs have most conspicuously failed. And it is the purpose of this bill to enlist the energies and resources of private enterprise in this great remaining task.

Though complex in detail, the bill we introduce today

[25] Address, luncheon of the Federation of Jewish Philanthropies of New York, New York, N.Y., January 20, 1966.

is simple in purpose and method. Its aim is to create a mechanism by which private enterprise can and will build and rehabilitate large numbers of low-cost housing units in urban poverty areas. It drives toward this goal by two means. First, it attempts to lower costs by providing an extended interest rate subsidy similar to that existing in some current housing programs, and by authorizing payments to municipalities in lieu of real estate taxes on this housing. Second, it aims to attract large-scale private enterprise investment through a system of tax incentives, designed to make such investment possible at competitive rates of return." [26]

Admittedly, these are complex and intricate provisions. But their basic thrust is simple and clear. They have been designed, after extensive consultation with businessmen and tax experts, to achieve the following ends: To induce large equity investment in low-cost housing; to favor those owners who hold the property for long periods, rather than turning it over within a few years for a tax gain; to encourage investors to reinvest the proceeds of any sale in more low-cost housing; and to provide a competitive rate of return to make the investment attractive overall—thus minimizing any need for direct government participation in the ownership, construction, or management of the housing, or for any direct government financing. [27]

. . . I believe—after careful study—that these bills provide a far cheaper mechanism for improving the slums than purely government programs. Furthermore, the housing bill—S. 2100—provides low-income shelter without the dependency of public housing, and with the strong probability of home ownership. Most important, these bills provide no single solution—they offer projects as diverse and flexible as the private sector itself. . . .

They offer a partnership between industry and community to rebuild neighborhoods—instead of destroying them through short-sighted policy or wanton chaos. They can turn the dark

[26] Speech, U.S. Senate, July 13, 1967.
[27] Testimony, National Commission on Urban Problems, New York, N.Y., September 6, 1967.

corners of the American portrait into places of work and living and hope. I do not suggest my proposals are the only way—indeed, I am convinced that with your experience, your suggestions may well be better than mine. I would urge you to find out—to discover which fiscal tools are best suited to your own cities, your own communities, your own towns.[28]

. . . it is argued that by building in the ghetto, we lock its residents in and turn our backs on the goal of integration. But open occupancy is not inconsistent with ghetto rehabilitation. For open occupancy laws are not enough. An escape hatch for those who both want to and can afford to move away from the ghetto is desirable. But what about those who either want to or have to stay where they are? What about those who would build their own community, those who would take pride in their own neighborhoods if they could? Integration is a vital, an indispensable goal in an open society. But equally important, the vast majority of Negroes must be enabled to achieve basic financial and social security where they live now. Indeed, a new generation of Negroes is striving to establish a sense of community as a people, to gain a measure of control over their own destiny as a people. Sensitivity to that aspiration is at the heart of S. 2100. And it is in no way inconsistent with a total commitment to an open society.[29]

S. 2100 would not replace the Model Cities program, which has been designed to coordinate more fully the governmental efforts in the ghetto areas of our cities; indeed, it is only within such a framework that S. 2100 could achieve its aims. For that program, the 89th Congress authorized $400 million —and that is the sum which this Congress should be prepared to appropriate. The bill is not a substitute for the rent supplement program, which will assist those with extremely low incomes to pay for housing. Nor will the bill eliminate the necessity for the Administration's Rat Control and Extermination program. For decay will remain for many years, and all the residents of our urban ghettos will continue to feel

[28] Remarks, U.S. Chamber of Commerce, Washington, D.C., October 3, 1967.
[29] Testimony, Senate Finance Committee, September 14, 1967.

threatened so long as they know that they and their children may still be subject to attack from rats. Nor do these programs preclude the possibility of further governmental efforts. For example, you suggested the other day, Mr. Chairman, [Paul Douglas] one possibility which deserves serious consideration: the use of suburban homes on which FHA mortgages have been foreclosed to house low-income families. Similarly the Administration's announcement last week of plans for a new community on surplus federal land in the District of Columbia—and its intention to explore like possibilities elsewhere—are welcome signs.[30]

It should be added that the prospects for the enactment of S. 2100, or any similar proposal, at that time were bleak. The Administration was working on a new housing program of its own, and it was unlikely to support the personal creation of any legislator, particularly one as threatening as Senator Kennedy. Without such support, passage of a measure as controversial as S. 2100 became next to impossible.

Urban Transportation

During his Senate campaign in 1964, Kennedy made public his views on another key city problem. In a press release directed to the difficulties born of our reliance on automobiles, he suggested several courses of action:

1. Fringe-area parking lots with connecting high-speed mass transportation to downtown areas.

   In addition to improving existing transit systems, Kennedy recommends new methods where feasible including monorails, helicopters, and hydrofoils.

2. Construction of beltways and circumferential highways by shifting the emphasis of the Interstate Highway Program to the bypassing of cities and downtown areas.

   Kennedy also would . . . try to amend the interstate law to provide aid in moving traffic across downtown areas.

[30] Testimony, National Commission on Urban Problems, New York, N.Y., September 6, 1967.

He emphasized that careful planning and adequate financing would be required to make crosstown arteries effective.

They should, he said, have limited access, often elevated or underground, and be constructed so existing neighborhoods are not uprooted or destroyed.

To meet the needs of interstate or intercity travel in the northeastern section of the nation, RFK recommended:

A high-speed, limited stop rail system such as one recently built between Tokyo and Kyoto, Japan. A working committee should be set up to study financing for the plan. . . .[31]

He also recommended the continuance of federal subsidies to foster the development of urban helicopter service.

In my judgment, helicopter operations should be subsidized for another five years, on a phase-out basis. . . .

Helicopters can take a businessman from the center of town to his plane in seven minutes. No other available form of transportation comes close to this performance. The second point I offer is that the results of these experimental helicopter programs will be of great benefit to other cities, to the air transportation industry in general and to the national interest. The problems which now confront New York City, and the other cities in question here, will soon confront many others. In the next forty years, the urban population of the United States will double. This increase is bound to affect surface time—which means that we may produce a supersonic airliner only to find that it takes more time to get from the city to the airport than the aircraft spends in the air. Indeed this is already the case between New York and Cleveland, Detroit, Pittsburgh, and Washington.[32]

Suburbia, the "Sterile Bedroom"

For those who believe they can escape the morass of urban ills by running to the suburbs, there was warning and advice:

[31] Press release, October 31, 1964.
[32] Statement, Subcommittee on Aviation of the Senate Committee on Commerce, March 10, 1965.

The battle to return to the neighborhood, to reconstitute democracy on a "face-to-face" level, is not just a battle on behalf of the child of the ghetto. It is a battle for all of us, for all of our children, for the shaping of ideals of our nation.

For the child of the suburbs has suffered from the loss of community as well. He lives, after all, in a vast bedroom, removed by ribbons of concrete from the city, where his father's work and the cultural and social amenities that are the heart of the community life are located.

He, too, suffers as he grows up from a sense of being unable to be an active, determining force in his own life. If there has been a "drug scene" in the ghetto for years, we now read increasingly of the use of LSD and other dangerous drugs on college campuses. The suicide rate among children and teenagers is rising. If there is crime and violence among young people in the ghetto, there are also disturbances and increasing delinquency among the "teenie-bopper" children of the suburbs.

Let no man think, therefore, that he fights this battle for others. He fights it for his own children, for us all. The sense of community is essential to us all—for none of us can have an identity except in relation to his community, to his fellow man.[33]

The patterns of growth in our suburbs have brought counties like Nassau and Suffolk and Westchester—city bordering upon city, a collection of communities so interrelated that the county is the only logical unit of over-all government. And the patterns of growth have left us other counties so sparsely populated that no village or town within has the resources to engage in the kind of planning and development activity that is needed in the years ahead. There are, of course, many areas in which urban growth has caused the city to overshadow the county in importance. But in area after area in our state and around the country, the county remains more than ever the logical unit for local planning and development.[34]

[33] Address, Day Care Council of New York, New York, N.Y., May 8, 1967.

[34] Remarks, New York State County Officers Association, New York, N.Y., September 20, 1965.

If we want to stop suburban sprawl, we will have to create new towns; to build new industry in these towns; and create new transportation networks to serve them. If we do not do these things, then the woods will be progressively leveled, and replaced by unplanned and often unattractive developments which none of us desire but with which we will all have to live. The job cannot be done by individual communities. No single town, for example, can prevent nearby cities from growing toward it. No single state can keep the air from being polluted. No community can meet its transportation needs without the cooperation of other localities, of state and federal government, and of major nationwide industries.[35]

Kennedy continually stressed the need for increased urban planning and interagency cooperation at all levels of government if inroads into the tangle of metropolitan problems are to be achieved.

I hope the Senate will vote to approve the creation of a Department of Housing and Urban Development.

It is important to view this legislation not as an end in itself, but as a beginning. Cabinet-level status for all of the housing, urban renewal, and mass transportation planning functions of the Housing and Home Finance Agency is, of course, long overdue. Over 70 percent of our population now lives in urban areas. The federal programs which affect the growth and decay of the environments of 135,000,000 Americans deserve the added stature that Cabinet-level administration will give to them.[36]

And the solution of any one problem depends upon the solution of many others. New job opportunities without education are meaningless. New housing without adequate supporting community service is not good housing. Communities with poor transportation cannot attract industry. New classrooms that will not be filled when completed do not meet our education needs. Poor zoning and unplanned development

[35] Address, Suffolk County Industrial Development Symposium, L.I., N.Y.
[36] Speech, U.S. Senate, August 10, 1965.

result in ugly communities and suburbs that people do not want to live in.[37]

But let there be no mistake. We *will* have more people; they *will* need more space in which to live, and work, and play; the question is whether we control growth wisely—or whether it controls us. If you would preserve the beauty and amenity of this area—and it should be preserved—it will be necessary for you to take active part in the planning not just of this community but of the entire state, and indeed of the United States.[38]

The fact that one county, or one community, is prospering does not argue against its inclusion in a regional plan. In fact, their inclusion is necessary if the regional plan is to be successful. The advancing, prosperous counties are the base on which the region can build its development. Binghamton, for example, is the key market for the counties of Western New York. If Broome County were omitted from the regional plan, federal assistance for the roads from these Western counties would have to end at the county line.[39]

We must not permit the shape of urban America to hinge on the chaotic use of our land, and the unforeseen movement of millions; but begin to plan coherently for the land where we will build our homes, our factories, and our parks.[40]

It is safe to conclude that the cities, which Kennedy perceived as the nexus of our major domestic problems, would have been the subject of increasing numbers of his speeches and legislative proposals in the years ahead.

[37] Remarks, New York State County Officers Association, New York, N.Y., September 20, 1965.

[38] Address, testimonial dinner for Congressman John Dow (D–N.Y.), Sterling Forest, N.Y., May 2, 1965.

[39] Press release following passage of the Appalachian Regional Development Bill, February 1, 1965.

[40] Address, Ninth Constitutional Convention of Oil, Chemical and Atomic Workers, New York, N.Y., August 23, 1967.

KEY KENNEDY VOTES ON CITIES

Rent Supplements (HR 14921). Amendment to fiscal 1967 appropriations bill to delete language providing $20 million in rent supplement contract authority and $2 million in rent supplement payments. Rejected 38-51, August 10, 1966. (D 16-43; R 22-8.) Kennedy: AGAINST.

Demonstration Cities and Metropolitan Development (S. 3708). The bill authorized grants for "demonstration cities" (later known as "model cities") and other programs for orderly metropolitan development. Passed 53-22, August 19, 1966. (D 39-9; R 14-13.) Kennedy: FOR.

Chapter 5

Poverty

. . . we have seen the savage, bloody evidence that there is today an alien land within our borders—an "other America," with its people too long denied a share in our affluence, almost without hope for improvement, no longer willing to live out a nightmare distortion of the American dream. This is the other America which subsists today in the ghettos of our crowded, modern cities, with a legacy of deprivation and indifference. And its people are without two of the root elements of our own affluent society: adequate homes and jobs. Forty-three percent of their housing—more than four million units—are substandard and dilapidated. And five million more are either deteriorated or badly overcrowded. The people of this inner-city nation live with an unemployment rate far worse than the rest of the nation knew during the depths of the Great Depression. More than three out of five cannot find work above poverty wages—and two out of five have no work at all.

And the grim fact is, as the Department of Labor has told us, that "economic and social conditions are getting worse, not better." [1]

I believe that, as long as there is plenty, poverty is evil. Government belongs wherever evil needs an adversary and there are people in distress who cannot help themselves. [2]

America has poor people—40 to 50 million of them. No one denies this. We also have a consensus in this

---

[1] Remarks, U.S. Chamber of Commerce, Washington, D.C., October 3, 1967.

[2] Robert F. Kennedy, *The Pursuit of Justice* (New York: Harper & Row, 1965), p. 11.

country that poverty ought to be eliminated and, to prove it, we have declared war against it—though it is a decidedly more dovish affair than the one in Vietnam.

The problem with the various recent efforts to help the poor is that there is still no real agreement on a conceptual definition of poverty—even within a given agency like the Office of Economic Opportunity. And whenever you have policies based on operational definitions that lack a common conceptual progenitor, the result tends to be disparate goals, the diffusion of resources, programs working at cross-purposes, and a high probability of failure. In fact, this has been the case with the federal government's war on poverty and its less publicized municipal and private counterparts. They simply have not been effective (whatever the definition of poverty employed).

What is the best conceptual definition of poverty? Perhaps by poverty we mean a certain income level per year below which minimum needs cannot be met. If so, a guaranteed annual income would be a solution. Or is poverty to be viewed as a relative term which defines the poor as those who perceive themselves to be less well off with respect to the rest of the population? In this case we are talking about the need for a more equitable redistribution of income, which the first definition implies only to a limited extent. Or, referring back to the first definition, do we mean a minimum standard of consumption, so that poverty would be defined not by how much income a family receives but by how much it spends on the necessities of life?

Maybe by poverty we mean a psychological state of hopelessness and apathy which is not strictly associated with any particular income level. Or do we mean by poverty the type of culture which some scholars suggest characterizes low-income areas (and if we do, can this culture be eliminated by merely providing residents with more money)? Or do we mean by poverty the whole cycle of problems that prey upon and reinforce each other: unemployment, substandard housing, poor or little education, discrimination, bad health, lack of motivation, lack of efficacy to cope with the problems facing one? Indeed, it has been said that what we mean by poverty is simply this last one: lack of efficacy.

However one chooses to conceptualize poverty, it is difficult to rationalize the government's dominant operational definition of poverty as the condition of a nonfarm family of four with an annual income of less than $3,130. This figure is arrived at by taking the Department of Agriculture's "economy" plan for an "adequate" diet for four people (which some experts claim is not nearly adequate over the long run) and multiplying it by three (the average American spends one-third of his income on food). I doubt that many poverty warriors seriously believe that simply putting enough money in the hands of the poor to boost their annual incomes to the OES's $3,130 level will significantly alter the recipients' way of life. Depending on the conceptual definition, it might be possible for a family to buy its way out of poverty—but not on $3,130 a year.

So here we stand, five years after the declaration of war on poverty, unable to agree even on what we mean by "human poverty," and therefore unable to isolate and attack its causes in a comprehensive and concerted fashion. About the only encouraging sign recently has been the widespread admission by federal and local bureaucrats that their efforts to eliminate poverty have flopped, and that they know less about the "other America" than they had once supposed.

Robert Kennedy was one of those in government who did not hesitate to publicize this national failure and the depth and severity of the problems facing the poor.

. . . And the Poor Get Poorer

In city after city, we have felt the pain of infections too long left festering—idleness and ignorance, rats and disease and hopelessness. Yet even as we become more aware of the injustice, indeed the danger of serious convulsion in our urban order, our efforts to right injustice, to open opportunity, to build better lives for all our people—all these efforts have faltered and slowed. . . .

We have seen families on welfare rolls, their husbands and fathers and sons idle, when we knew they should be at work —but our job-training programs too often have not resulted in jobs, and the unemployment rolls have gone up, not down, in Harlem and Watts and Southside Chicago.

We have seen housing dilapidated and deteriorating, and we knew children should not grow up in such conditions—but too often our public housing projects have turned into slums, and urban renewal relocated families into deeper misery elsewhere.

We have seen children three years behind in reading, and known that lack of education would blight the whole course of their lives—but our education bills, passed with great fanfare and hope, have not educated the children.

The Economic Opportunity Act, the War on Poverty, for all its major accomplishments, has sometimes been mired in the guerrilla skirmishes of local politics and not always relevant to the greatest needs of those it aimed to serve.[3]

For the fact is that despite all our efforts, despite the uninterrupted rise in prosperity experienced by the rest of the nation these past seven years, the 1967 manpower report states flatly that: "Economic and social conditions are getting worse, not better, in slum areas"! [4]

The dilemma of poverty faced by the society and the polity is the gap between expectations and reality. Great expectations were the creation, not of idle political promises, but of the country itself and its history. We can no more change those high expectations than we can change our history. Therefore our only recourse is to change the opportunities for realizing the expectations. In this we have no choice, although all of us at one time or another have spoken and behaved as though we did.[5]

After he entered the Senate, Kennedy frequently discussed the characteristics of poverty, its causes, and the groups of Americans which suffer most.

[3] Speech, Bedford-Stuyvesant [a large Negro ghetto], Brooklyn, N.Y., October 10, 1966.

[4] Speech, U.S. Senate, July 12, 1967.

[5] Kennedy, *op. cit.*, p. 17.

Poverty has nothing to do with race. Eighty percent of the poor families in this country are white. But like other disadvantages, poverty hits the nonwhite population hardest.[6]

But we did not hear only from experts, cool and detached. We heard from the residents of the ghetto themselves, and from others like you, who share every day the cares and burdens of those our society too often forgets. *They* spoke, not of training programs and job opportunities, not of portable swimming pools and sprinklers, nor of police review boards and reapportionment—but of the life lived by the poor in our great urban centers: a life where arrest is common, where numbers and narcotics are facts of teenage life, a world of overburdened parents and children too soon robbed of security, or innocence, or childhood itself. It is a world, above all, of alienation—of lack of communication which threatens to make permanent that sullen second society—that "other America"—of which perceptive writers have warned us this past decade.[7]

The poor, in this America, are usually poor precisely because they are without education, without knowledge, without the means to take advantage of what help we offer.

It does no good to make prenatal care available—if mothers come to doctors for the first time when they are six months pregnant. It does little good to prescribe balanced diets—when mothers do not know how to prepare food properly. And it does little good to prescribe adequate rest, and the rudiments of comfort and hygiene—when expectant mothers live in crowded, filthy rooms, without heat in the winter or adequate plumbing. Everyone here today, I think, would agree that the application of what we know now would cut mental retardation in half. But we should all recognize that that application will require the elimination of poverty from our society. And if this is true for many of those whose retardation we think of as "biological," it is even more true for those millions of children who are called mentally retarded

[6] Speech, New York State NAACP Convention, Buffalo, N.Y., October 3, 1964.

[7] Address, dedication of Mt. Providence Junior College, Baltimore, Md., September 12, 1966.

but whose retardation is but an extreme case of an affliction that affects millions more.[8]

We know our rights. We know when those rights are abridged. And we know how to redress our grievances. But the poor often do not have the tools to protect their interests in a complex world. They are short of effective spokesmen; of plans, of organization, of knowledge; of hope itself.

Better laws cannot change this impotence which is the lot of the poor. Laws confer "rights" only on those who can articulate a claim before some authority who will enforce it. But it is precisely this ability that the poor do not have. They do not know what claims to present—or to whom to present them—or how to do it. Pure food and drug laws, building codes, welfare and social security programs, schools, all are designed to create rights in all citizens—to clean food and fair measure, to dignified age and training in youth. None create rights in the poor.[9]

The problem of poverty is the problem of the youth, whether they "hang around" at the side of a muddy road in West Virginia or on a street corner in Harlem. They can be found, differing only in number, in every city and hamlet in the United States.[10]

But however great our responsibility to help with money and manpower in these locally directed efforts, we must not forget that we have the same responsibility at home. It will do no good to talk about starving people millions of miles away if we do not have the courage and the wherewithal to do what is necessary to feed every American. The problems abroad are complex and difficult and will take a long time to solve, but no one can seriously argue that it is difficult for us to feed every American. The American farmer may not be able to feed the entire world with his own produce, but he can feed our country many times over. Such has been the

[8] Address, Albert Einstein College of Medicine of Yeshiva University, New York, N.Y., March 18, 1965.

[9] Address, Lexington Democratic Club, New York, N.Y., February 4, 1965.

[10] Kennedy, *loc. cit.*

miracle of the revolution in agricultural productivity. Yet we have not made what would seem to be the most fundamental possible commitment—to say that no one is going to starve in America. In the Delta of Mississippi and Arkansas, in the hills of Appalachia, in the barrio of San Antonio, in the slum of Cleveland, on Indian reservations—all across our nation there are hungry children.[11]

For despite the growth of our social security system over the years, a fifth of those living in poverty are over sixty-five. These years should bring them a life of peaceful comfort and dignity—but instead retirement means a life beset with financial problems, burdened with dwindling savings and unpaid bills. Millions more approach sixty-five with apprehension— they know that when they stop work they begin not the golden years but years of life in poverty.[12]

Jobs, the Heart of the Matter

Time and again Kennedy returned to the conclusion that unemployment and underemployment lie at the heart of the poverty problem in this country. Introducing his proposal to create jobs in center city areas, he eloquently explained:

We earn our livings, support our families, purchase the comforts and ease of life with work. To be without it is to be less than a man—less than a citizen—hardly, in a real sense, to be a father or brother or son, to have any identity at all. To be without function, without use to our fellow citizens, is to be in truth the "invisible man" of whom Ralph Ellison wrote so eloquently—the man who John Adams said a century and a half ago suffers the greatest possible humiliation—"he is simply not seen."

The crisis in unemployment, therefore, is significant far beyond its economic effects—devastating as those are. For it is both measure and cause of the extent to which the poor man lives apart—the extent to which he is alienated from

[11] Remarks, dinner for Senator Gaylord Nelson, Milwaukee, Wis., October 28, 1967.
[12] Testimony, Senate Finance Committee, August 29, 1967.

the general community. More than segregation in housing and schools, more than differences in attitudes or life style, it is unemployment which marks the urban poor off and apart from the rest of America. Unemployment is having nothing to do—which means having nothing to do with the rest of us.

Indeed, the effects go deeper—into the very heart of life, into the structure of the family and the souls of men. As Richard Cloward has said: "Men for whom there are no jobs will nevertheless mate like other men, but they are not so likely to marry. Our society has preferred to deal with the resulting female-headed families not by putting the men to work but by placing the unwed mothers and children on public welfare—substituting check-writing machines for male wage-earners. By this means we have robbed men of manhood, women of husbands, and children of fathers. To create a stable monogamous family, we need to provide men with the opportunity to be men, and that involves enabling them to perform occupationally."

But this is what we have not done. This simple task—affording men the opportunity to contribute to themselves, to support their families, to contribute to their community—this is the task we have failed to accomplish.[13]

During his Senate campaign in the fall of 1964, he spoke often of jobs and unemployment:

One of the major problems of our time—in a sense, the cruelest problem—is unemployment. It is a problem that causes other problems—social as well as economic.

Unemployment causes delinquency, poverty, injustice . . . it damages our purchasing power and increases our relief rolls.[14]

When we talk about employment, we are talking about a right that is basic to human dignity. We have to do something more about employment.[15]

But this is no time to be complacent [RFK had just finished

[13] Speech, U.S. Senate, July 12, 1967.
[14] Speech, International Association of Machinists, New York State Council, Buffalo, N.Y., October 17, 1964.
[15] Campaign speech, Welfare Club of International Brotherhood of Electrical Workers, Local 3, New York, N.Y., October 26, 1964.

lauding improvements under the Kennedy-Johnson Administration], for the twin forces of population explosion and automation threaten to outdistance even the very substantial progress we have already made. Two million new jobs must be created in this country each year simply to offset the labor-saving effects of rising output per worker, and an additional one million new jobs are required each year to provide for new persons entering the labor market.

We should never forget that unemployment statistics represent individual cases of personal hardship and suffering. In traveling through this state I find strong and able men idle by necessity, not by choice. Skilled and energetic workers are replaced by machines and so lose their self-respect and the respect of others. Decent, honorable men are ashamed because they are helpless while their families live in tarpaper shacks or broken-down tenements. And perhaps most tragic of all are the young people deprived of any meaningful chance for education or training because their parents are unemployed, unable to find respectable jobs themselves, drifting inexorably toward juvenile delinquency and crime.[16]

Each year, two million jobs are wiped away by automation and technology. We should view this with alertness, not alarm. There is nothing wrong with America's machinists turning out better machines. But better machines should enrich our lives, not lengthen our relief rolls.

We have a responsibility to see that every displaced worker gets a new job, and an equally good job. This is a challenging assignment. In 1975, we will have to have 88,000,000 jobs for full employment.[17]

The War on Poverty: A Losing Battle

Just as Kennedy gradually lost confidence in the ability and willingness of the federal government to guarantee Negro equality and lead the campaign to revitalize our decaying cities, he grew increasingly skeptical of Wash-

[16] Campaign statement, October 19, 1964.
[17] Speech, International Association of Machinists, New York State Council, Buffalo, N.Y., October 17, 1964.

ington's oft-repeated commitment to eliminate poverty as his Senate term progressed. The chronological series of statements that follows documents the souring of what began as a cautious optimism about the War on Poverty and related programs and Congress' desire to fund them.

We have shown that IQs in the slums can rise rather than fall, that training programs provide jobs for the idle, and that new educational approaches provide hope for the previously hopeless.

The hardest task is to appoint and incorporate in our work groups of men and women with the power and willingness to look at our community difficulties, dissect them, criticize areas of shortcoming and make meaningful suggestions.

Sometimes, too, it is hard to accept that sort of recommendation. For sometimes it carries with it announced or implied criticism of programs that have failed us in the past. Change means that someone's professional feathers will be ruffled, that a glass-topped desk might be moved to another office or abandoned, that pet programs might die.

Progress is a nice word. But change is its motivater. And change has its enemies.

The willingness to confront that change will determine how much we shall really do for our youth and how truly meaningful our effort will be. . . .

I firmly believe that the "domestic peace corps" is a significant new means of attacking these problems. In the same way that thousands of our people have volunteered to serve in remote, dangerous and almost unknown corners of the world, we are convinced that Americans are equally willing to take on the toughest jobs in this country, whether in a city slum, an Indian reservation or a mining town.

Corpsmen would not be technical assistance experts. The program would not be service *to* people, but working with people.[18]

We should not be disappointed that Community Action has not been an instant success. It has been a long time since most leadership in this country has spoken to the poor and tried to understand the problems of their existence. We should

[18] Kennedy, *op cit.*, pp. 19, 20.

not be disillusioned because spokesmen for the poor have not appeared overnight. It takes time for genuine leadership capable of action and results to develop. Nor should we fear the conflicts that have arisen as new power groups contend with old, as political leaders are forced to meet the slum dwellers instead of the ward leaders. Every department of city government dealing with social welfare problems should feel challenged to justify their traditional response to the problems of the poor. They may not like it but the price of their discontent may be progress—and stronger and safer communities for our children and ourselves.[19]

We will make clear, if we are to fulfill our role as leaders, that sacrifices must be made. The War on Poverty authorization just passed by the Congress, as a beginning, is totally inadequate—nowhere close to meeting the needs of all our people for jobs, and training, and health, and self-sufficiency and respect. It is all very well to support civil rights bills, and open-housing bills; but it is far more right and relevant to assure all our people decent and dignified conditions where they live now. But this cannot be done if we are unwilling to make the effort, to spend the money, to help people help themselves, to once and for all end debilitating and demeaning welfare programs and instead insure that every family has the means to support itself.[20]

Can we then spend more? The evidence is clear that we can—as it is clear that we must. Our gross national product, in the last year, increased by $40 billion, soaring over $270 billion. The demands of Vietnam purportedly responsible for the cutbacks in vital education, housing, and poverty programs, in fact still represent less than 3 percent of our national product; all military expenditures, even with the expected supplemental after the elections, still take less than 10 percent of the gross national product.

Our growth is so great that in two years, at present levels of taxation federal tax revenues will be $10 to $14 billion

[19] Address, Third Annual WGHO Human Relations Award Dinner, Ellenville, N.Y., April 19, 1966.

[20] Speech, Democratic State Committee Dinner, Columbus, Ohio, October 8, 1966.

greater than in 1966. By 1970, another $11 to $15 billion will be added, by 1975, a total of $50 to $75 billion over this year.

But with the growth in revenue, and even with the expenditures in Vietnam, the federal government today is spending a smaller proportion of our gross national product than it did three years ago. If we did no more, made no greater proportional effort than we did in the early 1960s, we would add $6 billion to our annual spending immediately.[21]

There are those—and I am one of them—who say that we will only begin to deal with these problems when we decide to commit vastly greater resources to the task. We have not shown that commitment up to now, although I believe we can despite the war in Vietnam. Only last year, for example, the Senate Committee on Labor and Public Welfare sought to add $750 million to the poverty program.

Congress and the Administration rejected this proposal. The additional $200 million proposed for Head Start would have nearly doubled the number of children in full-year Head Start programs. The added $195 million proposed for the Neighborhood Youth Corps would have provided 65,000 more part-time jobs to keep young people in school, and 25,000 more jobs for those who had already left school.

But the fact is that far more than money is involved.

We who are the fortunate ones, we who are the "establishment," we who control the institutions of government as they are now constituted, must begin to recognize that the answers we have provided up to now have not been completely successful.

We have created a welfare system which aids only a fourth of those who are poor, which forces men to leave their families so that public assistance can be obtained, which has created a dependence on their fellow citizens that is degrading and distasteful to giver and receiver alike.

We have built vast, impersonal high-rise public housing projects—ghettos within ghettos—isolated from the outside world and devoid of any sense of humanity.

We have cleared areas of slums in the name of urban re-

[21] Statement, Subcommittee on Executive Reorganization of the Senate Committee on Goverment Operations, December 10, 1966.

newal, with little sense of what would become of those whose homes we leveled.

We have provided health services in huge, unpleasant municipal hospitals—through emergency rooms and outpatient clinics where people wait for hours to see a doctor they have never seen before and are likely never to see again.[22]

Our answers to this crisis in housing, in employment, in education—have been inadequate. We simply have not done enough. In part, this is a failure of will, a sheer short-sightedness which has deprived the cities of badly needed resources. The House of Representatives, for example, has cut the Model Cities program by two-thirds—and it has tried to kill the rent supplement program so desperately needed in our cities. The House rejected—with jokes and scorn—a rat-control program which would have cost $20 million a year —a sum we spend every six hours in Vietnam.[23]

Toward Local Solutions

However, the Senator had gone on record as early as 1965 as personally committed to finding a solution to the problems of the poor.

Poor people cannot apply for assistance themselves, because they do not govern our cities and counties. If they had the education and the knowledge and the skills to govern, they would not be poor in the first place.

So those who govern—no matter how comfortable—must apply for aid for the poor.

We are our brothers' keepers. As long as the benefits of prosperity are denied to one-fifth of our number, there can be no complacency—there can be no stopping—there can be no pride of place nor quarreling over labels. Until poverty is eliminated; until education is truly universal; until the least among us is secure in freedom and opportunity, in the

[22] Address, Day Care Council of New York, New York, N.Y., May 8, 1967.

[23] Testimony, National Commission on Urban Problems, New York, N.Y., September 6, 1967.

inalienable rights for which this country was established, none of us can rest content.[24]

There must be solutions to the dilemma of expectations rising against a static reality. To believe otherwise is to toss in the towel of social responsibility. I believe not only that there are appropriate remedies, but that they are ultimately to be found locally rather than nationally. The national government has ample constitutional power to enter into its war on poverty. This cannot be too strongly emphasized; and those who claim that the situation is or should be otherwise are usually found to be merely against a given program but lacking in the courage to say so. I say the solution will be local because national power, however broad in reach and however responsible in use, is severely limited in grasp. In the fight for social justice national power can create and encourage but local power is determinative.[25]

At first he expressed the view that nothing radical was required.

In America we already have conquered the problem of scarcity. Once that is accomplished, poverty is a problem not of production but of distribution. The poverty of goods is a matter of a more rational distribution at the forgotten margins of society; no massive redistribution is necessary. The poverty of understanding and respect is a problem of university education and guidance in the rights and duties of man.[26]

Most of his suggestions in 1964 and 1965 centered on expanding federal public works programs to create more jobs, more effective job-placement services in the slums, and increases in the minimum wage to improve the lot of the employed poor (one of three families living in poverty is headed by someone with a job).

I advocate a standby Public Works Bill authorizing the President to provide additional funds, up to one billion dol-

[24] Address, Binghamton, N.Y., March 29, 1965.
[25] Kennedy, *op. cit.*, pp. 17, 18.
[26] *Ibid.*, p. 10.

lars, to bolster the economy and increase jobs. This bill would provide for public works such as federal buildings, water and sewage systems, and port facilities which are needed and which the federal government would help construct in any event. It would give the President the discretion to accelerate expenditures for these public works in depressed areas where they would be a significant help in creating needed jobs. . . .

I would introduce legislation providing for a comprehensive federal study to determine exactly what kinds of jobs are presently available and unfilled; where they are located; what education and training is necessary to fill them; and to predict what jobs will become available over the next ten years and what skills and education will be needed for them. Such a study would very significantly improve the effectiveness of existing programs.[27]

I think it's time different parts of this country stopped competing for business by depressing the standards of their workers. I think it's time industry stopped fleeing this state to go to states where the *daily* wage is $1.50. And to stop this flight, I believe we need a minimum [hourly] wage of $1.50 for New York and for the entire nation.[28]

The present minimum wage of $1.25 an hour amounts to 2,600 dollars a year—400 dollars less than the Congress has declared to be the poverty line, the absolute minimum income for health and safety. You know how little can be bought for 3,000 dollars a year; yet millions of American workers do not even earn that much.

This country can afford better wages than that—and we cannot afford not to pay better wages.

I support an immediate rise in the minimum wage to $1.50 an hour—and further increases compatible with our competitive position and our advancing standards of decent living.

This nation has declared a war on poverty.

This means job training and education and creation of new jobs.

[27] Campaign statement, October 19, 1964.
[28] Speech, International Association of Machinists, New York State Council, Buffalo, N.Y., October 17, 1964.

But the biggest immediate job in the war on poverty is to raise the wages of millions who have jobs now.[29]

The Bedford-Stuyvesant Plan: Pattern for the Nation?

Then, on December 9, 1966, Kennedy announced the formation of two public corporations to try to revitalize Bedford-Stuyvesant, an area of chronic Negro poverty in Brooklyn. Designed to operate independently from all government agencies, with Kennedy informally supplying the needed contacts and leaderships, the program was conceived as follows: One corporation is made up of people from the local community, and it is to act as sponsor of programs for housing and rehabilitation and renewal, for job training, and for the creation of cultural and recreational facilities. The other corporation is made up of big names from the business world, such as former Secretary of the Treasury Douglas Dillon, former TVA chairman David Lilienthal, William Paley of the Columbia Broadcasting System, and Thomas J. Watson, Jr., of IBM. This corporation is supposed to work on the economic planning and redevelopment of Bedford-Stuyvesant with the purpose of attracting industry and helping to arrange for the financing of companies that want to locate in the neighborhood.

This "Bedford-Stuyvesant Program" amounted to a private Kennedy war on poverty. Bold and imaginative in many of its approaches—particularly its pointed reluctance to depend on the federal government—it promised an opportunity to test many of the assumptions and ideas frequently mentioned in connection with the combatting of poverty. How sound the program's conception is and how consistent Kennedy would have been in investing the time and leadership to make it a success are matters that could only have been known with time. However, at present, the program appears to be moving quite slowly and many residents have begun expressing disillusionment.

The day after his Bedford-Stuyvesant announcement,

[29] Address, International Ladies' Garment Workers Union Convention, Miami, Fla., May 18, 1965.

the Senator presented a broader version of the program designed to combat poverty in center-city areas throughout the country. Of interest was the fact that he had finally arrived at a specific conceptual definition of poverty that helped give shape and consistency to his program. Implicit in the provisions of his program is the view that poverty is a vicious cycle of reinforcing disabilities—unemployment, inferior education, discrimination, poor health, lack of motivation, unstable family life, and so on—that renders its victims incapable of competing successfully in our society:

The plan begins with a perspective: that questions of technical or surface integration are far less important now than is the building of self-sufficiency and self-determination within the Negro community; in fact, that what is too often an undifferentiated mass must be helped to form a coherent and cohesive community. Thus it is important that Negroes who have achieved financial and social security should have complete freedom to choose where to live. But it is far more important that the vast majority of Negroes be enabled to achieve basic financial and social security where they live now. It will be the work of years, and of all Americans, white and black, to decide whether most people will live in substantially homogeneous neighborhoods. But there should be no question that black neighborhoods, as well as white, should be places of security and dignity and achievement and comfort. . . .

But I would concentrate now on my proposal for the ghetto. It begins with a base of employment, in a vastly expanded and accelerated program of urban reconstruction. Our cities are in dire need of rebuilding, especially at the core: in spite of the largest slum clearance and rebuilding program in the United States, the number of unsound housing units in New York, for example, increased from 420,000 in 1960 to 520,000 in 1965. In most major cities, great stocks of housing built to accommodate the influx of migrants, from rural areas and abroad, in the early part of this century are long overdue for rehabilitation or replacement. Our public facilities are in similar need of repair. . . .

And in the coming years, these needs will multiply almost beyond measure. Just in the next forty years, the urban population of the United States will double—which means we must build homes and hospitals, schools and shops and factories, roads and railways and airports, equal to everything we have managed to build in the two hundred years of this republic. . . . Given, then, the known needs of the next four decades, it is clear that if we begin now, with proper initiative and stimulation, to repair the decay of the past and meet the needs of the future, we can create hundreds of thousands of new jobs directly, and through the new demands stimulated by this addition, millions more indirectly.

But let us not make the mistake of regarding these just as jobs; and let us not erect buildings for their own sakes. Our needs, and the programs we will now undertake to meet them, are in fact an opportunity to make every government program, and many private efforts, more effective than ever before.[30]

Kennedy then explained the program he had outlined nearly a year earlier in a speech before the Second Borough President's Conference of Community Leaders in Harlem.

He went on to propose the creation of Community Development Corporations to insure the active participation of center-city residents in the program and to foster a greater sense of community among the poor.

The measure of the success of this or any other program will be the extent to which it helps the ghetto to become a community—a functioning unit. its people acting together on matters of mutual concern, with the power and resources to affect the conditions of their own lives. Therefore the heart of the program, I believe, should be the creation of Community Development Corporations, which would carry out the work of construction, the hiring and training of workers, the provision of services, the encouragement of associated enterprises.

Such corporations might be financed along these lines: they would receive an initial contribution of capital from the federal government; but for their ongoing activities, they should need and receive no significantly greater subsidy than is ordinarily available to nonprofit housing corporations under present law.

[30] Statement, Subcommittee on Executive Reorganization of the Senate Committee on Government Operations, December 10, 1966.

As with all other housing and commercial construction, the bulk of the funds would come as loans from the great financial institutions—banks, insurance companies, corporations. Government would enter by way of the common devices of loan repayment insurance, some subsidization of the interest rate, and in some cases, assistance in the acquisition of land.

These Community Development Corporations, I believe, would find a fruitful partnership with American industry; many firms, of which U.S. Gypsum is perhaps the farthest along, have actively undertaken the search for ways to bring the ghetto into the national economic market. Loans and technical cooperation from industry and commerce; trained manpower and organization from labor unions; academic and educational partnership with the universities; funds for education and training such as those provided under many present federal programs; these would be resources sufficient to mount a real attack on the intertwined problems of housing and jobs, education and income.

But a further and critical element in the structure, financial and otherwise, of these corporations should be the full and dominant participation by the residents of the community concerned. Through purchase of cooperative and condominium apartments; through subscription to equity shares; through receiving part of their pay on these projects in equity shares, such as has been done in farsighted private enterprises such as Sears, Roebuck—in these ways, residents of the ghettos could at once contribute to the betterment of their immediate conditions, and build a base for full participation in the economy—in the ownership and the savings and the self-sufficiency which the more fortunate in our nation already take for granted.[31]

Participation of the Poor

On several other occasions, both before and after this presentation, Kennedy approached the controversial issue of the participation of the poor in antipoverty efforts. Although he failed to discuss the relative pros and cons of such participation, he made it perfectly clear where he stood on the matter.

[31] *Ibid.*

We might do better than turning our backs in embarrassed anger when spokesmen for the poor blast the social structure that has left them out. We might listen to them. In the process, we will learn, and they will learn—and out of that simple courtesy, plans and dreams for better communities for everyone may well come to pass.[32]

Government is an institution too often set in ways accepted in the past—but the old answers have failed, and we need new institutions to shape new solutions. Most importantly, reliance on government is dependence—and what the people of our ghettos need is not greater dependence, but full independence; not the charity and favor of their fellow citizens, but equal claims of right and equal power to enforce those claims.[33]

But if you are to succeed, we must begin, here today, to chart the steps ahead, to turn promise into performance, plan to reality.

To do this we must combine the best of community action with the best of the private enterprise system. Neither by itself is enough; but in their combination lies our hope for the future.

Community action has been much maligned in recent months. Yet these last two years have demonstrated its essential rightness. For if there is to be any action, any true progress in a community, that community itself—men and women like you who are here today—must be prepared to take full and final responsibility for what happens—for the success or failure of any program.[34]

This cannot continue. It must not continue. For all around our nation, Negroes and Puerto Ricans, Mexican-Americans and Indians, poor whites in Appalachia and in blighted inner-city areas, are waking up to what we have. They are demanding their rights as human beings. They are demanding what

[32] Address, Third Annual WGHO Human Relations Award Dinner, Ellenville, N.Y., April 19, 1966.

[33] Address, NAACP Legal Defense Fund Banquet, New York, N.Y., May 18, 1966.

[34] Speech, Bedford-Stuyvesant, Brooklyn, N.Y., October 10, 1966.

the rest of us take for granted—a measure of control over their lives, over their own destinies, a sense of communication with those whom they have elected to govern them. If we do not yield, if we do not work a virtual revolution in the organization of our social services, the result could be the ripping asunder of the already thin fabric of American life. The stakes are indeed high.

Can we not respond to the aspirations of our fellow citizens? . . .

Do we not have the ingenuity to involve private enterprise in the process of providing adequate housing for the 43 percent of Negroes who now live in substandard dwellings?

Do we not have the wherewithal to bring health services to the poor on a neighborhood scale, with family physicians, and aides who bring preventive care to the ghetto for the first time?

Do we not have the ability to devise manpower programs which create not just jobs, but jobs with possibilities for further education and advancement over time?

Do we not have the capacity to reorganize our welfare system so the ghetto resident is not confronted with a bewilderingly fragmented array of agencies, but rather is served by a rational system he can understand, with expediters or workers from his own community to help him obtain aid?

Do we not have the skill to bring government back to the community, back to Lewis Mumford's "face-to-face" scale, before it is too late?

We have begun to do some of these things, here in New York and across the country. But having begun, we must do more. And in all of this there must be an overriding theme and goal—the involvement of the community, of those who have the greatest stake in the quality of the services they receive.[35]

Enlisting Private Enterprise

On July 12, 1967, Kennedy introduced a bill (S. 2088) to provide federal tax credits, accelerated depreciation schedules, and job-training programs as incentives for

[35] Address, Day Care Council of New York, New York, N.Y., May 8, 1967.

businessmen to locate industry in poverty centers, thus creating jobs for the unemployed. Like its companion measure S. 2100, which proposed similar devices to stimulate the building of low-cost housing in poverty areas, S. 2088 was notable for its replacement of the federal government with private enterprise as the principal institution in the fight against slums and poverty. RFK explained the purpose and operation of his plan:

The specific purpose of the bill is to stimulate investment— the creation of new jobs and income—in poverty areas. The entire program is to be carried out, not by government agencies, but by private enterprise. The federal government provides only a system of tax incentives, carefully designed to enable private enterprise to make its investments and carry out its operations in the urban poverty areas.

Thus the bill seeks to remedy the greatest failure in our existing poverty efforts: the failure to involve and rely on the private enterprise system which is the basic strength of the nation. By failing to involve the private sector, we have not only ignored the potential contribution of millions of talented and energetic Americans in tens of thousands of productive enterprises. More dangerously, we have created for the poor a separate nation: a second-rate system of welfare handouts, a screen of government agencies keeping the poor apart from the rest of us. That system—ineffective, inefficient, and degrading—must be changed. This bill would work toward the needed change. . . .

Because it operates through the existing private enterprise system, the bill does not require the creation of new government departments or agencies. It creates no new systems of welfare handouts. It requires no great new outflows of government spending. Rather, by generating new investment and creating new jobs, it will increase productivity in the nation as a whole—putting idle hands to work, turning welfare recipients into taxpayers, and decreasing present financial burdens on state and local governments. And greater productivity will result, in our judgment, in increased over-all federal revenues, even after allowing for the tax relief afforded to businesses which make the desired investment.[36]

[36] Speech, U.S. Senate, July 12, 1967.

This measure too lacked Administration support. Washington rumor says that Bureau of the Budget estimates indicate, despite Bobby's claims to the contrary, that the program would be prohibitively expensive for the government in terms of lost revenue. Nonetheless, it was an imaginative new attempt to rectify an old problem, and in the years to come it would doubtless have been followed by more Kennedy suggestions for eliminating poverty.

KEY KENNEDY VOTES ON POVERTY

Economic Opportunity Amendments of 1966 (S. 3164). Amendment to reduce the total authorization for the poverty program in fiscal 1967 from $2.5 billion to $1.7 billion, the sum proposed by the President. Accepted 45-27, October 4, 1966. (D 23-25; R 22-2.) Kennedy: AGAINST.

Appalachia Regional Development Act of 1965 (S. 3). Authorize $1.1 billion in federal aid for development of the economically depressed 11-state Appalachia region. Passed 62-22, February 1, 1965. (D 51-71; R 11-15.) Kennedy: FOR.

Chapter 6

Welfare and the Welfare State

> We have spent more and more on money on welfare;
> but will we be ready to admit that welfare has also de-
> stroyed self-respect and encouraged family disintegra-
> tion—will we be ready instead to do what we must to
> bring its recipients into full participation in our so-
> ciety? [1]

The American welfare state was constructed over the
past third of a century by liberals in the Democratic
party. Thus it is with some irony that the most fundamental criticisms leveled at our welfare programs during
the past few years have come predominantly from liberals
in the Democratic party. (Most conservative and moderate politicians in both parties finally appear to have accepted the limited welfare state in its present form.) Of
the present-day Democrats who are dissatisfied with this
New Deal creation, Robert Kennedy was among the most
outspoken.

While serving in his brother's administration, Kennedy
seemed quite willing to accept social security, aid to dependent children, and public housing policies in their
existing form as effective ways of sustaining the less fortunate. However, beginning with his campaign for the
Senate in 1964, his public disillusionment with these welfare programs grew steadily. Whether this rather sudden
transformation from advocate to foe was the result of
honest re-evaluation or alert political opportunism is
difficult to determine. Perhaps, no longer tied to his

[1] Address, Retail, Wholesale and Department Store Union Convention, Miami Beach, Fla., May 27, 1966.

brother's policies and searching for issues with which to dissociate himself from LBJ in the hope of winning the support of anti-Johnson Democrats, he simply uncovered programs—like our welfare programs—with which, after re-examination, he could take honest difference.

A Second-rate Program to Create Second-rate Citizens

In the quotations that follow, Kennedy explained his dissatisfaction with our present welfare system.

We are learning that the welfare answers we have provided in the past have not been completely successful. We have lived with a welfare system which aids only a fourth of those who are poor, which forces men to leave their families so that public assistance can be obtained, which has created a dependence on their fellow citizens that is degrading and distasteful to giver and receiver alike.

We must understand what we have done. We have said, "Here is what we are going to do for you." And in our generosity, we have created a system of handouts, a second-rate set of social services which damages and demeans its recipients, and destroys any semblance of human dignity that they have managed to retain through their adversity.[2]

In the long run, welfare payments solve nothing, for the givers or the recipients; free Americans deserve the chance to be fully self-supporting—and this requires education.[3]

I believe our welfare system is unsatisfactory, because, in general, it provides aid for broken families and not for whole ones.

I believe our welfare system is unsatisfactory, because it imposes degrading conditions on eligibility, and encourages the enforcement of those conditions by demeaning investigation.

I believe our welfare system is unsatisfactory because, once

[2] Report to his New York constituents, Washington, D.C., May 1967.

[3] Speech on behalf of Democratic candidates for state office, Detroit, Mich., October 29, 1966.

a family does penetrate the bureaucratic maze and qualify for aid, the benefits it receives are in many states not even enough to live on.[4]

. . . the effects of the shortage of meaningful employment are reinforced by a welfare structure which is frequently destructive both of individuals and of the community in which they live. "Thus," as one economist says, "we penalize old-age pensioners who get jobs, by cutting their social security benefits in correspondence with their pay; we terminate welfare payments when the wage-earner head of a large family gets even a poor-paying job, sometimes at a lower level of income than that provided by his welfare payments; we evict the dweller in a low-rent public-housing project who succeeds in raising his income above the level permitted for that housing, even if the increases in his rent costs will exceed his income increase. Instead of providing real incentives to self-help efforts, we in effect deter them by the equivalent of 100 percent taxation on the additional income the poor may earn."

And, in the midst of much hand-wringing about the disintegration of Negro families, we compel fathers to leave home so that their families may receive a federal assistance; this teaches their sons the lesson that the best way to provide for a family is to abandon it. Neither is the Aid to Dependent Children of Unemployed Parents program an answer; for where jobs are menial and pay too low, a father may still be forced to leave home to bring his family a living income.[5]

For too many on welfare and for the rest of the poor, there are only days of misery without enough food for their children, and nights of fear in substandard housing, warding off marauding rats. And for those receiving assistance, there are also complex and degrading procedures; there are rules designed to qualify eligible applicants which often serve to disqualify or discourage people in need; there are rules which force families to stay apart in order to receive aid. For too many, then, welfare is not only inadequate, but appears as a

[4] Testimony, Senate Finance Committee, August 29, 1967.

[5] Speech, Second Borough President's Conference of Community Leaders on the Revitalization of Harlem-East Harlem Community, New York, N.Y., January 21, 1966.

reluctant handout designed to screen the poor away from the rest of society.[6]

Social Security and Insecurity

The Senator expressed concern about the involuntary idleness and poverty that are the tragic lot of so many elderly persons in this country.

Advancing technology has forced earlier retirement, while advancing medical science has increased the life span. From retirement on, therefore, the elderly person now faces a substantial period during which he can still contribute significantly to his society but cannot find a way to do so through gainful employment. Unable to generate new income, the older person is forced to rely on his savings and social security for support. If these sources are inadequate—and I will point out just how inadequate they are in a few moments—he will be unable to afford adequate housing, adequate medical care, and an adequate standard of living in general. The challenge which faces us, then, is clear. Will we sit by and let the situation deteriorate further, accelerating the tragedies of enforced idleness and poverty, of inadequate housing and misery, or will we take steps to help our elderly live out their years in dignity and comfort and usefulness to their society?[7]

Happiness, according to an old Greek definition, is "the exercise of vital powers along lines of excellence in a life affording them scope." For too many, this exercise is denied abruptly and arbitrarily, at the age of sixty-five. The man who was perfectly qualified to run a drill press or fly a plane, to manage a sales force or drive a truck, is the next day placed on the other side of a barrier. He is marked as useless until death.

Nothing in our policy toward the aged is more cruel. Nothing makes less sense. Nothing am I more determined to change.

Compulsory work is prohibited by the Thirteenth Amendment to the Constitution. Compulsory idleness is as much a

[6] Testimony, Senate Finance Committee, August 29, 1967.
[7] Speech, Hebrew Home for the Aged, Washington, D.C., April 21, 1965.

diminution of freedom, and is as much to be avoided. Yet it prevails throughout American industry and business—to the point where only 13 percent of persons over sixty-five are now in the labor force. Older people are idle, in many cases, not because they want to be, but because no work is available. Sometimes, work is available but useless—as when modest earnings terminate Social Security benefits. . . .

People over sixty-five should be able to choose between a wide variety of work and leisure, full-time and part-time, rewarding in money and rewarding to the spirit. For this purpose, I propose the following:

First, that work be less severely punished by the social security system. At present, benefits are terminated if annual earnings exceed $1,200. I would advocate that the limit be raised to $3,000. This figure is chosen for two reasons. It is enough below the prevailing industrial and commercial wage rate to discourage excessive competition for jobs with younger workers raising families. And combined with social security payments, it would provide an annual income roughly equivalent to median family income in the United States. Those without retirement income other than Social Security would thus be enabled to live as well as most of their younger fellow citizens.

Second, that counseling and training services be improved so that older people can find work. A small appropriation would provide old-age counselors for each of the major offices of the federally supported state employment services.

Third, that a special revolving credit fund be established to make loans to older people. Many of the elderly, eminently qualified to own and operate small businesses, cannot get normal commercial loans solely because of their age.

Fourth, that intensive effort be devoted to the development of ways in which older persons can contribute their skills and experience to the pressing social needs of the nation. One direction is indicated by the present participation of retired persons in the Peace Corps.[8]

He favored the enactment of the Medicare plan.

[8] Speech, Senior Citizens Golden Ring Council for Medicare, New York, N.Y., October 1, 1964.

New Yorkers are concerned about their elderly citizens. Over one million of them live in poverty. Others have trouble meeting medical bills. The widowers in the state of New York over sixty-five live on an income of $880 a year. Congress is today considering, in Conference Committee [a committee to work out differences between the Senate and House versions of the bill] a plan to provide medical care to elderly persons through social security. I hope it is approved. [It was not.] If it is not, I will sponsor the full King-Anderson medicare program next year.[9] [Bobby did lend his name to this bill upon entering the Senate.]

He attacked social security benefits as inadequate and supported several Senate measures to raise them.

Social Security is not charity. It is a program of earned insurance. In it we recognize that those who contribute to our society in their early years have a claim of right to retirement income in their later years. Because he has earned it, no man need feel mean or degraded by accepting this benefit. Because he has earned it, he need seek no man's favor to receive it.[10]

But it is no longer adequate. Social Security benefits have not kept pace with the times, and the result is that more and more of our elderly simply cannot make ends meet on their pension checks. We have amended the original 1935 Act to broaden coverage and to create new kinds of benefits. But we have failed up to now to undertake the basic overhaul of our benefit structure that is needed to lift millions of older Americans out of poverty and into a retirement of dignity and self-respect.[11]

For these elderly people, social security has not lived up to its original promise to avert economic insecurity in retirement. We must now keep that promise. We must now provide adequate benefits, and we can do so with fiscal soundness, to all who are insured. We must explore the full potential of the so-

[9] Speech, New York State Publishers Association meeting, Queens, N.Y., September 15, 1964.
[10] Speech, Senior Citizens Golden Ring Council for Medicare, New York, N.Y., October 1, 1964.
[11] Statement, U.S. Senate, July 28, 1966.

cial security system to serve as a guarantor of the retired years of our people.[12]

Recognizing resistance to further increases in payroll taxes to finance benefit boosts, Kennedy recommended partial financing from general federal revenues.

It is plain, as I pointed out in my remarks accompanying the introduction of S. 3661 on July 28 of this year, that social security benefits have not kept pace with the times. We must undertake a basic overhaul of the benefit structure if we are to lift millions of our older citizens out of poverty and into a retirement of dignity and self-respect. . . .

Furthermore, I would hope that if any amendments to the social security system are considered, the Senate would include the section of S. 3661, which I introduced on July 28, providing for automatic adjustment of benefits geared to the cost of living. The opportunity to make social security inflation-proof should not be passed by if amendments are to be considered.[13]

Social Security was intended as a floor of protection for the elderly. It has become a floor which is sagging and badly in need of repair. Our present struggle against poverty must be broadened to include a full-scale effort to raise the incomes of our senior citizens. In order to do this, I think we are going to have to start financing social security partly from the proceeds of the income tax. The figures show that benefits paid to the lowest-income groups must be more than doubled to be adequate. An increase of that magnitude probably cannot be financed by the payroll tax. Using the progressive income tax instead is economically sensible when the social security system responds to genuine social needs by providing benefits to those lowest-income people who are not able to pay for them. Paying for these benefits out of the proceeds of the payroll tax creates a great burden on middle- and lower-income wage-earners who end up paying for the new benefits. Using the income tax to finance the guarantee of an adequate income for our senior citizens will ease this burden and allow the payroll

[12] Statement, U.S. Senate, February 16, 1967.
[13] Speech, U.S. Senate, October 14, 1966.

tax to be used as it was originally intended—as a basically contributory device under which the worker gets back during retirement what he put in during his working years. This is the essential choice which we must make about social security: Will we allow it to continue as merely a way of keeping many of our senior citizens from having to rely totally on public assistance, or will we do what we must to insure an adequate income for all retired Americans? [14]

In February of 1967, Kennedy and ten other senators introduced a bill to raise benefits substantially and to restructure social security financing. He explained the bill's provisions:

First, the bill is premised on the belief that it is essential now to plan for the introduction of general-revenue financing into the social security system if we are to provide benefits of meaningful scope.

Second, it stands for the proposition that the present levels of benefits, which average $84 a month for individuals and $142 for couples, are wholly inadequate. A minimum benefit of $100 a month is a realistic floor of protection in retirement. In addition, significant benefit increases are in order for all beneficiaries, including increases of the magnitude of 50 percent for lower-income beneficiaries.

Third, the bill provides for automatic adjustment of benefits geared to the cost of living. Social security should be inflation-proof, and congressional energy should not be expended on enacting benefit increases which do no more than make up for ground lost to rises in the cost of living.[15]

With ten Senators of both parties, I introduced legislation earlier this year to make up the ground we have lost. That bill, S. 1009, would provide benefit increases averaging over 50 percent, and, crucially, would finance these increases by a gradual infusion of general revenues. It envisioned a leveling off of general revenue contribution at 35 percent of the cost of social security by the late 1970s. . . .

[14] Speech, Hebrew Home for the Aged, Washington, D.C., April 21, 1965.
[15] Speech, U.S. Senate, February 16, 1967.

General revenue financing would be a far more equitable way to raise revenues for the social security system, particularly revenues which would be used to provide additional benefits for low-income people—for those who worked either so irregularly or at such low wages that their contributions do not really finance the benefits they receive. . . .

I emphasize this because the proposal I shall make this morning to broaden the scope of HR. 12080 would give relatively more help to the poorest of our elderly, to those who have the most difficulty in finding dignity and comfort in their retirement. If we are to provide a meaningful floor of protection for older people as a matter of social insurance, I believe it is only fair to other workers that we finance it through general revenues.

I propose that the committee raise the across-the-board increase in benefits to 25 percent, weighting it, if possible, toward those beneficiaries at the lower end of the spectrum. I propose, in addition, that the minimum benefit be raised to $100 a month, $150 for couples. These proposals combined would produce an average benefit increase of 25 percent. . . .

First I would urge that the committee consider a cost-of-living provision to make social security inflation-proof, and to insure that future benefit increases granted by Congress do more than just make up for lost ground.[16]

When the House omnibus social security and welfare bill failed to incorporate the increases and financial restructuring proposed by his Senate version, Kennedy offered two amendments to the House measure, explaining:

The 12½ percent increase in retirement benefits enacted by the House would barely get beneficiaries back to the level of real income they had in 1954. The two increases of 7 percent each which we enacted in 1958 and 1965 actually fell short of restoring the 1954 purchasing power of benefits—for the cost of living has risen about 25 percent since that time. Thus four-fifths of the increase which the House provided would be used up just to get back to 1954 levels. Meanwhile, wages in our nation have steadily increased, but our older citizens have not

[16] Testimony, Senate Finance Committee, August 29, 1967.

shared in that affluence. Instead, many elderly couples retire each year—into a life of poverty.[17]

The Family Allotment That Breaks Up Families

Apparently accepting the much-debated thesis of Daniel Moynihan that an unstable family is a major determinant of poverty, particularly Negro poverty, Kennedy attacked the aspects of our welfare system that tend to weaken family bonds and drive the husband out of the home. Much of his criticism was leveled at the Aid to Dependent Children Program.

Mr. President: I want to commend the Senator from Connecticut [Mr. Ribicoff] for his stand on this matter. There really is very little to be said on the merits of the question, since our failure thus far to make the program of Aid to Dependent Children of Unemployed Parents applicable to the District is so lacking in any reasonable basis.

The so-called "man in the house" rule has not only prevented needy children from receiving assistance which they deserve to have, but has also had heartbreaking effects in causing the splitting up of families and the most degrading kinds of deception and subterfuge. By making Aid to Dependent Children of Unemployed Parents applicable in the District, we shall be allowing the father who cannot obtain employment to keep on living at home without depriving his children of welfare support. That seems like the most elementary of principles, and yet here we are on the floor of the United States Senate talking about it as though there were really some question. I hope we resolve this matter once and for all today. The continuance of the present situation is simply intolerable.[18]

Of the 7.3 million welfare recipients, 850,000 were female heads of families, and 2.6 million were minor children from these same female-headed families. Thus over 50 percent of the federal welfare rolls are made up of families whose

[17] Press release, October 25, 1967.
[18] Remarks, U.S. Senate, June 22, 1965.

husbands and fathers are absent precisely because they are unemployed, and unable to support their families. Leaving the house—to allow their families to qualify for welfare—is the only way these men can insure that their families will have food to eat and a roof over their heads. Thus it is the welfare system itself, in combination with the lack of decent job opportunities, which produces the welfare families who are asserted to be permanent dependents of the government. But providing real job opportunities—for the absent fathers and husbands of the future—will enable many of these families to reunite, and others to remain together. It is my firm conviction, therefore, that this bill will help to reduce welfare and dependency—and their costs both financial and personal." [19]

In the summer of 1967, Congress did move to revise the ADC program, but hardly along the lines Kennedy had suggested. It was proposed that all mothers receiving assistance be compelled to accept jobs and leave pre-school-age children in public nurseries, and that states be given incentives to take custody of illegitimate children. Testifying before the Senate Finance Committee against these proposals, Kennedy declared:

The amendments to our public assistance program which the House of Representatives enacted will not help, in my judgment, to solve the crisis in employment which grips the ghettos of our cities and the most impoverished of our rural areas. It will not help us to lighten the increasing fiscal burden of public assistance in any constructive way. Public money might be saved, but only because people badly in need of assistance would be eliminated from the welfare rolls without having anywhere else to turn. In short, House proposals seem to punish the poor because they are there and we have not been able to do anything about them. But if this is our approach, they will still be there when we are done. And the problem will be no closer to solution. The package of public assistance amendments which I propose would eliminate the most objectionable features of the House bill: the arbitrary freeze on payments under the Aid to Dependent

[19] Speech, U.S. Senate, July 13, 1967.

Children Program, the blanket compulsions on mothers and children to work, and the restrictions on assistance available to children of unemployed parents.[20]

The objective of enabling welfare recipients to obtain productive employment is of course laudable; indeed, as I have indicated, I believe it is the only hope we have for avoiding the deep division in our society which the creation of a permanent class of welfare poor would bring. But attempting to bring about employment by compulsion is not the way to do this. There are many mothers who should not work. Some, particularly in progressive states and cities, will be excused from working. But in other states with less enlightened welfare programs, many will either be driven off the welfare rolls or will be discouraged from applying, and *they will still be poor*—a little more invisible, for the time being, than they are now, but no less poor, no less miserable. . . .

. . . the provisions giving states an incentive to provide custodial care for illegitimate children are also punitive. Once an illegitimate child is born, although we may have wished to discourage that from happening, his best hope is to grow up in some kind of family structure. Study after study shows that the worst thing that could be done is to consign him to an institution. So we punish illegitimacy by punishing the illegitimate child. . . .

In the meantime, also, we must not continue to place a premium on broken homes as the condition for obtaining public assistance. And we must not end up by venting our own frustration in a measure punishing the poor because they are there and we have not been able to do anything about them. . . . It is not as though people choose to be poor, to need welfare assistance. . . .

We cannot afford to bury our heads in the sand. Our nation has been ripped apart this summer by violence and civil disorder that have taken dozens of lives and caused billions of dollars of property damage. We face in our cities the gravest domestic crisis to confront this nation since the Civil War. We are not going to solve that crisis by forcing welfare recipients to accept training for jobs when we have

[20] Press release, October 25, 1967.

absolutely no idea whether jobs will be available to them after their training. We are not going to solve that crisis by punishing the poor and hoping that they will bear that punishment silently, invisibly, graciously, without bitterness or hostility for their "benefactors." [21]

Three months later a bipartisan group of fifteen Senate liberals, including the junior Senator from New York, offered a series of amendments to the welfare revisions that was then before the Senate. In a joint press release, they described their proposals:

The most important of the amendments relates to the work incentive program which the committee adopted. While constructive in aim and purpose, this program also contains the most dangerous features of the bill. It will force mothers to work even though they have children in school who need their attention. As drafted, it may even force some mothers actually caring for preschool children to work. The first of the coalition amendments will eliminate any coercion on mothers actually caring for preschool children, and will require mothers of school-age children to take jobs only during school hours. A second amendment would require the federal minimum wage to be paid on all special work projects established under the work incentive program. Another would require that ADC children get the same increases in welfare which the bill provides for other welfare recipients. Others would make the Aid to Dependent Children of Unemployed Fathers Program a mandatory part of the state plan, and would liberalize the earnings incentive provided by the committee. [22]

None of their amendments were accepted.

KEY KENNEDY VOTES ON WELFARE

Social Security Amendments of 1965 (HR 6675). Passage of the bill authorizing the Medicare hospital insurance program for the aged. Passed 68-21, July 9, 1965. (D 55-7; R 13-14.) Kennedy: FOR.

[21] Testimony, Senate Finance Committee, August 29, 1967.
[22] Press release, November 21, 1967.

Unemployment Insurance Amendments of 1966 (HR 15119). Passage of bill requiring states to meet minimum federal standards for the amount and duration of state unemployment compensation benefits. Passed 53-31, August 8, 1966. (D 45-11; R 8-20.) Kennedy: FOR.

Chapter 7

The Failure of Our Schools

> And we have to think, above all, of the need for
> education. Education is the key to the jobs of the fu-
> ture. Education is the key to preserving individual
> capacity to act, to provide for oneself without depen-
> dence on government. And education, in the last an-
> alysis, is the key to understanding the world about us,
> the world of new nations and nuclear weapons, afflu-
> ence and starvation, war and peace.[1]

If education is the key to success and understanding,
as Robert Kennedy claimed, most of America's slum children are condemned to spend their lives in poverty and
darkness. For while limited successes are being recorded
in certain outer-city and suburban areas where home environments can compensate for school deficiencies, it is
impossible to overstate the failure of our schools in the
slums of the big cities.

Those children of the poor who do graduate from high
school—in some "inner-city" schools as many as 70 percent drop out before commencement—are not prepared
to compete with any hope of success in the world they
are about to enter. Most read at levels three or more
years behind the national average (it is not unusual to
find seniors with fourth-grade reading proficiency). Few
can compose an essay in acceptable English or perform
simple arithmetic operations accurately. Even more tragically, their thirteen years of formal education have left
them with only vague, misshapen conceptions of life

[1] Speech on behalf of Democratic candidates for state office, Sioux
City, Iowa, October 9, 1966.

beyond the ghetto's boundaries (of 175 graduating seniors in a Detroit ghetto high school, in 1968, more than 80 percent believed that between 60 and 95 percent of the U.S. population was Negro).

Predictably, the failure to master basic verbal and quantitative skills severely cripples the graduates' opportunities for gainful employment. A majority are not equipped to pass the qualifying examinations required for most better-paying jobs, and the absence of adequate counseling systems in the schools means that few of these students are directed to the job-training and remedial programs they so desperately need. Thus their education leads them nowhere but into the menial jobs and welfare offices that have maintained their parents in poverty over the years.

The causes of the public schools' inability to educate the children of the poor are many and complex. Educators have been slow to recognize that techniques and materials that produce results in middle-class areas often do not motivate and engage the interest of slum kids. Too many "inner-city" teachers have convinced themselves that slum children are "uneducable," thus providing a handy rationale for their own failures and unwillingness to devote the time and imagination necessary to create relevant, interesting, and demanding classes for their students.

There also is a tendency among these same teachers to take literally the "culturally deprived" label affixed to their students by sociologists. The label was intended to indicate the absence in many lower-class children of certain attitudes, habits, and experiences associated with success in a middle-class society, not the total lack of a culture. Unable or unwilling to recognize the existence of a vital lower-class culture, many teachers in slum schools bypass the opportunity to use this culture as a pertinent subject of study and as a bridge to topics beyond the untutored purview of ghetto students.

Accepting for the moment the questionable supposition that intelligent, committed members of the middle-class employing traditional techniques can teach lower-class kids basic verbal and quantitative skills, many of the schools' shortcomings are nevertheless traceable directly to the caliber of persons attracted to the field of teaching. Teachers—particularly the men—tend to be the dregs of the educated labor force, often drawn to the profession by its lack of competition, utter security, short work day (for those who do not take their preparation seriously), and long summer break. However, given the status and salary of teachers in this country, the prospects for improving the quality of our school personnel in the foreseeable future are not very promising.

What should be done about these and the numerous other inadequacies of our educational system? Simply pouring more money into education, which is what educators have been demanding, is not the solution. The *Coleman Report*—a massive federal study of American education—found that student achievement is not significantly related to school plant or teacher-student ratios, the two areas most frequently cited by education lobbyists as requiring more funds. In other words, even if we had a good deal more money to expend on education, we really do not know which are the most efficient ways to invest it.

It may be that we will not find the answers to many of these problems until we set up private experimental schools in the slums which are free from the stultifying direction of our urban boards of education, which rarely represent the parents of the children concerned. Possibly, human instructors with their literacy aids may have to be replaced with electronic audiovisual devices which reduce the teacher to a technical administrator. Whatever our solutions, one thing is clear: the time for boldness is here, for we have made little progress since the educational panic following Sputnik a decade ago.

"To Blame Themselves Instead of Their Students"

Although education was not one of Robert Kennedy's principal domestic interests, he recognized that our schools were failing to meet their responsibilities.

New York City already spends far more for education than does the average American community. But this money does not buy enough. When New York already spends an average of $550 per pupil each year—with a total operating budget of over 750 million dollars—the answer to this problem is not more money. The problem is that the schools have too often failed in their responsibilities—have not been willing to change, to innovate, to blame themselves instead of blaming their students.[2]

In principle, our commitment has been that every child should have an adequate education. But this commitment has been subordinated to the demands of the educational system. In the simplest terms, this means that when a child has failed to learn, we have assigned him a label—whether "slow," or "unmotivated," or even "retarded." But if we mean our commitment—if we mean that every child shall learn—then we must be willing to change a system which does not work, and find one which does. Josiah Royce once said that education is "learning to use the tools which the race has found to be indispensable." At that minimum level, at least, our commitment—and our system—must be total.[3]

Clearly, the most important problem in Harlem is education of every kind. Fathers must learn job skills, and mothers how to buy food economically; students must learn to read, and little children how to speak—and teachers must learn how to teach. . . .

But our educational efforts have thus far not been sufficient. For this there have been many reasons, which by now are familiar to all of us: segregation; lack of stimulation or stability in many homes; lack of preschool preparation; lack of adequate resources in the schools themselves; lack of effort in the schools which have not been determined that all children *must* learn.

All these shortcomings exist; all are destructive and wasteful; all must be changed.[4]

[2] Address, Lexington Democratic Club, New York, N.Y., February 4, 1965.

[3] Address, dedication of Mt. Providence Junior College, Baltimore, Md., September 12, 1966.

[4] Speech, Second Borough President's Conference of Community Leaders on the Revitalization of Harlem-East Harlem Community, New York, N.Y., January 21, 1966.

Surely it is significant that the parents of the young rioters in Harlem, in Rochester, in Philadelphia, had on the average no more than a fifth-grade education. Surely it is significant that the schools attended by the rioters themselves were significantly inferior to schools elsewhere. Surely it is significant that these schools were living reminders of the despair and degradation of their surroundings.[5]

If we have any greater responsibility than giving our children the best possible education, then I don't know what it is. I think the answer to civil rights, the answer to employment, the answer to slums, really rests with education. If we have a good education, we can break out of any of these prisons.

We are going to have to spend a billion dollars more by 1970 just in lower education, without even getting into higher education. I think there has to be help. I think the federal government has to play a role in this because the tax structure is already so high. And I am strongly in favor of that kind of an effort and if I am elected to the United States Senate, I am going down to Washington to fight for that. . . .

Fourth, I would fight to insure free tuition as the pattern for all public colleges. . . .

Eighth, we should test the feasibility of providing income tax credit for tuition expenses.[6]

Federal Money, Local Involvement

Kennedy was a strong advocate of increased federal aid to education as a necessary condition for a solution to our schools' shortcomings.

With education costs, particularly in both of our states [Iowa and New York]—the industrial states—going up and up and up, I think that the federal government has to play a role. The role can be played without control of education by the federal government, but I think that there has to be

[5] Campaign speech, University of Syracuse, Syracuse, N.Y., October 20, 1964.

[6] Speech, Westchester Women's Groups luncheon, New Rochelle, N.Y., October 16, 1964.

financial assistance given to the state and to the local communities to finance the cost of education. And I think every child in the United States who has the ability should have the right to go to college and not be prevented from attending the university because of lack of financial means.

First, we should continue and accelerate present efforts to expand federal support for education of every kind. Until now, the local property tax has been the primary source of financing for education. But local property taxes, especially in states like New York, have reached their upper limit to raise money. And local taxes of the present magnitude, though worth every penny in education they buy, still penalize those willing to sacrifice for education by driving business and income away to those areas which are willing to shortchange education by raising less than their fair share of taxes. In this mobile society, with most Americans moving across state lines at least once in their lifetime, the education of a child in Iowa contributes to the whole nation—and a stunted education elsewhere can force Iowa to spend more on welfare and police and housing. Education is a national resource; it should be paid for on a national basis, with each paying his share as a citizen of the nation. Second, we should also continue and expand our efforts for the education of the poor and disadvantaged. In the long run, welfare payments solve nothing, for the givers or the recipients; free Americans deserve the chance to be fully self-supporting—and this requires education. Third, we must vastly expand opportunities for college study for all our children. This means, among other things, the creation of 3,469,000 new places in the next ten years alone. We must also move to meet the swiftly rising cost of a college education. Just in the last eight years, the cost of four years at a private college has gone from $7,000 in 1956-1957 to over $10,000 in 1965; clearly, few families can send two or three children to college at costs like these. By expanded programs of student loans, by providing part-time earning opportunities for students, and by direct aid to colleges, we must lower the financial burden of college education. And I believe the time has already come when the first two years of college—just like elementary school or high school—should be free to all qualified students. Fourth, we must equalize educational opportunities among the generations. The graduating high school senior of ten years ago—whose opportunities for higher education were far more restricted than those his taxes help make available to the students of today—is still only twenty-seven or twenty-eight, a young man in the prime of his life, with over thirty years of productive life and work ahead. If that young man, for financial reasons, went to work instead of to college at the age of eighteen, there is little chance that he will ever get a college education. Yet giving him a college education now would add as much to our national wealth, and to his individual and family welfare, as would aiding many present high school seniors. This year, the Congress took one major step in this direction with the passage of the Cold War GI bill—and this fall, over 250,000 former servicemen, previously unable to attend higher education, are already enrolled in colleges all over the country. But we should go further—so that the assembly-line or construction worker of today may become the engineer or architect of tomorrow.[7]

But he warned against exclusive reliance on Washington as a source of programs and funds for improving our educational system.

But this commitment cannot be a governmental one alone. Not only must we reckon with the limitations imposed by priorities and logic upon taxation and spending of all kinds, but we are coming to understand that much of what is wrong with our education system is precisely that it is too much involved with government. Impersonal bureaucracies, however well-intentioned, operating from efficient remote headquarters, are no substitute for the intimate involvement of community, of home or church, of local voluntary association, and in the last analysis—the active concern of individual human beings.[8]

On occasion he offered proposals—some vague, some specific—as to what should be done.

So you and I, and all Democrats in this state, and all citizens of this state, must assume the responsibility for other children that we willingly accept for our own. We cannot do it just by

[7] Speech on behalf of Democratic candidates for state office, Sioux City, Iowa, October 9, 1966.
[8] Address, dedication of Mt. Providence Junior College, Baltimore, Md., September 12, 1966.

passing laws. For only people educate children. Only people like you can insist on the necessary changes in our schools. Only informed and active citizens can hold the schools—as we hold every other agency of government—to account for the results of their activity. And only those with the advantages of education and ability can provide the direct help these children need—in preschool programs, in remedial tutoring, in awakening them to the world around them. There are children living six blocks from the ocean—who have never seen it. You can take them. There are children of three and four who have heard nothing but one-syllable words, barely in sentences. You can talk to them. There are children of all ages who have never felt love, or concern, who have never known anyone to care. We can care. . . .

We must learn to accept individual differences and work with them—not to search for magic potions, trying to transform all children into facsimiles of suburban youth who fit our system.[9]

To change this sense of alienation we must reapproach the whole question of cooperation among educational institutions. Here we are not discussing an arrangement for sharing of faculties, or even of students, but rather of fundamental rearrangements. For example, we have discovered in the elementary grades that the "ungraded" school or class has great advantages. A child who can perform with his peers or beyond in one field may lag behind in another. Even many labeled as mentally retarded have sometimes performed near-genius work in particular areas. Operation Head Start has taught us that remedial work can begin before there is anything to remedy. Why not, then, apply this learning to the entire process? Why not view all of the schools as one school, one education? High school seniors do college work in some experimental situations. Indeed, some university teachers complain that *their* students do high school work. Study should be offered to students at the highest level at which they are able to perform—in classes and curricula adapted to helping them learn. Students with motivation problems, untaught as to the value of learning, might best learn on-the-job—in spe-

[9] Address, Annual Political Conference, Women's Division, New York State Democratic Committee, Albany, N.Y., March 1, 1965.

cial employment tailored to their abilities, in which they could at once learn that learning pays, and that we care enough to help them learn and perform productive tasks. Others, depressed by the general conditions of slum schools, might well benefit significantly from interchanges of teachers or students with junior colleges or universities. And we must reach out as well to those who have been passed by in the past—those already out of school, the fathers and mothers of young children, the unemployed and the abandoned of this entire nation. Here we must recognize that education is not something—and cannot be allowed to be something—which, once interrupted, is over for life. We need new kinds of universities and colleges—able to teach, not only in fine buildings, but in community centers and parks and even in homes —colleges which are no more than groups of people determined that learning shall be brought to all those who need it.[10]

[If elected to the Senate] I would fight to insure free tuition as the pattern for all public colleges.[11]

Decentralization

It was not until mid-1967, however, that he suggested some bold new approaches. In his speech before the Day Care Council of New York City, he asked:

Can we not decentralize the administration of our schools, offering parents a voice in the policy of the institutions which are supposed to educate their children?

Can we not encourage the development of laboratory schools, in the ghetto, with master teachers and parent teacher aides? Can we not devise a way to give such teacher aides the chance to further their education and move up the career ladder?

Can we not accept the development of competitive schools as a yardstick—what the TVA has been in the field of electric

[10] Address, dedication of Mt. Providence Junior College, Baltimore, Md., September 12, 1966.

[11] Campaign speech, Westchester Women's Groups luncheon, New Rochelle, N.Y., October 16, 1964.

power generation—to measure the performance of our traditional school system?[12]

[12] Address, Day Care Council of New York, New York, N.Y., May 8, 1967.

Unfortunately, these provocative questions were never pursued in subsequent speeches or legislative proposals.

KEY KENNEDY VOTES ON EDUCATION

Elementary and Secondary Education Act of 1965 (HR 2362). Provides a three-year program of grants to states for allocation to school districts with large numbers of children from low-income families in public and private schools. Passed 73-18, April 9, 1965. (D 55-4; R 18-14.) Kennedy: FOR.

Chapter 8

Health and Safety

This multifaceted and often technical field is one in which Robert Kennedy invested a good deal of time and interest while in the Senate. We will examine his views and proposals in the following areas: health care, mental retardation, drug use and addiction, physical fitness, automobile and highway safety, and cigarette smoking.

Health Care

In a speech at Albert Einstein College of Medicine on November 19, 1967, he discussed the problem of inadequate health care in this country and outlined his own prescription for improving the situation.

But I come here to offer you not congratulations, but a challenge. For in New York and across the nation, the condition of American medical care is grave—in fact, it is critical. We—and you—confront a grim scene of the neglected, the ill, and the dying—the thousands, the millions of victims of our indifference. . . .

The cost of health care in America is staggering: more than 6 percent of our gross national product. And with Medicare and Medicaid, these costs have soared. But consider what we have bought with these billions: In 1950, we ranked fifth in the world in our infant mortality rate. Today, we rank fifteenth—below all of the industrialized nations of Europe. And here in New York, during the last decade, infant mortality *increased*—by 4 percent.

—12 other nations have higher life-expectancy rates than we do.

—15 other nations have higher ratios of hospital beds to patients than we do.

—43 percent of our hospital care, according to Columbia's School of Public Health and Administrative Medicine, is only poor to fair.

But these figures—and countless others—cannot measure the full impact of our double standard of medical care. It cannot measure the disappearance of family physician care for poor families—and its replacement by the emergency rooms of huge impersonal municipal hospitals. . . .

It cannot measure the minor illnesses which spawn major diseases—because regular checkups are unknown, and continuing medical care an illusion. It cannot reflect the children whose education is useless—because they are too weak to work, or too ill to listen. Figures cannot measure the indignities, the inefficiencies, the lost lives, but they at least tell us how much remains to be done, beyond the spending of massive sums of money. . . .

The result of providing more money to compete for the same supply of services has been an astronomical increase in the cost of care. Daily rates in hospitals are up over a third in less than two years. Physicians' fees have risen over 10 percent, 8.5 percent in the past year alone. Hospital charges of $100 a day will soon be a reality in New York City. There is no real mystery about why this has happened. Wages are two-thirds of the cost of running a hospital, and there was a huge backlog of wage demands in our hospitals. Nurses and other personnel had worked too long at substandard pay, and now there are funds to offer a more adequate wage. But there are other matters. Hospitals are run essentially as they were fifty years ago. They have been neither forced nor even encouraged to innovate. Patients are still wheeled from one end of the hospital to the other for surgery. Costly services are maintained for vast numbers of patients not seriously enough ill to need them. Physician fees have risen so sharply because more dollars cannot by themselves produce more doctors. That, coupled with the fee-for-service approach of Medicare and Medicaid, has allowed some specialists and even some general practitioners to reap exorbitant benefits from these tax-financed programs. Serious as these matters are, the fundamental problem is one of structure—one which goes to the heart of our system of delivering health care. We are pumping billions of dollars of new money into the health industry—but without the slightest effort to change the existing system, under which people are taken care of in the costliest institution, the hospital, and by the costliest man-power, the doctor. It is no wonder that the cost of health care has risen so sharply. . . .

An effective program of action requires at least four steps:

First. We must tap new sources for recruitment into the health field and develop new health careers for our recruits. We all know we have a grave shortage of medical personnel. We know that each year we educate 2,000 fewer doctors than we need just to keep pace with present ratios; and we know we need more nurses of all kinds, and more technical aides. We can find many of these people in the same com-munities of the poor which most need medical help. We can find—and train—non-professional people to care for fellow members of their own communities. And this source of em-ployment—a source you have tapped with your health careers program—can find worthy service and increased job oppor-tunity within the medical profession.

Second. All of our medical resources must be put to work more effectively in the communities themselves. To structure the future of medicine solely around large, impersonal hos-pitals will not only insure poor quality care, but also guarantee even more excessive demands on these overcrowded institutions —and thus produce higher and higher medical costs. If we are to use our funds wisely—if we are to deploy our health manpower efficiently—we must decentralize medical care. We must bring health services to the people through a system of community and neighborhood health centers which provide comprehensive family care in a dignified, responsive setting.

Third. The program must go beyond narrowly defined "health needs." For all of the energy—all of the commitment— of the medical profession will not be enough, unless we also meet the sources of disease.

It is an illusion to think we can cure a sickly child—and ignore his need for nutritious food. It is foolish to pour in funds to minister to the effects of filth-ridden slums—without recognizing the undeniable fact that these slums breed disease. It is profitless to establish community mental health services— if we do not understand that a community of the jobless, the purposeless, the hopeless spawns frustration and agony in the minds of its victims. We will never have enough doctors to cure the children of Mississippi who have not eaten nourishing food since their birth. There will never be enough therapists for all the brain-damaged children of Bedford-Stuyvesant. We will not cure the pathology of individuals, unless we—and you—begin to come to grips with the pathology of these communities.

Fourth. As this is true for the communities of poverty, it is just as true for the whole society. All the cancer research, all the hospitals in the nation may be less important than the single simple step of making sure that fewer children are enticed into becoming cigarette smokers. All our programs for training new doctors may not mean as much to the health of the city of New York as courageous and forceful action to eliminate the pollution of our air. All our emergency rooms will not not be adequate to care for the victims of the carnage on our highways, if we do not enforce far more rigid safety standards on the makers of automobiles. And the same is true for the dozens of health hazards we have allowed to persist, through ignorance and inattention and sloth:
—the meat packed amid dirt and disease;
—the drugs sold without adequate testing;
—the pesticides carelessly sprayed onto our crops.

These are not for the medical profession alone—these are challenges to all of us. But you of the medical profession, the concerned and active doctors and leaders such as are here today, you can take the lead.[1]

Kennedy also supported legislation calling for the creation of regional medical centers to diagnose and treat major diseases such as cancer and stroke.

Mr. Chairman, I would like to address a brief statement to the subcommittee concerning my interest in this bill, S. 596, designed to combat heart disease, cancer, stroke and other major diseases. The deliberations of the Subcommittee on Health are of concern to all citizens of the country, for when 71 percent of all deaths in the nation are caused by the diseases under discussion, almost no family evades their scourge.

[1] Address, Albert Einstein College of Medicine of Yeshiva University, New York, N.Y., November 19, 1967.

The high incidence of these diseases, particularly cancer, among the young means that we are losing people who may not have reached their most productive periods of activity or are being struck down in the prime of their lives. For these individuals, as well as for the many individuals reaching the period of their lives when they can enjoy the fruits of retirement, we owe a full-scale attack on these outriders of the four horsemen of the apocalypse, heart disease, cancer and stroke. However, as I understand it, the three recommendations of the commission that are embraced in S. 596 are designed primarily to bridge the gap between the fund of research knowledge that we have developed on heart disease, cancer and stroke and the patient of the average practitioner who would like to receive the benefits of that research tomorrow. These recommendations provide for:

1. regional centers concerned with either heart disease, cancer or stroke, conducting clinical investigation, teaching local practitioners, and patient care.

2. a national network of diagnostic and treatment stations aimed at bringing the highest medical skills within the reach of every citizen.

3. medical complexes based on university medical schools where advanced medical equipment, teaching, and the school's research activities would be available to doctors affiliated with the regional centers and the diagnostic and treatment stations.

A program of this size is a major step in making the benefits of medical knowledge available to all.[2]

He introduced legislation to provide grants for expanding existing hospital facilities.

A survey taken by the United States Public Health Service reveals that there are now 143 hospitals serving 97 communities in 29 states and Puerto Rico that are in "critical" condition. These are hospitals that do not have sufficient beds to keep up with daily demand. The Public Health Service estimates that the immediate threat could be alleviated by the construction of 3,000 new beds in the "critical" hospitals.

Existing federal programs cannot solve this current crisis.

[2] Statement, Senate Committee on Labor and Welfare, February 10, 1965.

The hospitals involved have either exhausted the federal funds presently available or lack the financial resources to supply the required nonfederal portion of the estimated construction costs.

Under that [the one he is introducing] bill's provisions, hospitals threatened by immediate bed shortages could obtain direct grants and loans from the federal government. The grant program—providing up to 66⅔ percent of the cost of expansion or renovation to provide new bed space—is patterned after the successful Hill-Burton formula except that federal aid is given directly to the hospitals and is not distributed by the states. The intent of the legislation is not to supplant the Hill-Burton program. Rather, it attempts to correct an emergency situation with a single short-term infusion of federal assistance and without embarking on a massive continuing new federal spending program. Over the next three years, a total of $40 million is authorized to be appropriated for grants.

To meet the needs of those hospitals serving communities without adequate financial resources to supply the remaining 33⅓ percent nonfederal portion, the Act authorizes the Secretary of Health, Education and Welfare to make long-term, low-interest loans of up to 90 percent of the nonfederal share of the construction cost. Interest on these loans shall be charged at 2.5 percent and the hospital would have up to 50 years to repay.[3]

In 1966, Kennedy called for an investigation of the federal agencies which provide services for the handicapped.

One area which has not yet been examined, and one where the inquiry is long overdue, is the role of the federal government in programs for the handicapped. At the federal level no less than 28 agencies, bureaus, divisions, and commissions are charged with responsibility for major programs for the disabled. Between these agencies, there is totally inadequate communication and coordination. For example: two men heading programs for juvenile delinquency in two separate departments of HEW were at their jobs for two years—and had never met, talked on the phone, or even corresponded. . . .

[3] Statement, U.S. Senate, October 20, 1966.

Congress has demonstrated an amazing sensitivity to the many very real and critical needs in the fields of health and rehabilitation services, but I say that "confusion, duplication, fragmentation, and the absence of coordination in planning and administering these programs place the objectives of Congress, and the welfare of this nation, in jeopardy." We must now consolidate our gains—and end the losses of duplication and fragmentation. I have therefore asked the Senator from Connecticut to institute an inquiry into the role of the federal agencies which provide services to our handicapped citizens. He has, in turn, asked me to take the leadership in this effort. I welcome this opportunity to conduct full hearings into this critical situation through the Subcommittee on Executive Reorganization.[4]

Mental Retardation

The Kennedy family has a personal commitment to the fight to understand and treat mental retardation; one of the Senator's sisters has passed most of her life in an institution for the retarded. Kennedy spoke frequently about this often politically ignored problem.

Mental retardation, after all, is but a word—a word we use to describe those whose IQs are under 70, or 75; who do not relate normally to the people around them; who do not support themselves economically. But these characteristics are shared by millions of those we have come to call "the deprived" or "the disadvantaged."

It is vital that we recognize this. For we are beginning now to address ourselves to the problems of educating the disadvantaged. I have said before that our educational failures have been, more than anything else, a failure of commitment; that we have in effect told children to adapt to a fixed system, and weeded out those who did not fit the pattern.

What I want to stress now is that this is no less true for those we call mentally retarded. Whatever their differences from other children, there is one respect in which they are the same—they can be taught, they can be helped, they can lead

4 Statement, U.S. Senate, April 28, 1966.

normal lives, contributing to the society instead of burdening it—if we will it.

If we are prepared to accept responsibility for these children, to work with them—not to what we think is the limit of *their* abilities, but to the limit of *our* abilities—they can be helped. That is why I regard today's action [establishment at Albert Einstein of the Center for Research in Maternal and Child Health and Human Development] as so significant.[5]

Everyone here tonight, I think, would agree that the application of what we know would cut mental retardation in half. But we should all recognize that this application will require a revolution. It will require, as a beginning, the elimination of the conditions of poverty and ignorance under which millions of Americans live. Equality of opportunity is a mockery to those whose birth and early experiences—or lack of experiences—handicap them throughout life. It will require a revolution in our educational system as well. Mental retardation, after all, is not a single, well-defined disease. It is a symptom, a word we use to describe those whose IQs are under a certain level, who do not relate normally to the people around them, who do not as adults support themselves.

Up to now, we have allowed our educational system to function like a sieve—sorting out those who fit a predetermined pattern, and neglecting the rest. But we know that virtually every child—however retarded, however handicapped—can be taught.

We know that 85 percent of retarded children can become self-supporting. We know that whatever difference there is between the mentally retarded and other children, there is one respect in which they are the same—they can be taught, they can be helped, they can lead normal lives, contributing to the society instead of burdening it—if we will it.[6]

Total commitment is a commitment to *all* retarded children —whatever the cause of their retardation, whatever the kind of action necessary to deal with it.

[5] Address, Albert Einstein College of Medicine of Yeshiva University, New York, N.Y., March 18, 1965.
[6] Speech, Rhode Island Association for Retarded Children, Providence, R.I., April 24, 1965.

For too long, we have allowed our efforts to be fragmented. Some try to concern themselves only with "brain-damaged" children, some even with particular kinds of brain damage or disease. Others are willing to concern themselves only with children over a certain IQ level. There are those who will contribute only to research to prevent retardation, neglecting those who are already afflicted; and there are others who cannot be bothered to use the knowledge gained by research already done.

One result of these divisions is that the voices of concern for retarded children are not heard as plainly and loudly as they deserve to be heard—and as the lives of our children demand that they be heard. . . .

Dr. Leonard Duhl, for example, has suggested a whole new concept of institutional and semi-institutional care. He proposes the establishment of whole communities dedicated to the care, education and training of persons such as the retarded.

There are thousands of smaller towns, all over America, from which industry has fled. The people in these towns are some of the finest we have—hard-working, stable, capable and compassionate. These towns could be turned into service communities—composed of the existing community and its people; a facility for institutional care, employing local residents; and a branch of a nearby university, with departments of education, medicine, psychology, psychiatry and social work.

In such a community many retardates now institutionalized could live in foster homes, because it would be possible to train those who kept the homes more adequately than we now are about to do. The schools in such a community would have a greater consciousness of the special educational needs of the retarded; and they would benefit from constant contact with the university. In such a community, furthermore, a total community education program would be possible; all employers—for example, in stores and laundries—could make maximum use of the retarded, again because of close connection with trained staff; and bus drivers and salesgirls, policemen and housewives, all could be brought to understand the special needs of the retarded who would now walk freely about the streets. The university's research would not just be

in an impersonal laboratory; teachers and students would work
every day with real problems helping real individuals.[7]

Drug Use and Addiction

Until recently, drug use and addiction were primarily
lower-class afflictions. For that reason, few influential
citizens were concerned about the problem; it was too
remote. However, the sudden surge in narcotics consumption on college and high-school campuses has given
this problem a middle- and upper-middle-class dimension, resulting in the growth of effective political interest
in increased control of drug sales and treatment of the
addicted.

A central controversy in the field of narcotics control
has been whether addict-pushers should be treated
principally as criminals or as physically and emotionally
sick persons. As Attorney General, Kennedy spoke on this
question at a White House conference in 1962:

We have somehow assumed that the narcotics problem is so
intensely dangerous and vicious that the solution is principally
punitive. This field reaches across many disciplines—psychology, sociology, economics and medicine, as well as criminology
—and yet we have persisted in letting almost the entire burden fall on the Federal Bureau of Narcotics. . . .

For example, one particularly promising approach you have
analyzed here is civil commitment—giving an addict treatment rather than just a prison term, with an intensive period
of institutional care followed by closely supervised parole and
aftercare. Throughout the period of prospective rehabilitation,
criminal charges are kept pending. . . .

While the criminal should be given a prison sentence, I
think we also agree, however, that the addict should be given
treatment. The mandatory sentencing law applies equally to
racketeers and to others, who may be peddlers only to support the cost of their own addiction. As a result, rigid appli-

[7] Speech, National Association for Retarded Children, New York,
N.Y., October 1965.

cation of the law has produced some notable and dramatic sentencing disparities.[8]

He raised the issue again during his campaign for the Senate in 1964.

This is a danger to our youth. It endangers all of us—for it probably contributes to 50 percent of our street crime. . . .

But law enforcement is only part of the problem. We were also deeply concerned with the need for improved treatment of addicts, and their restoration to society. With James V. Bennett, then Director of the Federal Bureau of Prisons, we were convinced that simply to lock up prisoners, without offering incentive for rehabilitation and parole, was useless and cruel. . . .

The findings of the President's Commission and of the White House Conferences show that narcotics is not an "either/or" question. It is not crime *or* a medical problem. It is both, and success depends upon a coordinated attack, with the cooperation of many individuals and organizations.

The essential components of this attack are:

First, an all-out legal effort against illicit trafficking in drugs, utilizing the full power of the federal and state governments. Big-time traffickers should receive the most severe penalties possible.

Second, the addict himself should be given every opportunity for treatment and rehabilitation, to permit his restoration as a useful member of society. The addict-criminal, or the small-time addict-peddler, is responsible for his crimes against the community. But he should not be specially penalized for his addiction, and should be given every opportunity to cure himself.

The present mandatory minimum penalties for those convicted of violating the federal narcotics laws should be made flexible, thus allowing judicial discretion to provide incentives for rehabilitation and cure. Severe penalties could be imposed on traffickers, but addicts and minor addict-peddlers could receive more realistic and humane sentences. . . .[9]

[8] Speech, White House Conference on Narcotic and Drug Abuse, September 28, 1962.

[9] Campaign statement, October 21, 1964.

In the same statement, he called for more "adequate safeguards on the production, distribution, and sale of the so-called psychotoxic drugs (amphetamines, barbiturates, and tranquilizers)."

In 1965 Kennedy and seven of his Senate colleagues introduced two bills aimed at reforming present treatment procedures. RFK explained the provisions of this legislation, along with his views on the proper care of addicts:

I introduce, for appropriate reference, on behalf of myself, Senator Javits, Senator Erwin, Senator Hart, Senator Williams of New Jersey, Senator Tydings, Senator Kuchel, and Senator Case, two bills concerning the problems of narcotics and drug abuse—a bill providing certain reforms in the federal criminal law as it relates to narcotics, and providing a post-conviction sentencing program by which convicted persons may be sentenced to a treatment program instead of to prison, and a bill to assist states, political subdivisions and private nonprofit organizations in providing treatment and rehabilitation services for drug abusers. . . .

We have somewhere between 50,000 and 100,000 narcotic addicts in this country. Their affliction affects not only their own lives, but the lives of their families as well. As a result of the crimes they commit to get money to support their addiction, they cost society hundreds of millions of dollars annually. We need to do much more to get at the roots of this problem than we have done up to now, and that is why we introduce this legislation today. . . .

Let me turn to discussion of the bills we introduce today. One of the most important efforts which the federal government can make to help in connection with narcotics and drug-abuse problems is to stimulate increased efforts by states, cities, and private individuals and organizations to treat and rehabilitate addicts and to engage in research into the problems of drug abuse.

That is the basic purpose of the services bill which I am introducing. It authorizes $7,500,000 a year for grants for treatment and rehabilitative services, not only for narcotic addicts, but for users of depressant and stimulant drugs—like the barbiturates and the amphetamines. . . .

We cannot ever lose sight of the fact that many of the

problems underlying addiction are the same ones that under-
lie much of the problem of crime in the streets and delinquency. We will never erase addiction until we erase poverty
and discrimination—until we can give the addict adequate
educational and employment opportunities as an alternative
way to turn.

Nevertheless, since the addict's personal problems are
psychological and should be susceptible of treatment as is any
mental illness, there is much that can be accomplished through
better and more extensive treatment programs and better and
more extensive research. Monetarily, the bill is oriented
primarily toward the former category, since research money
is available under Section 303 of the Public Health Service
Act, but in over-all purpose, the bill's point is to encourage
greater efforts in both the research and treatment areas.

I hope that the aid provided by this bill will be used for
all types of treatment programs, since we do not yet have any
one sure-fire way to bring addicts permanently into organized
society. In general, I think it is safe to say that it would be
extremely useful to devote a substantial portion of the aid
which the bill offers to the critical period of aftercare—making
sure that the former addict has close attention, over an extended period of time, both psychiatric and vocational, to
make sure that he always has someone and something that
can offer tangible reason for not slipping back.

Beyond this, however, there are many questions. Should the
addict be removed from his original environment and placed
in drug-free surroundings for a long period of time while he
is getting psychiatric help and vocational training? Or should
an attempt be made to place him in some kind of halfway
house or other facility in his home environment once he is no
longer physically addicted, where he will live and participate
while he gradually attains membership in organized society?
Or is the addict such an inherently weak personality that he
can never successfully return to his original environment, so
that the only possible program is one which removes him permanently from his original surroundings and gradually makes
him a part of an entirely new and permanent social arrangement, of what might be called a reservation village? To what
extent should the rest of his family be brought into it as well?

All of these approaches deserve a full look. . . .

Turning to the other bill of which I am the principal sponsor, its design is twofold:

1) to enhance prosecutorial discretion in the enforcement of the federal narcotics laws, and

2) to provide incentive for addicts convicted of federal crime to involve themselves successfully in a treatment program in the prison system.

The person who violates the federal narcotics laws is ordinarily guilty of two violations: violation of the Narcotic Drugs Import and Export Act, the provisions of which are in Title 21 of the United States Code, and violation of the regulatory tax provisions of Internal Revenue Code, while retaining the mandatory minimum provisions in the Narcotic Drugs Import and Export Act. Since the latter is the more stringent act, this reform would give prosecutors a discretion to decide whether an accused is a major peddler of narcotics and should be tried under the stringent provisions of the Narcotic Drugs Import and Export Act, or is an addict who has been arrested for what amounted to be a possessory offense and deserves more lenient treatment. The over-all point of this reform, and of the other reforms which the bill accomplishes, is to give the addict-violator some incentive to rehabilitate himself successfully while he is in custody. As long as he faces a long mandatory minimum sentence that incentive is practically destroyed.

Along these same lines, the bill extends the flexible sentencing provisions of the Federal Youth Corrections Act to all violators up to the age of twenty-six, regardless of whether a mandatory sentence is involved for the violation. In addition, the bill extends the possibility of parole, on a limited basis, to those convicted of offenses for which there is a mandatory minimum. It makes them eligible for parole once they have completed their minimum sentence, assuming they are otherwise eligible at that time. These changes all provide a useful and important flexibility without jeopardizing the effectiveness of the strong penalties of the Narcotic Drugs Import and Export Act. . . .

Hopefully, the provisions of this bill will result in far greater flexibility in the administration of the federal criminal law and in far more effective treatment and rehabilitation of addicts who are convicted of a federal crime. We all agree that we must continue to spare no effort in trying to stop the illegal traffic in narcotics and to apprehend those involved. I was certainly deeply involved in that effort while I was Attorney General. Nevertheless, better protection and incentive for the addict-violator are needed, and I think the bill which I introduced today can provide that without in the least jeopardizing the law-enforcement effort against major traffickers in narcotics.[10]

The bill eliminates mandatory minimum sentences for marihuana violators and for violators of the regulatory tax provisions of the Internal Revenue Code. . . .

The bill also has a Title II, the purpose of which is to broaden the definition of narcotics and narcotic drugs in the Public Health Service Act, so that the efforts of the Public Health Service in this area will extend to the barbiturates, amphetamines, and other dangerous drugs, instead of merely to the opiates and other narcotics. Specifically, these amendments would result in broadening the mission of the Public Health Service hospitals at Lexington, Kentucky, and Fort Worth, Texas, to include research into and treatment of the problems of dangerous drug users.[11]

A year later he discussed the newest drug in vogue on college campuses and in the burgeoning hippy colonies, LSD.

Here is a drug which has been available for well over twenty years. Research on its effects and possible therapeutic uses has been going on for a long time. Yet suddenly, almost overnight, irresponsible and unsupervised use of LSD for nonscientific, nonmedical purposes has risen markedly. Such use carries with it grave dangers. Panic reactions or temporary personality changes may cause a person to harm himself or others while under the influence of the drug. And without careful psychological screening, the drug will be used by some who suffer permanent damage as a result. In a word, what was an experimental drug has become a social problem. We must be prepared to deal with that problem, and to educate people —particularly young people—about the dangers of LSD.

[10] Statement, U.S. Senate, June 9, 1965.
[11] Press release, June 9, 1965.

And as LSD has become a problem, the possibility has arisen that public reaction will discourage and dry up legitimate research into and therapeutic use of LSD. Experiments indicate that LSD may be useful in treating alcoholics—one of the largest groups of the handicapped. And it has been helpful in some cases as an adjunct to psychotherapy for mentally ill people. If we in the federal government allow these legitimate uses to be interfered with, the loss to the nation in hopes of help for the handicapped would be serious indeed.[12]

Physical Fitness

To Robert Kennedy, physical fitness was not a good habit but a way of life. His athletic feats and escapades—fiercely contested touch-football games, kayak paddling, fifty-mile hikes, climbing Mt. Kennedy—were inherent elements of both his private and his public existence.

In 1962 he expressed his concern over the declining physical vigor of American youth:

More is at stake than muscles for our children. In my judgment physical fitness is basic to all forms of excellence, and to a strong, confident nation.[13]

His keen interest in competitive sports caused him to intervene in a long-standing jurisdictional dispute in amateur athletics between the NCAA and the AAU.

The NCAA and the AAU have been locked in a silly and destructive dispute in recent years which has disrupted our track program, caused great harm to many young men, and done no credit to either organization. . . .

The NCAA has no business and no right to penalize Gerry Lindgren or any athlete for wishing to represent his country. I join with Senator Jackson in calling the situation to the

[12] Statement, Subcommittee on Executive Reorganization of the Senate Committee on Government Operations, May 24, 1966.

[13] Speech, American Association for Health, Physical Education and Recreation, Cincinnati, Ohio, April 6, 1962.

attention of the Senate and I call upon the NCAA to say here and now that it will not penalize Gerry Lindgren or his school. That is the least it can do.

What it can and should do, and what the AAU can and should do, is resolve this dispute before there is further threat to the careers of our young athletes. The country is being hurt, track is being hurt, but most important of all, many fine young men are being hurt through no fault of their own.

There have been suggestions that the way out of this impasse is for the government to establish a sports organization. I have some reservations about this, but I certainly think that as time goes by, and the NCAA-AAU dispute deepens to the point where a boy like Gerry Lindgren may be penalized for wishing to represent his country against the Soviet Union, then I think that perhaps the time is here for the Congress to look into this alternative very closely.[14]

I would like to make a settlement proposal this morning, or at least draw the broad outlines of one.

What I propose is that the United States Olympic Committee amend its constitution or bylaws to create a permanent arbitration board which would decide all athletic disputes among USOC's members. The arbitration board might, for example, be composed of five members—all outstanding Americans, not necessarily sports figures and not necessarily members of the United States Olympic Committee, but all knowledgeable in sports. These distinguished arbitrators would be empowered to decide disputes among USOC members in a compulsory and binding way.

The basic point, however, is this: The Olympic Committee approach is a feasible way to get a permanent arbitration body established. Every amateur sports body in the country has an overriding interest in continuing to participate in the USOC. . . .

In the long run, sports development will require much more from each of us than merely ending the present dispute and finding a way to solve other disputes which may arise. The goal of giving every youngster in this country, whether he goes to college or not, a chance to participate fully in amateur competitive sports is what is really important. For the long

[14] Statement, U.S. Senate, June 30, 1965.

run, we should be considering the establishment of a national sports body—an amateur sports foundation comparable to those in Canada and the United Kingdom—the basic purpose of which would be to insure that every young man and woman in America does have a chance to participate. Legislative action might be necessary to set up such a body, but once it is set up it should be free from governmental control.[15]

Automobile and Highway Safety

With the publication of Ralph Nader's muckraking best seller, *Unsafe At Any Speed*, Robert Kennedy, like a great many other public figures, began calling for legislation and voluntary industrial controls to reduce our staggering highway fatality rate.

Ironically, our highway death rate for 1965 is 27 times greater than the number of Americans killed in action in Vietnam since 1961.

The rising traffic accident rate reinforces the need for better solutions to our traffic safety problems. With increasing numbers of cars and drivers on our highways, new techniques must be found to reduce the carnage on our highways.

The most amazing aspect of this problem is that we have not fully used our scientific and technological skills to help reduce the highway accident rate. It is incredible that although we have a space technology that permits two Gemini spacecraft to rendezvous within several feet of one another while traveling at speeds of 17,500 miles an hour, we have not developed the techniques for protecting the driver going at average speeds of less than 60 miles an hour. It is our strong belief that we do have the technical expertise to solve our traffic safety problems and dramatically reduce the fatality and accident rate on the highways. But we have not yet made it a national policy to effectively use this know-how.[16]

I am pleased that President Johnson has recommended to Congress a bill designed to strengthen the federal role in high-

[15] Testimony, Senate Commerce Committee, August 26, 1965.
[16] Joint statement with Senator Abraham Ribicoff (D–Conn.), U.S. Senate, December 31, 1965.

way traffic safety. It is fitting recognition of Senator Abraham Ribicoff's efforts to highlight this problem during the hearings of his Subcommittee on the Federal Role in Traffic Safety. I am particularly glad that this bill recommends the construction of a traffic safety research and development laboratory along the lines suggested by Senator Ribicoff and others last year. The research and test program at this laboratory can give the public the facts on the effectiveness of various auto safety devices, highway safety regulations and practices, and the gains that can be made with new safety technology. The traffic accident information program discussed in the message can be highly useful in pinpointing the causes of the thousands of fatalities and millions of injuries resulting from auto accidents each year. Our modern computer technology coupled with easily obtainable accident information should do much to identify the true causes of these accidents. With this information, we will find ways to eliminate some of these causes.[17]

Carrier pilots and astronauts experience shocks much greater than those involved in many fatal collisions. But our automobiles are simply not designed to protect the passengers under these shocks. For although the human body can withstand a tremendous amount of force applied evenly over the surface, it cannot withstand a sharp object applied with only a fraction of this force. A first step to protect automobile riders from these hazards was the introduction of the waist safety belt. This device, first emphasized in a Cornell Aeronautical Laboratory Report of 1956, protects the occupant from some aspect of the second crash. But we can do much more. Metal parts could be recessed inside the car, and instrument panels designed for safety. But they have not been. Nor have passengers been adequately protected against other hazards. Seat belts are no answer to steering columns or even engines that are driven back toward the driver, or to frames that collapse, or brakes that give out. But these hazards too can be avoided. The motor can be mounted so that it is not shoved into the driver's legs during a crash, but is rather pushed down toward the highway. Steering columns can be positioned so that they are not jammed back into the driver's chest. There are brakes that do not give out under heavy use. And

[17] Press release, March 3, 1966.

car frames that do not collapse but gradually absorb collision shock are readily available. In view of this evidence, I think it is clear that the federal government should set minimum safety standards for automobiles just as it now does for planes, ships, and trains. . . .

For each other's sakes, and for the benefit of all our children, we must together set standards for safe automobile manufacture. Safer automobiles will not eliminate all accidents. We know that driver education and licensing systems must be improved; that stronger law enforcement can limit drunken driving; that safer roads can be built. There must be state and local efforts; and they must be pursued with vigor. And even if all these things are done, and cars improved a thousandfold, accidents will still occur. Human beings are fallible. Some people will put their foot on the accelerator when they meant to hit the brake. Others will signal left and turn right—or misjudge a curve—or be momentarily blinded by onrushing headlights. Some will just be careless. But carelessness, in our legal system, should not be punished by death. A momentary lapse in alertness should not result, if we can help it, in bodies smashed and families broken. Still less should another's mistake result in death or injury. But if the driver in the next lane swerves, or if another goes through a red light, there is no way we can avoid a crash. But we can limit, even avoid, much of the death and injury that come from that crash. . . .

It is important most of all as a forthright recognition that the federal government has a major responsibility to act—to curtail the needless death and injury and waste on our highways. For we have come to realize how heavy is the toll we pay to the automobile.[18]

When military commanders want money to improve safety at air bases, they place the boots of dead pilots on the conference table before them. The boots of millions of traffic victims—past and future—are on the table before us. It is time to act.[19]

[18] Statement, Senate Commerce Committee, March 30, 1966.
[19] *Time*, April 8, 1966.

Cigarette Smoking

As his days with the McClellan "Rackets Committee" and as Attorney General revealed, Bobby relished an occasional crusade. His latest expedition was aimed at a reduction in the incidence of cigarette smoking, particularly among the young.

However, his opponents in this joust—the cigarette and broadcasting industries—were not pushovers.

The cigarette industry and the advertising and broadcasting industries which it helps to support, are a powerful block of economic power in this country. But the fact is that they are dealing in a lethal product. I would wager that if the economic power of the cigarette and related industries were as minuscule as that of the marihuana industry, cigarettes would long ago have been prohibited and their sale saddled with severe penalties as a health hazard. Still, cigarettes are a multibillion-dollar industry and we must frame whatever action we take in that practical context. . . .

I am glad to co-sponsor Senator Magnuson's bill again this year. Requiring the disclosure of the tar and nicotine content of cigarettes will, I think, encourage the development of lower tar, lower nicotine cigarettes. And, since the amount of tar in a cigarette is associated with the incidence of cancer, and the amount of nicotine is related to heart disease, encouraging the development of lower tar, lower nicotine cigarettes is a worthwhile endeavor. . . .

I believe we must take significantly greater action to discourage people from smoking at all and especially to discourage young people from starting to smoke.

. . . we simply must begin to regulate cigarette advertising. The advertising and broadcasting industries have, in my judgment, done an unsuccessful job of self-regulation. I believe their respective codes are inadequate. I think it is time the Federal Communications Commission started showing an interest in this matter. There is a strong argument that the FCC has the power, in connection with its power to refuse to renew license, of stations that do not operate in the public interest, to prevent or limit the advertising of products which are harmful to health. It would also appear that the FCC could—

and should—require the acceptance of advertising detailing the hazards of cigarette smoking as a public service under the rubric of the "fairness" doctrine. At the very least, the FCC should begin applying pressure on the broadcasters and the tobacco industry to adopt a more stringent code of self-regulation. Similar action has been effective in keeping hard-liquor advertising off the air. If the FCC has not taken any action by the end of this year, and the cigarette companies and the broadcasters have not taken any further self-regulatory action in the same period, I plan to introduce legislation to mandate an experimental one-year ban on all cigarette advertising on radio and television. I might point out that this is not a drastic step. Great Britain has had exactly such a ban since August 1965, and the figures so far, although still quite tentative, seem to show a steady drop in cigarette consumption since that time.

Finally, I think it would be useful to have a sliding scale tax on cigarettes so that higher taxes are paid for cigarettes which contain more tar and nicotine. This would effectively encourage the development of relatively less harmful cigarettes. I plan to introduce such legislation in the near future.[20]

Something must be done now to control the advertising which encourages young people to start smoking at the rate of 1,500,000 a year. In my judgment, industry self-regulation of advertising has been totally inadequate. Therefore, today I am introducing two bills relating to cigarette advertising. The first —and this is the bill on which Senator Moss has joined with Senator Randolph and me—would require a warning in all advertising—"Warning: Cigarette Smoking Is Dangerous to Health and May Cause Death from Cancer and Other Diseases." . . .

The second bill I am introducing today would authorize the Federal Communications Commission to regulate cigarette advertising in three additional ways. First, the FCC would be allowed to determine the times at which cigarette advertising might appear. The National Congress of PTA recently resolved that advertising be discontinued before 9 P.M. That would seem to be a sensible beginning. Second, this bill would authorize the FCC to determine the kinds of programs on

[20] Press release, May 17, 1967.

which cigarette advertising might appear. Sporting events, for example, have a sizable audience of young people and the FCC may deem it necessary to prohibit cigarette advertising on such programs. Third, the FCC would have the power to set the over-all volume of cigarette advertising.[21]

[21] Speech, U.S. Senate, September 12, 1967.

Chapter 9

Civil Liberties: McCarthyism to Student Dissent

I told [Senator Joseph] McCarthy that I disagreed with the way the committee was being run, except for the work that Flanagan had done, and that the way they were proceeding I thought it was headed for disaster. . . .

I told him I thought he was out of his mind and was going to destroy himself. He disliked Schine and said he was going to get rid of him. He asked me to stay on for a month. But I said I would have to resign. But he kept me on the payroll for a month.[1]

MR. RESTON: During the last session of Congress you introduced what was widely regarded as a very tough wire-tapping bill. What was the theory in your mind at that time, and why do you think this was rejected by the Congress?

RFK: It hasn't been rejected by the Congress.

MR. RESTON: It never got out of Committee, did it?

RFK: No, but it hasn't been rejected yet. It hasn't been voted on.

We feel that in the field of espionage, in the field of some areas of organized crime, that there is a growing problem. We are having a more and more difficult time fighting it. We have suggested and recommended that with the approval of a court, approval of a judge, in cases of espionage, which is much more active now than it has ever been in the history of the United States —the Communist espionage here in this country, run and operated by representatives of bloc countries, is much more active now than it has ever been, much more active now, for instance, than it was five or ten

[1] R. E. Thompson and H. Meyers, *Robert F. Kennedy: The Brother Within* (New York: Macmillan, 1962), pp. 111-112.

years ago. We need the weapons in order to deal with that, to be able to present this evidence in court, so we have asked that with the permission of the court we should have the right to put wire taps on—also in the field of kidnaping, where kidnaping takes place. So it is not a very wide or broad bill that we have suggested or recommended. It is restricted in these areas, where we think it is particularly needed.[2]

Civil liberties was the issue that continued to hamper Robert Kennedy most in his campaign to capture the liberal wing of the Democratic party. Even his enthusiastic liberal supporters, who applauded his stand against the Vietnam war and his calls for accelerated efforts to meet the urban crisis, cringed and grew silent when his ties with Joe McCarthy were recalled. Many who found themselves in basic agreement with the Senator on most issues, but who were sensitive to questions of civil liberties, were kept aloof and uncertain by their memories of his early views on wiretapping and his alleged abuse of witnesses invoking the Fifth Amendment before the McClellan "Rackets Committee."

Many of the events and statements that earned Kennedy the reproof of civil libertarians occurred a decade or more ago. Politically, the hardest to live down was his brief association with the Senate Government Operations Permanent Investigations Subcommittee, chaired from 1952 to 1954 by Senator McCarthy.

Joseph McCarthy and RFK

After graduation from the University of Virginia Law School and a short stay in the Criminal Division of the Justice Department, Kennedy joined the McCarthy Subcommittee in January 1953. Apparently his eagerness to uncover corruption and Communist subversion left him impervious to his brother John's prophetic counsel that a close association with the Wisconsin Senator might return to haunt Bobby someday.

[2] "Meet the Press" (NBC-TV), September 24, 1961.

Working at first under the respected general counsel of the subcommittee, Francis Flanagan, Kennedy conducted an investigation of Allied trade with Red China during the Korean War. At no time was he involved in anything that might be distinctly labeled as "McCarthyism." In June of the same year, McCarthy kicked Flanagan upstairs to the full committee and placed Roy Cohn in charge of the entire staff. The Democratic senators on the subcommittee walked out in protest, and a month later Kennedy resigned.

Whether he quit out of disgust with McCarthy's objectives and tactics or as a result of his strong personal dislike of Cohn and his side-kick Schine is not clear from his statements at the time. His feelings about McCarthy were definitely mixed. Remembering his first meeting in 1951 with the controversial Senator on the University of Virginia campus, Kennedy said:

I liked him almost immediately. . . . He was always so nice to me. I never had any personal disputes with him.[3]

He emphasized McCarthy's complexity:

I liked him and yet at times he was terribly heavy-handed. He was a very complicated character. His whole method of operation was complicated because he would get a guilty feeling and get hurt after he had blasted somebody. He wanted so desperately to be liked. He was so thoughtful and yet so unthoughtful in what he did to others. He was sensitive and yet insensitive. He didn't anticipate the results of what he was doing. He was very thoughtful of his friends, and yet he could be so cruel to others.[4]

Of the subcommittee and his own brief stay:

He said he wanted to reconstruct the committee, to go into all kinds of investigations—communism and elsewhere. He wanted to find people who could help him do a good job.[5]

[3] Thompson and Meyers, *op. cit.*, p. 100.
[4] *Ibid.*, p. 121.
[5] *Ibid.*, p. 106.

In his first book, Kennedy attempted to clarify exactly what happened during that controversial part of his career.

I was an assistant counsel to the Senate Permanent Sub-committee on Investigations when Senator McCarthy was its chairman. I lasted only six months. With two exceptions, no real research was ever done. Most of the investigations were instituted on the basis of some preconceived notion by the chief counsel or his staff members and not on the basis of any information that had been developed. Cohn and Schine claimed they knew from the outset what was wrong; and they were not going to allow the facts to interfere. Therefore no real spade work that might have destroyed some of their pet theories was ever undertaken. I thought Senator McCarthy made a mistake in allowing the committee to operate in such a fashion, told him so and resigned.[6]

He got so involved with all the publicity—and after that it was the number one thing in his life. He was on a toboggan. It was so exciting and exhilarating as he went downhill that it didn't matter to him if he hit a tree at the bottom.
Cohn and Schine took him up the mountain and showed him all those wonderful things. He destroyed himself for that —for publicity. He had to get his name in the paper. I felt sorry for him, particularly in the last year, when he was such a beaten, destroyed person—particularly since many of his so-called friends, realizing he was finished, ran away from him and left him with virtually no one.[7]

He found time to praise McCarthy as one of the few congressional committee chairmen who fully supported and protected the members of his staff.

The record will show that, aside from Senator McCarthy— one of whose greatest mistakes was that he was loyal beyond reason to Roy Cohn and G. David Schine—Congressional committee members as a rule have been unwilling to stand up

[6] Robert F. Kennedy, *The Enemy Within* (New York: Harper & Brothers, 1960), p. 307.
[7] Thompson and Meyers, *op. cit.*, pp. 120-121.

and be counted on behalf of a staff member who meets with difficulties.[8]

Yet Kennedy claimed that had he sat in the Senate in 1954, he would have been forced to vote to censure McCarthy.

I thought he had brought the Senate and the United States into disrepute by his operation of the committee. The whole operation of Cohn and Schine was the core of it. To censure him for not appearing before a committee [the Privileges and Elections Committee chaired by Senator Watkins] prior to his re-election or because of what he said about other senators [on the Watkins Committee] was not so significant.[9]

As William Shannon reported in *The Heir Apparent,* Kennedy maintained a warm personal relationship with the Senator even after his censure.

Kennedy remained on friendly terms with McCarthy, whom he regarded as more sinned against than sinning. When the Junior Chamber of Commerce chose Kennedy as one of the nation's "ten outstanding young men," he stayed out of the banquet hall during the main address by Edward R. Murrow because the speech was critical of McCarthy. In McCarthy's last months, when he continued to drink despite a serious liver ailment, Kennedy was one of those who visited him and tried to sustain his morale. At McCarthy's death in 1957, Kennedy not only attended the funeral Mass in Washington but also flew to Appleton, Wisconsin, for the interment.[10]

Six months after his resignation from the McCarthy staff, Kennedy returned to the Permanent Subcommittee, this time as counsel to the Democratic minority (the position he held during the Army-McCarthy hearings [1954], when occasionally he was caught by the TV camera, a grave boyish figure seated behind Senators

[8] Kennedy, *op. cit.,* p. 172.

[9] Thompson and Meyers, *op. cit.,* pp. 121-122.

[10] William V. Shannon, *The Heir Apparent* (New York: Macmillan, 1967), p. 57.

Symington and Jackson). When the Democrats assumed control of the Eighty-fourth Congress in January 1955, Bobby was elevated to chief counsel and staff director and Senator John McClellan replaced McCarthy as sub-committee chairman.

Counsel to the McClellan "Rackets Committee"

In 1957, when jurisdictional problems arose because of the subcommittee's preliminary investigations of labor racketeering, the Senate set up a Select Committee on Improper Activities in the Labor and Management Fields to carry out the labor investigation. McClellan was appointed chairman of the Select Committee and Kennedy served as counsel. It was in this capacity that he became involved in his second major row with civil libertarians.

The Select Committee's investigation centered on corruption and hoodlumism within the leadership of the powerful Brotherhood of Teamsters.

In his efforts to secure enough information to implicate Teamster president Dave Beck and his successor James Hoffa with the violence and racketeering that characterized the union's operations in many areas of the country, Kennedy often became tough and abusive with the witnesses he called to testify. The incessant invocation of the Fifth Amendment by many Teamster officials and known gangsters connected with the union particularly angered and frustrated him.

Finally, the American Civil Liberties Union began to protest that he frequently was not zealous enough in protecting the rights of witnesses. Exchanges before the committee were cited like the following one with Joey Glimco, president of a Chicago Teamster local:

KENNEDY: And you defraud the union?
GLIMCO: I respectfully decline to answer because I honestly believe my answer might tend to incriminate me.
KENNEDY: I would agree with you.
MCCLELLAN: I believe it would.
KENNEDY: You haven't got the guts to [answer], have you, Mr. Glimco?

GLIMCO: I respectfully decline . . .

MCCLELLAN: Morally you are kind of yellow inside, are you not? That is the truth about it?

GLIMCO: I respectfully decline . . .[11]

Kennedy Witnesses and the Fifth Amendment

Some of Kennedy's statements during the late "fifties" and early "sixties" suggested that perhaps he accepted the Fifth Amendment, but with certain qualifications.

It has been said that one should not reach any conclusion about the guilt or innocence of a person claiming the Fifth Amendment. In a legal sense, I would agree. But certainly, if testimony is given that a man has violated his trust, misappropriated union funds or made a pay-off to a union official, and he then appears before the committee and refuses to answer on the grounds of self-incrimination, it is less than human not to reach some conclusion. At the least, the witness's employer or colleagues should begin an immediate investigation into his affairs to determine his fitness to hold his position. Furthermore, although the Fifth Amendment is for the innocent as well as the guilty, I can think of very few witnesses who availed themselves of it who in my estimation were free of wrongdoing. I know of several who took the Fifth Amendment out of fear, but aside from them, for whom I felt immensely sorry, I know of none whom I should like to work for or have work for me—or have anything at all to do with.[12]

Angered by Dave Beck's refusal to testify fully before the Committee in 1954, Kennedy argued:

There's a big difference between a petty crook who takes the Fifth Amendment to protect himself and a man like Dave Beck. Both certainly have a right to, but because of his responsibility to a million and a half Teamsters and to sixteen

[11] Nick Thimmisch and William Johnson, *R. F. K. at 40* (Boston: W. W. Norton, 1965), p. 71.

[12] Kennedy, *op. cit.*, p. 317.

million people in organized labor, Beck, I believe, has an obligation higher than just to himself and should answer whatever questions are asked him about his operation of the union.[13]

As concern mounted over Kennedy's mode of operation—he was being labeled a "ruthless inquisitor" with no sense of fundamental individual liberties—he moved to defend himself and the committee. Seeking to set the record straight about his support of the Fifth Amendment, he wrote:

Unquestionably the Fifth Amendment has been misused and, on occasion, abused. Hoffa turned it on and off for his subordinates as he felt it would help him. However, I would not have it changed. It is an important safeguard written into the Bill of Rights of our Constitution at the insistence of James Mason of Virginia. It grew out of the abuses practiced in the Star Chamber days in the reign of the Stuarts, and it is one of the rights that a free people possess against the potential abuses of government. It is part of our heritage, and should not be abandoned. No dictatorships recognize it, and we certainly cannot pay too high a price to protect ourselves from statism of that type. The Fifth Amendment does make the work of law enforcement, grand juries and congressional committees more difficult, but it does not prevent them from accomplishing their objectives. And after all, it is not the Fifth Amendment that is causing the graft and corruption in the country, or even preventing it from being cleaned up.[14]

He discussed the responsibilities of a congressional committee:

I think, therefore, that a congressional committee must, to a considerable degree, take responsibility for the testimony of its witnesses. You cannot put a man or woman on the stand, allow him to hurl accusations indiscriminately and, when his testimony is found to be untrue, disown him and accept no responsibility. . . .

[13] Thimmisch and Johnson, *op. cit.*, p. 72.
[14] Kennedy, *op. cit.*, p. 316.

However, the most important advantage of checking and rechecking testimony is that it lessens tremendously the possibility of damaging an innocent person's reputation. A prospective witness who intended to make a charge against another person had his story checked from every possible angle. On quite a number of occasions, after checking, we did not permit him to testify. More than once a witness who had information that was easily documented also offered other information that we could not corroborate. If we could prove the truth of a major portion of his testimony, we would, in most instances, permit him to testify about anything within his knowledge. However, if the uncorroborated part could not be supported and was not in context with his other testimony and was of a damaging nature, we could ask him not to go into it. If he did not agree, we would not permit him to testify.[15]

However, these disclaimers of his reputed disregard for the rights and privacy of witnesses and those about whom they testified did little to placate the critics.

Wiretapping

In 1959 Kennedy left the Select Committee to manage his brother's presidential campaign. A little over a year later he was appointed Attorney General, the youngest man to fill the position since 1814, and almost immediately became embroiled in yet another civil liberties controversy, this time over the use of wiretapping.

Like most of the attorney generals who preceded him, Kennedy favored the virtually unrestricted use of wiretapping and electronic "bugging" devices because they are effective for gathering information about underworld operations. And as Shannon points out, "Kennedy's zeal to break up the crime syndicates was reminiscent of a sixteenth-century Jesuit on the hunt for a heresy. . . ."

In his third book, Kennedy defended the need for legislation to enable law-enforcement officials to make broader use of wiretapping.

[15] *Ibid.*, pp. 304-305.

Finally, if we are to make maximum progress in our drive on organized crime, I am convinced that we need legislation to permit the use of wiretapping by law-enforcement officials. The urgency for revision of present and ineffective provisions of the wiretapping statute is emphasized by the fact that the latest electronic improvements are easily available to the criminal. The advantages these can give him over law-enforcement officers are plain. Leading racketeers make almost unrestricted use of interstate facilities, particularly communications, to direct their illegal activities.

Here lies the anomaly: the present statute fails to protect the right of privacy over the telephone, because anyone can *listen in* without violating that statute. At present, to convict someone of illegal wiretapping, we must prove not only that a tap was made, but also that there was unlawful disclosure of the conversation. At the same time, disclosure *by federal officers* of evidence gained from wiretapping violates federal law.[16]

Commenting on a rackets probe by New York District Attorney Frank Hogan, which the latter was forced to abandon due to existing limits on the use of evidence obtained by wiretapping, Kennedy remarked:

In other words, the men could not be prosecuted because of the present federal wiretapping statute, which should permit reasonable use of wiretapping by responsible officials in their fight against crime, but does not.

Thus the present law neither prevents indiscriminate wiretapping nor recognizes the legitimate needs of law enforcement for authority, closely circumscribed, to use this means of gathering evidence.

In 1963 the Department of Justice resubmitted to Congress a carefully worded bill, S. 1308, with strong procedural safeguards, which would afford a clear-cut basis for the legitimate and controlled use of wiretapping by law-enforcement officials. At the same time, the bill would expressly forbid all other types of wiretapping. Section 5(b) of this bill empowers the Attorney General, or an Assistant Attorney General, to au-

[16] Robert F. Kennedy, *The Pursuit of Justice* (New York: Harper & Row, 1965), pp. 54-55.

thorize application to a federal judge for a wiretap order. The section empowers the judge to issue an order permitting wiretapping in cases involving national security, murder, kidnaping and racketeering cases.[17]

But as groups like the American Civil Liberties Union and certain liberal politicians became increasingly vocal in their opposition to legislation to extend the use of wiretapping of any sort, Kennedy began to back down from his initial position.

Early in 1961, the Department of Justice was asked for its views on pending wiretap legislation. At that time I supported a bill which would have permitted state and local law-enforcement agencies to tap wires in any way permitted by state law. It would have permitted agencies of the federal government to tap wires under court order any time that they could show reasonable grounds to believe that the tap could be used for evidence in a criminal case. The bill which we mistakenly supported was introduced by Senator Keating.

I have always been opposed to wiretapping except under the most confined circumstances and pursuant to court order. And so I asked lawyers in the Department of Justice to review the problem with me and to draft legislation which would preserve the principles of privacy and due process. I realized that the Keating bill was far too broad and had far too little in the way of safeguards.

The Department of Justice offered such a bill in 1962. Those who are opposed to all wiretapping under all circumstances— and I am not unsympathetic to their view—continue to oppose this legislation. But it was supported by former Attorney General Francis Biddle and by *The New Republic. The New York Times* called this bill the best drafted and most responsible legislation ever offered in this field.[18]

Kennedy also tried to disengage himself from the widespread use of electronic eavesdropping by the FBI during his tenure as Attorney General. This led to a

[17] *Ibid.*, p. 56.
[18] Speech, Ansonia Independent Democratic Club, New York, N.Y., October 8, 1964.

somewhat disgraceful public exchange between him and J. Edgar Hoover in late 1966 in which each saddled the other with the full responsibility for authorizing all eavesdropping activity. Hoover claimed that he never did anything along this line without the explicit approval of Kennedy, and dismissed Kennedy's reply that he had known nothing about FBI "bugging" practices as "inconceivable." The Senator countered:

It may seem "inconceivable" to Mr. Hoover that I was not aware of the "bugging" practices of the FBI during my term as Attorney General, but it is nonetheless true. Perhaps I should have known, and since I was the Attorney General I certainly take the responsibility for it, but the plain fact of the matter is that I did not know. I believe that this will be confirmed by every Deputy Attorney General, Assistant Attorney General and the head of the Organized Crime Division during my administration of the Department of Justice. The first time I became aware of these eavesdropping practices, was when they were described in the press in connection with the Las Vegas investigation, and I promptly ordered it ceased. It is curious that Mr. Hoover does not recall this. Although Mr. Hoover says that this activity was "intensified" while I was Attorney General, and implies that we discussed it, the fact is that he never discussed this highly important matter with me, and no evidence exists supporting his recollection that we did. Indeed, there is no indication that Mr. Hoover ever asked me for authorization for any single bugging device, in Las Vegas, New York, Washington, or anywhere else.[19]

Over the past decade Kennedy addressed himself to other issues related to civil liberties. Here is a selection of some of his more interesting statements arranged by topic:

Civil Liberties and the Law

The law has played a great role in the development of American society. In the law, in our constitutions and statutes

[19] Statement, U.S. Senate, December 11, 1966.

and decisions, we have deposited our most cherished freedoms. To its protection we have committed the delicate balances upon which society rests—the tension between free speech and public order, between the rights of individuals and the rights of the group, between the right to worship and the right not to have others say how we shall worship. We decide whether a man goes free or is deprived of his liberty—by law. We decide whether a man shall be punished, and in what way—by law. But we do not always do so by reason. For there are other kinds of law than that of which Lord Coke spoke. One is the law that is a set of rules, old and unchanging —their purpose forgotten, their reason lost—which we yet observe, like the ancient rituals of a lost tribe. Justice Holmes called it "revolting" to have no better reason for a rule of law than that it was laid down in the time of Henry the Fourth. We still have some such rules. Another kind of law is the law of poverty—the law that sentences men at birth to a life of imprisonment in ignorance, in helplessness, in fear; the law of poverty and the law that is outworn too often operate together to negate the law of reason.[20]

Equality of justice in our courts should never depend upon the defendant's wealth or lack of resources, but in all honesty we must admit that we have failed frequently to avoid such a result.

It was not until March of 1963, with the Supreme Court's decision in *Gideon v. Wainwright*, that the poor man's right to appointed legal counsel was held to be applicable to all courts in the land, at the state as well as the federal level. I think the story of the Gideon case gives us a profound insight into the nature of our judicial system at its best, and into the basic sense of human justice on which it is founded. . . .

But in general practice the problem remains: the rich man and the poor man do not receive equal justice in our courts.[21]

Senator Goldwater said the other day in St. Petersburg, Florida, that the Court's decisions on criminal law were pampering criminals. He promised to try, if elected, to overturn

[20] Address, Governor's Conference on Bail and the Right to Counsel, Louisville, Ky., January 22, 1965.

[21] Kennedy, *op. cit.*, pp. 95-96.

some of those decisions. The one he particularly criticized was the Court's ruling in 1961 that illegally seized evidence may not be used in state criminal trials.

That case involved a lady in Ohio, a Miss Mapp. One day the police walked into her house and said they were going to search it for evidence of crime. They had no warrant. When Miss Mapp protested, they handcuffed her to the banister in her own house and proceeded to ransack it from cellar to attic.

The Supreme Court held that the material gained in that illegal search could not be used against Miss Mapp. The Court did so because years of experience had shown that there was no effective way of discouraging such searches except to suppress their fruits.

Can anyone reasonably argue that the Supreme Court was destroying our liberties when it protected Miss Mapp—and all of us—from that misuse of official authority? Surely not. Surely we can all feel safer in our homes because the Supreme Court is there to provide that kind of protection. Louis Brandeis wrote in 1890 of the right to be left alone. He called it one of the most important rights in civilized society.

Of course, crime is a serious problem in this country. We do need greater dedication to law and order. But the way to achieve that end is not to make the courts approve illegal actions by the government. Official lawlessness does not make the people law-abiding. On the contrary, it encourages disrespect for law. The end does not justify the means in law enforcement. That is the way of the third degree and other practices defended on the ground that anything goes in the name of fighting crime. The Supreme Court has fortunately rejected that view.[22]

Dissent and Free Speech

Discussion and dissent, the quest for truth and the need for reason—these matters are particularly relevant as I speak to you tonight.

We in the Senate are even now engaged in consideration

[22] Speech, Free Synagogue of Westchester County, Mt. Vernon, N.Y., September 20, 1964.

of an issue which has caused some to suggest that there are limits on our traditional freedom to discuss and debate as a nation. I speak, of course, of the war in Vietnam. This is not the first time we have debated the issue of free discussion in crisis. Abraham Lincoln was reviled for opposing the war of 1848. The citizens of his own state called Daniel Webster traitor for proposing a compromise to avoid civil war. Those who saw the storm, and tried desperately to prepare the nation for World War II, were cursed as warmongers, enemies of mankind, subverters of democracy—and worse. Of course, there *are* hazards in debating American policy in the face of a stern and dangerous enemy. But those hazards are the essence of our democracy. Full and informing debate is the basis of our system. We take the chance of freedom because we believe reasoned argument can move us to reasoned action. That is why we have always believed the right to dissent to be so fundamental to our system.[23]

As for me I am glad of Berkeley, and I am glad to be here with you. For I am sympathetic, and I welcome, the passionate concern with the condition and future of the American nation, which can be found on this campus.

The future does not belong to those who are content with today, apathetic toward common problems and their fellow man alike, timid and fearful in the face of new ideas and bold projects. . . . It will belong to those who see that wisdom can only emerge from the clash of contending views, the passionate expression of deep and hostile beliefs. Plato said: "A life without criticism is not worth living."

This is the seminal spirit of American democracy. It is this spirit which can be found among many of you. It is this which is the hope of our nation.

For it is not enough to allow dissent. We must demand it. For there is much to dissent from.

We dissent from the fact that millions are trapped in poverty while the nation grows rich.

We dissent from the conditions and hatreds which deny a full life to our fellow citizens because of the color of their skin.

We dissent from the monstrous absurdity of a world where

[23] Address, Jewish Theological Seminary of America, Hollywood, Fla., February 28, 1966.

nations stand poised to destroy one another, and men must kill their fellow man.

We dissent from the sight of most of mankind living in poverty, stricken by disease, threatened by hunger and doomed to an early death after a life of unremitting labor.

We dissent from the willful, heedless destruction of natural pleasure and beauty.

We dissent from all those structures—of technology and of society itself—which strip from the individual the dignity and warmth of sharing in the common tasks of his community and his country.

These are among the objects of our dissent. Yet we must, as thinking men, distinguish between the right of dissent and the way we choose to exercise that right. It is not enough to justify or explain our actions by the fact that they are legal or constitutionally protected. The Constitution protects wisdom and ignorance, compassion and selfishness alike. But that dissent which consists simply of sporadic and dramatic acts sustained by neither continuing labor nor research—that dissent which seeks to demolish while lacking both the desire and direction for rebuilding, that dissent which contemptuously or out of laziness casts aside the practical weapons and instruments of change and progress—that kind of dissent is merely self-indulgence. It is satisfying, perhaps, to those who make it.

But it will not solve the problems of our society. It will not assist those seriously engaged in the difficult and frustrating work of the nation. And when it is all over, it will not have brightened or enriched the life of a single portion of humanity in a single part of the globe.[24]

The Berkeley students of the Free Speech movement made a contribution to academic freedom, and helped also to remind universities all over the country that schools are for teaching.

But when a few students turned Free Speech into the scrawling of dirty words on placards, they discredited not only themselves, but the initial protest.[25]

[24] Speech, University of California at Berkeley, Calif., October 22, 1966.
[25] Address, Queens College commencement exercises, Queens, N.Y., June 15, 1965.

Turning first to communication: if our Constitution had followed the style of St. Paul, the First Amendment might have concluded—"But the greatest of these is speech." In the darkness of tyranny, this is the key to the sunlight. If it is granted, all doors open. If it is withheld, none. But a truth unheard is as much a social force as a tree falling in the lonely forest is sound. *Truly* free speech implies a guarantee of the right to listen. . . .[26]

Cities of millions are not New England villages, and probably less than 1 percent of our population has ever taken part in a town meeting.

The sense of face-to-face community, the marketplace in which Greek democracy flourished, the forum of Rome—all these are seen as history, irrelevant to our present concerns.

But the sit-ins and the teach-ins, the summer projects, the civil rights vigils and civil liberties protests, organizing the poor and marching on Washington—all these may be helping to return us to a politics of public participation—where individual citizens, without holding political office, may still contribute to the public dialogue—where they do something more than write letters to the newspapers or answer yes or no on a public opinion poll.

If the forms of action we have seen on our campuses can help to bridge the difference between government and its citizens, you of this generation will have made a major contribution to all of us.[27]

On my recommendation, President Kennedy vetoed a bill which would have permitted the Washington police to seize printed material on the ground that it was "obscene" without prior hearing on the issue of obscenity.[28]

If there is a racial incident in any corner of the United

[26] Speech, Tenth Anniversary Convocation of the Center for Study of Democratic Institutions of the Fund for the Republic, New York, N.Y., January 22, 1963.

[27] Address, Queens College commencement exercises, Queens, N.Y., June 15, 1965.

[28] Speech, Ansonia Independent Democratic Club, New York, N.Y., October 8, 1964.

States, within hours it is flashed around the world. The Communists seize upon it for their propaganda mill.

We don't hear of the East Europeans who are daily whisked to jails for seeking only a fraction of the freedom we enjoy.

But we would not have it any other way. Our newspapers must be free to report every facet of American life for this is not only a freedom guaranteed to them but a guarantee of freedom for all Americans.

With liberty for the press, as with all liberties, comes responsibility. Newspapers occupy a position of trust to the public to report to them all the news—not just that which they wish to read or that which an editor thinks they should read.[29]

I do not believe that newspapermen are self-appointed judges of what's right or wrong, or what's good or bad. But I believe in and greatly admire those who are competent to seek the truth and inform the people. In my opinion, the newspapers are equal to the courts—and sometimes ahead of the courts—in our system—in protecting the people's fundamental rights.[30]

However, your success is not measured by complete understanding between press and government. That is not possible, and it is probably not desirable. Nor is it found in the particular laws or policies you can influence. Yours is a more spacious and majestic part than that. In our wise and elaborate constitutional structure of checks and balances, the press is a check on government itself; giving content and meaning and force to that popular judgment and will which is the soul and design of democracy. Your obligation is not in your relationship to government but to the people; never confusing the nation with those who are its temporary leaders; serving ideas and purposes rather than men. Those of us in public life often call upon the press to be more understanding, sometimes with justice. But we also know that the day you are unanimously joined in praise of officials or policies, when

[29] Speech, National Newspaper Publishers Association Convention, Morgan State College, Baltimore, Md., June 22, 1962.

[30] Speech, Annual Luncheon of the Associated Press, New York, N.Y., April 23, 1962.

power is held in awe and skepticism disappears—on that day democracy will begin to wither.[31]

Loyalty Oaths

We are today reintroducing in the Senate a bill to repeal the loyalty oath provisions of the National Defense Education Act. This bill was originally introduced in 1959, with the then Senator John F. Kennedy as its principal sponsor, and Senator Joseph S. Clark as co-sponsor.

This bill would wipe off the statute books the requirement that recipients of student loans under the NDEA program swear or affirm allegiance to the United States and disclose criminal convictions for any offense greater than a minor traffic violation. It would also strike out a provision making it a crime for any person who belongs to an organization which has registered or been ordered to register under the Subversive Activities Control Act to apply for a student loan or other aid under NDEA.

The elimination of these provisions is long overdue. They are meaningless as a weapon against subversion; they gratuitously impugn the loyalty and integrity of our young men and women. Other government programs of grants and loans to individuals such as the Small Business Administration loan program, and the Soil Conservation and Rural Housing programs have no loyalty oath requirement. We are willing to assume the loyalty of our businessmen and farmers. We should be willing to do so for our youth.

In addition, it seems particularly unfair to us to require an affirmation of loyalty from the student whose financial circumstances force him to seek aid from the federal government, while no such requirement is made of his more affluent classmate who can pay his own way. Not only is this illogical, but it has the effect of degrading the recipient of federal assistance into a kind of second-class citizenship.

Loyalty oaths are particularly inapposite as a condition for receiving a college education. What most clearly distinguishes the universities of the free world from their Communist counterparts is our insistence that the university—and its

[31] Address, American Society of Newspaper Editors, Washington, D.C., April 22, 1967.

students—be free. Ideological tests and oaths have no place in this great tradition.[32]

Separation of Church and State

Finally, New York will have—for the first time—full separation of church and state in all areas. This constitution embodies the language of the federal First Amendment—which bars unconstitutional direct aid to religious schools. That is the position I take now. With this stringent protection of the federal First Amendment, and the right of any citizen to sue against invalid state acts, we will have the same protection that has kept church and state separate in America for one hundred years.[33]

QUESTION: How do you feel about the school prayer decision?
RFK: Well, I think it would have been better for those in political life if it hadn't happened. (Laughter.) But I think that if I were on the Supreme Court and that case had come to me I would have reached the same decision as they had reached, and it seems to me the answer now is for those who want to pray in school to do so quietly. (Laughter and applause.) [34]

The Attorney General's List of Subversive Organizations

QUESTION: General, there is an outstanding so-called Attorney General's list of subversive organizations which is admittedly meaningless because it has not been revised in five and a half years. Are you going to continue that list?
RFK: Well, I would say that there are problems, legal problems, in connection with any additions that might be made to that list. We have had some conferences and conversations and discussions about that, and there has not been a final determination as of yet.[35]

[32] Press release, June 10, 1965.
[33] Address, Rochester, N.Y., October 25, 1967.
[34] Speech, West Georgia College, Carrollton, Ga., May 26, 1964.
[35] Press conference, U.S. Department of Justice, April 6, 1961.

Right of Foreign Travel

I do not believe our national security gains—and I am sure that our national freedom loses—when we restrict the right to travel freely. I recall in this connection a bill introduced by Senator Keating in 1958 which would have permitted the Secretary of State to have denied passports to members of the Communist party and to others whose travel abroad is determined, by administrative fiat, to be inimical to the national interest. This bill, in my judgment, was unconstitutional. It was rejected as ill-considered and hasty by the Chairman of the House Foreign Affairs Committee. During my tenure as Attorney General I successfully opposed such bills. . . . I do know that I would restrict travel only in rare cases compelled by the most pressing national security needs, such as the prevention of espionage.[36]

House Un-American Activities Committee

QUESTION: Do you feel that the House Un-American Activities Committee is doing a good job in its effort to uproot Communists and Communist sympathizers and Communist activities?

RFK: Well, I think that this is primarily a matter for the Federal Bureau of Investigation. I think that on occasions they have made a contribution also.

QUESTION: Do you find any area where you disagree with the operation or the function or the method of functioning of the House Un-American Activities Committee?

RFK: Well, that is a legislative committee and they can proceed under the setup established by the Congress. That is outside of the executive branch of the government.[37]

KEY KENNEDY VOTE ON CIVIL LIBERTIES

School Prayer (S J Res 144). Proposed constitutional amendment to permit voluntary prayer in public schools (a substi-

[36] Speech, Ansonia Independent Democratic Club, New York, N.Y., October 8, 1964.

[37] Press conference, U.S. Court House, Columbia, S.C., December 12, 1961.

tute for a bill to designate a National UNICEF Day).
Accepted 51-36, September 21, 1966. (D 24-33; R 27-3.)
Kennedy: AGAINST.

Chapter 10

Crime and Law Enforcement

> The point I want to make is this: If we do not on a national scale attack organized criminals with weapons and techniques as effective as their own, they will destroy us.[1]

Crime prevention and control was the area of government responsibility in which Robert Kennedy possessed the most experience and expertise. Twelve of his sixteen years of public service were devoted to the investigation and prosecution of persons engaged in illegal activities.

Organized Crime

Kennedy's principal focus throughout this period was organized crime, though the unorganized variety—"crime in the streets"—has occasioned much greater public attention and indignation. He believed strongly that the powerful crime syndicates in this country pose a real threat to our efforts to maintain a healthy society, with institutions capable of commanding the public's trust. The quotations that follow represent his view of the nature and scope of organized crime in America:

In too many major communities of our country, organized crime has become big business. It knows no state lines. It drains off millions of dollars of our national wealth, infecting legitimate businesses, labor unions and even sports. Tolerating

[1] Robert F. Kennedy, *The Enemy Within* (New York: Harper & Brothers, 1960), p. 265.

organized crime promotes the cheap philosophy that everything is a racket. It promotes cynicism among adults. It contributes to the confusion of the young and to the increase of
juvenile delinquency.

It is not the gangster himself who is of concern. It is what
he is doing to our cities, our communities, our moral fiber.
Ninety percent of the major racketeers would be out of business by the end of this year if the ordinary citizen, the
businessman, the union official and the public authority
stood up to be counted and refused to be corrupted.

This is a problem for all America, not just the FBI or the
Department of Justice. Unless the basic attitude changes
here in this country, the rackets will prosper and grow. Of
this I am convinced.[2]

The picture is an ugly one. It shows what has been aptly
described as a private government of organized crime, a
government with an annual income of billions, resting on a
base of human suffering and moral corrosion.[3]

QUESTION: Do you feel that organized gambling is the biggest
crime problem that we have in this country?
RFK: That finances most all the other operations.
QUESTION: What would come after organized gambling, in
your opinion?
RFK: Well, I think there are a number that—there are a
number that are linked closely: Narcotics, prostitution, illegal
liquor—are all three major areas that are of concern, and
throughout all of this is the effort, and it is successful in many
cases, of infiltrating into legitimate businesses and into some
labor organizations.[4]

The financial cost of organized crime is not limited to the
vast illicit profits of gambling or narcotics. When racketeers
bore their way into legitimate business, the cost is borne by
the public.

When the infiltration is into labor relations, the racketeer's

[2] Speech, Law Day exercises, University of Georgia Law School,
Athens, Ga., May 6, 1961.

[3] Robert F. Kennedy, *The Pursuit of Justice* (New York: Harper
& Row, 1965), pp. 42-43.

[4] Press conference, Dallas, Tex., November 15, 1961.

cut is paid by higher wages and higher prices—in other words, by the public.

When the racketeer bribes local officials and secures immunity from police action, the price exacted by corrupt law enforcement, incalculable in dollars, is paid, again, by the public.[5]

The results of the underworld infiltration into labor-management affairs form a shocking pattern across the country. We found and duly proved that the gangsters of today work in a highly organized fashion and are far more powerful now than at any time in the history of the country. They control political figures and threaten whole communities. They have stretched their tentacles of corruption and fear into industries both large and small. They grow stronger every day.[6]

QUESTION: Do you think gambling and other organized criminal activities can exist successfully without connivance and collusion with public officials and police officials?
RFK: If it takes place on a major scale, there has to be some corruption.[7]

QUESTION: Do you recognize the Mafia as one of the big factors in organized crime?
RFK: I never get into the terms of it. The crime is organized on a local basis. Everybody has their own name for it. I don't think so. I don't believe that.[8]

But when asked three years later why anyone would want to kidnap the gangster known as Joe Bananas, he was no longer so certain there was not a national crime organization of some sort.

There are conflicts that are going on within the higher operation of the underworld and there is a commission that runs the organized crime across the United States, and con-

[5] Kennedy, *op. cit.*, p. 57.
[6] Kennedy, *The Enemy Within*, p. 240.
[7] Press conference, U.S. Attorney's Office, Boston, Mass., November 27, 1961.
[8] Press conference, Dallas, Tex., November 15, 1961.

flicts that break out, and there continuously are gangland kill-
ings of this kind. I suppose there must have been more than
100 last year alone.[9]

He mused over the difficulties of combating the big
crime syndicates.

QUESTION: Do you think—talking on the gambling, do you
think that perhaps you might eliminate the corruption involved with gambling by legalizing gambling?
RFK: Well, that's up to someone other than myself. Obviously
if it's legalized, if it's not a violation of law, you are not
going to have the corruption of public officials and have it
admitted to exist.
QUESTION: Would you favor legalizing it?
RFK: No, I would not.[10]

The work of local law-enforcement officials in many com-
munities has been outstanding, notably in Los Angeles under
Police Chief William Parker, in Cincinnati under Police Chief
Stanley R. Schrotel and in New York under Commissioner
Michael J. Murphy.

All these efforts notwithstanding, we have yet to exploit
properly our most powerful asset in the battle against the
rackets: an aroused, informed and insistent public.

In the words of the old saying, every society gets the
kind of criminal it deserves. What is equally true is that every
community gets the kind of law enforcement it insists on.
Regardless of new laws and old, regardless of resourceful and
dedicated federal investigative efforts, and regardless of how
well rounded a picture of organized crime our intelligence
helps us to secure, the only force that can conquer organized
crime is the vigilance of citizens in every community.[11]

A National Crime Commission?

Though law enforcement traditionally has been regarded as a state and local function, Kennedy was con-

[9] "News Conference" (WINS), October 25, 1964.
[10] Press conference, Cincinnati, Ohio, April 6, 1962.
[11] Kennedy, *The Pursuit of Justice*, pp. 46-47.

vinced that underworld operations have become so far-reaching and sophisticated that an active federal role now is required. He called for the establishment of a National Crime Commission as a key to a successful drive to reduce the effectiveness of organized crime.

The situation now is that the major figures of organized crime have become so rich and so powerful that they and their operations are in a large part beyond the reach of local officials.[12]

The methods of our law-enforcement agencies have not kept pace with the improved techniques of today's criminals. We are still trying to fight the modern Al Capone with the weapons that we used twenty-five years ago. They simply are not effective. And the result is that within ten years our whole economy will be drastically affected. I think that there are steps that can and should be taken to deal with the problem. One very effective move would be for each state to set up an agency that would periodically inspect the way law enforcement is being handled in the various localities within its jurisdiction. This has been done in England, and I think it would be most beneficial here. The agency's reports should be made public, so that everyone would know whether his officials were adequately meeting their responsibilities. And each law-enforcement officer would know that his work was being subjected to close scrutiny. In my opinion, however, our first and most urgent need is for a national crime commission. This commission would serve as a central intelligence agency, a clearing house to which each of the seventy-odd federal agencies and the more than ten thousand local law-enforcement agencies throughout the country would constantly feed information on the leading gangsters. The commission would pool and correlate all its information on underworld figures and disseminate it to the proper authorities.[13]

A national crime commission could alert the law-enforcement bodies in the various sections of the country to the

[12] Speech, Associated Press Managing Editors meeting, Dallas, Tex., November 15, 1961.
[13] Kennedy, *The Enemy Within*, pp. 263-264.

movement of gangsters and hoodlums and provide detailed information on their backgrounds . . . It would not be a national police force but a national information service for local police. With such an organization, even a one-telephone sheriff could prevent a hoodlum, well known in New York or Los Angeles, from coming into his community and taking over a local union or business.[14]

Immunity for Witnesses

Kennedy contended that a major obstacle to effective crime control is the difficulty of obtaining information about underworld activities. As Attorney General, he asked for two pieces of legislation to facilitate government intelligence gathering, a wiretap law (discussed in Chapter 9) and a measure to strengthen legal immunity for government witnesses.

. . . one of our most important weapons in the fight, at the federal and local level, is criminal intelligence. Intelligence, the most detailed information obtainable on the background and activities of suspected criminals, is essential to all law enforcement. It is even more important to successful action against racketeers.

Evidence concerning their clandestine operations is particularly hard to uncover. A witness who will testify in the face of threats to himself and his family is rare.[15]

The problem of obtaining testimony is nowhere more acute than in establishing violations of the racketeering travel act (Section 1952 of Title 18, United States Code, interstate and foreign travel or transportation in aid of racketeering enterprises), which the Congress enacted in August, 1961. Immunity here would materially assist our investigations of interstate racketeering in gambling, liquor, narcotics, prostitution, extortion and bribery. For example, the power of immunity under the bribery provision of this statute could be used to advantage in our investigations of political corruption. To assist still further our investigations of political corrup-

---

[14] *U.S. News & World Report,* January 9, 1961.
[15] Kennedy, *The Pursuit of Justice,* p. 42.

tion, which is such a serious by-product of organized criminal activity, Congress should also provide for the use of immunity in the general bribery and conflict-of-interest statutes. In the Eighty-eighth Congress [1963–1964] this was embodied in S. 1246, and this bill should be passed. This change would make an important tool available in certain political corruption situations where we are unable to establish connection as required under the travel statute.[16]

However, to those who might be misled into believing that these, or any other, bills would totally defeat organized crime, he warned:

I don't think these bills will end organized crime. You're going to have these problems of crime and corruption no matter what the laws are unless the attitude of the country changes. But these bills will give us tools for doing an essential job.[17]

"Coddling Criminals" vs. "Police Brutality"

As the nation's leading law-enforcement officer during his attorney generalship, it was inevitable that Kennedy should become involved in the bitter controversy over the proper rights of those accused of a crime. Much of the academic community and many representatives of civil liberties organizations berate the police for alleged disregard of individual rights and "police brutality." Police officials retort that their critics are "soft on criminals" and that they fail to understand the difficulties of successfully enforcing the law. The Supreme Court's decision in the case of *Gideon v. Wainwright* and related judgments regarding the rights of the accused merely exacerbated the dispute. Kennedy added his voice to the debate on several occasions.

For years now, the dispassionate figure of blind justice has been treated to a singular debate between the two schools.

[16] *Ibid.*, p. 54.
[17] *U.S. News & World Report*, July 10, 1961.

One side expresses its logic in such phrases as "coddling of criminals" or "knee-jerk sob sisters." Then, in ringing rebuttal from the other side, come such phrases as "savage police brutality" or "hanging judge."

The heat of this debate might be entrancing if it were not for the urgency of the problems which it obscures. The present problems of the field of criminal law are deep and serious. The application of criminal law to an increasingly concentrated, complicated urban society affects the life of every citizen. But because the debate has become so emotionally polarized, there is no common ground for communication or understanding. . . .

I mean no criticism of prosecutors or professors or policemen or of either side of this debate. But I *do* mean to condemn the emotional obstacles all of us have allowed to develop, obstacles which block intelligent—and perhaps even fruitful—appraisal of the problems. I became familiar with these obstacles soon after becoming Attorney General, in connection with wiretapping. Wiretapping is a subject of the deepest concern to me. I do not believe in it. But I also believe we must recognize that there are two sides to the argument.

We sought to do so in the Department of Justice by proposing revision of the present law on wiretapping. That law is widely acknowledged to be ineffective. It is not preventing widespread and indiscriminate wiretapping nor is it aiding law enforcement. Our effort was to bridge the gap.

We wrote a legislative proposal forbidding all wiretapping, except that by law-enforcement officials in connection with a small number of specified crimes. This exception was rigidly fenced in by a number of safeguards, administered by the courts and Congress. In my view, this was an excellent bill, balancing the need to protect individual privacy with the needs of law enforcement.

And yet, once introduced, discussion of the merits of the measure was instantly submerged in a flood of criticism so emotional and so bitter that rational debate is, at least so far, impossible. I found that many of the critics had not even bothered to read the bill. And I was interested by the fact that the American Civil Liberties Union strenuously opposed it,

while the ACLU's own President, former Attorney General
Biddle, testified in favor of it.[18]

Perhaps, above all, it was my hope that this Office of
Criminal Justice [an RFK creation in the Justice Department
to deal with the whole spectrum of the criminal process, from
arrest to rehabilitation] would be only the first step in dealing
with what I believe is one of the most aggravating problems
of criminal law: the wide, and widening, gulf between law-
enforcement officials on the one side and other legal figures
concerned with protecting the rights of the individual on the
other.

Differences of opinion between schools of thought on the
balance of justice are not only helpful, but desirable, for the
dialogue can be creative. But there is little creativity in
the present dialogue. . . . There are those quick to criticize the
police, without even attempting to comprehend their large
responsibility and the difficult condition under which police
often must work. And there are dedicated police officials who
believe that the courts are letting them down by erecting all
kinds of technical hurdles that interfere with law enforcement. . . .[19]

Rights to Counsel and Bail

Of the *Gideon v. Wainwright* decision, Kennedy said:

In the case of *Gideon v. Wainwright*, decided in 1963, the
court held that every poor man was entitled to have a lawyer
provided for him when he was charged with a serious crime.

The Gideon case put a burden on states and localities to
find lawyers for the poor in criminal trials but there was no
outcry about the Supreme Court invading states' rights. The
reason is clear: it is so obviously right to have a national
standard of equal justice for the poor in criminal trials.[20]

[18] Speech, American Bar Association, Criminal Law Section, New
York, N.Y., August 10, 1964.

[19] Kennedy, *op. cit.*, p. 99.

[20] Speech, Free Synagogue of Westchester County, Mt. Vernon,
N.Y., September 20, 1964.

Another injustice facing the poor in court is the American system of bail. As Attorney General, Kennedy worked diligently to reform that system.

One of the plainest of these problems [of the poor in court] is bail. Its legitimate purpose of insuring that defendants appear for trial has been distorted into systematic injustice. Every year thousands of persons are kept in jail for weeks and even months following arrest. They are not proven guilty. They may be innocent. They may be no more likely to flee than you or I. But they must stay in jail because, bluntly, they cannot afford to pay for their freedom.

. . . the present bail system exacts an incalculable human price. And it is an unnecessary price. Repeated recent studies demonstrate that there is little, if any, relationship between appearance at trial and ability to post bail. The pioneering work of the Vera Foundation in New York has disclosed that only 1 percent of persons released on recognizance have failed to appear for trial. This compares with a 3 percent default rate for those out on bail.

I have been deeply concerned about the effect of bail on the poor man. The Allen Committee [a committee of law professors examining the question of bail chaired by Professor Allen of the University of Chicago] looked into the question extensively. It recommended that release on recognizance be incr?ased wherever possible at the federal level, and we have followed that recommendation. In March, 1963, shortly after receiving the committee's recommendation, I instructed all United States attorneys to recommend that every possible defendant be released without bail. In the first year thereafter, such releases tripled. The default rate, 2.5 percent, is about the same as that for those released on bail.

Even if the default rate were higher, there would still be strong reason to encourage a maximum of pretrial freedom.[21]

Take, for example, the law of bail, which you have come here from five states to discuss. Bail is a device to insure that a person accused of crime will appear at trial. Our system of justice presumes that all are innocent until proven guilty. And it guarantees that no penalty, no imprisonment, no punishment shall be imposed without a trial at which the accused

[21] Kennedy, *op. cit.*, pp. 97-98.

is afforded every protection of the Constitution and the Common Law. In such a system, bail can have only one permissible purpose. Not punishment; not harassment; not even the prevention of some other act by the accused; but only to insure that the accused will be present at his trial. But that singleness of purpose has been forgotten. Every year, all over America, hundreds of thousands of people are deprived of liberty, subjected to punishment, simply because they are unable to pay for their freedom. In 1963, the federal government alone held 22,000 prisoners in jail—pending trial, before any adjudication of their innocence or weighing of their guilt. On any given day in 1963, the city of Los Angeles alone kept over 1,300 persons in jail awaiting trial. In Montgomery County, Maryland, nearly one-third of all prisoners have not been tried; and they may stay anywhere from three to six months waiting for trial. There is one primary reason for these people to be in jail. They are without the money to meet bail—or even to pay the bondsmen's fees. Our affluent society does not consider $500 as a lot of money; surely there is no one here who could not, if ordered to post that bail, afford at least the $50 or $75 the bondsman would charge. But in New York City, 25 percent of those whose bail is set at $500 cannot meet it.

As these and countless other examples make clear, punishment is imposed in thousands of cases simply because the defendant is poor. In most jurisdictions, from one-third to one-half or more of those accused of crime will be acquitted, or have their charges dismissed. Many more will have their sentences suspended, or be allowed to pay a fine. In fact, less than 10 percent of those arrested in New York City can expect to be sentenced to prison terms. But for thousands of these, the 90 percent who the *law* decides should not serve in prison, poverty will rule that the mere act of arrest will result in imprisonment—and in loss of job, self-respect, separation from family, and possible ruin. This is not the law of reason.[22]

By our concern for the abuses of the bail system, we can

[22] Address, Governor's Conference on Bail and the Right to Counsel, Louisville, Ky., January 22, 1965.

see to it that America does not unjustly punish the man who is already serving a life sentence of poverty.[23]

Juries, Judges, Prisons, and Capital Punishment

Kennedy also discussed several other aspects of our judicial system.

. . . I think all of us, bench and bar alike, have a most serious responsibility to assure that the method of jury selection, as well as the determination of the qualifications of jurors, conforms in every respect to the law.

The Department of Justice has urged the adoption of a statute fixing ultimate responsibility over the jury commissioner. A bill approved by the Judicial Conference was sponsored in the Eighty-sixth Congress [1959–1960], and an identical bill is now before the present Congress. It would provide that in the performance of all duties of his office, the jury commissioner shall act subject to the instructions of the Chief Judge of the District.

The importance of a properly functioning jury system to our American concept of equal justice cannot be overemphasized; neither can its effectiveness be weakened by a failure —whether innocently or through laxity, ignorance, indifference, local prejudice, or reluctance to depart from established habits—to apply the statutes and case law which govern that system. The injury which results, if I may quote from the Supreme Court in the Ballard case, "is not limited to the defendant. There is injury to the jury system, to the law as an institution, to the community, and to the democratic ideal reflected in the processes of our courts." [24]

I do not believe that previous political activity should disqualify anyone for judicial office. But judicial office should never be the reward for political service alone, without regard for other more important qualifications. Lawyers with political experience can and have made fine judges. But law-

[23] Speech, National Conference on Bail and Criminal Justice, U.S. Department of State, Washington, D.C., May 29, 1964.

[24] Speech, Fourth Judicial Circuit Conference, Roanoke, Va., June 30, 1962.

yers whose only distinctions are their character, scholarship, and legal experience must also be encouraged to undertake judicial public service. Partisan political activity has weighed too heavily in our considerations. We have avoided devising methods by which non-political merits would receive the attention they deserve.[25]

The time has come for another Wickersham Commission [the informal name of the National Commission on Law Observance and Law Enforcement created by President Hoover in 1929], another comprehensive survey designed to study and strengthen enforcement *of* and obedience *to* criminal law all over the country. The Wickersham Commission report had a marked effect on criminal law for many years. There are similar rewards to be gained from a new effort.[26]

Kennedy demonstrated a concern about the effectiveness of prison rehabilitation programs and efforts to treat those crimes linked to mental illness.

The data coming to light now shows that we have done all too little to rehabilitate and reintegrate into society those who have once run afoul of the law-enforcement process. . . . The rate of recidivism for released criminal offenders is far too high. . . . The difficult question that now faces our nation is how best to deal with this recurrent cycle which continually brings those who have once had a taste of the criminal process back into contact with that process. From the little information that we have, the answer appears to lie in a greater commitment to rehabilitation. We must educate and vocationally train those who are in prison; and we must be prepared to supply guidance and help find employment for those who are released from incarceration facilities.[27]

All of these rulings reflect a judgment that those whose crimes occur because of mental illness should be treated for their illness rather than punished for their conduct. Based on the application of modern psychiatry to the law, these decisions reflect a retreat from the archaic practice of just im-

[25] Press release, July 20, 1966.
[26] Kennedy, *op. cit.*, p. 101.
[27] Press release, May 17, 1967.

240
240   ROBERT F. KENNEDY: APOSTLE OF CHANGE

prisoning the mentally ill, which was the effect of the
M'Naghten Rules. But in the federal area, this change has
occurred without accompanying assurances to the acquitted
defendant that he will receive the medical attention he needs,
and to the public that it will be protected from unwise release
of dangerous individuals. Federal law—apart from a special
provision applicable in the District of Columbia—contains no
provision for the commitment and treatment of those acquitted
in the federal courts on the ground of insanity.[28]

On one occasion in 1962, he was asked about capital
punishment:

QUESTION: Would you abolish capital punishment?
RFK: No, I would not.[29]

J. Edgar Hoover: The Untouchable

Despite recurrent rumors that Kennedy and FBI director J. Edgar Hoover could not stand each other, with the
exception of their brief exchange over who was responsible for authorizing FBI electronic eavesdropping
(Chapter 9). Bobby had only kind words for Hoover and
the Bureau in public.

QUESTION: Mr. Kennedy, you said that Mr. Hoover would be
head of the FBI longer than you would be Attorney General.
Are you planning to resign and run for the governorship of
Massachusetts?
RFK: No, I have had great admiration for J. Edgar Hoover
and that respect for him and his organization has increased
since I have been Attorney General. And I think that he has
demonstrated outstanding leadership in that organization, and
that the American people owe a great deal to J. Edgar Hoover
for all that he contributed; but, I didn't mean to imply that I
am going to resign and run for something.[30]

[28] Statement, U.S. Senate, August 4, 1966.
[29] Press conference, Crime Prevention Conference, Los Angeles,
Calif., March 24, 1962.
[30] Address, Sigma Delta Chi [journalism fraternity], New Mexico
Chapter, Albuquerque, N.M., February 14, 1963.

During the whole life of the committee the advice and help that J. Edgar Hoover gave to me personally and to the Committee were absolutely invaluable.[31]

This morning you heard from J. Edgar Hoover, a man whose record of service and dedication to his country cannot be surpassed. I doubt that any of you who heard Mr. Hoover could really question that the forces of this government are alertly arrayed against the danger of Communist subversion here at home.[32]

The type of service which J. Edgar Hoover and Jim Bennett, the Director of the Bureau of Prisons, have given to this country is unique and outstanding. Their careers are somewhat parallel in the fact that both have taken federal agencies and completely overhauled them and made them models to be followed not only in the United States but all around the world.[33]

QUESTION: Mr. Kennedy, have you taken any steps to investigate the charges that the FBI does less than it might do in civil rights cases?
RFK: I have never found that problem. I heard that before I became Attorney General, and there were articles written about that. I have never had an instance since I have been Attorney General that we have asked the Federal Bureau of Investigation to do something that they haven't done it with great diligence and great integrity and tremendous effort, and I think it is the best investigative body in the world. . . .[34]

Juvenile Delinquency

Kennedy always enjoyed a warm relationship with children. Therefore it is not surprising that he dis-

[31] Kennedy, *The Enemy Within,* p. 177.
[32] Speech, National Commanders' Dinner, American Legion Convention, Las Vegas, Nev., October 9, 1962.
[33] Speech, Fourth Judicial Circuit Conference, Roanoke, Va., June 30, 1962.
[34] Press conference, Atlanta, Ga., April 26, 1963.

played a keen interest in the problem of juvenile delinquency throughout his career. As Attorney General he was a guiding force behind the enactment of the Juvenile Delinquency Control Act, which authorized $30 million for a three-year study of the causes and prevention of crime among youngsters. And when John F. Kennedy created the President's Committee on Juvenile Delinquency and Youth Crime, his brother was put in charge.

In *The Pursuit of Justice* he discussed the problem of kids and crime at length:

In 1960 the average number of youths aged sixteen to twenty-one who were out of school and out of work was a disturbing 450,000. But by last year [1964] that number had grown to a whopping 700,000. They are forming the core of a new lost generation which is growing up in our country with no skills and little hope. Many of its members turn to the short cut of crime to get the things others get by hard work and study. . . .

Crime, violence in the streets and the dissolution of families and personalities are not eliminated by calling them evil and blaming them off onto "some other" party. Nor are they eliminated by sloughing them off onto "some other" level of government. We begin by *accepting* the blame and the responsibility, not by displacing or disregarding them. Federal programs for delinquency prevention will work and should be expanded to help give the juvenile his birthright. . . .

What is needed now is a systematized and intense effort to mobilize the resources of federal, state and local governments and the private agencies, schools, and churches which have done so much pioneer work. The federal government ought to have a part in such programs, although ultimately it is up to city, state and private agencies to carry most of the load. . . .

Clearly, an increased federal role is not going to solve the problem either. But it can stimulate local community interest and investment in finding out how to do a better job of prevention. We can encourage development of programs that are effective and we can get this knowledge to those who need it.

There are many good programs already being tried in different parts of the country. There are many new ideas being proposed. Our job is to help put these programs together so their full impact can be felt. In the President's Committee on Juvenile Delinquency and Youth Crime we had a means for mobilizing federal resources to meet this challenge. Throughout the country we must continue to encourage agencies to get together to make these new programs work.[35]

After citing some figures on the soaring incidence of juvenile crime, RFK remarked:

These might be totally discouraging statistics if we did not have proof that modest efforts on the part of the community, *if concerted,* can pay off in enormously beneficial results. . . . One never finds more than a few hardy souls making a serious contribution to the war against the corruption of youth. Today we are confronted with large increases in delinquency, particularly in major urban areas, and correlated with these increases is the high incidence of delinquency among minority groups. The results are disastrous, with the disintegration of many American families through either the inadequacy or the nonexistence of parents raising children in their own homes.[36]

The answer to the problem, he argued, is not simply more police and better juvenile courts and institutions.

The problem of juvenile delinquency—and this is so extremely important—is not just better policemen or better prisons—it's a wide range of things. It's more opportunities for housing. It's better education; it's recreation; it's family. It deals with law enforcement, deals with opportunity. If you can't give young people an opportunity for a better life, so that they think they can improve themselves, they're going to turn to narcotics, they're going to turn to stealing, they're going to have some excitement if they can't go and play baseball, or figure that they're going to finish school and going

[35] Kennedy, *The Pursuit of Justice,* pp. 23, 24, 27-29.
[36] *Ibid.,* p. 23.

to get a job. They're going to figure, well, we have to do something, let's go steal a car and take a ride.

Oh, yeah, I think there's no question that it's a national problem—that's how we've gotten into it. What we're trying to do, though, it's not just—what I mean to say is that the federal government just by having a lot of money is not going to cure this. This is going to have to be cured at the local level. What we can do, and what the President is attempting to do, is to give some leadership, so that the communities take some action. They have in New York; they're beginning to in other communities.[37]

In formulating our program on juvenile delinquency it quickly became clear to us that the emphasis could not be upon law violations and law violators, but upon the cause of violation.

To put it differently, youth offenses are not the illness to be dealt with. They are merely symptoms of an illness that goes far deeper in our society.

To arrive at this conclusion one need not be a sociologist, or a social worker or a planner. One simply needs to walk the slums of Washington, or New York, or Chicago, or in the communities of Appalachia, and talk with the young people.

For many of these young people law violation is not the isolated outburst of a social misfit. It is part of a way of life where all conventional routes to success are blocked and where law abidingness has lost all meaning and appeal.

You cannot look into their eyes or look up and down the asphalt jungle or the desolate hollows in which they live without sensing the despair, the frustration, the futility and alienation they feel. One is strongly impelled to do something, to make some gesture that says: "People do care; don't give up."

Surely the answer to this problem is not simply to provide more and better juvenile courts, more and better juvenile institutions, or more and better lawyers to prosecute or defend young people, who then return to the same desolation which caused their difficulty in the first place.

What is needed are programs which deal directly with

[37] "Today" (NBC-TV), Washington, D.C., June 4, 1962.

the causes of delinquency. These are programs to impart skills, to instill motivation, to create opportunity. These are programs which urge young people to stay in school.

These are summer job programs for high school students. These are programs to provide decent recreational facilities. These are, in short, programs which indicate that people do care, that there is hope, and that all young people do count in this society.[38]

[38] Speech, University of Chicago, Chicago, Ill., May 1, 1964.

Chapter 11

Big Business and the
Federal Government

Early in his career Robert Kennedy acquired a reputation for being antibusiness, but it is difficult to understand why. He had made some strong statements about business ethics and had questioned the wisdom of permitting the merger boom of the last decade to go unchecked, but few of his actions and recommendations as Attorney General or as a U.S. Senator threatened business interests in any discernible way.

The Steel Price Hike

The Kennedy Administration's pressure on the steel industry to rescind its 1962 price increases—in which the Attorney General bluffed a major Justice Department investigation of pricing procedures within the industry—raised the ire of many businessmen and the cry of "government interference." RFK discussed the Administration's view of the "steel crisis" shortly thereafter on television:

QUESTION: Turning to a more recent controversy, the recent steel price rollback in the face of the President's action, some have contended that the President and the Administration exercised too much power and did it too ruthlessly. What is your answer to that?

RFK: The President and the Administration were committed to attempting to stop the inflation in the United States and in that effort of course steel plays a major role. With the concurrence of steel executives, management, the President and Mr. Goldberg, Secretary of Labor, had many meetings with representatives in the steel union to attempt to prevail upon them not to make their demands excessive. It was understood in the meetings with the steel executives, Mr.

Blough [president of U.S. Steel] and others, that this effort was to be made so that with the union's demands being reasonable that the price of steel would not have to be raised. It was with this understanding that the President and Arthur Goldberg went ahead and finally, I think, through their efforts prevailed upon the union to keep their demands in extremely reasonable level which was recognized by all throughout the United States and a contract was signed on very reasonable terms and recognized as such, and then a short time later the steel companies, led by U.S. Steel, raised their prices. Thereafter, realizing what the effect would be on the economy generally, what the effect would be on all of the other industries, if this remained, the President did what he could to exert the public interest and the various branches of the departments, various branches and departments of the executive branch of the government were brought into play. I think he had a responsibility to defend and protect the public interest.

QUESTION: Well, if there was not an understanding, Mr. Kennedy, there was at least an assumption on the part of the Administration that there would be no steel price rise after this noninflationary wage agreement was signed?

RFK: That is correct.

QUESTION: And it was on this feeling of an assumption rather than an understanding that the President felt in effect that he had been doublecrossed, right?

RFK: That is correct. The steel company executives, however, never said, never indicated, said or stated that they would not raise their prices, but it was an understanding as you described that if we were successful in keeping the union demands at a low level and a contract was signed which was noninflationary it was the understanding that the price of steel would not be raised. Shortly afterwards the price of steel was raised.[1]

The crisis did not, as many had feared, represent a major turning point in government-industry relations. Once the price hikes were canceled, nothing was ever heard again of the Justice Department's investigation of the steel industry.

[1] "Issues and Answers" (ABC-TV), June 17, 1962.

Antitrust Enforcement

As Attorney General, Kennedy liked to contend before business audiences that his commitment to enforce antitrust laws vigorously was a sign of his probusiness proclivity.

Furthermore, I might add that I look upon the antitrust laws as being "probusiness." I believe firmly that the purpose of the antitrust laws is to protect and promote the competitive interests of business—small and large—as well as to protect the public.

Fortune Magazine several years ago stated that proposition extremely well.

"Now that socialism and planning have failed wherever they have been tried abroad, it is all the more necessary that Americans look to those institutions which have tended to preserve their own flexible, dynamic and competitive society. . . . Whatever the difficulties that surround the enforcement of the Sherman Act today, it remains, in the words of former Chief Justice Hughes, a charter of freedom standing for something precious in American life."

This statement correctly declares what the antitrust laws are.[2]

The Kennedy-Johnson Administration has not been antibusiness primarily because there is every good reason why we should be probusiness. Furthermore, I might add that I think upon the antitrust laws as being "probusiness." I believe firmly that the purpose of the antitrust laws is to protect and promote the competitive interests, small and large, as well as to protect the public. . . .

Yet there is talk that enforcement of the antitrust law is evidence that the Administration has been "antibusiness." Much of the criticism has centered on merger cases brought under Section 7 of the Clayton Act. This section is intended to avoid the creation of barriers to entry into the market and the loss of competitive vigor which may result through excessive concentration in a particular industry. It is not intended

[2] Speech, Economic Club of New York, New York, N.Y., November 13, 1961.

to prevent all mergers. Many mergers promote vigorous competition just as some mergers have the opposite effect.

The record shows that mergers have not been attacked indiscriminately. The number of mergers challenged by the government is very small compared with the total number of mergers which are completed. During the first eight months of 1961 the Department filed only eleven antimerger cases. In the same period 757 mergers or acquisitions were recorded by the Federal Trade Commission. Included in the mergers we opposed were five bank mergers.[3]

On "Issues and Answers," he called for action to curb monopoly, but he seemed to exempt the growing number of conglomerate mergers from his concern.

We are not against and can't be against bigness per se, but we are against, under the law, in this country, we are against monopoly and we have to examine this subject continuously.[4]

However, for all his talk, Kennedy seemed bored by antitrust issues and the record of that division during his tenure as Attorney General was not significantly better or worse than under his Republican predecessor, William Rogers. In fact, his most effective work in this area was probably his active support of a proposed merger between the Pennsylvania and New York Central railroads.

I have supported the concept of a merger between the Pennsylvania and New York Central railroads since the time that I was Attorney General. It has been and is my belief that such a merger is the first step forward in the development of a modern and integrated transportation system in the eastern part of the United States. Such a system must exist if we are to satisfy the growing needs of this region's citizens for swift and efficient service from city to city and from city to suburb. That is why early consummation of the merger, with adequate provision for inclusion of vital service now

[3] Robert F. Kennedy, *The Pursuit of Justice* (New York: Harper & Row, 1965), pp. 59-60.

[4] "Issues and Answers" (ABC-TV), April 21, 1963.

being provided by other carriers, is so important to the public.[5]

Furthermore, he recommended that these merged giants be granted government aid to maintain the New Haven line's commuter service.

As I said three months ago, I hope that the proposed merger of the Pennsylvania and New York Central railroads will be approved and that the New Haven will be made a party to that merger. However, I am also convinced that it would be unwise and uneconomic to saddle the merged entity with the New Haven's passenger operation. Therefore, I think that, concurrent with the merger, we must move ahead to put the entire passenger operation into the public domain for the long run. As it is, however, the only immediate source of funds for the New Haven are the states concerned. There is certainly precedent for state involvement. The Commonwealth of Massachusetts only recently, through the Massachusetts Bay Transit Authority, began an arrangement whereby the Boston & Maine Railroad will receive some $3 million a year so that essential commuter operations can be preserved. Senator Pell's bill, together with the merger, may solve the long-run problem, but the states, particularly New York and Connecticut, must act, and act immediately, if drastic cuts in commuter traffic are to be avoided in 1965.[6]

As I testified before the Senate Commerce Committee on March 2, the long-haul passenger service should also, in my judgment, be included on an absolute basis, and perhaps the full commission will still consider this. When I last considered the matter as Attorney General, it was my view that the Department's objections to the merger on antitrust grounds should be withdrawn if the ICC made appropriate provision for the New Haven. I think that if these provisions were extended to the long-haul passenger service, the public policy considerations favoring the merger would be made even stronger. I do agree, however, that insofar as the commuter service is concerned, governmental participation is essential. It

[5] Statement, U.S. Senate, September 1966.
[6] Press release, January 7, 1965.

is on this point that the conditional inclusion provisions of yesterday's decision point the way to a course of action.[7]

Government Regulation of Private Enterprise

In defending the public accommodations sections of the 1964 Civil Rights Act, Kennedy made clear his belief in the government's right to regulate private enterprise in the national interest.

. . . Federal action in this field involves no novel constitutional concept. Congress often has regulated private business enterprises to remove burdens from the national commerce. The National Labor Relations Act, The Taft-Hartley Act, the Fair Labor Standards Act and the Agricultural Adjustment Act—these are only a few that come readily to mind, and there are countless others.[8]

Consumer Protection, Labor-Management Ethics, and Price-Fixing

He justified the propriety of federal legislation to protect consumers on similar grounds.

I am thoroughly convinced of the need to provide a federal umbrella of protection for the American consumer.

The efforts of the government should be to help those who cannot help themselves. That was the theme behind the Poverty bill, the Criminal Justice bill, the Civil Rights bill, and many other undertakings of the Kennedy-Johnson Administration.

Many people purchase on credit. Often they are the least able to pay exorbitant interest rates which are charged in some instances. Often they are not given the full facts or they are misled about what the true cost of their purchase will be. This has happened again and again and, therefore, I am fully in support of the two bills which are now before the Senate, as part of general programs to insure federal protection of con-

[7] Statement, U.S. Senate, March 30, 1965.
[8] Kennedy, *op. cit.*, pp. 78-79.

sumers. These bills are popularly known as the "Truth in Lending" and "Truth in Packaging" bills.[9]

As his record as a Senate investigator affirms, Robert Kennedy had a very low tolerance for dishonesty and corruption in the private as well as the public sector. His more than two years as chief counsel for the McClellan Committee [Senate Select Committee on Improper Activities in the Labor and Management Fields] were devoted to the task of uncovering illegal and unethical practices in the field of labor-management relations. The focus of his investigation was the Teamsters Union, which led many to conclude that Bobby placed most of the onus for economic corruption in this country on organized labor. In fact, he viewed the problem as a "crooked two-way street."

We found there is often a thin line between bribery and extortion, shakedown and payoff. Labor-management corruption is a crooked two-way street. That is why company officials who conspire with union officials won't talk. They have bought something, just as the labor leader has sold something. And those management officials who aren't involved themselves are usually satisfied to let things go along with everybody happy. They don't want anyone to rock the boat. I believe 90 percent of the corrupt deals between business and labor could be eliminated if business officials would simply talk to proper authorities.[10]

Kennedy did not mince words in condemning such illegal but widespread business practices as price-fixing and other conspiracies to limit or eliminate competition.

We are talking about clear-cut questions of right and wrong. I view the businessman who engages in such conspiracies in the same light as I regard the racketeer who siphons off money from the public in crooked gambling or the union official who betrays his union members.

A conspiracy to fix prices or rig bids is simply economic

[9] Campaign statement, September 17, 1964.

[10] Robert F. Kennedy, *The Enemy Within* (New York: Harper & Brothers, 1960), p. 217.

racketeering and the persons involved should be subject to as severe punishment as the courts deem appropriate. When possible, I believe that we should not only take action against the corporations or companies involved, but against the individuals who have participated in these frauds. I am against granting immunity to the individuals, with the result that the cases end with their companies paying a fine. I think those responsible should be held responsible.[11]

I feel very strongly about groups that get together to fix prices to put competitors out of business and defraud the public. Where there is evidence of that, I think it should be vigorously pursued. It is harmful for small groups to gain control of an industry or a segment of the financial community.[12]

He repeated what he had said to the businessmen at the Economic Club in his book, *The Pursuit of Justice*, adding:

In such cases as price-fixing, or illegal merger or other business techniques for "beating the system," a powerful and vigorous government is not the enemy of the free market. The real enemy is the very businessman who engages in such practices and his colleagues who condone his actions because "business is business." He is the enemy not only because he is stealing, but also because he is destroying the confidence and trust that make a vigorous, free-wheeling economy possible.[13]

QUESTION: General, one of the top officials of Westinghouse has said that the electrical industry ought to adopt a code of ethics industry-wide now; have you any comments on that?
RFK: Yes, and I think they should. I think it is a little bit after the horse has left the barn, but I think it would be very worthwhile, and I think it should go beyond that. I think that the National Association of Manufacturers and the Chambers of Commerce should adopt some code of ethics. I made some

[11] Speech, Economic Club of New York, New York, N.Y., November 13, 1961.
[12] *U.S. News & World Report*, July 10, 1961.
[13] Kennedy, *The Pursuit of Justice*, p. 64.

suggestions along these lines over the period of the last several years, where we revealed, when I was counsel to the committee, some 50 companies and corporations which acted improperly and no management group, despite the fact that they were major companies and corporations, or perhaps because they were, no management group took any action against any of them.

. . . I would hope that . . . the various employer groups throughout the United States would take some action and start looking into their own homes. I would say that based on what I have seen since I have been here in the Department of Justice, and the work that I did with the committee, that the corruption within management is something that should concern everybody in the United States, and it is extremely serious.[14]

However, he conceded that federal action taken against these sorts of business activities has often failed to meet acceptable standards of justice. Kennedy was interviewed about the problem and pointed out areas requiring reform:

We are properly concerned today about the rights of indigents, of those accused of crime and of individuals suing and being sued in civil court cases. But we should also be concerned about federal administrative agency action against business, large and small. . . .

Despite giant strides in recent years in the quality of justice dispensed by these agencies, we still have not achieved the high degree of fundamental fairness to which business concerns are entitled. There are two aspects of needed reform, although many more can be mentioned. The first is delay in adjudication, and the other is a more precise and universal application of the simple rules of ordinary justice that have long been enforced by our courts. . . . Actually the vehicle by which many of these problems can be met and ameliorated is already at hand. . . .

Congress passed and President Johnson signed a bill [which RFK's brother originated] in 1964 which established a permanent Administrative Conference. . . . Perhaps most im-

[14] Press conference, U.S. Department of Justice, April 6, 1961.

portantly the Act provided for the appointment of a full-time conference chairman. . . . A suitable man has not yet been found. . . ." [15]

The Need for Government-Business Partnership in Today's Vital Tasks

Beginning in 1965, most of Robert Kennedy's statements addressed to the American business community emphasized the need for greater government-business cooperation in meeting the problems confronting the nation. As Chapter 5 makes clear, his steady retreat from the New Deal faith in "reform by bureaucracy" led to his advocacy of an expanded private role in the efforts to eliminate poverty and rebuild our cities. Far from being antibusiness, his most recent pronouncements and legislative proposals (for example, his 1967 bills calling for federal tax incentives to stimulate private development of low-income housing and the creation of new jobs in inner-city areas) revealed a solid respect for the vigor and strength of American free enterprise and a high expectation of the part it will play in shaping the country's future.

Our entire defense establishment, including the most secret and sensitive installations, is the best evidence of business and government bringing together the very best talent and ingenuity to keep this country strong, vigorous and prosperous.[16]

Yet we know that in a survey last year only 12 percent of all graduating college seniors hoped for a career in business, or thought such a career would be worthwhile and satisfying.

Why? Part of the answer, surely, is that the great corporations which are so large a part of American life play so small a role in the solution of its vital problems. Civil rights, poverty, unemployment, health, education—these are but a few of the deep crises in which business participation, with a few important exceptions, has been far less than might be

[15] *Nation's Business*, June 1967.
[16] Kennedy, *op. cit.*, p. 65.

expected from such an important part of the society. We can recognize, and applaud, the work of the NAM in job training, or the work of the foundations like Ford and Rockefeller, or the efforts of individuals like Paul Hoffman or Thomas Watson, or corporations like Smith, Kline & French. But certainly business as a whole has not sought out the challenge of the nation's frontier. Of course, it may well be argued that the business of business is to make a profit, that to attempt more is to do less than its stockholders deserve. But does such an argument have relevance, ask the young, when a single company, like General Motors or IT&T, has annual profits greater than the gross national product of any one of seventy nations in the world? [17]

To rely exclusively, even primarily, on government efforts is not only to ignore the shaping traditions of American life and politics. To ignore the potential contribution of private enterprise is to fight the war on poverty with a single platoon, while great armies are left to stand aside. For private enterprise is not just another part of America; in a significant sense, private enterprise is the very sinew and strength of America. Our productive assets, our machines and money and plants are owned by private enterprise. The entire intricate chain of economy—the means by which we join with our fellows to produce goods and roads, to bring food to our tables and clothes to our backs—all this is organized by private enterprise. Private enterprise has built our cities and industries; it has created jobs for over 60 million Americans now at work. But it has not rebuilt the centers of poverty, nor put their people to work. And in my judgment, the lack of private enterprise participation is the principal cause for our failure to solve the problem of employment in urban poverty areas.

In what way should private enterprise now be encouraged to join the fight against unemployment? For us, the answer is simple and direct: it should create new jobs, and hire and train unemployed and poor people to fill them. [18]

[17] Address, Americans for Democratic Action, Philadelphia, Pa., February 27, 1967.

[18] Speech, U.S. Senate, July 12, 1967.

Chapter 12

Organized Labor and the Hoffa Crusade

The Hoffa-Kennedy feud surely was one of the most famous and vitriolic in the annals of congressional investigations. Neither principal sought to conceal his utter contempt for the other nor hesitated to hope publicly for the other's downfall. His campaign to "get Hoffa," which dominated Kennedy's career with the McClellan Committee (1957-1959) and assumed a high priority during his Attorney Generalship (1961-1964) provided him with his first intimate contacts with national labor leaders, their unions, and the complexities of labor-management relations. Thus his statements regarding Hoffa and the mode of operation of the International Teamsters Union are a logical starting point for a survey of Bobby's views of the American labor movement.

"A Bully Behind a Façade"

The Senate Select Committee on Improper Activities in the Labor Management Fields, with Senator McClellan of Arkansas as its chairman and Robert Kennedy as counsel, began its investigation of James Hoffa and the Teamsters in 1957. It did not take Kennedy long to form some definite opinions about the character of the man who was to become his star witness and public *raison d'être* over the next few years. In his first book he recalled a dinner meeting with Hoffa at the home of one of Hoffa's lawyers early in the investigation:

On my way home I thought of how often Hoffa had said he was tough; that he destroyed employers, hated policemen and broke those who stood in his way. It had always been my feeling that if a person was truly tough; if he actually had strength and power; if he really had the ability to excel, he need not brag and boast of it to prove it. When a grown man sat for an evening and talked continuously about his toughness, I could only conclude that he was a bully hiding behind a façade.[1]

In reference to a case in which he attempted unsuccessfully to prove that Hoffa had sought to bribe a committee investigator named Cye Cheasty, who, according to Hoffa, was being paid to frame him, Kennedy wrote:

The truth was and is that Cye Cheasty is an honest man—and Jimmy Hoffa had failed to recognize that there is such a person.[2]

Gradually Kennedy grew to see Hoffa as wickedness incarnate, complete with an "evil eye."

In the most remarkable of all my exchanges with Jimmy Hoffa not a word was said. I called it "the look." It was to occur fairly often, but the first time I observed it was on the last day of the 1957 hearings. During the afternoon I noticed that he was glaring at me across the counsel table with a deep, strange, penetrating expression of intense hatred. I suppose it must have dawned on him about that time that he was going to be the subject of a continuing probe—that we were not playing games. It was the look of a man obsessed by his enmity, and it came particularly from his eyes. There were times when his face seemed completely transfixed with this stare of absolute evilness. It might last for five minutes— as if he thought that by staring long enough and hard enough he could destroy me. Sometimes he seemed to be concentrating so hard that I had to smile, and occasionally I would speak of it to an assistant counsel sitting behind me. It must have been obvious to him that we were discussing it, but his expression would not change by a flicker. . . .[3]

[1] Robert F. Kennedy, *The Enemy Within* (New York: Harper & Brothers, 1960), p. 43.
[2] *Ibid.*, p. 40.
[3] *Ibid.*, pp. 74-75.

Jimmy Hoffa dealt with the congressional committees in 1953 and 1954 as he deals with everything and everybody; he believes that money, or influence, or political pressure, or a combination of all three can fix any problem that faces him. As he once said to Washington newspaperman Clark Mollenhoff: "Every man has his price. What's yours?" . . .[4]

I think he saw the whole investigation simply as a fight between the two of us—Bobby Kennedy and Jimmy Hoffa don't like each other. To him, it was a personality clash, not the United States versus corruption. . . .[5]

In our August, 1957, hearings, when the committee began to spread on the record Hoffa's close ties with racketeers, the nation got its first look at the man who in little more than a month would be elected to succeed Dave Beck as president of the most powerful union in the country—and at the convicted killers, robbers, extortionists, white slavers and sodomists who were his chosen associates. . . .[6]

. . . there was no group that better fits the prototype of the old Al Capone syndicate than Jimmy Hoffa and some of his chief lieutenants in and out of the union. . . .[7]

By August of 1958, the McClellan Committee had uncovered a mass of crookedness and wrongdoing in the Teamsters. There were demands that Hoffa take steps to clean up his union. However, I was convinced by this time that he was completely incapable of doing the job—had he cared to. He was dependent on the racketeers and ex-convicts with whom he had surrounded himself.[8]

He accused Hoffa of corrupt management of the Teamsters, of maintaining ties with numerous underworld figures and of "selling out" his own rank and file on many occasions.

[4] *Ibid.*, p. 55.
[5] *Ibid.*, p. 74.
[6] *Ibid.*, p. 72.
[7] *Ibid.*, p. 75.
[8] *Ibid.*, p. 52.

First of all, we discovered that Mr. Hoffa has made side deals with his friends in the trucking business throughout the Central Conference of Teamsters, deals advantageous to the management; he also has made sweetheart contracts with management in his home city of Detroit. And, worse, he had tried to bring down the higher standards of Teamster contracts in other parts of the country, where he cannot control the terms, to make them conform to his own. . . .[9]

I am the first to admit that the record we uncovered is only a portion of the evil wrought by Hoffa, his men or associates. But what we did uncover shows clearly that the Teamster membership has been betrayed; democratic processes have been stifled; money, including pension and welfare funds, has been misused to the tune of at least $9,500,000; Hoffa and some of the men around him have got fat off enterprises they promoted with union backing. Perhaps worst of all, this potentially great institution, the Teamsters Union, has been turned over to the likes of Johnny Dio and Joey Glimco and Bert Brennan and Babe Triscaro and Sam Goldstein, and others who have spent their lives shifting in and out of the Teamsters and in and out of trouble with the law.

In 1957 Hoffa promised to clean up the Teamsters if he became president. In 1958 he said he had not had time to do a complete job. In 1959 he said the Teamsters were clean. Hoffa has abandoned any pretense that he will clean up. He has not—and because of the men around him, he cannot.

The Teamsters Union is the most powerful institution in this country—aside from the United States Government itself. In many major metropolitan areas the Teamsters control all transportation. It is a Teamster who drives the mother to the hospital at birth. It is the Teamster who drives the hearse at death. And between birth and burial, the Teamsters drive the trucks that clothe and feed us and provide the vital necessities of life. They control the pickup and deliveries of milk, frozen meat, fresh fruit, department store merchandise, newspapers, railroad express, air freight, and of cargo to and from the sea docks.

Quite literally your life—the life of every person in the United States—is in the hands of Hoffa and his Teamsters.

[9] *Ibid.*, p. 143.

But, though the great majority of Teamster officers and Teamster members are honest, the Teamsters Union under Hoffa is often not run as a bona fide union. As Mr. Hoffa operates it, this is a conspiracy of evil.[10]

We have shown that Mr. Hoffa has made collusive deals with employers . . . betrayed the union membership . . . sold out the union membership . . . put gangsters and racketeers in important positions of power within the Teamsters Union . . . misused union funds.

If Mr. Hoffa wishes to sue me, I think we can take that to a court . . . and if he loses that case he should resign as president of the Teamsters.[11]

Democracy had been destroyed in the union by Hoffa and his thugs, Kennedy contended, and there was. virtually nothing that honest rank-and-file Teamsters could do about it.

This, then, is the story of democracy in the Teamsters Union—or, rather, the story of the complete absence of democracy in the Teamsters Union where Hoffa exercises control. Can anyone familiar with it still ask why the decent, honest, hard-working rank-and-file Teamsters don't rise up and throw out Jimmy Hoffa and his gang? The answer is simple:

They have tried in dozens of towns and cities across the country—and they can't. . . .[12]

Editorial cartoonists portray "the Teamsters" as a grasping octopus, a tidal wave of corruption about to engulf the nation's capital, a brass-knuckled fist, a shadowy underworld figure. Such images are accurate symbols of Hoffa's rule, but they attach an unfair stigma to the real Teamsters, the men who load the freight, and drive the trucks and deliver the milk. As a group the rank and file are decent, honest, hardworking men who, like Emil, [Teamster who dared to testify in Washington against Hoffa] hate what Hoffa is and what

[10] *Ibid.*, pp. 161-162.
[11] *Newsweek, August* 10, 1959.
[12] Kennedy, *op. cit.*, p. 138.

he stands for. Given half a chance they would indeed "rise up and throw him out." . . .[13]

People who ask why the rank and file put up with gangsters and corruption have only to look at what happened in Local 808 to realize the terrible truth of the matter is that the rank and file are powerless.[14]

However, when Kennedy resigned from the McClellan Committee in 1959 after more than two years of investigating Hoffa, the latter was still in full control of the Teamsters. Despite all the witnesses called and all the evidence collected, Hoffa was more powerful than ever—a fact about which he never tired of reminding Kennedy. Never one to accept defeat easily, RFK was not reticent about expressing his longing to see Hoffa behind bars and the Teamsters Union in new hands.

We have fought the evil that Hoffa represents for two and a half years. It's been a hard grind all along—for the people who work on our committee and for myself. I am not going to lie down and see all that work go to waste.[15]

And Hoffa's days are numbered. Because of recent court decisions the Teamster monitors have the power to press for his removal. I believe they will. Even if this does not prove true, a man with Hoffa's power and position, and so corrupt, cannot survive in a democratic society if democracy itself is going to survive. I believe the country, not Hoffa, will triumph.[16]

QUESTION: Mr. Kennedy, what do you think the Justice Department is going to be able to do with Jimmy Hoffa this year, I hope? (Laughter)
RFK: I'll tell you, if there isn't a reporter here—I'll tell you. (Laughter)
Well, he's under indictment at the present time, and so I think that it would be improper for me to make any com-

[13] *Ibid.*, p. 121.
[14] *Ibid.*, p. 138.
[15] *Newsweek*, August 10, 1959.
[16] Kennedy, *op. cit.*, p. 320.

ments on him or on his activities. I would say that nothing that I have learned since I became Attorney General of the United States has lessened my interest or concern about this matter. (Laughter) [17]

I'm not satisfied when I see men like Jimmy Hoffa, in charge of the largest union in the United States, running around free.[18]

Senator Robert F. Kennedy said today he was "pleased" by today's action of the Supreme Court in affirming the conviction of James Hoffa. The prosecution began when Kennedy was Attorney General in 1964. "I hope and believe that this final decision will facilitate the return of the Teamsters to the mainstream of the trade union movement," Senator Kennedy said, "where their strength can be a great force for a better life for all of our citizens." [19]

The Labor Movement, "Backbone of a Democracy"

Although Kennedy had nothing but contempt for Hoffa and his associates, he was careful to point out that he did not believe they were representative of the American labor movement as a whole. He frequently stressed the importance of organized labor to the survival of democracy and commended the integrity of labor leaders like Walter Reuther and George Meany.

A true democracy, to survive, to prosper, must have a strong, dedicated, militant labor movement. Its leaders must be devoted to their members, to an ideal. In my judgment a labor movement is the backbone of a democracy.[20]

The labor movement in America is a huge, living, human machine. It is subject to human error. But with a few excep-

[17] Question and answer following address, Associated Press Managing Editors luncheon, Dallas, Tex., November 15, 1961.
[18] *U.S. News & World Report*, March 16, 1964.
[19] Press release, December 12, 1966.
[20] Robert F. Kennedy, *Just Friends and Brave Enemies* (New York: Harper & Row, 1962), p. 84.

tions, the men who run our great labor unions in this country are honest, dedicated men. . . ."[21]

Senators Goldwater, Mundt and Curtis and others in the United States, because they disagreed with Reuther politically and economically, wanted him and the union investigated. It would follow automatically, they believed, that Reuther would be portrayed just like Beck and Hoffa. Why didn't you do to Reuther what you did to Beck and Hoffa, I have been asked. The reason is very simple and is the answer to this whole question. Reuther and the UAW have made mistakes, as I have pointed out, but as a general proposition the UAW is an honest union and Walter Reuther is an honest union official who attempts to run an honest union. For some people that is unfortunate but nevertheless it is true. Any attempt to equate the UAW with the Teamsters or Reuther with Hoffa will fail—and in fact, did fail. The sooner this fact of life is accepted in the country, the better off we shall all be. . . ."[22]

At a time when the faces of Beck and Hoffa stood out in the public mind as an image of labor corruption, George Meany and some of those around him stood out just as clearly as symbols of what was right and decent and honorable at the head of the American labor movement. Meany is a gruff, stubborn man. It is my belief that he sometimes depends on people around him who give him only those reports that they feel will be best for themselves, or that he wants to hear. But he is incorruptible and the labor movement was fortunate to have him in an hour of crisis. So was the country."[23]

But the question remained: What could be done in those cases where union corruption did exist? Kennedy believed a change in attitude on the part of many of the nation's businessmen would provide a good beginning.

The great concentration of power that rests in some of the unions in this country should be a matter of concern, just as should the great concentrations of power in some companies

[21] Kennedy, *The Enemy Within,* p. 211.
[22] *Ibid.,* p. 298.
[23] *Ibid.,* p. 214.

and businesses in certain sections of the country. But the answer to the problem of powerful unions is not to be found in a breakdown of morality in the nation's business community. Unfortunately this is the answer too many businessmen are willing to accept.

I recognize that the majority of American businessmen are above crookedness and collusion in labor-management negotiations. But we found that with the present-day emphasis on money and material goods many businessmen were willing to make corrupt "deals" with dishonest union officials in order to gain competitive advantage or to make a few extra dollars.[24]

He called for new legislation to eliminate corruption and a re-examination of existing laws such as the Landrum-Griffin Act (legislation enacted in 1959 to lessen corruption and strengthen democracy within labor unions).

The most important thing is to get legislation. That transcends everything else. You can get rid of Beck or Hoffa, but, in four or five years, they or their equivalents will be back unless there is law controlling the situation. Unless deficiencies in the law are rectified nothing is accomplished. What I think of Jimmy Hoffa is unimportant. I just think there is a tremendous amount of power concentrated in the hands of evil people. Hoffa is the epitome of it. We can't deal with it at the present time.[25]

I believe the time has come to review the provisions of the Landrum-Griffin Act. The bill that passed the Congress in 1959 was very different from the one that my brother proposed and that George Meany and the AFL-CIO supported.

The Law's provisions which expose and prevent corruption are necessary, as your own Al Hayes, the chairman of the Ethical Practices Committee of the AFL-CIO, would agree.

But he would also agree that five years of experience with this law shows that the overwhelming number of trade unions

[24] *Ibid.*, p. 216.
[25] *U.S. News & World Report*, August 31, 1959.

are run honestly, efficiently and fairly. And that there are provisions of Landrum-Griffin which have nothing to do with the main purposes of the law and in my opinion are anti-union.

For example, the handicaps imposed on organizational picketing and so-called secondary boycotting—these are attacks on legitimate weapons in labor's arsenal—and I am opposed to those restrictions.

I do not believe—and my brother did not believe—that those provisions were in accordance with the objectives of the bill. I believe we have to act on that. . . .

I believe some other provisions of Landrum-Griffin, while legitimate in their objectives, have worked a hardship on trade unions—particularly the small local. The reporting and bonding requirements are expensive and often burdensome. I believe we should consider very carefully whether they should not be relaxed in certain cases or even removed.

I would propose in the next Congress—and I would fight for—a formal review of the Landrum-Griffin Act. I think we should examine its provisions and remove its burdens to the labor movement.[26]

The "Right to Work" Law

Legislatively, the cardinal objective of organized labor's lobbyists on Capitol Hill during the past decade has been the repeal of section 14(b), the so-called "right-to-work" section, of the Taft-Hartley Law. Robert Kennedy lent his full support to the repeal campaign.

It is my view that collective bargaining demands strength on *both* sides of the table. And it is my view that Section 14(b) of the Taft-Hartley Act must be repealed.

Some have tried to justify the so-called Right to Work Laws that have grown out of 14(b) by saying they preserved liberty but to weaken labor unions. And I will fight for the repeal of 14(b).[27]

[26] Speech, International Association of Machinists, New York Council, Buffalo, N.Y., October 17, 1964.
[27] *Ibid.*

Beyond this is the question of whether 14(b) should be repealed. I believe that it should. At the outset, we must realize what the issue really is. A vote for 14(b) is not a vote to make the union shop compulsory. Rather it is a vote to allow unions and management to freely reach agreement on whether a union shop should be instituted. In those states which do not have right-to-work laws and in the nation, should we repeal 14(b)—no union shop can be imposed without the consent of management. No union shop can be instituted over the objection of a majority of the workers in a bargaining unit. . . .

Having said this, the question is, Why should 14(b) be repealed?

The first reason is the need to return to a uniform national labor law. Uniformity is no abstract goal; it has real and immediate consequences. It was originally sought in the Wagner Act of 1937 because we realized that ours is a national economy. Our great companies operate in every state in the Union. Their manufacturing operations are often spread over dozens of states; they buy their products everywhere. The unions which represent their employees are also national in scope. For such a national economy to operate efficiently and with a minimum of discord, it is necessary that the laws affecting collective bargaining and union organization do not differ from state to state. Lack of uniformity encourages states to compete with others for industry by making union organization more difficult. Even a senator from New York, which has lost large amounts of industry to other states in recent years, cannot criticize the efforts of less-developed states to attract industry and the new payrolls it brings. But that competition should not be fought out at the expense of American workers, or of their rights to bargain freely on the terms and conditions of employment—including the union shop. A third reason for the repeal of 14(b) is that it contributes to wage levels which are unacceptably low. Average weekly wages in manufacturing enterprise in states without right-to-work laws in 1963, for example, were $101.52. For comparable enterprises in states with right-to-work laws, the average weekly wage was $91.80. . . .

Let us, then, be clear as to what the issues are. No one, as a result of repeal of 14(b), will be forced to join a union—only to contribute with his dues toward the work of the union which improves his own wages and working conditions. The only "States' right" which is at issue is the right to compete for industry with other states by hindering union organization and keeping wage levels low. What the repeal of 14(b) would mean, and all that it would mean, is that labor and management would bargain throughout the United States in a more uniform manner—unhampered by restrictive state laws. It would help to improve wages and working conditions for millions of Americans. It would remove artificial incentives for industry to change its location. It would serve a national economy with national rules. For these reasons, I shall vote for the repeal of 14(b), and vote for cloture on the debate which has held up the work of the Senate these past weeks.[28]

For in Louisiana—the only non-right-to-work state in its region—the average weekly wage in manufacturing was $100.62 per week, 23 dollars more a week than the average for the region and as much as 30 dollars a week more than wages paid in some neighboring states; a wage on a par with states like New York, Pennsylvania, and Illinois.

I submit to you that a weekly wage of 77 dollars—just 4,000 dollars a year—is not adequate in this country, in the year 1965. . . .

These figures demonstrate what you know in the marrow of your bones—that where unions are strong, the cause of progress and social justice is advanced; and where unions are kept weak, the whole society suffers.

The consequences of 14(b) cannot be denied.

But still there are those who say—in well-financed publicity campaigns—that the issue is not material welfare, but individual freedom; that unions are authoritarian, that workers should not be forced to join them in order to earn a living.

But they are not talking about the freedom of labor and management to set their own relationships by collective bargaining.

They are not talking about the freedom of workers to live in decent housing and educate their children and provide for their old age.

The freedom they are talking about is the freedom to buy

[28] Statement, U.S. Senate, February 8, 1966.

cheap and sell dear—to depress wage rates all over the country by threatening to move operations to states with right-to-work laws—the freedom to deny to labor the fruits of more than a half-century of devoted and courageous struggle and sacrifice.

That does not fit my definition of freedom.

That is not what we mean by justice.[29]

He came out against placing organized labor under antitrust legislation as a way of improving union operations:

I don't think that putting labor organizations under the antitrust laws is the answer.[30]

Compulsory Arbitration

In the summer of 1966 a Senate proposal for a forced settlement of the airlines strike brought to the surface Kennedy's thoughts on the controversial question of compulsory arbitration of strikes where the public interest is involved.

When the Labor and Public Welfare Committee began consideration of the airline strike last week, my initial position was in favor of congressional intervention. The strike has unquestionably disrupted and inconvenienced many people and a part of the business and commercial sector. It therefore appeared that special measures might be needed. During the hearings, however, the Secretary of Labor twice testified that there is no national emergency. And twice he told the committee that the administration requests no legislation, and makes no recommendations for legislation.

No major administration official—not one—has suggested that the Congress should enact legislation. Indeed, it has been indicated in today's debate that the President might not even

[29] Address, International Ladies' Garment Workers Union Convention, Miami, Fla., May 18, 1965.

[30] Remarks, Associated Press Managing Editors luncheon, Dallas, Tex., November 15, 1961.

sign such a bill if we were to pass it. I am, therefore, opposed to legislation at this time. . . .

First, there is no national emergency, as that has been defined traditionally. Second, this legislation would be unprecedented. Never before, in nearly two hundred years, has Congress ordered striking men back to work. Only twice has Congress prevented men from striking—in 1916 and 1963. And the contrast between those cases and this is one demonstration why action now is inappropriate.

Third, this legislation would be a far-reaching precedent for intervention by the Congress into dozens, perhaps hundreds, of major labor disputes: intervention on an emergency basis, in the midst of bargaining, without the sober and considered judgment of expert and experienced opinion in or out of the Congress. I submit that those earlier judgments of the Congress not to intervene were completely sound and correct. Whatever the short-run effects of congressional intervention in particular labor disputes, Congress knew that the long-run effect could only be injurious to a free economy and a free collective bargaining system. We have stood firmly behind that principle in far more serious situations than the present. There is nothing—in the facts or in the position of the administration—which compels us to be the first Congress in the history of the United States to thus intervene in a labor dispute. . . .

I favor new legislation to deal with strikes that affect the public interest. I believe our laws are inadequate to handle the problems which have emerged in this area in the last few years. Too frequently the public interest is not sufficiently taken into account as the parties bargain. This is an ingredient which cannot be overlooked, and I believe we should act expeditiously to assure more effective assertion of the public interest in labor disputes. I would urge that the Labor and Public Welfare Committee undertake to hold hearings at an early date on this problem and on the form which new legislation should take.[31]

[31] Statement, U.S. Senate, August 4, 1966.

The Migrant Workers

During his last three years Kennedy had become one of the most outspoken supporters of union drives to organize migratory agricultural workers. In 1965 he flew to Delano, California, to encourage striking grape pickers seeking recognition for their union from the powerful growers' association. Commenting on some forthcoming hearings by the Senate Subcommittee on Migratory Labor, on which he sat, he remarked:

What will emerge from the hearings, if previous experience is any guide, is further evidence of the pressing need to enact legislation which allows the farm worker the right of other workers to organize in order to secure adequate wages and working conditions.[32]

Upgrading Skills

For those who are employed and organized he proposed a massive plan to upgrade the skills of the American worker. He called for transferable pension funds, job training for those already employed, and financial aid to enable older workers to go to college.

Our society changes rapidly, but we have not provided enough opportunity for people to change with it. We are proud, and justly, of the opportunities we offer to our young people now as never before, the lives of most of them are their own to determine. But what we have tended to overlook is that most of our people have, between the ages of fifteen and twenty, been forced to make a choice—of life and education and career—and that one choice has sharply limited later opportunities. . . .

If we are to allow new mobility to our people, we will have to assure them that rights they have earned—equities built up in pension funds are not lost. . . .

First. We should now begin to study ways in which

[32] Speech, U.S. Senate, September 6, 1967.

workers presently in the labor force could be assisted and encouraged to resume their education, continuing through college. Such a policy would require new methods of financial support for students. Most workers have families, and have assumed mortgages and other financial commitments on their behalf; to return to school, they would need income close to that they are now receiving throughout their study period. . . .

Third. Federal and state job-training programs should be made available, as resources permit, to persons now employed. If there is a need for workers in a particular skill, and none with that skill available, training of lower-skilled workers who now are employed will add as much to our economic growth as will training of persons not now employed. The latter can find the jobs vacated as the former move up the ladders. Efforts should be made to regulate training programs so as to allow presently employed workers to retain their present jobs while training.[33]

Today's Unions and Youth

Pondering the future of organized labor in this country, Kennedy warned that many of today's young activists no longer view the unions as a positive force for social and economic change:

Most of us at this dinner, when we think of labor unions, have as a frame of reference the long struggle to establish labor's basic rights—to make the workingman something more than an industrial serf. Labor has been in the forefront of many a great battle; it has always been a major part of this organization. But youth looks with other eyes, and their view is very different; They think of labor as grown sleek and bureaucratic with power, sometimes frankly discriminatory, occasionally even corrupt and exploitative; a force not for change but for the status quo, unwilling or unable to organize new groups of members, indifferent to the men who once worked the coal mines of Appalachia, a latecomer to the struggles

[33] Address, Joint Conference of Regions 9 and 9A, United Auto Workers, New York, N.Y., January 22, 1966.

of the grape pickers of California or the farm laborers of the Mississippi Delta. This is a one-sided picture, without the dimensions of fifty years' struggle, and the undramatic yet vital work of labor in many parts of the nation today. But there is too much truth in it for us not to understand our children's view—or to ignore the need for change.[34]

[34] Address, Americans for Democratic Action, Philadelphia, Pa., February 27, 1967.

Chapter 13

Conservation: Urban and Rural

Until recently conservation did not command a high priority on the list of our national tasks. Depleted and deteriorating natural resources were regarded primarily as a limited rural concern. Reforestation, wildlife management, and soil erosion prevention failed to ignite the imagination of most Americans, particularly those who lived in the cities.

Within the past few years all this has changed. Today conservation is recognized as lying at the heart of urban America's struggle to survive. For we have discovered that our technology and industry, the creators of our impressive affluence, are rapidly transforming our urban areas into death traps. Insufficiently treated human and industrial wastes dumped into our lakes and rivers are destroying our fresh-water supply. Smoke from industrial and municipal plants and incinerators, along with the exhaust from our automobiles, is poisoning the air we breathe. Our cities are becoming stinking, smog-ridden, unhealthy wastelands which, if nothing drastic is done to conserve our air and water, will soon be unfit to sustain human life.

It is no longer the senators from North Dakota and Idaho who lead the conservation fight in Congress, but men from industrialized states like New York and Connecticut. Conservation now is clearly an urban concern and a climbing national priority.

Air and Water Pollution

When Robert Kennedy was elected senator from an area with the pollution problems of New York City, it was only natural that he became an active urban conservationist. During his campaign for office in the fall of 1964, he discussed the problems confronting conservationists and suggested some of the remedies he would support if elected to Congress.

In its most profound sense conservation means to care about the public good over private gain.

In New York City it is the difference between the green respite of Central Park and the millions to be made there in real estate. In the great Adirondack and Catskill preserve it is the difference between an area guaranteed "forever wild" by our State Constitution and the constant encroachment of commerce. . . .

Expediency is the enemy and everywhere it threatens us with congestion and blight. Against it, we must fight to provide each citizen with breathing space and at least a minimum contact with the land and its creatures. We must insure that everyone can find self-renewal in what was once a frontier and always a wellspring of America's greatness. . . .

But we face problems today that conservationists of another day never dreamed of.

We face a crisis in urban conservation. We have suddenly awakened to find ourselves living in megalopolis—in the grips of urban and suburban sprawl, worsening slum conditions and mounting mass transit difficulties.

We even face a crisis in the very air we breathe and the water we drink. Fantastic amounts of soot, ash and stinking chemical masses, much of it from industrial areas of New Jersey, engulf New York City every day. Urban residents inhale the equivalent, in toxic substances, of two packs of cigarettes a day. . . .

The Clean Air Act of 1963 [federal act to provide funds and standards to combat air pollution] was an initial and significant step in this direction but much more in the way of federal appropriation and guidance is needed. . . .

Water pollution problems need more attention, too. . . . The federal Water Pollution Control Act has been extended and strengthened these past three and a half years. . . . But further expansion of federal participation is needed, particularly in the area of providing effective sanctions against the industrial raiders who pollute our streams and lakes and harbors.

And we must have a further expansion of the program of federal grants to help communities build sewage-treatment facilities. The need for such plants in our nation is immense.

The bill for a federal conservation program isn't going to be cheap. But it must be paid if we care—if we believe in a livable space for each person among the shoddiness, the noise and the profiteering, the impersonality of our cities and our suburbs, the destruction of our countryside.[1]

If the nuclear age has made us aware of anything—it is that we simply cannot continue to take for granted the purity of the air we breathe and the water we drink.

Harmful gases from auto exhausts and industrial fuels permeate the air. Polluted water affects some of our finest beaches, and intermittent water shortages are felt here and in many other states.

The cost of air and water pollution is staggering.

President Kennedy estimated in 1963 that air pollution costs Americans $11 billion annually in wear and tear on machinery, clothing, buildings and in light bills. Of even greater concern are the obvious health hazards. Heart disease, cancer, respiratory ailments are all higher in incidence where air is polluted. The bacterial threat of polluted water is manifest.

State and local authorities have taken some remedial purification measures—but the problem, in simple fact, outstrips their resources. Furthermore, air and water masses move interstate, so one weak link—one state which allows pollution to increase—weakens the whole chain of effort. . . .

I propose the following measures:

1. Tax relief via outright deduction or rapid amortization, encouraging private industry to utilize the expensive air-pollution control devices that exist and are available. . . . The cost of control equipment is high—it can run up to 25 percent of the cost of a plant's production machinery. Public-spirited firms should not be penalized financially for keeping the air clean.

[1] Speech, meeting of conservationists, Croton-on-Hudson, N.Y., October 22, 1964.

2. A fine, larger than the $100 a day which the federal Clear Air Act now imposes on those who do not file the reports it requires. Big polluters would rather pay this token fine indefinitely than invest in control equipment.

3. A federal standard establishing hazardous levels of sulphur dioxide, nitrogen dioxide, hydrocarbons, and other air-borne pollutants, and a means for publishing the existence of hazardous conditions.

4. A careful observation of the California requirement of afterburners to curb exhaust fumes on automobiles, with federal legislation to require them nationally if and when the California experiment proves workable.

5. Federal encouragement of the formation of more interstate air-pollution control agencies (there is only one now, the New York-New Jersey and Connecticut-Interstate Sanitation Commission) and of more extensive local regulation of air pollution.

6. Increased federal participation in the effort to find water resources for the nation's future needs, including more emphasis on efforts to develop a viable saline water conversion program.

7. Expansion of the program of federal grants to fight water pollution and expansion of federal regulation of industrial water pollution.[2]

After his victory, Kennedy wasted little time in joining the fight to abate pollution of the nation's rivers and lakes. Less than a month after taking the oath of office, he rose in the Senate to support the creation of a Federal Water Pollution Administration:

Senator Muskie, my distinguished colleague from Maine, has long recognized the dangers of pollution of our water resources. He recently introduced, for the Committee on Public Works, S. 4, a bill to amend the Federal Water Pollution Act, and under his able floor leadership the Senate enacted this bill on January 28, 1965. Passage of S. 4 is a significant step in the battle to abate the pollution of our streams, ponds, lakes and rivers. The creation of a Federal Water Pollution Administration provides focus for strong

[2] Campaign statement, October 16, 1964.

federal action in the field of water pollution abatement. The increase in the size of federal grants available for construction of sewage treatment plants makes its possible to meet the needs of the smaller and medium-sized communities. Yet Senator Muskie recognizes that S. 4 does not solve the problem of water pollution. He stated at the time of passage of S. 4 that his Special Subcommittee on Air and Water Pollution would consider further legislation. He also stated that his subcommittee would consider whether the federal government is providing sufficient funds to fulfill the obligations recognized under the Federal Water Pollution Act.[3]

In fact, most of the Senator's antipollution activity occurred in 1965. At a series of water pollution conferences and symposiums that year he made his views on the problem known.

Lake Erie is in danger of becoming polluted to the point where cities can no longer draw drinking water from this tremendous reservoir, where commerce on its shores is endangered, where the growth of algae and other aquatic plants threatens those who wish to enjoy the lake for boating, swimming or just the magnificent scenery.

We need more political innovation at the state and local levels, particularly in relation to industrial pollution. Of course, no town or state government likes to tell an industry that they must eliminate their pollution. The economics of plant investment often lead a firm to reply that it will relocate its plant in another state if local pollution controls are enforced. Because there are major differences in state regulations and enforcement of pollution laws, industry can play one municipality or state off against another. . . . Unless common standards are applied it is difficult to require action from communities and industry.

Yet New York, Massachusetts, Vermont, Maine and many other states opposed the establishment of federal interstate water quality standards recommended in the water pollution legislation brought before the Congress this season.

The water quality standards passed by the Senate this year but rejected by the House should be adopted by Con-

[3] Statement, U.S. Senate, February 8, 1965.

gress. I have urged the House conferees to join the Senate in adopting these interstate water quality standards. They are a critical underpinning for state and local antipollution efforts.

We must go beyond the establishment of standards that apply only to interstate waters, and establish and enforce quality standards for all waterways.

I do not believe that continued federal aid to fight the contamination of water will be available until the states are willing to enforce pollution regulations. There are a number of ways in which better pollution control can be exercised.

In Germany and England, for example, which are countries that have already faced the water shortage that we are now experiencing, each source of pollution is licensed by the appropriate river or water basin commission so that there is full knowledge of the pollution that is going into the waterway. And certain kinds of pollution are prohibited.

We could well do the same in the United States. We might, for instance, have a federally established licensing or permit system, with enforcement generally to be accomplished by states and municipalities. The control agency could be given a right of entry and inspection for all licensed sources of pollution. Such a system of licensing would insure that competing firms with pollution problems would be treated alike.

Another source of control might be a user fee applied to each source of pollution on the basis of the cost to the government of removing the pollutants that are discharged. Since collective treatment of waste is less costly, this user fee might cost the polluter less than installing his own purification unit would cost.

I also believe that federal economic assistance to industry in meeting new pollution standards can be provided through rapid federal tax write-offs of the cost of acquiring and installing adequate pollution control equipment. Assistance of this type could be useful if coupled with a broad attack on water pollution.[4]

I also want to stress today that water pollution is an interstate problem. The body of water on which a community or industry is located does not have to cross a state border to

[4] Statement, Buffalo Session of Water Pollution Conference for Lake Erie, Buffalo, N.Y., August 10, 1965.

make the problem an interstate one. As long as widely different standards of water quality and water pollution regulation enforcement exist, individuals, industries, municipalities, counties, and states will find it difficult to take the steps to eliminate pollution. Runaway industry, lax enforcement of pollution regulations, public apathy toward new bond issues, and a more dreary natural environment will haunt our lives.

I hope that the subcommittee will indicate at the end of their study whether they think it is possible to maintain 50 different water quality systems and meaningfully enforce these systems. I hope that they will suggest some of the ways in which a more uniform system can be evolved. I think that such a system would permit effective enforcement of water quality standards. Without this enforcement we will not have the water resources that we require for the future.[5]

The present crisis is largely of our own making. In parts of the country we have continued to allow streams to flood without adequate control, thereby losing billions of gallons of water which could be stored for future use. We have stood by while our lakes and rivers have been polluted by cities and industry to the point where they cannot be safely used as a water supply. In some places we have planned our reservoirs badly, making no provision for a reserve capacity sufficient to see us through extreme drought. We have been inattentive to the development of new sources of supply and the conservation and economy in the use of our water. . . .

And if we now see crisis in the midst of plenty, we may shortly see a deeper crisis. The total amount of rain which falls in the United States is 560 billion gallons a day. Some of this we capture for use—in reservoirs, after it falls; from streams and lakes as it makes its way to the sea; from wells as it seeps into the ground. We use 320 billion gallons of water a day. Of this water, our industry uses 51 percent, agriculture uses 40 percent, and individual use accounts for only 9 percent. But by 1980, unless we radically change our present patterns of water consumption, we will use the equivalent of all the water which falls in the country—as fast as it falls.

Clearly, we cannot hope to capture all the water which falls.

[5] Statement, Subcommittee on Air and Water Pollution of the Senate Committee on Public Works, June 17, 1965.

But our effective supply of water must be increased. We have, then, two great tasks. One is to develop, to the fullest extent possible, our capacity to capture usable water. The second is to make our water use more efficient—to make each gallon serve as many purposes as possible, to retain it within our control as long as possible. . . .

What is required now is a careful matching of water resources and water uses—of what we have and can develop, and what we need—an assessment weighed, in each case, according to the monetary and social cost of each course of action. . . .

We must plan and develop all available sources of water supply. This is a matter for action at all levels of government. Water resources problems do not stay neatly within state, let alone city lines. Streams and watersheds are often interstate in nature. Cooperative planning and development activity are essential. . . .

Perhaps the major problem with use of run-off water in lakes and streams in much of the United States is pollution. Our municipal sewage systems are for the most part hopelessly out of date and our industries continue to pour wastes and heated water into our streams at rates that prevent the natural cleansing processes from working.

We must clean up the streams and lakes. In addition to obvious reasons of health and recreation for doing so, the fact is that this is the most economical way to get at significant sources of water. The Hudson River pours 20 billion gallons a day into the Atlantic, all of which is too polluted to use except in the case of emergency. . . .

We vitally need interstate water quality standards. The multiplicity of state and local laws and practices has dulled incentive to clean up pollution. The need for uniform standards on interstate bodies of water, to which all will be held, would seem obvious. Yet this measure has encountered serious opposition in the Congress this year. . . .

I might say a particular word about desalinization. Its current costs—30 to 50 cents a thousand gallons—are too high to allow immediate reliance on this technique for much of our water needs. Indeed, the desalinization plants that have been built up to now are far too small in size to make even a dent in, say, New York City's needs. But we must continue to push the cost down, as President Johnson said so cogently recently.

The technology of desalinization is not just important for this country. In the arid countries of the world an ample supply of water could grow food and arrest starvation. A cheap enough way of processing salt water could give life and hope for the future to millions of people all over the world. . . .

In this connection, we must realize that there is no such thing as "free water." Water costs money; if it is not paid for on a user basis, it must be paid for by general taxation. Lack of metering means that small users tend to subsidize large industrial and agricultural users, which may or may not be an acceptable policy. I think the question of metering deserves a thorough discussion of the pros and cons if we are to make the right decision. In any case the waste of water which lack of meters encourages may be too costly.

A more fundamental goal is multiple use of all the water we have. We now, of course, use water more than once; the simplest example is the river water which is taken out by an upstream town, used, and replaced in the river—only to be taken out, purified, used again, and returned at towns lower down. But we can, and must, do more in this regard. First, only multiple use will allow us to meet our needs, which will increase, while rainfall remains at its present level. Secondly, multiple use can reduce our costs sharply—as in the Bethlehem steel plant.[6]

In 1966 Kennedy and Senator Muskie of Maine co-sponsored a bill to greatly expand existing water pollution control efforts:

To meet this need, I co-sponsored with Senator Muskie this year a Water Pollution Control bill that will provide a total of $6 billion over the next six years to assist communities in meeting sewage treatment plant and sewer needs. . . .

What becomes clear is that we no longer can afford to provide only primary treatment. We need to provide secondary treatment for municipal sewage if we are to keep from being outdistanced by our population and this costs money.

[6] Speech, International Water Quality Symposium, Washington, D.C., August 26, 1965.

I also believe that we may want to offer federal tax credits to older industries that are required to add treatment facilities because of a change in water quality standards. These credits could be made available to existing plants on rivers or lakes where water quality standards are raised. In this way, a comprehensive plan insuring higher water quality standards could be placed in effect. These credits would help older industry meet those costs and reduce the incentive to relocate. If we found, however, that an enforcement of water quality standards was causing a relocation of industry, we would have to enact federal standards to insure that industry was treated equally in every state.[7]

It was during this same period when he was urging Congress to attack the problem of water pollution that Kennedy began proposing legislative action against air pollution.

We are beginning to find the evidence showing a direct connection between air pollution and lung cancer; it has been shown that our air contains highly carcinogenic substances in quantities that often more than equal the amount that an individual would be exposed to in smoking several packs of cigarettes in one day.

In addition to the direct danger to health, air pollution takes a tremendous economic toll from each individual who lives in the New York metropolitan area. New York residents pay a high cost to clean up the soot and dirt that the air daily brings into their homes and places of business. Cars in New York must be washed more often than in other areas because of the high dustfall. As Commissioner Benline has pointed out, the economic cost to New York City alone is estimated to be $520 million per year. In deterioration of stone building fronts, rusting of metal, costs of cleaning clothes, weathering of paint, and many other similar costs, each one of us bears an unnecessary economic burden.[8]

[7] Statement, House Subcommittee on National Resources and Power, Syracuse, N.Y., August 19, 1966.

[8] Statement, New York City Council Special Committee on Air Pollution, New York, N.Y., June 25, 1965.

In discussing another health problem, cigarette smoking, it was pointed out that the individual had a choice as to whether he would smoke. There was no choice, however, for the 360 people in New York City who died in 1963 in one incident because of an increase in the pollution of the air. And there is no choice for the millions who will have their lives shortened because our air is contaminated. It is our responsibility to reduce the level of pollution to a point where no individual's health is threatened.[9]

He offered some specific suggestions for abatement:

Another federal action that can assist in eliminating air pollution in New York City is to halt the emission of pollutants by automobiles and other motor vehicles. A bill currently pending before the Congress, S. 306, would require the installation of antipollution devices on all new automobiles, by September 1, 1967. The Senate has already passed S. 306 and it is now pending before the House. I am hopeful that S. 306 will be passed during the current session of Congress so that this particular source of air pollution may be eliminated.[10]

We can make progress in our efforts to control air pollution if we establish a federal safety code for the major pollutants. This code, establishing an adverse and a serious level for each of the significant pollutants, could be used as a guideline by communities concerned with this problem. This code should set a level for a pollutant that will protect all members of the community, the very young and the old and those most sensitive to the effects of this pollutant as well as those more able to withstand the effects of pollution. For these groups suffer most when pollution levels rise. There is no doubt in the minds of our doctors that pollution takes a toll of these groups —a toll that is reflected in the death records of most major cities.[11]

However, he subsequently lost faith in the efficacy of

[9] Statement, U.S. Senate, July 12, 1966.
[10] Statement, New York City Council Special Committee on Air Pollution, New York, N.Y., June 25, 1965.
[11] Statement, U.S. Senate, July 12, 1966.

certain of these control devices and at one point actually called for the elimination of individual automobiles:

The Clean Air Act of 1966 requires pollution control devices on all new cars starting in 1968. But at the current rate of car replacement, it will take almost ten years to equip most cars with these devices. In addition, test information from Los Angeles states that the new devices do not meet the standards established by the Clean Air Act. This means that we cannot expect a significant decrease in pollution from cars in the near future.

As a result, we need to substitute mass transportation systems for individual cars if we are to obtain a significant reduction in the amount of carbon monoxide and hydrocarbon in the atmosphere. A conference recommendation for a regional transportation plan designed with this problem in mind would meet this need.[12]

Wildlife Protection

Occasionally he addressed himself to the more traditional concerns of conservationists.

This is a task that requires the utmost care and farsightedness on the part of the subcommittee's members. We must both exert every effort to prevent the destruction of fish species by indiscriminate action on the part of man, and also take the necessary steps to accommodate modern technology to our environment.

Unfortunately, the record in the United States is not one of which we can be proud. The destruction of animal, bird and fish species over the centuries is testimony to our lack of foresight. I hope that we are better prepared today, both with knowledge and strength of conviction, to prevent the destruction of our remaining fish and wildlife.

In the larger sense, the task we face today is the difficult job of insuring that our modern atomic energy installations,

[12] Public letter to Secretary of Health, Education and Welfare John Gardner, March 11, 1967.

power plants, chemical industries and municipalities do not contaminate and desolate our environment.

At the same time that we introduce new techniques to improve our well-being, we must also insure that we do not kill off other life on our planet. As mankind grows in numbers and as our requirements for housing, energy, food and sewage disposal grow proportionately, we face the possibility that we may not only destroy animal, fish, and plant life but that we may destroy ourselves as well. Problems of air and water pollution, nuclear fallout, and misuse of pesticides are not idle threats to human life.[13]

Potomac Palisades

I was dismayed to read recently that permission has been given for the building of a high-rise motel addition near the Virginia end of Key Bridge. I was also dismayed to read of the Interior Department's position, which was expressed in a letter signed by Assistant Secretary Stanley Cain. That letter, while expressing concern about the future development of the Potomac palisades, offered no objection to the motel proposal.

Now, in addition, the motel firm has been given permission to erect a pair of neon signs on top of the motel addition.

I believe this matter merits your personal consideration. I know you agree that we in the District of Columbia area are extraordinarily lucky to have a vista as attractive as the Potomac palisades so close at hand. The proposed motel addition will mar that vista, and the proposed neon signs will add to the intrusion. Even more important, because the tower would be the first high-rise building on the river side of Interstate Highway 66, it could well be the first step toward a series of encroachments which permanently deprive us of the beauty of the palisades.[14]

After late 1966, Robert Kennedy said almost nothing about conservation, rural or urban. The reason for the late Senator's sudden loss of interest is not clear.

[13] Statement, Fisheries and Wildlife Subcommittee of the House Merchant Marine and Fisheries Committee, May 11, 1965.

[14] Letter to Secretary of the Interior Stewart L. Udall, February 20, 1967.

Chapter 14

Agriculture and the Farm Problem

Essentially, the American "farm problem" is that a sizable group of people who are trying to make a living in agriculture are not earning an adequate income. Of the 3.7 million farms in this country, 21 percent produce 72 percent of the nation's agricultural output. Needless to say, the men and women and corporations who operate these large farms are doing well (these are also the farmers who receive the bulk of the roughly three billion dollars a year spent by the federal government for agricultural income stabilization). At the other end of the scale are the 44 percent of the farms that account for only 5 percent of the produce. Most of the people who own these farms depend on nonagricultural employment to provide or supplement their incomes; for the most part, this group doesn't warrant any national concern.

To locate the hard core of the "farm problem" we have to turn to the middle 35 percent of the farms which transact only 23 percent of the business. This group, which relies entirely on farming for its livelihood, has been finding it increasingly difficult to compete with the bigger farms because of lack of capital. These are the people who have to be induced either to enlarge their farm operations or to give up farming if American agriculture is to become entirely self-sufficient. As time goes on, many of the children of these farmers can be counted on to find nonagricultural jobs. To facilitate this process, the federal government has been attempting to attract industries to these nonproductive agricultural areas through development programs such as the Appalachia project.

Another aspect of the "farm problem" which has become increasingly visible during the past few years is the tragic plight of the migrant farm laborers. Living in much the same deplorable conditions so poignantly portrayed in *The Grapes of Wrath* a third of a century ago, these modern nomads have received scant help in their struggle to escape the horrors of rural poverty.

From statements such as the following, it is evident that Kennedy was not well acquainted with the difficulties of American agriculture in the early sixties.

Well, I could say that that is a domestic economic problem which is very high on the list. It has been high for a long period of time. The cost to the American taxpayer . . . I guess, it's four billions of dollars, and it is a continuous drain on the treasury, which is not going to be liked by any administration, Republican or Democratic. We have just increased our productivity here in the United States.

I was in the Soviet Union in 1955 and they were producing manpowerwise at most, 20 percent of what an individual farmer could produce here in the United States. This is a continuous problem, based on our increased productivity, and we haven't got the answer to that, and it's going to continue to cost money, and it's going to be a continuous fight and effort to try to pay them, but again, it's not going to be successful immediately, and again, there is a concern by the administration and by the President of the money that's going into this program. If anybody has an answer to the farm problem, however, we certainly would welcome it.[1]

The Need for a Rural Revival

Beginning with his Senate campaign in 1964, he made reference at times to a need for a rural revival in this country.

[1] Answer to question following address, Associated Press Managing Editors luncheon, Dallas, Tex., November 15, 1961.

The family farm—long a vital institution in the fabric of American life—has been placed in serious danger by the momentous changes that have occurred and are occurring in agricultural technology.

This is the challenge facing us. We must see to it that the rural America which emerges from the agricultural revolution is a healthy one. We must insure that our rural community continues to contribute to and enrich our great nation.

What is needed is a program for rural America—a program which encompasses not only an answer to the question of how each of you can make a better living from producing milk and other products, but also a way to bring new industry to your towns and to keep present industry there.[2]

But today I want to say that the time has come when the movement to the cities must slow down, even stop—that the rural areas of this state and the United States should not be further stripped of their people and their pride—and that we must act to revitalize these areas, to make use of their great resources for the benefit of all of us.

For I believe that rural America means much more than farms or produce. I think that the traditions—the values— the sense of rootedness and the fundamental decency, to be found in our small towns and farms, are essential to a healthy nation. And I think that we have lost as much of these traditions and values as we can afford to lose.

Furthermore, the evidence is clear that any continued move to the cities will only increase our already staggering urban problems. Our cities are already more crowded, less able to clear their air and their water, less able to educate their children properly than is good for the people who live in them. Jobs are increasingly reserved for the highly educated and trained; and many of those now moving to the cities are unable to find adequate jobs there.[3]

But there is simply not enough room in the big cities; and it is not more bigness that should be our goal. We must

[2] Speech, farm meeting outside St. Johnsville, N.Y., October 19, 1964.

[3] Speech, Western New York Publishers Association, Painted Post, N.Y., October 9, 1965.

attempt, rather, to bring people back to places such as this—
back to the warmth of community, to the worth of individual
effort and responsibility. Therefore, every step we take to
make our rural areas more attractive and viable—participating
in the economy, giving their children the finest possible
education, affording their citizens the stimulus and excitement
of thought and learning and entertainment—every such step
is a gain for all America. For it was Athens, the very mother
of cities, which showed us that greatness does not require
size—even as others have shown us that size does not
necessarily bring greatness.[4]

The Plight of the Migrant Workers, East and West

In 1966, Kennedy became publicly involved with the
issue of migrant labor when he flew to Delano, California,
in June to support a strike of migrant grape pickers (see
Chapter 5). At that time he called for a revision of the
National Labor Relations Act to enable farm workers to
organize and bargain effectively with their employers.

We would add this: If ever there were a classic case for
bringing farm workers under the collective bargaining provisions of the National Labor Relations Act, this is certainly
it. The lack of legally constituted, orderly procedures upon
which labor and management may rely created chaos in this
situation. And if, as seems inevitable, the union movement
among farm workers is going to spread, the chaos also will
spread unless we enact legislation to extend the rights and
obligations of our national collective bargaining laws to the
farm industry.[5]

He raised the issue again several times:

I was delighted to hear today that Schenley Industries
has agreed to bargain with the National Farm Workers
Association, which represents agricultural workers who work in
the fields for Schenley and other firms which grow grapes
in central California. This right has now been recognized in

---

[4] Speech, Worthington, Minn., September 17, 1966.
[5] Statement, U.S. Senate, June 28, 1966.

the fields of one grower in California, but only under the most difficult circumstances and after great effort. It should now be recognized under the law, for two reasons: first, so that field workers who want a union to represent them do not have to endure the hardship of a long organizational strike every time they have sufficient support for a union to bargain with one particular grower, and second, so that growers will have the protection of having an established machinery to determine without disruption whether there is in fact sufficient support among the workers for designation of a bargaining representative.[6]

Though the plight of the migrant workers in the West was receiving the most publicity, Kennedy was quick to remind his own constituents that New York, too, shared this problem.

The legislation will help, but we can and must do much more. We can help, now, by making the public aware of the fact that the average migrant family earns $1,200 a year from farm work and that, more often than not, these families live in conditions more wretched than the worst urban slum. The public should know that the young children of these families often are uneducated, because they must work the way children worked fifty years ago before there were laws to protect them. The public should also understand the dilemma of the small farmer. Many farmers intend to improve conditions in their camps, but lack the resources to build new housing and health and sanitation facilities. Public concern and understanding are essential because the migrant workers are an unorganized, voiceless minority. Public indignation and pressure will be necessary to force the kind of action, by government and by farmers, which is so long overdue.[7]

[6] Statement, U.S. Senate, April 7, 1967.
[7] Statement, U.S. Senate, September 18, 1967.

The American Farmer, His Needs and His Role in the World

But it was not until he delivered a major address at the National Farmers Union convention in Oklahoma City in March 1967 that anything that might be called a Kennedy farm policy emerged. What follows is a number of excerpts from that important speech:

Still, for these great contributions, you have not been equitably repaid. We can be glad that net farm income last year reached $16.1 billion, up from $11.7 billion just six years before. But this great increase still leaves farm income 17 percent lower than it was in 1947—while income in the rest of the economy has more than doubled.

It is sometimes said that the decline in total net farm income is not so bad because more than 2½ million farmers have left the land since World War II. But farm income per person, or per farm family, is over 50 percent below income in the rest of the country—just as far as it was twenty years ago. Two-thirds of the nation's farms return less than $4,000 a year to their owners and operators, for all their sweat and sacrifice and investment.

And as one economist has said: "It is not good enough to save half the people on a ship by casting the other half off into the sea. . . ."

Farmers deserve—and the nation can afford to pay them—a fair price for what they produce. All of us must come to realize that no one is the gainer—and all of us lose—when farmers are not paid a fair return for their investment and their labor. Better farm prices would benefit consumers—as workers and businessmen—far more than they would cost at the retail level. That, after all, is one reason why we have minimum-wage laws and social security, and why we encourage labor unions to organize for better pay. If the farm economy allowed farmers to bargain collectively as labor does, the farm problem would be very different than it is today—and farmers might not think of it as a problem at all. . . .

The first aim of our policy must be to bring greater income to farm *families*. We can applaud the 200,000 family farmers who have moved into the more adequate size group [bigger profits] in the last eight years. But these more prosperous family farms have not taken their proportionate share of the market—too much has gone instead to giants, not necessarily more efficient, but with advantages of better access to capital and credit, bargaining power and tax advantages. Ways must be found to direct government support, as much as possible, to the family farms which need it and to help them realize opportunities for growth by providing realistic credit in adequate amounts. . . .

Second, we need more—not less—farm production. Private consumption within the United States must rise even faster than the population. Twenty percent of all Americans still subsist on inadequate diets. Assuring them enough to eat—both through expansion of direct aid like the Food Stamp and School Lunch programs and through vastly expanded efforts to eliminate poverty—would also be of great assistance to the farm economy.

Government efforts to export food to the hungry of the world must also increase. World population will double by the year 2000. The underdeveloped world will grow even faster—Latin America will triple in size. Asia's population by itself will exceed the present world total. . . .

But if we are to meet these responsibilities abroad, we will first have to rid ourselves of one of the most misleading myths in public debate: the myth of "surpluses." We restrict food shipments to India's famine areas, in large part because American food stocks are now below adequate reserve levels. Our production-reducing policies have been so successful that the present wheat and feed grain reserve of the United States would scarcely meet our own needs for six months if a catastrophe wiped out a single year's crop.

Still, millions of Americans believe that farmers overproduce and depress farm prices, and that the taxpayer is unfairly required to "bail out" the farmer through government payments. But for those who look clearly at facts, there is a different story. During the decade 1953-1964, when the outcry over surpluses was at its greatest, farm production exceeded consumption only 1.8 percent. . . .

So rather than talk about surpluses, we could do better to think of the children of Appalachia and Harlem, the young mothers of Latin America, the villages of East Asia—of the food forever lost to them, which was not produced in the past; and of the food which will be lost to them in the future unless we produce much more today. Acres left fallow are, to this starving world, as consequential as pigs or potatoes plowed under the ground. And as Owen Young warned in the 1920s in a prophecy all too accurate: "If America starts to burn surplus wheat or cotton . . . when people are hungry elsewhere in the world, the fire will start a conflagration which cannot stop." Now, as we look to the millions of India and Pakistan and Latin America, to half the world's population without enough to eat, we know that that fire cannot be allowed to burn. . . .

We must, therefore, rid ourselves finally of the idea that Food for Peace is a surplus disposal program. We must not only utilize all existing Food for Peace authority, but we must act now to plan the production of food at a level which will enable us to begin meeting our responsibilities adequately. Such planning—together with appropriate pricing policy— will not only help feed millions of malnourished children, but will help the farmer finally to know that he will be able to dispose of the crop he plants at a fair price. . . .

Third, the farmer, a classical free competitor, cannot continue to buy his needs from and sell his goods to giant industries with vastly superior bargaining power. Farmers must buy tractors and harvesters and fertilizers, spending up to 60 percent of the value of their produce. But these prices do not fall in bad years. The steel industry, for example, did not reduce its prices even during the Great Depression, and every recession since has seen many industrial prices rise even as workers were laid off and plants shut down. On the other side, in the market where you sell, we have all watched the miller and baker, the wholesaler and retailer, raise their prices again and again while your prices were rising far less, or even falling—as they are doing now. . . .

Part of the answer to the cost-price squeeze facing the farmer is in vigorous and vigilant enforcement of the antitrust laws. Another—perhaps more fundamental—is in encouragement and assistance to the principle of cooperative action which the Farmers Union has already done so much to further. The continued growth of institutions like your Central Exchange, which saved you $11 million last year, will be of benefit to us all. And if processing firms can reach back to grow their own raw materials, perhaps family farmers can also reach forward together to process what they grow.[8]

[8] Address, National Farmers Union Convention, Oklahoma City, Okla., March 13, 1967.

Chapter 15

The Radical Left and Right

And there have been those, throughout our history—
and particularly in times of crisis—who have preached
intolerance, who have sought to escape reality and
responsibility with a slogan or a scapegoat. Religious
groups have been the first targets but they have not
been the only ones.

There are those who suspect their neighbors because
they pray to a different God—or because they pray
to none at all. And there are those who bellow that
a former President of the United States is a tool of
the Communist conspiracy.

There are those who preach that desegregation of
the schools will destroy our society. And there are
others who believe that calamity will occur because
of the way we may treat our drinking water.

There is a freedom in this country to be extreme, to
propose the most reactionary or the most utopian
solutions to all the problems of the country or even
the world. There is freedom here to believe and act
with passion, whether for the cause of religion, or
party, or personal welfare. . . .

What is objectionable, what is dangerous about extremists is not that they are extreme, but that they
are intolerant. The evil is not what they say about
their cause, but what they say about their opponents.
The intolerant man will not rely on persuasion, or
on the worth of the idea. He would deny to others
the very freedom of opinion or of dissent which he
so stridently demands for himself. He cannot trust
democracy.

Frustrated by rejection, he condemns the motives,
the morals, or the patriotism of all who disagree.

Whether it is inflamed by politics or religion or drinking water, he still spreads selfish slogans and false fears.[1]

It was apparently this rejection of the "gentlemen's agreement" to approach affairs of state in a trusting, tolerant, open manner—an agreement which many argue is the essence of liberal democracy—that most disturbed Robert Kennedy about the politics of the far left and right in America.

The Extreme Left

Of the far left, particularly the American Communist party, Bobby stated the following over the years:

The Communist party as it exists in the United States and in other countries is not a legitimate political party. It is a group whose policies, decisions and movements are directed and controlled by a foreign power. This is why the Soviet Union and the Communist party are so inimical to the activities of free men everywhere. It is the Trojan Horse assuming the form of a so-called political party in democratic countries around the world—agrarian reformers in China, guerrillas in SouthVietnam or rioters in Japan.[2]

But the FBI has been dealing with this menace [the U.S. Communist party] for many, many years. If it hadn't been for the work of Mr. Hoover and the FBI, the Communist party would have achieved much greater power in the United States.[3]

First, I think that the Communist party as a political organization is of no danger in the United States. It has no following and has been disregarded by the American people

[1] Speech, dedication of John F. Kennedy Interfaith Chapel, West Georgia College, Carrollton, Ga., May 26, 1964.

[2] Press release, June 10, 1961.

[3] Press conference, U.S. Court House, Columbia, S.C., December 12, 1961.

for many, many years. It has been studied; attention has been given to it by newspapers, by congressional committees, and so everybody in the United States has had the opportunity to analyze it. The result is that it is down to a bare minimal following.

Number two, an organization even as small as the Communist party is in the United States, of about 10,000, where it is dominated and controlled and financed by a foreign power as the Communist party is in the United States, poses a danger at all times, because they are taking instructions and orders from an outside government. But the danger exists not in numbers, not in their political power in the United States, but the fact, as the Supreme Court has held eight to one, that they are dominated and controlled and financed by the Soviet Union.

Any time that you have a group or an organization in a country that exists and takes instructions from an outside power, that poses a danger.

The greatest danger, as far as communism in the United States, in my judgment, is not the Communist party, but comes from representatives of the Communist bloc countries who are here within the United States. I think that is the great danger. The great danger for the United States in the long run is not the Communist party and the small membership that it has here in this country, but the problems and the difficulties that we have overseas.[4]

The Communist party here in the United States has had the vigilant attention of the Federal Bureau of Investigation. That is necessary and that will continue. And the FBI is the organization that can deal with this operation in the best possible fashion. This is not a job for self-appointed patriots or office-seekers working in a hurry or part-time though well-intentioned sleuths.[5]

In 1962, on a visit to the Far East, Kennedy attempted to explain to a Japanese audience the U.S. legal requirement that all Communists must register with the federal

[4] Press conference, Los Angeles, Calif., March 24, 1962.
[5] Robert F. Kennedy, *The Pursuit of Justice* (New York: Harper & Row, 1965), p. 70.

government (the McCarran Internal Security Act of 1950).

An act was passed in 1950, with the overwhelming support of the American people, defining the Communist party as a representative, not of American citizens, but as following the orders and instructions of a foreign power in the United States, and that it therefore should register. . . .

There is overwhelming evidence that this is true, and that the Communist party in the United States is financed by the Soviet Union. And I think that is true of most Communist parties in the world. They follow the leadership of the Soviet Union. They are not looking out for what is best for the Japanese people or the American people, but what the Soviet Union tells them.[6]

The ADA

The Americans for Democratic Action, a national ultra-liberal group currently chaired by John Kenneth Galbraith, has frequently been accused of extreme left leanings by conservatives of both parties. In a speech before the ADA, Kennedy made it plain that he discounted any such extremist charges about the group:

Americans for Democratic Action is a young organization, on the scale of history. But in its passion for excellence, it is as old as the impulse which gave this nation birth.[7]

The Extreme Right

In time, Kennedy came to view the radical right in this country as a greater threat to American democracy than the left.

I have no sympathy with those who are defeatists and who

[6] Robert F. Kennedy, *Just Friends and Brave Enemies* (New York: Harper & Row, 1962), p. 74.

[7] Address, Americans for Democratic Action, Philadelphia, Pa., February 27, 1967.

would rather be "red than dead." Nor do I have sympathy with those who, in the name of fighting communism, sow seeds of suspicion and distrust by making false or irresponsible charges, not only against their neighbors, but against courageous teachers and public officials and against the foundations of our government—Congress, the Supreme Court and even the Presidency itself. As a vigilant, experienced American, who has real credentials as a Communist fighter—J. Edgar Hoover—has said, such actions play into Communist hands and hinder, rather than aid, the fight against communism.[8]

QUESTION: . . . what is your opinion of the danger on the political level of some of those who react most violently to the Communist problem . . . the extreme right-wing groups?

RFK: Well, I think that I have said before that there is a real sense of frustration in many parts of the United States about communism, about the Soviet Union. In an effort to try to do something about it, the efforts, in my judgment, are virtually misdirected. For that reason, I think that they perform, those who participate in those activities, a disservice to the United States and to the American people.

Number two, I think that as a general proposition, this can get into an area where there is harmfulness and unfairness to people's reputations, and I think that that is most unfortunate. I think that if these groups would direct themselves in a positive fashion to positive matters, to making a positive contribution, instead of making a negative basis, they could be a help against communism rather than a hindrance, which I think that they are at the present time. . . .[9]

The danger of such views is not that they will take control of the American government. In time, the consensus of good sense which characterizes our political system will digest and discard frozen views and impossible programs. But there is a *short-term* danger from such voices. If they cause enough confusion, stir enough irrational fear, and attract enough political allies, they can restrict and inhibit a

[8] Speech, Associated Press Managing Editors meeting, Dallas, Tex., November 15, 1961.

[9] Press conference, Los Angeles, Calif., March 24, 1962.

President's freedom to take maximum advantage of the openings which the future may present.

The answer to these voices cannot simply be reason, for they speak irrationally. The answer cannot come merely from government, no matter how conscientious or judicious. The answer must come from within the American democracy. It must come from an informed national consensus which can recognize futile fervor and simple solutions for what they are—and reject them quickly. . . .

To say that the future will be different from the present and past may be hopelessly self-evident. I must observe regretfully, however, that in politics it can be heresy. It can be denounced as radicalism or branded as subversion. There are people in every time and every land who want to stop history in its tracks. They fear the future, mistrust the present and invoke the security of a comfortable past which, in fact, never existed. It hardly seems necessary to point out in the United States, of all places, that change, although it involves risks, is the law of life.

Nevertheless, there are those, frustrated by a difficult future, who grab out for the security of a nonexistent past. Frustrated by change, they condemn the wisdom, the motives and even the patriotism of those who seek to contend with the realities of the future. They search for the haven of doctrine.[10]

There are others who would tear down what all of you have worked so hard to build—those who think education a luxury and cooperation between Americans a socialist plot. They are for education, if the federal government has no part in it; for education, but they must say what will be taught and what will not; for education, except if it costs money.[11]

In his conclusion, Bobby quoted from the speech President Kennedy had planned to deliver in Dallas on the day of the assassination. The President would have said that while dissident voices will always be heard in our

[10] Speech, California Institute of Technology, Pasadena, Calif., June 8, 1964.
[11] Speech, dinner honoring Congressman James C. Corman (D–Calif.), Los Angeles, Calif., October 21, 1966.

country, other kinds of voices are being heard in the land today, "voices preaching doctrines wholly unrelated to reality, wholly unsuited to the sixties, doctrines which apparently 'assume that words will suffice without weapons, that vituperation is as good as victory and that peace is a sign of weakness." President Kennedy's undelivered speech was, in part, critical of extremist positions which were being voiced in increasing numbers in late 1963. Bobby himself concluded, at Pasadena:

"President Kennedy felt we deserved better—that as a people and as a country, we had the strength, courage and fortitude to face the future." [12]

Of the John Birch Society, specifically, Kennedy said:

Well, I think that they are ridiculous and I don't think that anybody should really pay too much attention to them. I think that they make no contribution, in my estimation, to the fight against communism here in the United States, and in fact I think, if anything, that they are a hindrance. I don't know any of the top officials personally, but from the statements that I have read by them in the newspapers, it seems to me it is an organization that is in the area of being humorous, and I don't think so much attention should be paid to them.[13]

QUESTION: Mr. Kennedy, the John Birch Society has been in the news quite recently. Is this organization in any danger of winding up on the Attorney General's list of organizations? RFK: No, I wouldn't say so. I would say it's a group of individuals who are trying to accomplish and deal with a problem. I think they are misguided . . . the Communist party poses a problem but it is not as great a problem in my judgment as international communism, and the way to deal with it is not . . . to label everyone who disagrees with you as a Communist or a Communist sympathizer. As I've pointed out before, the only real live Communist that the John Birch, or

[12] Nick Thimmisch and William Johnson, *R. F. K. at 40* (Boston: W. W. Norton, 1965), p. 156.

[13] Press conference, U.S. Department of Justice, April 6, 1961.

its head, has seemed to uncover so far is President Eisenhower, so I don't think that's a great contribution.[14]

The New Right and Left

Why the marked resurgence of radical and reactionary political organizations in this country over the past decade? Kennedy pondered that question in a speech delivered in the summer of 1967:

Everywhere I go in this country I find people groping for answers to these other problems we barely understand; searching for purpose in the midst of baffling change; confusion and danger. We are losing many of our most active and committed young—losing them to extreme movements or to public indifference. We are losing members of the older generation who lack confidence in their ability to protect their future—and turn to the past in an effort to protect what they already have. The extreme-right Minutemen, and an extreme-left group calling itself the "Revolutionary Action Movement," agree on only one thing: that they have the right to arm themselves and use guns and violence against their fellow citizens with whom they disagree.

Radicalism and reaction—and the New Right and the New Left—reflect a common theme: the desperate desire of individuals to find a sense of inner significance, by sharing in some larger common purpose. And does not all this reveal what danger there is in feelings of helplessness, of impotence, in a lack of direction—polarizing groups and individuals, creating a nation of strangers; until even those with whom we sympathize, glare at us across an impassable barrier of hostility and mistrust.[15]

[14] Press conference, U.S. Court House, Columbia, S.C., December 12, 1961.
[15] Address, Salt Lake City, Utah, June 28, 1967.

Chapter 16

The American Economy

Robert Kennedy was not an economist, either by formal training or by avocation. I think he would not have taken issue with the statement that his understanding of the American economy and the fiscal and monetary devices available for managing it was superficial at best. Yet he did possess a set of beliefs about the advantages of a capitalist system and the constraints which should be placed upon it, and he frequently suggested the use of various fiscal measures and government economic controls for securing public goals. To the extent that it can be gleaned from his scattered statements on the subject, it is important that we comprehend Kennedy's conception of the economy if we are successfully to define him as a public figure.

Private Incentive and Public Control

To begin with, he was firmly convinced that private enterprise, with certain public controls, is responsible for much of America's freedom and affluence.

We in the United States regard highly the importance of private incentive. We see it as a mainspring for social action. This does not mean that state enterprise is incompatible with freedom. Our public power, our nuclear energy development and similar undertakings are proof that we can utilize, where desirable, the credit of the state in lieu of private capital.

But our history has been primarily that of private enterprise—controlled by the government wherever necessary in the public interest.[1]

Our enemies assert that capitalism enslaves the worker and will destroy itself. It is our national faith that the system of competitive enterprise offers the best hope for individual freedom, social development and economic growth.[2]

The vital difference has been the free individual American farmer, producing abundance by himself—while the compulsory work of state collectives, throughout the Communist world, produced only minimal subsistence. For all the efforts of the mighty Soviet State—all their grandiose schemes and lavish investments—could not equal the achievement of individual American farmers.[3]

Yet he realized that the mix of private initiative and government regulation that has worked in this country in the past may not have held in the same proportion for other nations or for America in the years ahead.

Other nations may not have the time to wait or the resources to do so. But the degree of private and public control is not the test of freedom, either economic or political.

Complete economic activity by the state can stifle freedom, but the point at which a balance is struck between the use of promoting the two methods of producing wealth will vary from time to time and from nation to nation.[4]

When it was proposed recently that the jurisdiction of the Federal Power Commission be diminished, RFK appeared before the Senate Commerce Committee to speak out against this suggested reduction of public control.

[1] Robert F. Kennedy, *Just Friends and Brave Enemies* (New York: Harper & Row, 1962), p. 106.
[2] Speech, Portland City Club, Portland Ore., October 6, 1961.
[3] Address, National Farmers Union Convention, Oklahoma City, Okla., March 13, 1967.
[4] Speech, University of Indonesia, Djakarta, Indonesia, February 14, 1962.

I oppose enactment of S. 1365, a bill to amend the Federal Power Act with respect to the jurisdiction of the Federal Power Commission. I take this position because I do not believe that it is in the public interest to decrease the authority of the Federal Power Commission in regulating private power companies; on the contrary, if any change is to be made, I believe that the regulatory powers of the FPC need to be expanded and strengthened.

The bill under consideration today would exempt from regulation by the Federal Power Commission about two dozen of the 200 large private power companies which transmit or sell power at wholesale in interstate commerce. The FPC currently insures that many of these companies market electricity for resale at reasonable rates, that service is adequate, and that financial information on the finances and management of these monopolies is available to the public. Elimination of FPC regulation of these companies could in many cases remove them from all regulation because a number of state public service commissions are either unwilling or unable to effectively perform these functions.

In a period when electric power needs are growing rapidly, when nuclear energy offers the promise of sizable rate reductions, and when interconnections and pooling make individual power companies increasingly interdependent, I believe that an emphasis should be placed on more effective regulation, and not on less regulation. . . .

The Federal Power Act has been law for over thirty years. It was enacted following congressional investigations which showed that many private power companies used their monopoly status and economic power to exploit consumers and investors. I have seen no evidence that the situation has changed—on the contrary, high electricity costs and weak state public service commissions argue more than ever for a vigilant and aggressive FPC. The reasons for enactment of the Federal Power Act—protection of the public interest—remain as valid today as in 1935. I urge the committee to recommend against enactment of S. 1365.[5]

Similarly, when Governor Rockefeller recommended that the Power Authority of the State of New York

[5] Statement, Senate Commerce Committee, June 8, 1967.

(PASNY) be denied a role in the development of nuclear power plants in the state, Kennedy protested loudly that the public's interests were being sacrificed for private gain.

I hope the legislature will reject the Rockefeller proposals concerning PASNY. The Power Authority should have a role in the development of nuclear power plants—the Governor would deny the Authority that right. He would amend the Public Power Act to favor industrial users over domestic and rural consumers of power produced by any new hydroelectric facilities which PASNY develops. He would have PASNY pay taxes on any new hydroelectric projects it constructs, and curtail the Authority's growth by forcing it to become a customer of the private utilities for the power it needs to meet its growing commitments. Every aspect of the Rockefeller proposals can only add to the cost of electricity for the citizens of New York. And our electric costs are practically the highest in the country already. . . .

I have no argument with private investment in and development of nuclear power. I welcome that, and it should be encouraged, but not by destroying the historical protection that public power has given to the people of New York. If the Power Authority does not participate in the development of nuclear power it will lose its position as yardstick and lever in connection with private power costs, for as much as 80 percent of new power facility construction between now and 1980 will be in the nuclear field. And because the combination of nuclear and hydroelectric power is the cheapest use of nuclear power we now know, excluding PASNY means foregoing important savings to New York consumers. . . .

The exceptions are crucial because utilities in most cases are monopolies, and it has proven difficult for government to insure adequate service and reasonable rates by mere inspection, supervision and regulation. Most power is produced by private capital, subject to the conditions that quality service be provided at low rates and limited profit. But every community has the basic right, *if it chooses*, to own and operate its utility services. And to provide a yardstick by which the efficiency and effectiveness of the private utility monopolies can be measured, the state and the federal government have developed power sites which permit comparisons of the relative cost of public and private power. Thus the people of the state are protected by "the birch rod in the cupboard," as FDR called it—the right of their government to control the cost and, if necessary, the transmission and distribution of electrical power. What Governor Rockefeller proposes and the Republican party now supports is that we throw away the key to the cupboard. . . .

His proposals are supported by the Republican leadership, and they focus in new form one of the most important consumer issues of this century—the struggle between public and private power.[6]

I criticized the Governor's power program last week not only because I believed that it would deprive New York State of the benefits of the nuclear power revolution now in progress by turning over its development exclusively to private companies, but also because it would make our people in effect pay twice—once, as taxpayers to help the private utilities monopolize future power needs in the state, and later, as consumers in the form of largely uncontrolled higher rates.[7]

Taxes

John Kennedy's faith in the "new economics" apparently rubbed off on his younger brother, who did not hesitate to recommend fiscal measures—changes in the tax rate and in levels of government spending—as means of managing the economy. In 1964, when administration economists were recommending an excise tax cut to "heat up" the economy, Kennedy supported this measure in his Senate campaign.

A cut in excise taxes within prudent budgetary limitations would stimulate consumption expenditure and encourage investment in output of products.

As have the 1964 income tax cuts, it would over the long run increase our revenues through pushing our economy to higher levels. Excise tax cuts would at the same time result

[6] Press release, March 20, 1967.
[7] Press release, March 30, 1967.

in price reduction. Thus the noninflationary stimulus to the economy begun in 1964 would be continued in 1965. . . .

Our excise taxes have been enacted piecemeal in a confusing and chaotic manner. The burden of many of them falls most heavily and unfairly upon those with the least ability to pay. . . .

I favor giving priority of reduction by eliminating first the taxes which discriminate against those least able to afford taxation and which are costly to enforce and collect. The taxes I mentioned fall in that category (women's purses, matches, and light bulbs). . . .

An orderly elimination of arbitrarily imposed excise taxes would help keep our economy moving, would restore more equity in our tax structure, and would eliminate those taxes which are costly for businessmen in compliance and for the government to collect.[8]

Two years later, when an overheated economy and inflation were the principal threats, he raised the possibility of a tax increase:

But the problem does not end there. The airline problem [see Chapter 12] is really just one example of the problems which confront our economy in this time of war and increasing inflation. In the labor area, the increasing complexity of our economic problems only means that there will be more disputes like this one, a fact which only emphasizes further the need for an over-all examination. The questions are numerous. How are we, for example, to develop wage guidelines which help chart the direction of development in an expanding economy without unduly constricting the bargaining process in particular disputes? How are we to make sure that unforeseen cost of living increases do not make a mockery of our guidelines? More broadly, with the increasing inflation and the increasing profits being generated by the war, should we now be considering a tax increase to help maintain economic stability? And, too, if we are going to pay for programs to deal with the problems of our cities, with poverty, with the plight of our elderly, and with a dozen other domestic

[8] Press release, October 24, 1964.

problems, should we not begin considering a tax increase for that reason as well? [9]

The following year he suggested changes in President Johnson's proposed 10 percent surtax which he contended would render this increase more equitable.

That is a minimum income tax, a minimum percentage which would prevent the wealthy from continuing to get away completely. We might, for example, require all who earn over $50,000—in ordinary income, in tax-exempt interest, in capital gains, and so on—to pay at least 20 percent of that income in taxes. This is not a complex proposal. It is just. It is fair. It should be enacted now. And as we consider the proposed surcharge, we must also take special care to see that it is not unfair in itself. It would now require every tax-payer—corporate and individual alike—to pay 10 percent more in tax, except for those with very low incomes. For the man with an income of $7,000, the surcharge will be a burden. If he gets a 5 percent pay raise after the surcharge is imposed, that raise will be more than eaten up by the tax increase and the expected increases in the cost of living and in state and local taxes.

I believe we must consider increasing the exemption to the surcharges so that it would exempt a family of four with an income of $7,000 instead of the present $5,000 exemption proposal. The minimum income tax I have suggested will help make up for the revenue loss involved in this. And we might also consider graduating the surcharge as we do the basic tax rates, and perhaps imposing a higher surcharge as we do the basic tax rates, and perhaps imposing a higher surcharge on corporations, which have been helped so much by the investment credit and other tax benefits granted them over the past six years. [10]

He was disturbed by the loopholes in our income tax system which vitiate its progressive design:

We must not be satisfied with a tax system which lets

[9] Statement, U.S. Senate, August 4, 1966.
[10] Address, Civil Service Employees Association, New York, N.Y., September 7, 1967.

many of our wealthiest escape their share of the burden—
while new taxes are proposed which fall most heavily on those
wage earners who can least afford it. We must build a system
which is fair to all, and will thereby provide us the resources
we need for the tasks ahead.[11]

But we cannot rest content with a tax system which compels those who can least afford it to bear the brunt of sacrifice—while those with greater financial resources escape into
the maze of loopholes. Today, because of the gaps in our tax
structure, the wealthiest of our citizens—those who earn more
than $200,000 annually—pay an average of only 27 percent
in taxes; the same proportion as those earning about $13,000
a year pay on every additional dollar they earn. Thus the
very people who earn the least—those who depend upon
wages and salaries—pay the full amount required by law,
while the wealthiest find refuge from responsibility in our
tax shelter. We must raise the resources we need. But we
must do so in ways which are fair to all.[12]

Tax Incentives

Because Kennedy's proposals to involve private industry
in the efforts to rebuild the nation's center cities relied on
federal tax incentives to make such undertakings com-
mercially profitable, he was forced to justify these incentives, or subsidies.

The concept of government incentives to induce desired
investments by private industry is neither new nor radical.
Rather it is a concept honored by practice since the founding
of the Republic. . . .
Of course, exceptional tax incentives should not be lightly
given. Any exception and departure from a uniform tax base
should be required to meet two tests. First, as President
Kennedy said in submitting the original investment credit

[11] Address, Ninth Constitutional Convention of Oil, Chemical
and Atomic Workers, New York, N.Y., August 23, 1967.
[12] Remarks, Rotary Club luncheon, Poughkeepsie, N.Y., September 6, 1967.

bill, we must ask if the provision will "promote desirable social or economic objectives of overriding importance." Second, if certain preferential tax treatment is to be given to certain members of a class, then we must be sure that these benefits are not creating a special, privileged group, but are only compensating for additional risks and burdens.[13]

For structural problems in the economy which were not responsive to moderate changes in aggregate economic performance, he advocated direct government spending and private investment such as that proposed in his recent bills on housing and on industrial investment in urban poverty. During his first two years in the Senate, he backed existing development programs to revive depressed areas, not only in Appalachia, but all over the United States.

There is pending in the Congress now legislation which can make a major difference to the development of your entire region. I speak of the Public Works and Economic Development Act of 1965, which has already passed the Senate and will, I am sure, soon pass the House of Representatives.

This bill is one of the major items in the program of our Democratic administration. It provides for an extension of the Area Redevelopment Program and, in modified form, of the Accelerated Public Works Program, both of which made such a major difference to so many depressed areas these past four years. Even more important, however, is an entirely new provision in the bill. This allows counties to plan together and to apply for aid together, so that regional problems are attacked on a unified basis. This can make a difference to you. But you have to do something about it. You have to make sure that your county has a professional planner, a man who can determine what your county needs, a man who can serve as your liaison with your neighboring counties and with the federal government. I cannot emphasize too strongly the importance of these multicounty planning provisions to your area. A solid effort by an entire region to develop its resources collectively is on much firmer ground

[13] Speech, U.S. Senate, July 12, 1967.

than a county-by-county effort. A cooperative effort by a whole area to attract industry is bound to be more effective than the efforts of counties acting singly. Cooperative applications to the federal government for economic aid are bound to have a greater impact than a series of isolated, uncoordinated single applications.[14]

However, as Chapters 4 and 5 show, he began to switch his emphasis to federal subsidies for private investment in underdeveloped areas of the country.

Human Resources and Deficit Spending

On the question of America's future economic growth, he sided with most economists in stressing the development of human resources rather than capital formation:

We must work for education, the prime capital of a technological society. Defense Secretary Robert McNamara once said, "The contracts go where the brains are"—and for good reason. Eighty percent of our industrial growth in the twentieth century has been the result not of capital formation; not of increased population; but of invention and innovation. That invention, that innovation, come directly from education—from the resources of great universities, and from the people they educate.[15]

Unfortunately, Bobby lined up with most politicians against most contemporary economists in his unwillingness to admit to the public that deficit spending by the federal government could be a sound economic tactic for managing the economy in certain circumstances. On this issue he earned no profile in courage.

Yes, there is a deficit of almost 7 billion dollars, but they had a deficit in 1957, and the deficit in 1958 was over 12

[14] Speech, Cayuga County Democratic Committee Dinner, Auburn, N.Y., June 5, 1965.
[15] Address, Greater Syracuse Chamber of Commerce, Syracuse, N.Y., April 21, 1965.

billion dollars under President Eisenhower. Yes, we are all against deficit spending, and President Eisenhower, and I'm not making a partisan speech, he's most against spending, but he did pretty well with the problem involved. So, I think that the whole facts—that all the facts involved in these matters should be kept in mind, that this is where the money is going—that the money is going into defense and going into space, where we need it.[16]

How Robert Kennedy's view of the economy would have evolved in the future is difficult to determine, for his proposals and actions appeared to lack a coherent theoretical base.

[16] Answer to question following address, Associated Press Managing Editors luncheon, Dallas, Tex., November 15, 1961.

Chapter 17

The Federal Government:
Its Prerogatives and Performance

This chapter is a collection of Robert Kennedy's statements regarding the proper functions of the federal
government—the operations of the judicial, executive and
legislative branches, important federal issues such as
"one-man, one-vote," home rule for the District of Columbia, our immigration laws, and miscellaneous items which
do not fall logically under the book's other subject head-
ings. In other words, it is a potpourri of the Senator's
views on issues and problems related to the theory and
operations of the national government and the rules that
define its activities.

The Federal System

The responsibilities of the federal government have not
changed basically over the years. In essence they are three:
—to uphold the rule of law and protect our basic rights;
—to maintain our military strength and defend our security;
—to stimulate the well-being and prosperity of our people.[1]

Kennedy indicated that he did not fear a greater concentration of power on the federal level, for he believed
that the division of powers between the states and the
national government often impeded the solution of
problems.

[1] Speech, University of Virginia Law School, Charlottesville, Va.,
May 4, 1963.

In the United States we have a federal system and this creates some problems and difficulties in our efforts to make progress. There are areas of action where the states are dominant and the federal government is powerless. There are other areas which the states cannot invade. The political destinies of states are never all controlled by the same political party, and their political outlook can differ state by state from that of the national administration. This makes for problems and difficulties in realizing certain national goals. In civil rights matters, our federal government has a direct responsibility to combat discrimination in voting but can move against discrimination in transportation only when the interstate transportation system is involved. The federal government can intervene directly in school desegregation cases only at the direction of the federal courts.

Thus, constitutional barriers can impede efforts at the national level. . . .[2]

And in response to a question about the effectiveness of federal legislation and court orders as a means of obtaining equality for Negroes in this country, he made the point again.

I think, however, in the last analysis—the laws are important, the court orders are important, and they are important in and of themselves and they are also important because they give the President of the United States greater power and give the federal government greater power, and I think that it is important because that can give leadership throughout the United States.[3]

To the charge that federal interference in state voting registration procedures was an abrogation of states' rights, he replied simply:

Well, first we have the fact, that federal elections are involved, elections for federal officers—the President, Vice-President, the Senate and Congressmen.

[2] Speech, University of Gadja Mada, Jogjakarta, Indonesia, February 15, 1963.
[3] "Press Conference USA" (Voice of America), June 4, 1963.

Beyond that, and under the Fourteenth Amendment, and other legislation that has been passed, I think it is very clear that we also have a responsibility in state-wide elections.[4]

At the same time he maintained that government must be brought closer to the people by strengthening it on the state and local level.

First, in this time of giant organizations—sprawling government bureaucracies, huge impersonal corporations, universities as big as cities—we must find ways to return the focus of government and society to the individual citizen. For thirty years, we as Democrats have concentrated on the urgent national problems which required national solutions: the problems of war and peace in the world, economic crisis and regeneration at home, conservation to protect our heritage and education to create an inheritance for our children.

Now it is our responsibility, as believers in the individual spirit, not to undo the accomplishments of the past; but to engage in an even more creative effort to return the levers of power and decision to places we can reach as citizens: in the state house, the city hall, in our own neighborhoods and communities.

One great and necessary step in this direction is the revitalization of state and local government, making its service again a proud and innovative and lively career—as you and Governor Rampton are doing in Utah today. I hope your example is followed all over the country.

Alongside this new effort at the state and local level, we in Washington must work to assist you with the burdens of an ever more complex society: by increasing local control and participation in all government programs; and by helping you raise the revenue which is so desperately needed by every state and city in the nation.[5]

The Judicial, Legislative, and Executive Branches

Since its 1954 school desegregation decision, the Supreme Court has come under particularly heavy con-

[4] "Washington Report" (CBS-TV), March 3, 1963.
[5] Address, Salt Lake City, Utah, June 28, 1967.

servative criticism for judgments which allegedly ignore both the letter and the spirit of the Constitution. However, Kennedy never hesitated to defend both the legality and the wisdom of the great majority of the Court's decisions.

[Barry Goldwater] has said, within the last week, that the Court is not faithful to the Constitution. He has criticized the Court's decisions on criminal law, race relations and apportionment of state legislatures. He has said he would appoint new Justices who would vote the other way.

I think Senator Goldwater is completely wrong.

The Supreme Court in our time has done more than any other institution to protect the liberties of American citizens. It is a courageous Court dedicated to the Constitution. Its decisions point the way to a just and a responsible society.[6]

QUESTION: Mr. Kennedy, what is your view of the role of the present strong Supreme Court vis-à-vis the Senate?

ANSWER: I support the Supreme Court. I basically agree with its decisions. I basically think that in the field of civil rights its efforts have been extremely important. In the area of reapportionment there was no relief that the people themselves could obtain. I think that that effort has been important. Those have been the two areas particularly criticized as far as the Supreme Court is concerned. I would support the Supreme Court in both of those areas.[7]

He favored a liberal or broad interpretation of the Constitution, which permits the Supreme Court maximum freedom in applying the 180-year-old document to the legal questions of the day.

Now as always, when the Constitution is too narrowly interpreted on a word-for-word basis, it can too easily become a crutch for reaction, a rationalization, an excuse for maintaining the status quo.

[6] Speech, Free Synagogue of Westchester County, Mt. Vernon, N.Y., September 20, 1964.

[7] Question and answer following speech, University of Rochester, Rochester, N.Y., September 29, 1964.

This is the very thing that Jefferson feared, so long ago, when he urged us not to regard the wording of the document with "sanctimonious reverence."

My point is that the Constitution was never meant to specify every detail, every individual right in the relations of man to man in this country.

It was intended to set forth certain duties of government and certain restrictions on government—nowhere in its working does it pretend to tell us, as individual citizens, how to treat our neighbors.

But what Woodrow Wilson called the *spirit* of the Constitution does, and has always done, just that.

Interspersed throughout the Constitution and its amendments—written in between the lines, if you will—are the basic moral principles of democratic justice by which we all try to live.

Surely we don't need a new court decision to tell us that the Negro is entitled to decent housing, and that his right to have such housing must not be denied or abridged because of his color.

Surely we don't need a court ruling to insure the Negro equal opportunities in employment, or equal opportunities to advance from unskilled into skilled and responsible jobs.

These are moral issues, not legal ones, and their constitutionality is a matter of common sense.[8]

When people criticize the courts for invading spheres of action which supposedly belong to other parts of our constitutional system, they often overlook the fact that the courts must act precisely because the other organs of government have failed to fulfill their own responsibilities.

This surely is the moral of the recent decision in *Baker v. Carr*, the Tennessee reapportionment case. For half a century the urban voter of Tennessee had been systematically underrepresented in the state legislature—and for half a century political and legislative remedies had proved inadequate to re-establish the substance of democratic equity. And the same unfair situation exists in many other states.

In *Baker v. Carr*, the Supreme Court held that a system of

[8] Speech, ceremonies celebrating 175th anniversary of the ratification of the Constitution, Philadelphia, Pa., June 21, 1963.

apportionment could be so unfair and irrational as to require judicial cognizance under the Fourteenth Amendment. Exactly what judicial standards will emerge no one can say as yet; but, if legislatures continue to evade their primary responsibility, there can be no alternative but to work these standards out, as so many of our constitutional principles have been worked out, on a case-by-case basis. . . .

Some of the protest has been addressed to the role of the Supreme Court itself as the final arbiter of our constitutional system. This is a powerful role—but let no one suppose that it came about lightly or by accident. It was a role foreseen by the authors of the Constitution, and this role of the Supreme Court was established by one of the greatest of all Virginians, John Marshall.

Because no constitution is self-expounding, there must be some agency to expound it. And the job of exposition is not that of citing a rigid and unchanging set of theorems, like repeating a mathematical table.

"We must never forget," said Marshall, "that it is a *Constitution* we are expounding . . . intended to endure for ages to come and consequently to be adapted to the various *crises* of human affairs."

In following Marshall's injunction, the Supreme Court has acted as the conscience of the nation. It has been one great means by which our constitutional framework has responded to the ethical imperatives of our people. . . .

This, of course, is precisely why we have a Supreme Court —to adjudicate disputes laden with concern and emotion. The American Constitution would indeed be a sterile document if the Court in its labors did not recognize the truth so well stated by Justice Cardozo:

"The great generalities of the Constitution have a content and a significance that vary from age to age." [9]

Most of Kennedy's comments on the legislative branch were directed at the operations of congressional committees. His service as chief counsel on two Senate investigating committees helps to explain this focus.

[9] Speech, Law Day ceremonies, Virginia State Bar, Roanoke, Va., May 1, 1962.

When a congressional committee abuses its power, the remedy is to point it out and to get rid of those responsible. For this, it seems to me, we have a built-in safeguard in the public press. All congressional committees' work is subject to public scrutiny, more so really than the work of any other group. If a witness is abused, if an investigation is unfairly or improperly conducted, if senators or staff members stoop to unethical practices, the press is always present to expose it. The press serves as a sort of safety valve against the violation of civil rights. This is not the ideal, obviously, because often there is a delay in obtaining a cure for the abuses; nevertheless the press, the responsible part, is a potent and powerful safeguard. This is one of the reasons I am strongly against having committee proceedings in private. (I am discussing here our kind of operation [crime] and obviously not matters dealing with national security.)

In the first place they do not remain private, for the choice morsels are leaked to the press. Certainly we saw that during the days of the McCarthy Committee and even in our own committee. I don't remember one executive session where anything of any significance that we discussed did not get out to the press. This can be extremely unfair, for invariably only one side of a story is leaked. Secondly, I think the public is entitled to know what is going on and should have as full information as is possible. Public knowledge is a major deterrent to abuse. This is a serious matter. It seems to me that where a public body is dealing with persons' reputations as we were, the press has an obligation and responsibility to remain vigilant. . . .[10]

In my estimation, rules and regulations can do very little to cure the major faults that exist in congressional committees. What rule can you pass to prevent a congressman or senator or counsel from asking an unfair question? What regulation can you write to prevent a committee member from yelling at or browbeating a witness? To set up a system under which all questions are cleared with the chairman, as though he were judge, would not only be too cumbersome but completely unacceptable to individual committee members. Furthermore,

[10] Robert F. Kennedy, *The Enemy Within* (New York: Harper & Brothers, 1960), pp. 312-313.

the fault with many investigating committees has been their chairman. (In the case of our committee [McClellan] he was a lifesaver.) However, there are basic rules that ought to be followed. For instance, every witness should have the right to have counsel whether he appears in executive or open session; he should have full knowledge of the purpose of the hearing and of why he is being called as a witness. . . ."[11]

Because the investigative power has been misused, some people, as I have said, have advocated abolishing investigating committees. In view of the commendable record of most such committees, this suggestion is hardly justified. It is the old remedy of shooting a person to cure his cold. The stock exchange and investment banking, Teapot Dome, the five percenters, Alger Hiss, conflict of interests and hundreds of . . . worthwhile investigations have been conducted with dignity and honor. More than this, much of our most important legislation has grown out of the factual basis laid by congressional investigations. . . ."[12]

The result is that the caliber of staff investigators on Capitol Hill is often not of the highest. Added to all else, you have the problem of political appointees whose jobs are based on whom they know, not what they know. You have some men who, aware of the risks of being involved in a controversial subject, figure very early that the way to keep one's job is to do nothing—just keep out of sight and don't stir up anything or anyone. Then you have the crusader who will dynamite everything in sight to get over his point. There is little room left for the professional dedicated public servant. . . ."[13]

The committee decided, however, that from then on any approach made to a member of the staff should be brought to its attention. My brother and Senator Church suggested that it should also be reported if an approach of this kind was made to any member of the committee. However, Senator Mundt was against this and it was left that only approaches to the staff were to be reported. Approaches to the senators

[11] *Ibid.*, pp. 309-310.
[12] *Ibid.*, p. 311.
[13] *Ibid.*, p. 172.

were to be kept confidential. There must be a distinction but it was too subtle for me.[14]

Kennedy had written and spoken very sparingly about the executive branch and the role of the President. The following statements deal with two different and relatively minor matters, presidential disability and executive privilege.

I call to the Senate's attention a most important aspect of Senate Joint Resolution 1 which has not received as much notice as it should have. That is the provision, in Section 4, which gives Congress authority to provide by law for a body other than the Cabinet to determine the inability of the President to exercise the powers and duties of his office when he is unwilling to make the declaration of inability himself.

This provision was wisely added by the framers of Senate Joint Resolution 1 because of the doubts which some people voiced as to the workability of using the Cabinet as the body to determine the President's inability. Now that we are finally enacting Senate Joint Resolution 1, we must not cease thinking about this aspect of the inability problem. We must keep in mind that we have given Congress the power to provide a different body to determine presidential inability, and we should engage in a continuing study of whether there is some better way to handle this very difficult matter.[15]

MR. RESTON: Mr. Attorney General, in two fields you seem to have introduced in the last eight months a new principle or a new emphasis. First, in the field of executive privilege where you seem more willing than previous presidents and administrations to give information sought by the Congress. . . .
RFK: First, as far as executive privilege is concerned, I was associated with a congressional committee for five or six years and had battles with the executive branch of the government regarding obtaining information. I think it is terribly important to insure that the executive branch of the government is not corrupt and that they are efficient, that the legislative branch

[14] *Ibid.*, p. 171.
[15] Statement, U.S. Senate, June 30, 1965.

of the government has this ability to check on what we are doing in the executive branch of the government. So in every instance that has been brought to our attention in the Department of Justice so far by various departments of the executive branch where this question has been raised, we have suggested and recommended that they make the information available to Congress. We will continue to do that. I don't say that there might not be an instance where executive privilege might have to be used, but I think it is terribly important with the executive branch of the government as powerful and strong as it is that there be some check and balance on it. And in the last analysis the group that can best check and insure that it is handling its affairs properly is the Congress of the United States. So we will lean over backwards to make sure that they get the information they request.[16]

In response to a question about the Billie Sol Estes scandal [in 1962, Estes was accused of defrauding the government], Kennedy talked about the delicate subject of corruption in government.

We are going to have corruption . . . over the period of the next few years. I mean you have a lot of people that are working for the federal government. You have other people on the outside who are willing to attempt to corrupt them, and as long as you have human beings, you are going to have some kind of corruption. I think the important thing is whether you take action to deal with it, whether you cover it up, whether you push it under the rug, whether you act as if it doesn't exist. I think that it is serious, but the fact is that you are going to have corruption. Every administration has had corruption. I think that the criterion by which this should be judged is not whether you have it, but whether you move and take action against it. If corruption is found, the administration has to take the responsibility for it and has to take the blame for it. This I recognize, this I accept, but I think beyond that is a question of whether we move against it, whether we try to cover it up.[17]

---

[16] "Meet the Press" (NBC-TV), September 24, 1961.
[17] "Issues and Answers" (ABC-TV), June 17, 1962.

One-Man, One-Vote

Legislative apportionment is one of the crucial constitutional issues of our times. On the outcome of this
bitterly contested question rests the future distribution of
political power in this country between urban, suburban,
and rural areas, and the nature of the coalitions that will
control Congress and the state legislatures. No less is at
stake than the determination of which voices will
dominate in the formation of public policy in the decades
ahead.

Robert Kennedy was an influential participant in this
debate, both as Attorney General and as a senator. In
January 1963 he argued before the U.S. Supreme Court
in a case involving the constitutionality of Georgia's
county-unit system of tabulating votes in primary elections. This case established the principle of "one-man,
one-vote," which underlay the Court's subsequent reapportionment decisions.

Bobby championed the strict application of this principle in all legislative apportionment cases. In the quotations that follow, he discussed the social cost of malapportionment and the wisdom of the Court's decision
demanding redistricting along "one-man, one-vote" lines:

These disparities in representation had deprived urban
citizens in particular of effective state help in meeting their
problems. The malapportioned legislatures had really, in fact,
ceased to provide progressive legislation for the people of
their states generally. This failure had caused urban communities to look to Washington to help, but it was obvious
that the federal government could not solve all the problems
by itself. We concluded, therefore, that we should urge the
Supreme Court to reverse its previous refusal to adjudicate
apportionment cases. We felt that if the Court did agree with
the plaintiffs in *Baker v. Carr,* and with us, the log jam created by malapportionment might be broken and the state
legislatures might recapture their proper status in our federal
system.

The arguments which we made to the Supreme Court in
the Baker case regarding the effects of malapportionment reflected the discussion which had gone on in the executive

branch. We pointed out that state legislatures used to be effective formulators of policy on the domestic level. Thirty years ago, we said, Justice Brandeis had praised the state legislatures as laboratories which could "try novel social and economic experiments without risk to the rest of the country." Partly because of the failure to reapportion, the state legislatures had failed to adapt themselves to modern problems and majority needs, particularly in urban areas.[18]

In the distant past a legislature was divided into districts. Or an apportionment formula was written. Then, for ten or twenty or fifty years, the politicians who benefited from the existing system refused to change it. The people had absolutely nothing to say about it.

It was the Supreme Court that finally gave the people a voice. The Court said that a system in which it took the votes of a hundred or a thousand citizens in Atlanta to equal one vote in rural Georgia was not the kind of equality promised by the Constitution. Nor was a system by which one state senator in metropolitan New York represents 600,000 people while one upstate represents 166,000 people.

It will take time to adjust to the standard of equality laid down by the Court. Hasty measures are unwise. But I can see no way, in the long run, of escaping the common sense and the moral soundness of the idea that one man's vote should count the same as any other's.[19]

Thus it is not difficult to understand Kennedy's adamant opposition to the proposed constitutional amendment offered by Senator Everett Dirksen of Illinois to permit one house of a state legislature to be apportioned according to factors other than population.

This amendment would provide that nothing in the Constitution shall restrict or limit any state in the apportionment of representation in its legislature. It would add that no Federal Court shall have power to hear any reapportionment case. Observers have noted that if the amendment means what

[18] Statement, U.S. Senate, August 4, 1965.
[19] Speech, Free Synagogue of Westchester County, Mt. Vernon, N.Y., September 20, 1964.

it says, it is perhaps the most drastic change yet proposed to the United States Constitution.

By its literal words, representation could be drawn from or excluded from any group designated by the state legislature. This would be true whether the group were based on geography, religion, race or political or social affiliation. The religious or social bar would be only one step beyond the gerrymander. . . .

Were this constitutional amendment adopted, it could constitute a dangerous withdrawal of guarantees of liberty, justice and equality now contained in the Constitution. It would at the barest minimum throw away the gains we have begun to make at the beginning of this era that started with *Baker v. Carr*—this era of improving the representative quality of our democracy.[20]

Were I today a member of the United States Senate representing all New Yorkers, I would vigorously oppose as a matter of policy and principle the Dirksen rider to the foreign aid bill. This rider would unduly delay and frustrate implementation of the Supreme Court decision.

The Supreme Court has said that each citizen has a constitutional right under the equal protection clause to a fairly apportioned legislature. I pledge that I will do all in my power to protect and vindicate that civil right as well as all others guaranteed by the Constitution.[21]

I appreciate the opportunity of appearing before your subcommittee today to testify regarding the proposed constitutional amendment which would, in essence, overturn the decisions of the Supreme Court last June 15 in *Reynolds v. Sims* and related cases, and allow one house of a state legislature to be apportioned according to factors other than population.

In my judgment, the tendency of these amendments is a constitutional crisis of the deepest significance.

Utilizing the historically unprecedented approach of taking

[20] Speech, University of Virginia Law School, Charlottesville, Va., May 4, 1963.

[21] Letter to a prominent Democrat during Senate campaign, September 9, 1964.

away declared constitutional rights, the amendments would preserve a structure of malapportioned state government and would thereby have the most far-reaching effects on the future of our cities and the urban development process, and on the civil rights movement as well. . . .

This subcommittee well knows that the Colorado reapportionment plan which was before the Supreme Court last year in the Lucas case had been approved in a referendum. The Court nevertheless struck down the plan, saying, "An individual's constitutionally protected right to cast an equally weighted vote cannot be denied even by a vote of a majority of a state's electorate. . . ." The point is that no other of our freedoms is framed in terms of being deniable by a vote of the majority. Any suggestion, for example, that the First Amendment guarantee of free speech and freedom of religion should be "except when the majority votes otherwise" would be dismissed out of hand as totally absurd. . . .

I believe we cannot and must not let the majority of the voters dilute or deny the right to equal representation, particularly when we know that the majority may not appreciate the implications of what it is doing or, even worse, may not be given a realistic choice to make. . . .

What about the South? The Negro, of course, is still badly underregistered in many states. It will be entirely logical for the legislatures of those states to draft a plan which would protect their position against the day when Negroes obtain full voting rights. And, of course, the electorate as presently constituted is equally as interested in preserving the status quo. In much of the South, therefore, permitting a departure from reapportionment based on population will inevitably result in a serious stumbling block to the Negro's ever attaining equality in the political process. . . .

The perpetuation of minority, nonurban control, even though confined only to one house, could be catastrophic for the cities. The result at worst would be a continuation of the shortchanging of the cities, and at best a stalemate, a legislative paralysis caused by the differing apportionment bases in the two houses. . . .

It is argued also that the so-called federal analogy justifies these amendments. In my judgment [the federal government] was a union of previously sovereign states, which had to enter into a compromise as the basis for coming together at all.

There is nothing analogous to that at the state level. Counties and other political subdivisions have no independent significance whatever. . . .

In sum, to paraphrase Chief Justice Marshall, we must remember that this is, after all, a Constitution we are amending. What the proponents of the amendments are advocating is the introduction of an exception to the equal protection clause of the Fourteenth Amendment, an exception which says, in effect, equality is the rule except where representation in the state legislatures is concerned. What they are supporting is the removal of a right previously enjoyed—the taking away of a guarantee of equality—the equality of representation—which the Fourteenth Amendment has previously been held to encompass. They are talking about changing the basic fabric from which our government is woven and they are talking about doing so in a way which would diminish the rights guaranteed by the Fourteenth Amendment. To me this kind of venture is inconsistent with the ideal of equality for which we have always striven and which we have always held out to peoples of other lands as the principle which differentiates America from less democratic nations. And this whittling away at the Fourteenth Amendment represents a most troublesome precedent for the future. . . .

We are confronted with a proposal which could destroy that hope and which would in any event change the structure of our government for a long time to come. This is important and significant to all of us, and I believe we should not allow it to proceed any further.[22]

Unable to acquire sufficient support for the amendment in Congress, the Dirksen forces began exploring the alternate means of amending the Constitution—a constitutional convention requested by resolutions passed by two-thirds of the states (33 states). By early 1967, thirty-two states had already passed such resolutions, and a number of others reportedly were about to take action. Alarmed by the initial success of this tack, Bobby rose in the Senate on April 19 to denounce it.

[22] Testimony, Subcommittee on Constitutional Amendments of Senate Judicial Committee, May 6, 1965.

Because constitutional amendments do produce such fundamental changes in our political structure, the Founding Fathers intended that the amending process be both elaborate and exacting. Thus, in the case of resolutions passed by two-thirds of the states, they could hardly have intended that Congress not play a significant role in deciding whether the desired convention has been validly requested. This is not to say that Congress has complete discretion to disregard the wishes of the states. But it must possess power to rule upon the validity of the submitted resolutions as the basis for convening a constitutional convention. If for any reason these resolutions appear to be invalid either in regard to the circumstances of their enactment or their submission or the form of their request—then it follows that Congress must reject them. . . .

First, twenty-six of the thirty-two resolutions were invalidly enacted, since that many legislatures were malapportioned when they passed these petitions. Their hastily enacted and ill-considered applications are thus nothing more than attempts of malapportioned bodies to preserve their lost power. The vast bulk of these resolutions represent not the voice of the people but the special pleading of those groups and factions whose rule of our states has already been found inherently undemocratic.

I believe this Congress can and should refuse to sanction those efforts by the few to maintain power at the expense of the majority. Any attempt on the part of a malapportioned legislature to legitimize its own power and thwart the rights of its citizens to equal representation must—as the federal courts have recognized—be rejected. Changes which go to the very heart of our constitutional system cannot properly be set in motion by those whose right to govern has been overturned.

Second, these resolutions fail as a group to constitute a valid set of requests upon which Congress is required to act. It would make little sense if a convention could be convened on the basis of widely differing applications seeking consideration of disparate issues. And these thirty-two resolutions are not all the same. Thirty of them request a convention to pass an amendment permitting one house in a bicameral legislature to be malapportioned. The other two seek only to abrogate the power of the federal judiciary to deal with apportionment. . . .

Third, these resolutions do not accord with the intent of

Article V that the purpose of calling a convention is to "propose" amendments. The thirty-two resolutions not only request a convention but stipulate the texts of the amendments and the method for ratification. They are in effect an attempt by the various state legislatures to force Congress to call a convention which can only act mechanically to approve or disapprove a specific amendment. The attempt is to make the convention merely an initial step in the ratifying process instead of a deliberative meeting to seek out solutions to a problem. The word "propose" cannot be stretched to mean "ratify." This Congress cannot properly accept and become part of any prepackaged effort to shortcut the amendment process. . . .

The time is late, but public consideration and discussion of the dangers of a constitutional convention can still help. There are still states which have not yet passed a resolution but are considering one. There are other states in which a previous legislature passed a resolution, but where there is presently a chance to rescind it. And, most important, the people of our nation should know of this new assault on the principle of "one-man, one-vote," this attempt which could bring with it the destruction or inhibition of our basic liberties. For it is they who stand to lose in this effort to restore the "rotten borough" to the American political system. It is they who will lose if the Bill of Rights is eroded at such a convention. And it is they, in the end, who have the power to insure that such damage will never be done to our Constitution.[23]

That same year a congressional-district standards bill was introduced proposing a maximum variation of 35 percent between the highest and lowest populated congressional districts within a state. Bobby opposed this measure, contending that its enactment would delay the implementation of the "one-man, one-vote" principle.

Let me make clear that I personally do not regard the language of the bill as ambiguous. On its face, it seems clear to me that its meaning is that ascribed by Congressman Celler. It simply says, "The district with the largest population . . . shall not exceed by more than 35 percentum the district with the smaller population. . . ." That says to me that all Congress

[23] Statement, U.S. Senate, April 19, 1967.

is doing is enacting an outside limit, and that the power of the courts to review for their constitutionality schemes meeting the statutory standard is unchanged.

Why, then, am I concerned about the enactment of a 35 percent standard? The answer is that it invites litigation. It invites delay. It invites those who oppose application of the rule in *Wesberry* to use the statute and the remarks of some members of Congress in debate as an excuse to avoid as long as possible any need to conform with the rule of substantial equality in population.[24]

However, when it became clear that an outer limit would be passed, Bobby supported his brother Edward's successful amendment to the district standards bill, which replaced the 35 percent limit recommended by the Senate Judiciary Committee with a 10 percent limit.

District of Columbia Home Rule

One of Robert Kennedy's three committee assignments upon entering the Senate in January 1965 was the District of Columbia Committee. After that he was one of the principal proponents of home rule for the nation's capital in Congress. The following statement provides a good summary of his views on this matter:

There is little need to dwell either on the case for home rule or its importance. We have allowed a classic situation of taxation without representation to persist on our very doorstep for far too long.

The ramifications of this are enormous. It is not just a question of the District resident having no say in how much he is taxed and in what manner, although that is certainly important. The critical thing is that he has no elected official to turn to—no one to whom he can say, "I and others like me won't re-elect you unless you are more responsive to our needs."

Under the circumstances, the District Commissioners, working together with Congress, have done the best they could. But the limitations have been crippling. The Commissioners

[24] Statement, U.S. Senate, June 8, 1967.

can take no major action without turning to Congress, and most members of Congress, with some justification, act first in response to the place where the votes come from. The District resident, despite powerful advocacy on his behalf by a handful of interested senators and congressmen, always ends up at the end of the line.

This is really a national disgrace. . . .

But we should not be misled. Removing the automatic federal payment and replacing it with the annual ritual of consideration and approval by the House and the Senate appropriations committees cuts to the heart of the home rule concept. The very autonomy that S. 1118 seeks to create is thereby subverted. A major purpose of S. 1118 is to get us in Congress out of the business of analyzing the specific needs and problems of the District as though we were the rightful occupants of city hall. As written, S. 1118 would leave us ample supervisory power while relieving us of the need for day-to-day supervision of the operations of the District's local government. We certainly have a few other things to do.

Changing the automatic federal payment back to the status quo would subvert these purposes. And the arguments against the automatic federal payment are, in my judgment, without substance.[25]

Immigration Laws

A commitment Robert Kennedy inherited from his brother's administration was the struggle to revise our immigration laws. Enacted in 1924 during the isolationist reaction to Wilson's internationalism, the national origins quota system which shaped our immigration policy for forty years was clearly designed to exclude particular racial and ethnic groups from this country—notably Asians, Africans, and southern and eastern Europeans. Finally, in the fall of 1965, a more equitable system giving preference to those with relatives in the United States and those possessing necessary skills without reference to their national origin, first proposed during Kennedy's Ad-

[25] Statement, U.S. Senate, July 20, 1965.

ministration and steered through Congress by President Johnson, was passed.

Here are a series of statements during the campaign to revise the national origins quota system:

The existing immigration laws of the United States, incorporated in the McCarran-Walter Act of 1952, are, in my judgment, not only out of date but out of step with the realities of life in this city and this state. Based, as these laws are, on the United States population of 1920, they were born of restricting isolationism, and nourished by a politics of prosperity based on privilege. They are as Republican as they can be.

A quota system is employed in regard to human beings—a system deliberately designed to keep the United States population exactly as it was racially and ethnically in the year 1920. I am against this law for its philosophic error in conception, its unfairness in practice, and for the great positive contributions we are now losing because of it.

The immigration quota system we now have—based on country of birth—is fundamentally wrong. In a real sense, we are all immigrants, and we are unfair to ourselves and our beliefs in the equality of man before God and the laws when we perpetuate a human quota system as our basis for future immigration.

The law is impractical. Very large quotas have been allotted the countries of northern Europe because of the composition of the United States in 1920. Discriminatory small quotas are assigned southern European countries, and countries still enslaved by the Soviet Union. Consequently, more than one-third of England's and Ireland's quotas, for example, go unused each year. And the law makes no provision for reassigning these quotas.[26]

I support legislation which would abolish the national origins quota system and pool the present quotas to help cut down the waiting list in countries like Italy, Greece and Poland. This does not mean a great influx of immigrants in this, the state of New York, or in the United States. It means it is for and in the interest of the state of New York. It means those

[26] Speech, Nationalities Committee breakfast, New York, N.Y., September 23, 1964.

with relatives who are uneducated can come in with those relatives who are skilled. It means we can treat all countries alike. This is the legislation I support.[27]

There is now before the Congress an immigration bill, sent there two years ago by President Kennedy, which has found a great new advocate in President Johnson. It will eliminate the insidious discrimination of the national origins system. It will judge immigrants to this country not by their names but by their talents; not by where they come from, but what they bring. It will reunite tens of thousands of American citizens with their families—parents and children, brothers and sisters. It will return us to the best that is our tradition—by casting off one of the most shocking parts of our history, a product of bigotry—which is today ignorance, fear and narrow selfishness. And in doing so it will help to free this nation for the great tasks ahead.[28]

It gives me great pleasure to appear today to voice my support of the administration's immigration bill, S. 500.

This bill distills the accumulated experience and wisdom of forty years—the years since the institution of the discriminatory national origins system. That system was imposed during the postwar crisis in Europe, when many in the United States feared that a continuance of unlimited immigration would lead to the coming here of tens of millions of unlettered, poverty-stricken refugees—and of hundreds of thousands of revolutionaries.

Those fears proved unfounded. And ever since 1924, we have regretted the excesses of that day. Presidents of both parties—including every president for the last quarter-century —have deplored the presence in American law of discriminations directly opposed to the assumptions of our Constitution. Both political parties, for many years, have called for the repeal of this system.

They have done so because the follies and the random

[27] Speech, New York State Publishers Association, Queens, N.Y., September 15, 1964.
[28] Address, Hebrew Immigrant Aid Society, New York, N.Y., June 10, 1965.

cruelties the system imposes have become too clear to be ignored. . . .

What, then, *will* the bill do?

It will eliminate from the statute books a form of discrimination totally alien to the spirit of the Constitution. Distinctions based on race or national origin assume what our law, our traditions, and our common sense deny: that the worth of men can be judged on a group basis.

Our ancient struggle for due process of law, for equal protection and individual rights, is the story of the struggle for individual treatment—for the proposition that no disability may be imposed on men as members of a class.

Our law allows men to be judged only on a finding that an individual has committed some act, or has some characteristic, which bears a reasonable relation to some legitimate governmental end. . . .

Third—and to my mind most important—we *need* immigration. The history of America, as Oscar Handlin has said, *is* the history of immigrants. Our strength is in variety, not sameness. Our unity is that of the living, not the graveyard. Our greatness we owe not to the bayonet, or to the atomic bomb, but to our capacity to attract and absorb the richness of diversity—because to all men we attempt to secure the same measure of freedom and opportunity.

Yet our immigration policy has lagged behind the promise of our tradition and the progress of the world. Trade crosses borders ever more freely; capital flows by the mere entering of figures on ledgers; ideas spirit from one country to another as fast as the printing press and the airplane can carry them; news, protests, approvals, anger and gratitude travel with the speed of light. But people who make the goods, create the capital, think and live the ideas—move almost as slowly as if the airplane or even the railroad had never been invented.[29]

And for Americans who might have forgotten their not-so-distant origins, he reminded:

As St. Patrick's Day approaches, it is appropriate to remember our heritage as a nation of immigrants. As Professor Oscar

[29] Statement, Subcommittee on Immigration of the Senate Judiciary Committee, March 4, 1965.

Handlin has said, "Once I thought to write a history of immigrants in America. Then I realized that the immigrants *were* American." [30]

Federal Consumer Protection

On April 29, 1966, Kennedy testified before the House Committee on Government Operations on behalf of a proposal to create a Cabinet-level Department of Consumers. The following are excerpts from that testimony:

The excellent work of Assistant Secretary of Labor Esther Peterson, at the federal level, as well as the work of this committee, have dramatized consumer problems to the point where the idea of a federal Department of Consumers is now receiving serious public attention. The fact is, of course, that none of us will be very surprised if Congress does not establish a Department of Consumers during the current session or even during the next Congress. But, remembering the long struggle to establish the Department of Health, Education and Welfare, and the equally long fight to create the Department of Housing and Urban Development, we know that we must begin now to focus on the problems if we are to succeed later. We must begin to organize consumer groups in support of this legislation and we must carry the debate concerning the proposal to the country. We must do these things because the American consumer will never be properly protected against unsafe and unfair conditions until we create a Cabinet-level Department with a full set of protective legislation under its jurisdiction. Four years ago President Kennedy sent a special message to the Congress about consumer problems. He began it by reminding us that "consumers, by definition, include us all." In saying that, he recognized that consumer interests are so broad that we will never succeed in protecting all of them in a single institutional structure. But he laid down a fundamental challenge: to find the means by which the four basic rights of the consumer could be protected—the right to be safe, the right to choose, the right to be informed, and the right to be heard. In my judgment, meeting that challenge as

[30] Speech, U.S. Senate, March 17, 1967.

best we can ultimately depends on our creating an institutional framework for action—a Department of Consumers endowed with effective enforcement powers. That is why we must begin working toward its creation now. . . .

Of course one original purpose of the regulatory agencies was protection of consumer interests. Yet it increasingly occurs that the consumer's voice before these agencies is drowned out by the competition of one more particularized interest or another. Why shouldn't young people who will be enticed to smoke by cigarette advertising be spoken for when the tobacco interests are heard so clearly? Why shouldn't the users of electricity be heard when the giant utilities are spoken for so effectively? Why shouldn't those who borrow from banks be heard as well as the spokesmen for the networks and the manufacturers? Why shouldn't those who pay exorbitant prices for drugs be heard as well as the airlines? It is not easy to organize the consumers so that their point of view can be consistently and effectively set forth. But a federal department, specifically charged with that obligation, could give the consumer the voice he needs in the regulatory process. . . .

Under the terms of this bill the Department of Consumers would have the responsibility of preparing programs to inform and educate consumers. That kind of consumer education is in the best tradition of our free-enterprise economy. Furthermore, the department would act as a national clearing house for complaints. It would coordinate and dispense important consumer information to the general public and to local and state governmental bodies concerned with the problem. It would conduct economic research and surveys. In the process of doing these things, the department would help achieve the best protection possible against abuse of the consumer— namely an educated and informed public.

I am especially concerned about the protection of the poor. The disadvantages of the poor extend to every contact they have with the world of commerce. The quality of their food is lower and the prices they pay are often higher; the interest rates they pay are higher; they are more often the victims of the high-pressure tactics of deceitful salesmen. And they are the most frequent casualties of the various laws that protect the producing interests of our society: the poor suffer again and again through the entry of default judgments against them, through the repossessing of merchandise, and through misuse of landlord and tenant laws.[31]

The American Indian

Speaking before the National Congress of American Indians in 1963, Bobby addressed himself to the tragic plight of this country's original inhabitants, a subject politicians seldom raise.

Since the outset of this administration, our firm policy has been to consult with tribal groups and to work with them in determining every phase of the federal action in their behalf—in marked contrast to the long-standing custom of the past, when the wishes of the tribal organizations were all too often ignored.

The Indian may be technically free—to vote, to stay on his reservation or leave it, to take part in state and federal government—but that freedom amounts to precious little when he must struggle every day, against heavy odds, to feed and clothe and shelter his family.

He may be technically free, but he is the victim of social and economic oppressions that hold him in bondage. He is all too likely to become the victim of his own proud anger, his own frustrations, and—the most humiliating of all—the victim of racial discrimination in his own land.[32]

[31] Testimony, House Committee on Government Operations, April 29, 1966.

[32] Speech, National Congress of American Indians, Bismarck, N.D., September 13, 1963.

Chapter 18

American Society: Sick or Sound?

. . . I have had occasion to reflect upon what Burke would have called the "cause of our present discontents." The essential cause is poverty—poverty of goods and poverty of understanding. The consequences are loss of health, loss of dignity, loss of simple justice and loss of respect for law and order. While this may have been true of every age, there is a difference now, which is that for the first time in history we have every resource necessary to conquer all forms of poverty and their symptoms.[1]

I'm not doing this [campaigning for John Kennedy in 1960] only because of the family and because Jack is my brother. I sincerely do feel that this will make a hell of a lot of difference to the country. I really believe that we've gone soft in America, that we've got to wake up.[2]

Can it meaningfully be stated that a given society is either sick or sound? Although this kind of social judgment is by nature somewhat relative and subjective, most modern social scientists—particularly historians and anthropologists—would probably reply with a qualified yes. Sense of community and of national purpose and the physical and intellectual vigor of a people appear to be more than the figments of romantic imagination. They

[1] Robert F. Kennedy, *The Pursuit of Justice* (New York: Harper & Row, 1965), p. 10.
[2] Nick Thimmisch and William Johnson, *R. F. K. at 40* (Boston: W. W. Norton, 1965), p. 26.

seem to be real social characteristics which vary discernibly from nation to nation and time to time.

But a prognosis of societal health is a complex and subtle matter. Past societies tend to be judged in terms of today's values and national aspirations, and evaluations of contemporary societies almost invariably fall prey to the vanity which leads men to view their own times as a crucial "turning point" or "watershed" in history fraught with unparalleled crises.

Putting aside the question of the accuracy of most assessments of a society's health, it suffices for our purposes to point out that a politician with any interest in issues and programs can hardly avoid forming opinions about the relative sickness or soundness of his own society. The very nature of his political program (radical, moderate, or reactionary) is a function of his answer to the question, "Where is this society going and is this good or bad?" Thus publicly expressed opinions in this area, no matter how vague or tentative, supply us with useful information about the manner of public man with whom we are dealing.

Robert Kennedy long felt that all was not well with the Union. During the early years of his career he often expressed his discontent and foreboding in simplistic terms such as "moral decay" and "getting soft." Like Barry Goldwater, he apparently believed in reform by incantation—talk enough about declining American morality and physical fitness and things will improve. The following are typical of his statements during this period.

And I think that . . . in the last analysis, it's not going to be the federal government that's going to end this. The attitude in the United States must change. We must realize that there's a problem and difficulty—that management must be willing to stand up—and labor leaders must be willing to stand up—and people themselves must be willing to change their attitude toward corruption. For instance, in basketball alone you've got thirty players and seventeen or eighteen different colleges in the United States involved in gambling. I think Bob Cousy of the Boston Celtics said, the other day, that you can't really find fault with these people because this is the attitude that has permeated the United States lately. There's so much concentration on making a few extra dollars and being comfortable, and having the biggest car or television set, that it's pretty difficult, even if you have good laws, to get these things all altered or changed. If the attitude in the country changes—if we have a greater interest in our communities and the state and the nation—in our schools—in the fact that there should be good law enforcement, I think we'll make progress. But otherwise, we won't.[3]

But I think we all recognize that today sports, athletics and physical fitness are a cause as well as an interest. As a nation we have come too near forgetting our tradition of physical vigor and stamina. We have been spending too much of our time in the stands and not enough on the field. To put it bluntly, we are in danger of getting soft.[4]

Gradually his analysis became more sophisticated. His speeches were increasingly filled with references to individual alienation, loss of community, and the estrangement and disillusionment of our youth. Gone was the naïve faith that if Americans only understood what was happening to them, they could return the nation to a mythical golden age in which simple virtues reigned supreme and each American was at one with himself and his community.

Alienation and the Need for Community

Here is a broad sample of what Kennedy regarded as America's "present discontents":

This is no easy matter, no immediate vision turned into the next day's fact. For seldom have our historic goals and ideals seemed more difficult of achievement. We have passed civil rights legislation of a reach and detail unknown since the Civil

[3] Press conference, U.S. Department of Justice, June 20, 1961.
[4] Speech, "Dinner of Champions," New York, N.Y., October 17, 1961.

War; yet never has there been a greater sense of alienation or more open hostility between the races. We have found material wealth, and government programs, far beyond our dreams of a few years ago; yet perhaps we count the wrong things, for the forms of the new wealth seem to destroy as many pleasures as they bring to us—and the new programs seem irrelevant, even hostile, to many of the purposes they were designed to achieve. Most dangerous of all, millions of Americans—who can say how many?—have lost confidence in each other, and in their ability to shape their own fate, their community's development, or their nation's course. Everywhere I go in this country I find people groping for the answers to questions we barely understand: searching for purpose in the midst of baffling change, confusion and danger. We are losing many of our most active and committed young to extreme movements or public indifference. We are losing members of the older generation, who are turning to the past in order at least to protect what they have. The Minutemen and the Revolutionary Action Movement agree only on one thing—that they have the right to use guns and violence against fellow citizens with whom they disagree. More and more, debate is not an interchange of views but a dialogue of the deaf, often serving to demonstrate differences but not to reconcile them. We confront even those with whom we sympathize across barriers of hostility and mistrust.[5]

Most important, and yet hardest of all to achieve, or even to define: we—you and I, and the people of Harlem and Watts, and the factory worker of Detroit and Gary, the executive in New York or Washington, the college student at Iowa State or Berkeley—we, all of us, have to try to recapture our community, the sense of our country. Not from a foreign enemy, not from robber barons like those you fought a century ago, not from any man or men; we must recapture ourselves from the consequence of our own success. For the wonderful production machine we have built here in America is also a machine that sometimes sacrifices humanity on the altar of a seeming efficiency. The computers whir and glide—and another ten thousand men are doomed to lives of idle surplus,

[5] Speech, dinner in honor of ex-Senator Paul Douglas, Chicago, Ill., October 23, 1967.

their skills replaced by ever more efficient machines. Numbers go up and down on a board at the exchange—and another thousand farms are wiped out, to be absorbed by a corporation with a more favorable tax picture. A plant closes, and a town dies—churches and schools slowly emptying, shops boarded up, weeds growing in once-pleasant gardens.

We have grown perhaps too efficient at counting money, and not efficient enough at measuring what gives satisfaction to our own minds and hearts.

And even then, we have not achieved true efficiency. For what use is it that we save a fraction of a cent on the price of bread—if the result is that thousands of independent farmers become factory hands, and others must turn to idleness? What use is it that the government's books look better—if the result is starving children in the Punjab, and empty pockets at home? Or what use even is spreading prosperity—if the price is to abandon all decision-making power to a few men in far-away board rooms?

Our second great aim must be to begin to rebuild our sense of community, the simple facts of common experience and purpose, affection and respect, which tie us to our fellows. Pericles said of Athens that "we are a free democracy, but we obey the laws, more especially those which protect the oppressed, and the unwritten laws whose transgression brings shame." That is the creed of civility, of decency between men, which is indispensable to the good life, or even to the safe life. But it is those "unwritten laws whose transgression brings shame" which are most often violated in the United States today.

There is no written federal law against desecration of the American flag; but even the most bitter of protesters must recognize that it is only what that flag stands for that protects his right to protest.

There is no written law against the use of insulting or intemperate language in public debate. But there can be little dialogue between the races when one Negro leader refers to the President as a "honky" and a racist or when simple cries for racial justice are dismissed as "outside agitation" or "subversive." There can be no solution to the problems in Vietnam, if those who disagree with administration policy are accused of giving aid and comfort to the enemy, and those who support it are accused of pursuing the war because they enjoy blood and killing. There can be no national progress or security, no better life for our children, if we respond to our critics with denunciations or epithets—for only through the dialogue of criticism and response can we discover and remedy our own mistakes.

All these are both symptom and cause of a general lack of mutual respect which for a democratic society is the greatest danger of all. This sense of apartness, of selfish unwillingness to share the concerns of our fellows, or even to listen to them, simply must be ended.[6]

As the poet asks,
"When the Strangers say: What is the meaning of this City?"
What will you answer? "We all deal together
To make money from each other"
Or "This is a community"?

I know the answer the International has always given. And it is because you have always said, "This is a community"— because you have always acted to create that community— that all who would build a better America and a better world come here to draw strength from you as the giant Antaeus drew strength from the earth.

So long as you provide that strength, we need not fear the Strangers' question.[7]

The Individual

It is impossible to mistake the anguish of that voice. There may be many things in that cry, but one of them is surely a protest of individuality—against the university as corporate bureaucracy, against the dull sameness Miss Hamilton [Edith Hamilton, noted classicist] saw also—for in bureaucracy and sameness is the denial of individuality, and the denial that human beings matter; if all are the same, why listen to what

[6] Address, Salt Lake City, Utah, June 8, 1967.
[7] Address, International Ladies' Garment Workers Union Convention, Miami, Fla., May 18, 1965.

anyone says? And if we are not prepared to listen, then men cannot be recognized as more than numbers in statistical collections, a part of the gross national product like so many coffee cups or carpet sweepers.

The nonrecognition of individuality—the sense that no one is listening—is even more pronounced in our politics. Television, newspapers, magazines are a cascade of words, official statements, policies, explanations, and declarations; all flow from the height of government, down to the passive citizen; the young must feel, in their efforts to speak back, like solitary salmon trying to breast Grand Coulee dam. The words which submerge us, all too often, speak the language of a day irrelevant to our young. And the language of politics is too often insincerity—which we have perhaps too easily accepted, but to the young is particularly offensive.[8]

There will be some general restrictions, but the burden of justification must be on those who propose to limit freedom of action not on those who wish to enlarge it. In this way, too, we can strike at a dominant cause for mounting disaffection and discontent: the feeling of the individual citizen that he is impotent to overcome private degradations, public dangers, and official indifference. From the beginning the American citizen has believed he was part of the great enterprise. That conviction is rapidly fading as control over much which influences his life slips away, leaving a helplessness which must contribute to personal despair and social turmoil. Strengthening local government will also help enhance the opportunity for thousands more to seek personal fulfillment by sharing in the burdens and adventures of their society.[9]

The Young and the Disaffected

In his speech before the Americans for Democratic Action in Philadelphia, in February 1967, Kennedy discussed the discontent and disillusionment with America brew-

[8] Address, Americans for Democratic Action, Philadelphia, Pa., February 27, 1967.

[9] Address, New York State Constitutional Convention, Albany, N.Y., April 4, 1967.

ing among young people on our college campuses and in the black ghettos of our cities.

Yet for all the inspiration, all the freshness and imagination our young people have given us in the last few years, we are now profoundly troubled by them; and so we should be. For the gap between generations, always present in the past, is suddenly widening; the old bridges which span it are falling; we see all around us a terrible alienation of the best and bravest of our young; and the very shape of a generation seems turned on its head overnight. Bob Moses is gone, Stokely Carmichael stands in his place—and beyond him are others more militant, offering dark visions of an apocalyptic future. Peace Corps recruiting is not so easy as it was; and we read less of tutoring programs in the ghetto than of "trips," "festivals," and drugs with strange new names. There are riots on the Los Angeles "strip" and in dozens of colleges; hundreds of young men dodge the draft in Canada, and unknown numbers effectively do the same in years of graduate study; the suicide rate among young people is rising—and so is the rate of juvenile delinquency. The troubadour of their generation, who three years ago sang of the changes that were "blowin' in the wind," now dismisses our pronouncements as "propaganda, all is phony."

Clearly, there are different phenomena, different youth. But taken together, they mean that more and more of our children are estranged, alienated in the literal sense, almost unreachable by the familiar premises and arguments of our adult world. And the task of leadership, the first task of concerned people, is not to condemn or castigate or deplore—it is to search out the reason for disillusionment and alienation, the rationale of protest and dissent—perhaps, indeed, to learn from it. And we will learn most, I think, from the minority who most sharply articulate their criticism of our ways. And we may find that we learn most of all from those political and social dissenters whose differences with us are most grave; for among the young as among adults, the sharpest criticism often goes hand in hand with the deepest idealism and love of country. . . .

And if we add to the insincerity, and the absence of dialogue, the absurdity of a politics in which a Byron de la Beckwith can declare as a candidate for Lieutenant Governor of

Mississippi, we can understand why so many of our young people have turned from engagement to disengagement, from politics to passivity, from hope to nihilism, from SDS to LSD. . . .

If we cannot help open to them this sense of possibility, we will have only ourselves to blame for the disillusionment that will surely come. And more than disillusionment, danger; for we rely on these young people more than we know: not just in the Peace Corps, though the Peace Corps has done more for our position around the world than all our armed forces and foreign aid; not just in civil rights, though our youth have done more toward a solution of that problem than all the power and panoply of government; we rely on our youth for all our hopes of a better future—and thus, in a real and direct sense, for the very meaning of our own lives. If we would look back with pride at the lives we lead, we know above all that we will judge ourselves by the hope and direction we have left behind.[10]

The Ethnic Heritage

Using his Irish heritage as an example, he lamented the nation's fading diversity as third- and fourth-generation Americans lose touch with their ethnic traditions.

This is of course a familiar story. But it is worth tracing and retracing and retelling. The time is long past when men bowed their heads or looked away from our heritage because of shame; indeed, the long roll of senators and playwrights, poets and heroes, has given us full reason for pride. But there is a danger that this heritage will be lost—not from failure, not by an oppressor's hand—but from its own success. For even as we have taken our place in the general American community, as the fact of our Irish roots or religion ceased to be a handicap, it became perhaps too easy for our children to take it all for granted; not only to become—as they should become—Americans first and Irish-Americans second; but to lose entire touch with our tradition and its days of discomfort and danger.

[10] Address, Americans for Democratic Action, Philadelphia, Pa., February 27, 1967.

This problem has afflicted every group of immigrants, as the third and fourth generation went off to college, leaving behind old neighborhoods and the old way of thought. And as Americans, I think we can all sense that as the immigrant tradition dies, we lose one of our most precious possessions: the diversity and color, the rub of difference and discovery that have made this country more than the sum of all its particular heritages. . . . I want that tradition—and those of all the other immigrant groups that built this country—to live. I for one would not be happy to see this nation bland and homogeneous, its speech and literature reduced to the common denominator of mass-circulation magazines, its life settled down into a uniform suburb stretching from coast to coast. What would *Abie's Irish Rose* have been if Abie was Jewish and Rose Irish in name only? [11]

The "Ideal" Family

Addressing the graduating class at a girls' college in Washington, Kennedy questioned the prevailing view of the "ideal" American family.

The classic role of wife and mother as *just* a wife and mother is something that belongs, I believe, to simpler times than ours—and to simpler minds than yours.

The bland gospel of "togetherness," so sweetly and solemnly spread by merchants over the mass media of this country, can no longer be dismissed as a minor irritant in our popular culture.

It has come to reflect a real and present danger: a growing concept of ideal family life as containment within an airtight capsule of coziness and consumership, a bright plastic bastion from which all the range and clamor of the world is shut out —from which reality itself is forever held at bay.

Don't—as those other frightening advertisements used to say —don't let this happen to you.

Consider it imperative, for your own and your husband's and above all your children's sake, as well as the sake of your

[11] Address, Irish Institute, New York, N.Y., April 1, 1967.

countrymen, that you continue to make full and generous use of the mind your education has set free.

If only with part of your time and only in the region of your own community, you may find yourself able to work effectively against the forces of darkness around you.[12]

The Central Sickness

And he questioned the sanity of a society that permit poverty and despair in its midst while possessing th means to eliminate them.

Our scientists grapple with the difficulties of placing a ma on the moon, but the immediately troubling concern of ou society is whether men of different races can sit together at lunch counter. Automation provides us with wonders of pr duction and information but no answer to the question c what to do with the men the machines displace.

In short, the power and the resources of modern technology education and civilization do not enrich the lives of all me We do not all live in the same century.

The New York World's Fair exemplifies the scientific ac vances of the twentieth century and it offers suggestions abou the America of the twenty-first century. But less than an hoi away in Harlem, people live in squalor and despair mor closely resembling the nineteenth century. A few hundre miles away, in the remote hovels of Appalachia, the life of th people is, if anything, worse than it was a hundred years ag

Such disparity cannot be tolerated in a society which be lieves in free opportunity, or even in one which only tall about it. And I believe that our generation is committed t seeking an end to such disparity and solutions for the prol lems of the nation and the communities in which we live.[13]

[12] Speech, Trinity College commencement exercises, Washing ton, D.C., June 2, 1963.

[13] Speech, Marquette University commencement exercises, Mi waukee, Wis., June 7, 1964.

Toughness, Idealism, and the Modern American Revolution

Can we find cures for these societal ills? Kennedy thought so. But he warned that the traditional American panacea of economic growth could not be expected to do the job.

And let us be clear at the outset that we will find neither national purpose nor personal satisfaction in a mere continuation of economic progress, in an endless amassing of worldly goods. We cannot measure national spirit by the Dow-Jones average or national achievement by the gross national product.

For the gross national product includes our pollution and advertising for cigarettes, and ambulances to clear our highways of carnage. It counts special locks for our doors and jails for the people who break them. The gross national product includes the destruction of the redwoods, and the death of Lake Superior. It grows with the production of napalm and missiles and nuclear warheads, and it even includes research on the improved dissemination of bubonic plague. The gross national product swells with equipment for the police to put down riots in our cities; and though it is not diminished by the damage these riots do, still it goes up as slums are rebuilt on their ashes. It includes Whitman's rifle and Speck's knife, and the broadcasting of television programs which glorify violence to sell goods to our children.[14]

What, then, should be done? Early in his career, while still espousing a "rugged individualist" approach, he called on Americans to recapture their "toughness and idealism."

It seems to me imperative that we reinstill in ourselves the toughness and idealism that guided the nation in the past. The paramount interest in self, in material wealth, in

[14] Address, Jefferson-Jackson Day Dinner, Detroit, Mich., May 5, 1967.

security must be replaced by an actual, not just a vocal, interest in our country, by a spirit of adventure, a will to fight what is evil, and a desire to serve. It is up to us as citizens to take the initiative as it has been taken before in our history, to reach out boldly but with honesty to do the things that need to be done. To meet the challenge of our times, so that we can later look back upon this era not as one of which we need be ashamed but as a turning point on the way to a better America, we must first defeat the enemy within.[15]

However, by the time he reached the U.S. Senate, Kennedy's challenges to the American people to face the hard realities of the day began to assume the shape and tone of his brother's brilliant inaugural address. In 1966 he said:

What is required of us is that we do more than recite those accomplishments and talk of dreams fulfilled. For now we must be prepared to work a revolution at once as profound and as compassionate as the struggle of the past thirty years. The question is whether we have lifted our eyes to the new horizons of our days, and to the uncharted oceans beyond. The question is whether we are prepared to dare—whether we will risk our positions and our popularity, our intellectual and social comforts in order to make a world for our children which is truly better than the world our fathers passed on to us.[16]

We have triumphed not in spite of controversy, but because of it, not because we avoided problems, but because we faced them. We have won not because we bent and diluted our principles for the sake of political expediency, but because we stood fast for those ideals which represent the most generous and noble portion of the American spirit. If we forget this great lesson, if we place the claims of power ahead of the claims of justice, if we shrink from principle in the face of the passing winds of controversy of reaction or ignorance,

[15] Robert F. Kennedy, *The Enemy Within* (New York: Harper & Brothers, 1960), p. 325.

[16] Address, Retail, Wholesale and Department Store Union Convention, Miami Beach, Fla., May 27, 1966

then we will have lost the great purpose which has made us strong, and with it our claim to the allegiance and support of the majority of the American people. But I do not believe we will embark on so suicidal a course. I believe, rather, that we will remember that leadership in freedom does not rest in wealth and power, force or fear. It depends on fidelity and persistence in those shaping beliefs—democracy, freedom, justice—which men follow not from the enslavement of their bodies but from the compulsion of their hearts. We must cope with real dangers, overcome real obstacles, meet real needs; but always in a way which preserves our own allegiance to the fundamental principles and promises of the American Constitution. Otherwise we will preserve the shadow of progress and security at the expense of the substance of freedom here in America and all around the world.[17]

Have our triumphs and conquests erased the visions which adversity, struggle and danger could not dim? I do not think so. Everywhere I travel I meet a generation anxious to share, not only in elevation of their own society, but in taking part in the revolution now reshaping the world. The nature and course of that revolution are not dictated by abstract and unreal dreams. It is a dream, but it is compelled by the nature of our achievements and our problems. Think how our world would look to a visitor from another planet as he crossed the continents. He would find great cities and knowledge able to create enormous abundance from the materials of nature. He would witness exploration into understanding of the entire physical universe, from the particles of the atom to the secrets of life. He would see billions of people separated by only a few hours of flight, communication with the speed of light, sharing a common dependence on a thin layer of soil and a covering of air. Yet he would also observe that most of mankind was living in misery and hunger, that some of the inhabitants of this tiny, crowded globe were killing others, and that a few patches of land were pointing huge instruments of death and war at others. Since what he was seeing proved our intelligence, he could only wonder at our sanity.

[17] Speech, Democratic State Committee Dinner, Columbus, Ohio, October 8, 1966.

It is this monstrous absurdity—that in the midst of such possibility men should hate and kill and oppress one another —that must be the target of the modern American revolution.[18]

A Call to Youth

He called to youth to play a role in this new American revolution.

This group, if any, can reach across the gap—can reach out to the young of the sixties. And this group must. We may find some of their ideas impractical, some of the views overdrawn. But there is no question of their energy, of their ability, above all of their honest commitment to a better and more decent world for all of us. They have struggled and sacrificed alone too long. It is for us now to make the effort—to take their causes as our cause, and to enlist them in our own; to lend to their vision and daring the insight and wisdom of our experience; and to recapture for ourselves the sense of open possibility which they gave a nation for a few brief years. And if, when we reach out to them, we are tempted to dismiss their vision as impossible, or their indignation as naïve, let us remember, as the poet says, that

> "None can usurp the height
> But those to whom the miseries of the world
> Are misery, and will not let them rest." [19]

Your generation is the first with the chance not only to remedy the mistakes which all of us have made in the past, but to transcend them. Your generation has the chance to serve not only your state but to take up the troubling burdens of a great nation with global responsibilities. Your generation—this generation—cannot afford to waste its sub-

[18] Address, Columbus Day Dinner, New York, N.Y., October 11, 1966.
[19] Address, Americans for Democratic Action, Philadelphia, Pa., February 27, 1967.

stance and its hope in the struggles of the past when beyond these walls is a world to be helped, and improved, and made safe for the welfare of mankind.[20]

Knowledge and a Vision of Things to Come

Despite serious misgivings about past and present applications of science and technology to modern living, Kennedy maintained continually that further knowledge of our physical environment is man's only hope for survival.

Although we do make mistakes in the application of our technology, mistakes that effective public policy combined with technological knowledge can avoid, the promise of science and technology offers the only hope that man will live and prosper in our physical environment.

It offers the promise of sufficient food for all the people of the world.

It offers the promise of detection and prevention of destruction by natural phenomena.

It offers the promise of adequate housing and clothing for all mankind.

It offers the promise of a standard of living in which all mankind can live in dignity and civilization, freed of the brutalization of a daily scramble for animal existence.

It is these applications of science rather than science itself which is the promise of science to the man on the street and the citizen of a newly developing country. It is science and its application through technology that has created a revolution in expectations in the developing sectors between modern man and his physical environment.[21]

Robert Kennedy saw much in American society that was unhealthy and disturbing. But his faith in the basic rightness of our principles of government and the resilience of the nation's institutions and people—a faith he felt

[20] Address, University of Mississippi Law School Forum, Oxford, Miss., March 18, 1966.

[21] Remarks, Yeshiva University, New York, N.Y., May 23, 1965.

no need to justify—kept him sanguine about the future. All is in flux, he contended.

> . . . commencement speeches, in this year of 1967, must be different from what they have ever been before. They have always signified "Beginning" for the students who graduate—now they signify a new beginning for all of us. They have always been given by a representative of the settled order in which the graduates would take their assigned places—but there no longer is any settled order, and we must all find new places to take. All around us the old order of things is crumbling, and a new world society is painfully struggling to take shape. The pace of change has made of us all—your teachers and senators no less than yourselves—mariners on an uncharted ocean.[22]

But out of this incessant change he had a vision of what will emerge if Americans are determined enough to make it so.

> Every man must have his own vision of things to come. But many Americans, I believe, share broad and deep hopes for the world—the hope of a world without war—of a world where peoples now suffering in poverty and oppression can win a better life for themselves and their children—of a world where the imagination and energy of mankind are dedicated, not to destruction, but to building a generous and spacious future.
>
> And many Americans too, I think, share broad and deep hopes for our own land—and hope of a land in which every child born has a decent opportunity for education, medical care and employment—of a land where intolerance and segregation become a memory, and a Negro child born in a cotton field in Alabama is as secure in his rights as a white child born here in Washington—of a land where poverty is a thing of the past, and every American has a free and equal chance to realize his own individual talents and possibilities.
>
> If this is the vision of the future—if this is the direction in which we want to move—the next thing we must con-

[22] Speech, Fordham University commencement exercises, New York, N.Y., June 10, 1967.

sider is how we propose to get there, and what obstacles lie in our path. For such a vision is never self-fulfilling. We cannot stand idly by and expect our dreams to come true under their own power. The future is not a gift: It is an achievement. Every generation helps make its own future. This is the essential challenge of the present.[23]

Thus the question before us in the last third of this century will be not the magnitude of our wealth, but the way that we use it; less the health of our production than the health of the men and women who produce it; as President Johnson has said, not the quantity of our goods, but the quality of our lives. That quality will depend on our ability to serve four great ends, in the shaping tradition of our historic ideals.

These are the directions in which a new politics move.

First, we must above all find ways to liberate and enhance the importance of individual lives and actions; to protect ourselves against the great organizations—sprawling government bureaucracies, huge impersonal corporations, and universities as big as cities—which threaten to overwhelm and obliterate the importance and value of individual man.

We as Democrats have tended to look toward Washington for solutions to our perplexities—and for the most part this has been correct, for only national policies can create the conditions for the solutions of national problems. But now it is our responsibility as believers in the human spirit to afford our citizens the opportunity for personal participation and achievement on the great stage of public affairs: with levers of power and decision in places citizens can reach—in their state house, their city hall, indeed in their own neighborhood community.

Second, as we move to extend and deepen government protection of our people we must understand the new meaning of justice—ending the dependency which pervades our social programs, and which is the antithesis of democracy. Our greatest failure toward those who have been denied American justice is not simply that our poverty programs are pitifully and shamefully inadequate; our greatest failure has been our refusal to recognize their rights as citizens. We have given welfare handouts to mothers and their children—

[23] Speech, Seattle World's Fair, Seattle, Wash., August 7, 1962.

but we refuse to create jobs for husbands and fathers, and thus have forced families to break up in order to receive our bounty. We have told the poor to shop more wisely; but we have refused to help them build the stores or the credit institution at which they could do so. We have built public housing units by the thousands, in the depressed urban ghettos; but we have done nothing to help poor people own their own homes, free of bureaucratic management, and control over their locations.

In these ways and many more, we have enforced a dependence on their fellow citizens that is degrading and distasteful to giver and receiver alike. In the years ahead, through programs of economic reconstruction and development, we must move beyond welfare to self-sufficiency, giving less charitable doles—and substituting instead a full opportunity to contribute to the building and benefit of our society.

Third, we must begin to rebuild our sense of community, of human dialogue, of the thousand invisible strands of common experience and purpose, affection and respect that tie men to their fellows. . . .

Fourth and most important, arching over all else, must be our quest for world peace: not the quiet of desolation nor the stability of tyranny, but a world of diversity and progress, in which armaments and violence give way to the forces of reason and compromise which are man's only hope for survival on earth. These are also the forces which must one day bring an end to the war in Vietnam; but we should also look beyond that terrible conflict—to insure that it is not repeated; and to insure also that the world's inevitable conflicts of interest and belief do not become irrepressible conflicts of death and global destruction.[24]

An America piled high with gold, and clothed in impenetrable armor, yet living among desperate and poor nations in a chaotic world, could neither guarantee its own security nor pursue the dream of a civilization devoted to the fulfillment of man.

[24] Address, Jefferson-Jackson Day Dinner, Detroit, Mich., May 5, 1967.

Our true interest, therefore, is to help create a world order to replace and improve that shattered when World War I opened the doors to the twentieth century; not an order founded simply upon balance of power or balance of trade, but one based on the conviction that we will be able to shape our own destiny only when we live among others whose own expectations are unscarred by hopelessness, or fear of the strong, or the ambition to master other men.[25]

[25] Address, Columbus Day Dinner, New York, N.Y., October 11, 1966.

PART III

America Abroad

Chapter 19

United States Foreign Policy

Can a democracy in which public opinion plays a prominent part in executive decision-making frame a foreign policy predicated upon the realities of international power politics? And can such a democracy pursue the objectives of its policy with the reason and restraint both success and survival demand in a nuclear age?

These are not academic questions. Many reputable scholars and diplomats have charged that American foreign policy in this century has tended to be irrational, self-defeating and, most recently, a dangerous threat to world peace. Men of the stature of the columnist Walter Lippmann and George Kennan, former Ambassador to the Soviet Union, have suggested that a popular democracy may be incapable of rationally coping with the complex and constantly shifting realities of international politics. If they are right, American history may come to read like a classic Greek tragedy to succeeding generations—if there are succeeding generations.

Why this pessimism on the part of so many students and practitioners of United States diplomacy? Usually they begin by citing the unparalleled role public opinion plays in the shaping of our foreign policy. In no other nation does the "man in the street" exercise such critical influence over diplomatic and military decisions, and some critics regard this popular power over the conduct of our external relations as a grave liability. As Mr. Kennan has written, ". . . a good deal of our trouble seems to have stemmed from the extent to which the executive has felt itself beholden to short-term trends of public opinion in the country and from what we might call the erratic and subjective nature of public reaction to foreign-policy questions. . . . I think the record indicates that in the short term our public opinion, or what passes for our public opinion in the thinking of official Washington, can be easily led astray into areas of emotionalism and subjectivity which make it a poor and inadequate guide for national action."

Suggested structural antidotes for this state of affairs have been antidemocratic or else have called for the replacement of our separation of executive and legislative branches with a parliamentary system similar to Britain's —an unlikely prospect in the foreseeable future. This leaves us to deal with American public opinion, which, these critics contend, must be educated if we are to survive.

Throughout this century, it is argued, the American public has naïvely and self-righteously refused to accept conflict and power politics as permanent factors in international affairs. In addition, Americans have displayed a marked inability to relate military power to political objectives realistically. Force and diplomacy are regarded, as a rule, as mutually exclusive tactics to be applied independently in different contexts. The result: a myopic foreign policy which alternates a somewhat condescending lack of interest in world affairs with frenzied "holy wars" in which violence must know no limitations short of the enemy's unconditional surrender and in which the flexibility needed to attain our political objectives is destroyed.

Soviet control of Eastern and part of Central Europe after World War II—hardly a surprise to those familiar with traditional European power politics—shocked millions of United States citizens. According to their model of international behavior, the proper diplomatic moves should have prevented Soviet expansion. The point was that the Soviets controlled half of Europe by V-E Day because the Red Army had occupied this area on its drive to Berlin (as the western Allies controlled the other half of Europe because of our armies' advances). Nothing short of war could have been expected to dislodge them, certainly not pieces of paper signed at Yalta or Potsdam. Confused, many Americans could only conclude that our statesmen must have betrayed the nation by "selling out" much of Europe to the Soviets. This mass paranoia threatened civil liberties at home and further reduced what flexibility and sanity remained in our foreign policy.

Much of the blame for this persistent failure of large segments of U.S. public opinion to grasp the workings of international relations must be laid at the feet of our political leaders. For the most part they have preferred to remain the captives of an uninformed, often irrational public rather than run the political risks involved in confronting long-held prejudices and beliefs. Even today the public is told by many government officials and members of Congress that United States involvement in Vietnam is aimed at "defending freedom in Southeast Asia"—a ridiculous assertion that no sophisticated supporter or opponent of our current policy seriously believes.

Thus a cardinal criterion for judging the foreign policy record of a federal officeholder must be the degree to which he has succeeded in educating his constituents to the realities of international politics. For a more sophisticated public opinion is America's only hope.

Robert Kennedy's public record regarding foreign affairs was a rich, constantly evolving one. He entered public life with strong views and considerable experience in this area for one so young (his father had been Ambassador to Great Britain from 1937 to 1940, and his two older brothers had been avidly interested in international relations).

In the late forties and early fifties Kennedy and his brother John espoused the hard-line anti-Communist views of their father. However, in time their belief in an evil Communist monolith seeking to devour the West was shaken, and a more subtle analysis of the cold war took its place.

The quotations in this chapter are a collection of general foreign policy statements that Kennedy made over the past decade. Remarks dealing with specific policy questions are reserved for succeeding chapters; here this impressionistic pattern is meant to show the tone and perspective of his perception of world affairs.

A policy is not fear or hostility or wish. Policy is the establishment of goals and of a course of action rationally calculated to achieve those goals. It must be ready to yield to the overriding logic of events, yet striving to shape circumstances rather than belatedly reacting to them.[1]

I do not consider foreign policy a burden; or relations with other countries as at best a necessary evil. I do not believe, as the Republican candidate for President seems to believe, that half the world is our implacable enemy and that the other half is composed of beggars to be ignored, bullied, or castigated.

I see the foreign policy of the United States as an opportunity to turn adversaries into friends and ancient allies into modern partners.

It is an opportunity to help two billion human beings escape from poverty and misery; and to show that the American concepts of technology and individual dignity and enterprise can work around the world.[2]

When our time comes, we want to make sure that we bequeath to our descendants a better and safer world than the one in which we live today, a world in which people will be free from the terrors of war and oppression, free from the handicaps of ignorance and poverty, free to realize their own talents and fulfill their own destinies.

This has been the object of our foreign policy and of our defense policy.[3]

The foreign policy that I support is based on three principles. They are:

First, the achievement of strength adequate to defend our interests, and those who cannot defend themselves— coupled with the inner strength and wisdom not to use that military strength precipitately or indiscriminately. . . .

Second, we must work with other countries through the United Nations and other international groups. The U.N.

[1] Address, China Conference, University of Chicago, Chicago, Ill., February 8, 1967.

[2] Speech, University of Rochester, Rochester, N.Y., September 30, 1964.

[3] Robert F. Kennedy, *The Pursuit of Justice* (New York: Harper & Row, 1965), pp. 128-129.

is recognized by all countries as mankind's noblest experiment. It is the only major world organization in which the small nations and the new nations can play a part. Our support of the U.N. mirrors our interest in these countries, as well as our commitment to peace. . . .

Third, we must extend to the peoples of the world a vision of a better world, and the hope that it can be attained.

Over the years, an understanding of what America really stands for is going to count far more than missiles, aircraft carriers and supersonic bombers. The big changes of the future will result from this understanding—or lack of it.[4]

Our long-term objective obviously is to create an international system of law and order—to create a peaceful and productive society throughout the world. We are not going to succeed this year or next, and perhaps not for many years to come. But struggle we shall and succeed we must![5]

He consistently stressed the need for Americans to accept political and economic diversity in the world and to resist the desire to remake other nations in our own image.

The resources of the earth and the ingenuity of man can provide abundance for all—so long as we are prepared to recognize the diversity of mankind and the variety of ways in which peoples will seek national fulfillment. This is our vision of the world—diversity of states, each developing according to its own traditions and its own genius, each solving its economic and political problems in its own manner, and all bound together by a respect for the rights of others, by a loyalty to the world community and by a faith in the dignity and responsibility of man.[6]

It is not a world in which we can preserve all our advantages of wealth and position and comfort—but a world in

[4] Speech, University of Rochester, Rochester, N.Y., September 30, 1964.

[5] Speech, Portland City Club, Portland, Ore., October 6, 1961.

[6] Robert F. Kennedy, *Just Friends and Brave Enemies* (New York: Harper & Row, 1962), p. 55.

which we must use those advantages for the benefit of others. It is not a world with which all our contacts can be clear and antiseptic, in which we can insist that all people conform to our ideas of what is right and fitting. Rather it is a world of awakened diversity, of hundreds of nations asserting their right to self-determination and full participation in world affairs. To deal with such a world—to make it safe for diversity—to assure true security to our children—we will have to learn to accept the diversity, to disdain all stereotypes, to cast off all excess intellectual and social baggage. We cannot be ready for diversity abroad—until we return to its acceptance at home.[7]

I cannot leave this theme of our historic dedication to the freedom of the individual without commenting on its relationship to our international outlook. It is not we who insist upon other nations accepting our image or our philosophy. . . . Indeed, except by example, democratic ideas are almost incapable of export. To be vital and effective such ideas must be indigenous, developed by the experience of tears and toil rather than as a gift from some outside source.[8]

The resources of the earth and the ingenuity of man can provide abundance for all—so long as we are prepared to recognize the diversity of mankind and the variety of ways in which peoples will seek national fulfillment. This is our vision of the world—a diversity of states, each developing according to its own traditions and its own genius, each solving its economical and political problems in its own manner, and all bound together by a respect for the rights of others, by a loyalty to the world community and by a faith in the dignity and responsibility of man.

We have no intention of trying to remake the world in our image but we have no intention either of permitting any other state to remake the world in its image. Even

[7] Address, Hebrew Immigrant Aid Society, New York, N.Y., June 10, 1965.

[8] Speech, University of Gadja Mada, Jogjakarta, Indonesia, February 15, 1963.

given aims similar to ours, the institutions we have devised to achieve them may be inappropriate in another culture or another historic setting. The creation of the necessary political and economic machinery to achieve these aims must be performed by the people themselves.

We do not condemn others for their differences in economic and political structures. We understand, that newer nations have not had time, even if they so wished, to build institutions relying primarily on private enterprise as we have done. Our privately owned railroads, our airlines, our communications systems, our industries, were not created overnight. These enterprises developed as a result of private initiative at a time when life was far simpler than it is now. We thus had time to permit their slow growth and time to permit the intertwining of many small units into the great systems that the modern age requires, and, under government regulation, time to permit the continuation of private control. This we can understand and appreciate. It neither offends us nor can we deem it hostile.

It is the belief that the restriction of individual liberty is essential to economic growth, coupled with efforts to impose that formula on other nations of the world by subversion of force, that we feel is inimical to peace and liberty.[9]

But we do not believe in a system of government where the most powerful nation tells every other nation what to do.

We are not telling you. We are not telling England. We are not telling France.

Now the Communist system is entirely different. They order others to do certain things. If their instructions are not followed—as happened in Albania and Yugoslavia—they are expelled.

When we talk about strategy, our strategy is to get along with Japan. Our strategy is that the Japanese Government and the Japanese people should determine their own destiny, that they should not be dominated or controlled by any other power.[10]

[9] Speech, Nihon University, Tokyo, Japan, February 6, 1962.
[10] Kennedy, *op. cit.*, p. 36.

But Kennedy pointed out that, although the United States should harbor no intentions of trying to remake the world in its image,

We have no intention either of permitting any other state to remake the world in its image.

In the unending battle between diversity and dogmatism, between tolerance and tyranny, let no one mistake the American position. We deeply believe that humanity is on the verge of an age of greatness, and we do not propose to let the possibilities of that greatness be overwhelmed by those who would lock us all into the narrow cavern of a dark and rigid system. We will defend our faith by affirmation, by argument and if necessary—and heaven forbid that it should become necessary—by arms. It is our willingness to die for our ideals that makes it possible for these ideals to live. . . . Freedom means not only the opportunity to know but the will to know. That will can make for understanding and tolerance, and ultimately friendship and peace.[11]

He warned against the dangers of isolationism:

But there is one thing which Americans have come to understand in these last decades. That is, that we cannot hope to realize these purposes in isolation from the rest of the world (these purposes being the perfection of our own society). The turbulence of social change has long since begun to spill across national frontiers. The overriding development of the second half of the twentieth century is the awakening of peoples in Asia and Africa and Latin America—peoples stirring from centuries of stagnation, suppression and dependency. Now they are seeking through national independence the kind of economic and social development which both your country and mine have experienced. These are young nations, trying desperately in the quest for political and social progress to make up for lost centuries.[12]

They knew—and they led this nation to know—that we,

[11] *Ibid.*, p. 56.
[12] Speech, Nihon University, Tokyo, Japan, February 6, 1962.

who had been blessed with the riches of a continent, must develop its riches as a resource for the whole world; that the United States, which had developed its freedom behind the shield of an ocean, had a responsibility to reach back across the oceans to protect the freedom of those who stayed behind; and that we, who had developed a unique American community, must take the lead in the building of a world community.[13]

You are the last people whom anyone need warn against the dangers of narrow nationalism. The record of European history is the world's strongest argument against a policy of isolation.

Yet in troubled times there is always a temptation to grow one's own hedge and cultivate one's own garden. For either the United States or Europe to succumb to such a temptation would be unworthy of our past and unfaithful to our future.

We cannot—you in Europe and we in the United States— become fortresses within ourselves, dealing with and helping only one another.

If we do so, we will not be meeting our responsibilities to the rest of mankind, and very likely will be spelling our own destruction.[14]

Kennedy wrote that the peoples of the world were counting on the United States.

In every country I found a common strain of friendship for the United States. There were pickets and minor incidents and small misunderstandings in some countries but generally there was a tremendous undercurrent of good will. Wherever I went I met free men who want to remain free and who look to the United States for hope in the future.[15]

To the charge that the United States was pursuing an imperialist foreign policy, he replied:

[13] Speech, Four Freedoms Award Dinner, New York, N.Y., 1965.

[14] Kennedy, *op. cit.*, p. 174.

[15] *Ibid.*, p. 19.

I said to this [Japanese] labor leader, "Do you believe the United States is imperialistic?"

He said, "Yes I do. It is a different kind of imperialism. It is economic imperialism."

I said, "Do you believe that the Soviet Union was imperialistic when it went into Hungary, or do you believe that Communist China was imperialistic when it went into Tibet?"

He said, "No. The United States is imperialistic because they have economic imperialism."

I asked him what he meant by that—what it was in the United States. He said, "Well, the United States is run by the Morgan gang and the Rockefellers."

I said, "Well, not yet it's not!"

You can use guns and bullets and you shoot people down and you are not imperialistic. But because people have been saying or talking about capitalism for one hundred years, it has now become a dirty expression and you are going to accept everything that is said about it. "How could it possibly be true in the United States with Arthur Goldberg, the Secretary of Labor, or President Kennedy, backed by the labor organizations, as he was, that they are now run by the great monopolistic capitalists that you have described?"

But this was the first time he really had thought about it.[16]

After his brother's death, Kennedy gradually became less of a defender and more of a critic of American international behavior. At the China Conference at the University of Chicago in 1967 [a group of scholars and diplomats meeting to re-evaluate U.S. policy toward China], he attacked the hypocrisy of United States policy and challenged the sweeping nature of our "commitments" around the world.

More corrupting, if less dangerous, is the self-righteous assertion of sweeping moral principles as a substitute for policy, though we are willing to ignore those principles when our conception of national interest demands it. We proclaim our intention to assure self-determination, with American lives if necessary. Yet we support and defend a Formosa

[16] Speech, Philadelphia Fellowship Commission, Philadelphia, Pa., April 3, 1962.

whose indigenous people have no voice in government. We do not even raise our voice in protest against this most flagrant and outrageous situation. We are told that "nations must learn to leave their neighbors alone." Nor can we righteously announce that "we seek only freedom and human decency throughout the world," when we have supported, for what we felt was good cause, repressive and corrupt governments in every continent.

I do not quarrel with the necessity of some of the actions which were inconsistent with these principles but those actions do teach us that blanket moral statements cannot determine all strategic judgments, and that their enunciation is not a substitute for policy. It may well be that greater consistency with the moral principles upon which this nation rests might, in the long run, lead to a sounder policy and greater protection for the interests of the United States. I believe this to be so. Yet if we solemnly pronounce principles which will not or cannot be consistently applied, we delude ourselves and invite serious charges of hypocrisy from others. . . .

In Africa, I have tried to answer the question: If the United States is fighting for self-determination in Vietnam, then how can it not support the independence struggle of Angola and Mozambique? For those questioners, it is less our intention than our pretension which is objectionable. To this there is no answer. Thus does false principle destroy the credibility in our wisdom and purpose which is the true foundation of influence as a world power. . . .

The same is true of another kind of blanket formulation— that we must keep our commitments or meet our obligations. Of course, we must keep our commitments and obligations. But by what standards, and toward what ends, are those commitments made? How deeply do they extend, and what means will be used to fulfill them? Thus it is one thing to defend a commitment in Vietnam yet it is something else indeed to fulfill that commitment by extending military operations to Thailand in return making a new commitment to that nation as well. And what is to govern the form of the commitment—whether it is to be a commitment to help others help themselves or not? And when we make the first, do we slowly and inexorably and almost automatically accept the latter? None of these—sweeping statements, pious hopes, grandiose commitments—constitute . . . policy for the future.

That policy must be based on the reality and diversity of today's world; and on a discriminating evaluation of our own interests, capacities and limitations.[17]

Kennedy charged that too often our actions reflect a "narrowness of vision."

Far too often, for narrow tactical reasons, this country has associated itself with tyrannical and unpopular regimes that had no following and no future. Over the past twenty years, we have paid dearly because of support given to colonial rulers, cruel dictators, or ruling cliques void of social purpose. This was one of President Kennedy's gravest concerns. It would be one of his proudest achievements if history records his administration as an era of political friendships made for the United States.[18]

Nor has the narrowness of vision been confined to our conduct at home. We have too often ventured abroad without fully realizing the twisted paths our journeys would take. We built a foreign policy on the rhetoric of anticommunism—and found ourselves trapped by that rhetoric when the Communist monolith began to crumble. We saw good markets and stable governments abroad; and we did not realize that, to the victims of oppression, our support marked us as defenders of tyranny. And today in Vietnam, we spend three billion dollars every hour, and send half a million men into battle, but we do not seem to know how we came to a war of this breadth, nor the way to bring it to an honorable end. Nor did we see that this commitment abroad would drain us of resources so vitally needed at home; that it would cause us to retreat from the task of helping other nations build new societies; that we would have to consider levying new taxes to support this ever-widening war.[19]

He consistently maintained that United States foreign

[17] Address, China Conference, University of Chicago, Chicago, Ill., February 8, 1967.
[18] Speech, California Institute of Technology, Pasadena, Calif., June 8, 1964.
[19] Remarks, Rotary Club luncheon, Poughkeepsie, N.Y., September 6, 1967.

policy makers were not concerned enough with the motivations of other nations.

The essence of a foreign policy is results—which means that we should be concerned not just with our own judgment of our motives and actions, but as much with the judgments of those with whom we deal.[20]

On many occasions he stated that our failure to solve problems at home undermined our diplomatic efforts.

When Carlos P. Romulo, who is a great friend of the United States and the American people, came to my office just before he left Washington recently, he said that we were destined to continue to lead the world. However, he warned that the one thing that can stop us—the one thing that will stand in our way is if we don't deal with the important civil rights problems. People are just not going to believe that we live by the Declaration of Independence or the Constitution if we don't treat our fellow human beings as human beings. He said we have a responsibility and obligation to do this.[21]

On January 30, 1964, while he was still Attorney General, Kennedy held a background press conference at the State Department to answer questions about a diplomatic mission to Asia he had just completed. Since his remarks were "not for attribution," and could be credited only to "U.S. official sources," and because some were completely off the record at the time, the transcript of that conference yields some interesting insights into his view of international affairs, diplomacy, and many leading political figures in the Far East.

The purpose of Kennedy's trip had been to induce Malaysia, Indonesia, and the Philippines to settle their differences peacefully, thus avoiding the continuation of armed conflict between newly formed Malaysia and Indonesia, which was publicly threatening to crush the young state. One of the problems of the situation was

[20] Speech, Annual Luncheon of the Associated Press, New York, N.Y., April 23, 1962.
[21] *Ibid.*

an amendment to the foreign aid bill enacted by Congress forbidding aid to a nation committing acts of aggression against another nation. Pressure was mounting for President Johnson to cut off aid to Indonesia, which was clearly the aggressor. Kennedy commented:

But the problem was if the President made an announcement that we didn't feel it was in the national interest [to continue aid] it is not the fact that it would cut off the aid to Indonesia [which amounted to very little], but just the fact it would be a real break with Indonesia. And whatever you want to say about Indonesia and Sukarno, the fact is it is not Communist, and I will come back to that in a moment. But it is a nation of a hundred million people, and for the United States to cut off its relationship with Indonesia at this period of time—fighting in Vietnam, we have our problems in Cambodia, in Northeast Thailand and some of these other difficulties—to have this break with Indonesia—and Indonesia would consider it obviously an unfriendly act—it presents all kinds of difficulty.[22]

On his conference with President Sukarno in Tokyo:

I said I didn't see how it was possible to ask Malaysia to sit down while they continued their aggression against Malaysia, and I said that if he was in the position of the Tunku he wouldn't be willing to do so, and certainly any self-respecting nation wouldn't be willing to sit down under those circumstances, so that the aggression had to be really curtailed.[23]

Discussing his trip to Malaysia to urge the Tunku (head of state) to the conference table, he referred to Cambodia's controversial Prince Sihanouk:

I then went and saw the Tunku, and at that time Sihanouk arrived and through various suggestions that he was making in Kuala Lumpur almost torpedoed any success that we might have had of even having a conference. I think there were

[22] Press conference, U.S. Department of State, January 30, 1964
[23] *Ibid.*

probably two reasons: number one, he wanted to focus attention on him and on Cambodia; number two, he wanted to take attention off the United States and wanted to have some way of embarrassing or affecting the prestige or position of the United States in that part of the world.[24]

Asked by a reporter why he held out any hopes for this peace conference when others seeking the same ends had failed, Kennedy replied:

Well, I think you have to look at it from almost around the other side, from really a negative point of view, for the reasons . . . that it was escalating and getting more and more serious. This is the only chance of arriving at an agreement. The only chance of calling off what is an escalating war is for the parties to talk.

They are not going to end the war, that is not going to end, the problems are not going to disappear unless they talk and attempt to resolve their problems. And it is important that it be done at a time when it doesn't get so serious that even to sit down would be impossible for any of the countries because they have been so hurt.[25]

In response to a question about his earlier statement that Indonesia is not Communist, he explained:

Well, there is frustration in the United States and in other countries about Indonesia and the fact that President Sukarno doesn't always follow a course of which we approve or which we support. I make the point that he is frustrating perhaps to the United States. I would think he is perhaps even more frustrating to the Russians and to the Chinese. I believe the Russians have put in about five times as much aid and assistance in Indonesia as the United States. There is no question that the United States is far the most popular country in Indonesia. Just driving along in the car, the ambassador or myself, people pour into the streets, extremely enthusiastic about the United States and the American flag.

I think although it might be frustrating to us the situation

[24] Ibid.
[25] Ibid.

is far better than if—again looking at it from the negative
point of view—the situation is far better than if Indonesia
was Communist. They don't agree with us. Sukarno is looking
at it from what he feels is best for his own country.

As I say, it is frustrating at times, but it is a far better
situation than if the hundred million people spreading across
that part of the world some 3,000 miles were in the Communist camp.[26]

Asked if the recommendations he made were in any
conscious way part of a plan relating events in Indonesia
to those in Cambodia and Vietnam, he answered:

Just as far as our own policy is concerned I think that
there is a general feeling that if Indonesia went communistic,
was taken over by the Communists, that you wouldn't—any
struggle that you might have in the rest of Southeast Asia
would be futile. So that therefore a struggle in Vietnam, the
loss of American lives and others there would be all completely lost if Indonesia went communistic, and that is why
I think that also if we cut off our contacts with Indonesia it
would be such a serious step for both countries.[27]

Questioned as to whether he thought Sukarno was in
danger of being ousted, he made one of his less fortunate
predictions:

RFK: No, none. I mean I suppose one shouldn't ever say those
things, but I just don't think there is even a—
QUESTION: You get a lot of reports to the contrary that of
course the army is about to take over.
RFK: No, I don't think it is even conceivable. I mean at least
not in the immediate future . . . the army is anticommunist
and strongly anticommunist. The situation in this particular
struggle would not be improved by the army because the
army really is very enthusiastic about fighting Great Britain.
I mean it doesn't make any sense, but it has gotten involved
in a war and it is not unlike some things we have at home

[26] *Ibid.*
[27] *Ibid.*

[a reference to U.S. military pressure to remain in Vietnam?]. . . .

I might say also just incidentally that a number of governments said that the recognition by France of Communist China would pose serious problems for all of the countries in that part of the world, all of the free countries in that part of the world, make their stability or their possibility of survival more difficult.[28]

Kennedy offered a number of positive recommendations for improving the country's international position. One was to increase foreign aid (a topic handled in greater detail in Chapter 22).

But if this is true, we must ask, what has been our contribution to peace? How are we fulfilling our responsibility to feed the hungry and cure the sick and help the victims of oppression, in our own country and around the world? Which side are we on?

All too sadly, the answer comes: We have made a contribution—but it has not been enough. We have a commitment—but it is too often a commitment in name only. Our gross national product has tripled in a generation. But as we grow more wealthy, we make less of an effort. Fifteen years ago, rising to the challenge of a Europe devastated by war, we devoted 10 percent of our federal budget—fully 2 percent of our gross national product—to foreign aid. This year, we will devote less than 2 percent of our federal budget—less than one-third of 1 percent of our gross national product—to the starving and diseased of half a world. Even at home—where the building of a just society is important not only for itself, but if we are to be effective abroad—here at home, we spend more on our dogs, $3 billion, than we do to help our fellow citizens out of poverty, less than $2 billion.

If there would be peace at home, or in the world, all this must change.[29]

He consistently argued for lower trade barriers.

[28] *Ibid.*
[29] Address, Fordham University, New York, N.Y., June 10, 1967.

[President Kennedy] feels it is so important that the free people of the world be able to trade freely. He is attempting to have Congress accept an arrangement whereby the trade barriers will be lowered as far as trade with the Common Market and the United States is concerned. He had made it clear, however, that any benefit that comes from the lowering of barriers as far as the United States is concerned, or the Common Market is concerned, should be available to all of the other countries of the Free World.

The United States and the countries of the Western World should not become fortresses within themselves. As economically fortunate areas, we have responsibilities to countries who are not as fortunate as we are. So these benefits will come to Japan as well as other countries.[30]

And he consistently supported the Peace Corps.

Everywhere I have traveled, in Peru and Chile and Tanzania and Kenya and Ethiopia and Brazil, the Peace Corps is the point of the lance, the far-flung sentinel of American purpose. It has been matched by no Russian, overcome by no Chinese; and I believe that for millions of men it is the best evidence they have that the future of the world is not in compulsion and slavery, but in freedom and daring and individual responsibility.[31]

He placed a great deal of faith in the efficacy of "people exchanges."

In conclusion, I would pause for a moment over a question which has troubled us for many years. Ever since the onset of the cold war, we have been urged to "develop" a concise exciting American manifesto—a platform which would compete with the simple, rousing calls of the Communists. Such an effort I think pointless—for what matters about this country cannot be put into simple slogans; it is a process, a way of doing things and dealing with people, a way of life. There are two major ways to communicate what this country is

[30] Round-table discussion with labor union representatives, Tokyo, Japan, February 9, 1962.
[31] Remarks, Los Angeles, Calif., October 22, 1966.

really about: to bring people here, or to send Americans abroad.[32]

As for the larger question of world peace, he began to address himself to both the strategy and the tactics of this quest in 1964, during his campaign for the Senate.

First, there is the opportunity for negotiation with the Soviet world. Making the most of that opportunity is not easy. There are always demagogues and extremists ready to oppose any step toward peace. Still, with skill and patience, and a determination to achieve peace, progress can be made—and already has been made.

In that connection, I think of the Cuban missile crisis. For seven days, and for seven nights, President Kennedy and the small group of advisers he collected around him held the door open for peace. The fate of the world hung in the balance. There were those who called for bombing attacks. There were those who wanted an invasion. There were those who cried "soft on communism." But the door was kept open. And when the Soviet Union understood the alternatives, and withdrew the missiles, this country achieved not simply a diplomatic triumph. It achieved something far greater than that. It made the world a little safer, and it opened the way for new steps toward peace—especially the test-ban treaty.

No one knew in advance that agreement could be reached banning nuclear tests above ground. There were those who said the negotiation was a Soviet trap, designed to gain a military advantage. There were those who said it was a propaganda trick. But President Kennedy and Governor Harriman [leading American negotiator] persisted in exploring all avenues. And when that agreement was finally reached, it too was more than a diplomatic triumph. It too made the world a little safer.

With those examples as our guides, I believe that we can go forward in making the world a safer place.

We can see whether recent advances in the art of detection do not now make it possible to complete the test ban by ending testing underground. Such an agreement would

[32] Speech, Columbia University, New York, N.Y., March 12, 1966.

still further tend to arrest military developments at a level favorable to the United States. Such an agreement, by being made open for signature by other nations, would afford to those countries one more chance for contracting out of the race for nuclear arms. Finally, such an agreement, by adding still a new thread to the fabric of American-Soviet understanding, would create a climate for still further progress.

A second area of opportunity [for securing an enduring world peace] lies in our relations with the emerging nations— the newer countries of Latin America, Africa, the Middle East, and Asia. . . . I know that these nations have a great interest in peace, for they are vulnerable to war. And they can be an enormous force for keeping the peace in the United Nations where they hold the majority of seats, in regional councils where local disputes can best be settled, and in their own dealings with other countries.

But to play a peaceful role, the newer countries need help. I am not thinking simply of economic aid. It goes without saying that the newer nations need food, and technical assistance and investment credits. But far more than economic aid, they need political encouragement—encouragement to achieve working, democratic regimes. And here the United States can play a vital role, for it makes an enormous difference when the United States withholds its favor from corrupt, autocratic, aggressive regimes. It makes an even bigger difference when the United States favors regimes that are honest and democratic, and imbued with social purpose. . . .

The Republicans—even the so-called moderate Republicans—have never understood that the problem of these nations is essentially political. They see the world mainly in military terms. They try to press the newer nations into military alliances—thus imposing upon them a kind of loyalty oath. They prefer to give them military instead of economic aid. They want subservience rather than independence. That is why this country had so many ties to reactionary and dictatorial regimes when the Republicans held office in Washington. That is why American prestige fell so low in those years.

The Democrats have understood the need for helping the new nations to build economic growth and political independence. That is what President Kennedy had in mind when he initiated the Alliance for Progress. That is why he made such a point of backing great progressive leaders like Nehru in India and Betancourt in Venezuela. And that is why American prestige has revived so dramatically over the past few years.[33]

He maintained that the United States had to make a fundamental decision about its role in the world.

Our choice, in your lifetimes, will be whether to support the status quo, or the forces of change; whether to sit content in our fellow human beings around storehouses, or share our wealth with our fellow human beings around the world; in the last analysis, whether to recognize the rights of others to the ideals for which we have fought so long—even when they can be achieved only in opposition to the settled order in which we ourselves are so comfortable.

Yet these are not simple choices and there are no simple rules for their solution. Einstein was once asked why men could build an atomic bomb, but not a structure to control it. He answered that "nuclear physics is much easier than politics." And we could add that the tangled complexities of human nature are harder to analyze than are the particles of the atom.[34]

He warned that rhetoric and good intentions alone could not be expected to resolve conflict into harmony. Peace would require specific programs to solve concrete problems:

"Peace," as President Kennedy said, "is a process, a way of solving problems." And therefore peace in the last third of the twentieth century depends on the solution of concrete, specific, and difficult problems: whether we can limit the spread, and prevent the use, of the weapons of mass destruction that still wait in bomb bays and submarines and missile silos; whether we can fulfill in the seventies the failed pledge of the sixties, to create a decade of development in freedom for the dispossessed of the world, and continue thereafter to make a national effort equal to the towering magnitude of the problem; and above all, whether we can protect our security and yet understand and welcome change—whether we,

[33] Campaign statement, October 22, 1964.
[34] Address, Fordham University, New York, N.Y., June 10, 1967.

the heirs of the world's greatest revolution, can identify no
with potentates in their palaces or generals in their army
camps, but with peasants and villagers in their huts and
slums, whether we will refuse to be cast as the protector
of privilege and guarantors of the bankrupt and dictatorial
governments of the world.

For we dare not forget that leadership in freedom doe
not rest on wealth or power. It depends on fidelity and per
sistence in those shaping beliefs—democracy, freedom, justic
—which men follow not from the enslavement of their bodie
but from the compulsion of their own hearts. It is not realisti
or hardheaded to meet problems or take action unguided b
ultimate moral aims or values; it is thoughtless folly. For i
ignores the realities of human faith and passion and belief
forces ultimately more powerful than all the calculations o
economists or generals.

Fourth and most important, arching over all else, must b
our quest for world peace: not the quiet of desolation nor th
stability of tyranny; but a world of diversity and progress, i
which armaments and violence give way to the forces of rea
son and compromise which are man's only hope for surviva
on earth. These are also the forces which must one day bring
an end to the war in Vietnam; but we should also look be
yond that terrible conflict—to insure that it is not repeated
and to insure also that the world's inevitable conflicts o
interest and belief do not become irrepressible conflicts o
death and global destruction.[35]

The following month he made the same points, adding
that peace also depended on:

. . . whether we can reach an accommodation with Com
munist China—now suspicious and profoundly hostile, ye
the possessor of nuclear and hydrogen weapons.[36]

In characteristic Kennedy fashion, he often turned to
the world's youth—of which he always considered himsel
a part—as mankind's ultimate hope.

[35] Address, Jefferson-Jackson Day Dinner, Detroit, Mich., May 5
1967.
[36] Address, Salt Lake City, Utah, June 28, 1967.

Our answer is the world's hope: it is to rely on youth. Each nation has different obstacles and different goals, shaped by the vagaries of history and experience. Yet as I talk to young people around the world I am impressed not by the diversity but by the closeness of their goals, their concerns and values and hopes for the future. I have seen students in South Africa, risking position and daring imprisonment against the awesome power of a garrison state. I have met others in Brazil, seeking to return their nation to constitutional democracy. In Peru and Chile, I have seen students leaving the civilization of the university and the city for the danger and disease and squalor of the countryside, seeking justice and progress for peasants who have never shared in the life of their country.[37]

[37] Address, Fordham University, New York, N.Y., June 10, 1967.

Chapter 20.

Communism and the Cold War

Communism has been the preoccupation of American foreign policy since the end of World War II. The nature of this economic, social, and political system, the international intentions of those governments called Communist, and the best way to deal with those governments are the subjects of a debate which has held the center of the American political stage for nearly a quarter of a century. Today's bitter controversy over the wisdom of United States policy in Southeast Asia is merely the continuation of that debate in a new geographical setting.

At the risk of oversimplifying, it can be stated that three distinct points of view have emerged in this debate over the character of communism and the proper American response to it. The first regards communism as an evil, atheistic, international conspiracy singlemindedly seeking to enslave the minds and bodies of free men everywhere. This militant anti-Communist view, voiced by members of the far right, many domestic conservatives, and a large number of military men, maintains that accommodation is neither possible nor desirable with these anti-Christ, anti-capital forces. "The men in Moscow and Peking have never stopped letting it be known that Communist domination of the world is their ultimate and unyielding goal," the argument runs. "We and the Communists are pursuing contradictory ends and hold antithetical concepts of man and nature. The differences which distinguish freedom from tyranny and individualism from collectivism can never be subject to negotiation or compromise by either side because they are the very substance of both systems." In short, just as no righteous man can deal and coexist with the devil without losing his soul, the free world (the United States and her allies) cannot permit the continued existence of Communist governments and hope to survive.

From this analysis it follows that U.S. policy must seek the total destruction of communism if freedom is to be secure. The cold war thus becomes a fight to the finish. As Barry Goldwater, a leading militant anti-Communist, put it, "The cold war is a conflict where one side or the other must win, and no amount of wishful thinking can make it otherwise." In this light, American foreign policy, which has pursued a strategy of "containment" since 1945, is "no-win." Yalta is seen as a betrayal, failure to attack the Soviet Union after World War II as the waste of an extraordinary opportunity, Korea is considered a defeat, peaceful coexistence a dangerous delusion, and our current limited objectives in Vietnam and our hesitancy to engage China in war are further evidence that our diplomats still do not comprehend the true nature of communism and the cold war.

The second view, which has influenced post-World War II American policy more than either of the others, holds that communism is a constantly evolving national phenomenon. This "cold-war liberalism," which represents the thinking of most domestic moderates and liberals in both political parties and the vast majority of our diplomatic corps, sees Communist governments in the years immediately following their accession to power as operating in much the same way as the militant anti-Communists portray them. However, the cold-war liberals believe that these communist governments will significantly moderate their internal and international objectives and modes of operation, given sufficient time and the right conditions.

The technique devised by cold-war liberals for buying time and gradually inducing essential changes in Communist intentions has been labeled "containment." This strategy of militarily encircling a Communist state and repelling its every attempt to expand was first applied to the Soviet Union in the late forties. In 1947 one of its architects, George Kennan, described its aims: "[A successful containment strategy] has it in its power to increase enormously the strains under which Soviet policy must operate, to force upon the Kremlin a far greater degree of moderation and circumspection than it has had to observe in recent years, and in this way to promote tendencies which must eventually find their outlet in either the break-up or the gradual mellowing of Soviet power. For no mystical, messianic movement—and particularly not that of the Kremlin—can face frustration indefinitely without eventually adjusting itself in one way or another to the logic of that state of affairs."

Convinced that containment has successfully checked Soviet expansion and has led to improved relations with the U.S.S.R., most cold-war liberals are now counseling the application of this policy to China.

Believing that the essential character of communism can be altered, cold-war liberals do not regard war with the Communist states as inevitable. While they might prefer the elimination of communism, they argue that this is not a reasonable objective in a nuclear age. The best we can hope for, they contend, is a world in which different systems can coexist and compete peacefully.

Finally, the cold-war liberals argue that communism is more cogently explained in national rather than international terms, that Communist governments tend to put national objectives ahead of international ideological commitments. Thus the fragmentation of the so-called Communist bloc, which finds a widening chasm between the Soviet Union and China, and the countries of Eastern Europe beginning to assert their independence from Moscow. In other words, the cold-war liberals charge, the militant anti-Communist positing of a monolithic Marxist conspiracy directed from the Kremlin is no longer an accurate description of reality.

The third view of the nature of communism and the appropriate response to it we may call, for lack of a better label, the "post-cold-war" analysis. Though it traces some of its roots back to Henry Wallace's presidential campaign of 1948, this analysis has gained limited currency only in the past few years. Advocated by large numbers of academicians and intellectuals, New Left partisans, and a handful of senators, this approach maintains that the threat of Communist military expansion, if it ever did exist, has passed. In short, the cold war should be over.

The "post-cold-war" view considers the United States the principal obstacle to the relaxation of international tensions, due to its inability or unwillingness to recognize the "thaw" occurring in East-West relations. American belligerency and blindness are also blamed for much of the hostility we encounter in the world. Castro indicated an interest in working constructively with us following his overthrow of Batista, it is argued, but our anti-Communist zeal forced him to turn to others. Again, frightened by the specter of a "Red takeover," we sent the Marines into the Dominican Republic, further alienating the nations of Latin America. There is even good reason to believe, these critics of U.S. policy contend, that understanding could have been reached with the Soviets and the Communist Chinese if reason had prevailed instead of McCarthyism in that crucial decade after V-J Day.

Not recognizing the opportunities for reasonable and peaceful relations with the Communist nations because of other lingering paranoia or imperialist designs, U.S. policy is regarded by the post-cold-war group as *the* potential provocateur of World War III. Our current crusade to impose a Pax Americana on the world can only lead to more Vietnams and eventual military confrontation with Moscow and Peking. Not until the United States abandons the aim of remaking the world in its own image and recognizes both the moral and political limits of its power, these critics conclude, will the danger of nuclear holocaust subside.

Rather remarkably, Robert Kennedy held variants of each of these three views of communism and the cold war at one time or another while in public life. Using his own statements, we shall seek to document these dramatic shifts in his outlook and attempt to discern his underlying reasons.

During the late forties and early fifties Joseph Kennedy and his sons assumed a militant anti-Communist stance. As a newly elected congressman from Boston, John F. Kennedy toyed with the "betrayal" theory to explain Soviet control of Eastern and part of Central Europe, while his father and Bobby indicated a sympathetic interest in the charges of men like Richard Nixon and Joseph McCarthy that U.S. foreign policy was "soft on communism." In 1953, Kennedy translated interest into active concern by joining the staff of McCarthy's Permanent Investigations Subcommittee.

Two years later he accompanied Supreme Court Justice William O. Douglas on a vacation trip to the Soviet Union. In a *U.S. News & World Report* interview he reported his impressions.

We are dealing with a government to whom God, the family or the individual means nothing and whose practice it has been in the past to make promises and treaties to serve their purposes and to break them when it has been to their advantage. It can only be suicidal for us during this period on the basis of smiles to strengthen Russia and weaken ourselves. . . .

QUESTION: But people coming back from Russia are all singing hymns of praises . . . senators, congressmen saying that they found it much better than they had expected, and Russia they thought was fine, the people are getting along all right and so on. Did you come back with that highly favorable idea?

ANSWER: No, I think you can tell that I didn't like what I saw. . . .

QUESTION: Why were you interested in [the "human cost of progress"] particularly?

ANSWER: There was the serious allegation that there had been so much opposition to collectivization and that the Russians had taken stringent measures to crush the local people's resistance, that we wanted to find out the facts. You can go into this area as a visitor like Nehru [Prime Minister of India] and the degree to which it has been built up is impressive, from a materialistic point of view. But I think also the price that was paid in human beings in order to make this change and too, that the people have such a difficult life even now, should be considered. . . .

QUESTION: They say they are going to be our brothers—

ANSWER: That's fine—all I say is—and I'm all in favor of that, I think it's terrific, and I think we should have more trade and all of that—but all I say is: Before we do all those things let's get a quid pro quo on it. Just on the basis of a smile, I don't think we should make all those concessions. They have a system of government which is entirely different from ours, which is based on the rights and dignity of the individual. I'm not saying they aren't entitled to theirs, but they just don't believe in the same sort of things we do.[1]

Over the succeeding decade he continued to see the cold war as a life-and-death struggle in which one side must triumph and the other fall.

The Communist purpose, now as in 1917, is to remake the world in the Communist image. The Communist faith, now as ever, is that history inevitably will sweep all other forms of society, democracy included, into obscurity.

The Communist conviction is that any means is justified to undermine and capture free governments and free peoples. The enormous global struggle which we call the cold war is being fought at every level. Moscow remains energetic and alert, and its challenge to our freedom is dangerous and enduring. The Communist calendar of ambition is measured in decades, not weeks.

If the free world is to survive, it must above all resist aggression. Aggression today takes a multitude of forms. It requires a variety of responses.[2]

In an earlier book he had condemned contemporary Communist governments for their failure to provide the social justice Marx prophesied.

Marx's condemnation of the heartless laissez-faire capitalism of the early nineteenth century now—by an irony of history—applies with fantastic precision to twentieth-century Communism.

It is Communism, not free society, which is dominated by what the Yugoslav Communist Milovan Djilas has called the New Class—the class of party bosses and bureaucrats, who acquire not only privileges but an exemption from criticism which would be unimaginable in democratic society. Far

[1] *U.S. News & World Report,* October 21, 1955.
[2] Robert F. Kennedy, *The Pursuit of Justice* (New York: Harper & Row, 1965), pp. 129-130.

from being a classless society, Communism is governed by an elite as steadfast in its determination to maintain its prerogatives as any oligarchy known to history.

And it is Communism, not free society, which has become the favorite twentieth-century means of disciplining the masses, repressing consumption and denying the workers the full produce of their labor.

By this historical paradox, it is free society, and not Communism, which seems most likely to realize Marx's old hope of the emancipation of man and the achievement of an age of universal abundance.[3]

Speaking before a convention of the militant anti-Communist American Legion in late 1962, Kennedy made it evident that his views had not yet moderated significantly. He was still preaching the defeat of world communism as the cardinal objective of the United States policy.

I want . . . to take this occasion to report to you on the steps this administration has taken in the last twenty-one months to strengthen our country in every way—and thereby maintain the peace on honorable terms, protect freedom at home and abroad, and defeat Communism.

I need say very little to this audience about the character of the cold war and the Bolshevik Revolution in Russia, the Legion has been in the forefront of those determined to alert the American people to the dangers of Communism.

The Communist purpose, now as in 1917, is to remake the world in the Communist image. The Communist faith is that history inevitably will sweep all other forms of society into the dustbin of the past. The Communist conviction is that any means is justified to advance military, political, and economic policies designed to undermine and capture free governments and free peoples.

The enormous global struggle which we call the cold war is being fought at every level. Moscow remains energetic and alert and its challenge to our freedom is dangerous and determined.

[3] Robert F. Kennedy, *Just Friends and Brave Enemies* (New York: Harper & Row, 1962), p. 160.

Communism counts its opportunities in terms of decades—not of weeks. Its means of aggression consist not only of nuclear weapons and missiles with enormous boosters and not only of spies, agents and terrorists, but of great masses of men and women, deluded by a common ideology which inspires them with a false hope. . . .

Nothing is more false than the notion that the triumph of communism is inevitable or that the Communists are steadily pushing the free world into a corner.

The tide running against us roughly from the time of the first Soviet Sputnik to the early months of 1961 has been stemmed. We are moving forward while the Communist world is falling increasingly into turmoil and disarray.

Khrushchev's post-Sputnik offensive, based on nuclear blackmail, expanding Communist power in underdeveloped areas, and exploiting Soviet space feats psychologically and politically with vigor and imagination, has run out of steam.

The fact is that Mao's "Great Leap Forward" has fallen miserably short of its target. There is a major disaster inside Red China, demonstrating for all the world to see that Communist methods lead not merely to hunger for the people but to industrial stagnation.[4]

And similarly, discussing his brother's morale-boosting visit to Berlin in 1963:

Of course, it was more than just his visit that counted. It was our resolution to risk war, if necessary, to defend freedom in Berlin and South Vietnam and to force the Russians to back down during the Cuban missile crisis, plus the evidence on all sides that a free society serves its people best.[5]

However, at the same time he was becoming cognizant of the fact that the cold war was no longer the bipolarized affair of the immediate postwar period (though he chose to focus on decentralization only on the Soviet side of the iron curtain).

The attack on Berlin will be seen, in the long run, as the

[4] Speech, American Legion Convention, Las Vegas, Nev., October 9, 1962.
[5] Kennedy, *The Pursuit of Justice,* pp. 109-110.

Communist response to the growing unity of Europe. Indeed, the essential contest between the free world and the Communist world is which side can better manage its affairs, unite its purposes and concert its energies.

There are indications today that, while the free states are working ever more closely together, the Communist system is beginning to exhibit signs of discord and fragmentation.

Moscow says one thing, Peking another, and the still, small voice of Tirana compounds the clamor.

This discord is the inevitable result of the attempt to impose a single policy on a world dominated by national traditions and national interests. It confirms our own view that the world is moving, not toward a single centralized order, but toward a unity in diversity, with many nations developing according to their own traditions and abilities.[6]

Gradually, possibly because he believed we were winning the cold war, Bobby's views began to soften.

It would be quite wrong, and quite unlike a group such as the one assembled here, to become mesmerized by the present confrontation of the Soviet Union and the United States. Yet in this brief moment in time we can see some polarization of allegiance—some to the Communist way—some to the way of freedom.

This is the tug of the cold war. We should be excused if we venture the opinion we are winning. As the President said last week in his State of the Union Message: "Not a single one of the nearly fifty United Nations members to gain independence since the Second World War has succumbed to Communist control." In one case, a wall has gone up to prevent a great people from accepting the tug of freedom. History will record that while the Great Wall of Old China was built to keep barbarians out, this brooding ugliness by the Brandenburg Gate was built to keep civilized people in. And men may speculate on the current Soviet proficiency in the high jump.

But overall, we are winning—why? What is it we have that others will reach for, run for, die for? Surely it is more than houses, cars and dishwashers. Even Communism, with

[6] Speech, Bonn, Germany, February 24, 1962.

some rearrangement of production priorities and a few other sacrifices by the New Class, could provide these things. No, the attraction of the so-called materialist West is more a thing of mind than of matter. Why then do young foreign students become disaffected with iron curtain curricula and seek out our consuls? What is it that brings tears to the eyes of new Americans as they take the oath of citizenship? What is it they sought? What is it men want? Isn't it freedom of conscience and action conditioned only by the legitimate needs of private and public security? [7]

Every free nation has the capacity to open up its own new frontiers of social welfare and social justice. Communist leaders have sometimes spoken of peaceful competition as to which society serves the people best. That is a competition which free society accepts with relish.

I know of no better controlled experiment for such competition than Germany itself.

Only a superficial glance is necessary to see how this competition has come out. The contrast in progress speaks for itself. West Berlin has met the challenge of rehabilitation and the rebirth of justice and of freedom; East Berlin has not. In this city lies the answer to the question of competition. It is an answer so overpowering that it has had to be shut from sight by concrete and barbed wire, tanks and machine guns, dogs and guards. The competition has resulted in so disastrous a defeat for Communism that the Communists felt they had no alternative but the Wall. [8]

In the field of international trade, too, the barriers have been slightly lowered. The United States has sold large quantities of agricultural surplus to Poland, and Polish exports to this country have increased.

We hope to see a steady widening of these economic relations, and for that reason this administration is in favor of retaining authority to grant "most favored nation" treatment to Polish commodities entering our ports.

The United States has made it clear that we will continue

[7] Speech, Center for Study of Democratic Institutions of the Fund for the Republic, New York, N.Y., January 22, 1963.

[8] Kennedy, *op. cit.*, p. 109.

to welcome those actions of any country, Communist or otherwise, which respond to the basic needs of the people of that country and which seek to improve relations with us.

Our foreign policy is to encourage such developments, and to show our approval of any progress made along those lines.

But this in no way suggests a weakening in our fundamental position—and the Communists know it.

We as a nation will never retreat from our conviction that there can be no lasting justice in the world until people everywhere have the right to self-determination. And the cause of justice demands equal vigilance here at home.[9]

Communist Provocation Re-examined

In the year following his brother's assassination Robert Kennedy began to move perceptibly toward a new posture on the cold war. He criticized the negativism of U.S. policy and warned that guns and guerrillas would not be enough to deter Communist-inspired revolutions among the impoverished and exploited masses of the Third World.

Too often in the past we have relied on a negative response to communism and left the world with the illusion that only Karl Marx had a philosophy.

We have too frequently left people thinking that there are only two philosophies—communism on one hand and anti-communism on the other. And this is just not enough.

We have not been as tough, aggressive or articulate as we might have been in the war of ideals.

Beyond that we must acknowledge the temptations of self-satisfaction, indulgence and complacency at home.

Unless we resist these temptations in our own countries, and I think that frequently in the past we have not, we cannot speak with the ringing voice that will be heard by the young struggling for progress throughout the world.[10]

[9] Speech, Polish National Alliance Convention, Philadelphia, Pa., September 18, 1963.

[10] Speech, Canadian Press, Toronto, Canada, April 14, 1964.

Ultimately, communism must be defeated by progressive political programs which wipe out the poverty, misery, and discontent on which it thrives. For that reason, progressive political programs are the best way to erode the Communist presence in Latin America, to turn back the Communist thrust into Southeast Asia, and to insure the stability of the new African nations and preserve stability in the world. . . .

More importantly, perhaps, in a practical sense, we have not perfected the technique of training foreign nationals to defend themselves against Communist terrorism and guerrilla penetration.

Having an adequate defense against terrorism is only part of the answer, however. To the extent that guerrilla warfare and terrorism arise from the conditions of a desperate people, we know that they cannot be put down by force alone. The people themselves must have some hope for the future. There must be a realistic basis for faith in some alternative to communism.[11]

He then stated that the idea of a Communist monolith was no longer true and should not blind America to opportunities for affecting Communist behavior.

It is true, of course, that the world has its troubles—serious troubles. But it also has opportunities—opportunities for securing an enduring peace. These opportunities are richer than many believe. And there are two pieces of plain evidence to show that these opportunities are growing.

One piece of evidence arises from the breaking up of what used to be the monolithic Communist empire. It is not only that Soviet Russia and mainland China are now in terrible tension, or that Russia itself is in internal tumult. It is that many different kinds of Communist regimes have emerged.

Poland is different from Russia, and Rumania from Poland, and Yugoslavia from all the others. Between these different Communist states there are complex interreactions. Every time we deal with one of these states—whether by trade or by cultural exchange, or diplomatically—we affect the others.

We thus have at our disposal, perhaps for the first time

[11] Speech, California Institute of Technology, Pasadena, Calif., June 8, 1964.

since the Bolshevik Revolution, a potent means for influencing developments behind the iron curtain. We hold in our hands a true lever—not just a phony slogan—for speeding up the liberalization of regimes, for changing the hostile outlook, for achieving a reduction of tensions.[12]

For the next two years Kennedy's view of communism and the cold war continued to run along these lines, lines very similar to his late brother's cold-war liberalism. Then, in a much-quoted speech before the Americans for Democratic Action in early 1967, he struck out dramatically in a new direction.

But for our young people, I suspect, Vietnam is a shock as it cannot be to us. They did not know World War II, or even Korea. And this is a war surrounded by rhetoric they do not understand or accept; these are the children not of the cold war, but of the thaw. Their memories of communism are not of Stalin's purges and death camps, not even the terrible revelations of the Twentieth Party Congress, or the streets of Hungary. They see the world as one in which Communist states can be each other's deadliest enemies or even friends of the West, in which Communism is certainly no better, but perhaps no worse, than many other evil and repressive dictatorships all around the world—with which we conclude alliances when that is felt to be in our interest.

And even as the declared foreign policy of our government is to "build bridges" to this new Communist world, they see us, in the name of anticommunism, devastating the land of those we call our friends. However the war may seem to us, they see it as one in which the largest and most powerful nation on earth is killing children (they do not care if accidentally) in a remote and insignificant land. We speak of past commitments, of the burden of past mistakes; and they ask why they should now atone for mistakes made before many of them were born, before almost any could vote. They see us spend billions on armaments while poverty and ignorance continue at home; they see us willing to fight a war for freedom in Vietnam, but unwilling to fight with one-hundredth the money or force or effort to secure freedom in Mississippi

[12] Campaign statement, October 22, 1964.

or Alabama or the ghettos of the North. And they see, perhaps most disturbing of all, that they are remote from the decisions of policy; that they themselves frequently do not, by the nature of our political system, share in the power of choice on great questions which shape their lives.[13]

From this point on his criticism of the basic assumptions of the Johnson Administration's foreign policy grew increasingly vociferous. He began to reject the cold-war liberalism he had so vigorously championed a short time before. In statements like the following (and in his remarks on Vietnam quoted in Chapter 27), he argued that Communist governments must be evaluated in the context of real world politics, not on some simplistic scale of good and evil which we apply neither to ourselves nor to our allies.

Nor has this narrowness of vision been confined to our conduct at home. We have ventured abroad without fully realizing the twisted paths our journey would take. We built a foreign policy on the rhetoric of anticommunism; and found ourselves imprisoned in that rhetoric when the Communist monolith began to crumble. We saw good markets and stable governments abroad; and we did not realize that, to the victims of oppression, our support marked us as defenders of tyranny.[14]

In early 1968, it was not yet clear where Kennedy's critique would lead him in terms of specific policy alternatives. But one thing was certain: he had disassociated himself completely from the foreign policy of the Johnson Administration and would focus on this area of disagreement in his Presidential campaign against the administration's candidate, Hubert H. Humphrey.

[13] Address, Americans for Democratic Action, Philadelphia, Pa., February 27, 1967.
[14] Address, Ninth Constitutional Convention of Oil, Chemical and Atomic Workers, August 23, 1967.

The Soviet Union

In addition to his general remarks about communism, Kennedy devoted some attention to specific issues concerning the U.S.S.R. In his last book he singled out Soviet reluctance to engage in meaningful intellectual and cultural exchange with the West.

The proof of the power of freedom lies in the fact that Communism has always flinched from competition in the field where it counts most, the competition of ideas. The flight of scholars and jurists from East Germany shows the fate of intellectual freedom under Communism. To this day, nearly half a century after the Russian Revolution, one virtually never sees on a Moscow newsstand any book, magazine or newspaper exported from a democracy except Communist party publications. Yet one is free in Washington and London and Paris to buy all the copies of *Pravda* and *Izvestia* one wants.

As recently as two years ago a Russian leader, while saying that coexistence with democratic social systems was possible, asserted emphatically that coexistence with democratic ideas was "impossible and unthinkable." It would amount, he said, to Communist ideological disarmament.

I would have thought that he might have more faith in the capacity of Communist ideas to survive such competition. But he may well be right in fearing to let Communism stand on its own in a free forum. . . .

For many years we have steadily sought new ways and means of increasing the exchange of ideas with the Soviet Union. We proudly press the challenge: let the ideas of freedom have the same circulation in Communist states that Communist ideas have in free states. We can have formal peace without such reciprocal competition in the realm of ideas; but until we have full freedom of intellectual exchange, I see no prospect of a genuine and final relaxation of world tension.[15]

With a sizable Jewish constituency in his home state which is vitally interested in the issue, Kennedy was called upon to speak out against Soviet antisemitism.

[15] Kennedy, *op. cit.*, pp. 111-112.

. . . Russia has come to represent what the godless, anti-religious tenets of communism can do to corrupt the world.[16]

Today, after one hundred and nineteen years, we must still meet to protest the treatment of Jews in Russia. Today, more than fifty years after Nicholas II distributed the infamous "Protocols of the Elders of Zion," the Russian government continues to distribute vicious antisemitic propaganda. These are isolated incidents. The easing of particular restrictions does not alter the fact that the Jews of the Soviet Union are subject to persecutions and violations of human dignity that are beyond the capabilities of language to denounce. But these incidents demonstrate that our protests are heard. They prove that we not meet in vain, that our presence here is not an idle gesture.[17]

True recognition of the historic and religious identity of the Jewish people will have to involve much more: a thorough educational campaign by the Soviet government to eradicate antisemitism; and the allowance, even the support, of an entire set of communal institutions—schools and rabbinical seminaries, Yiddish and Hebrew books and periodicals—in short, a Jewish cultural identity.[18]

China, Plea for a Policy

Since Mao's capture of the Chinese mainland shattered United States plans for a Sino-American alliance to contain Soviet expansion and re-establish the balance of power in Asia, our China policy has been disappointingly barren. Aside from our commitment to Chinese exclusion from the United Nations and a position of diplomatic nonrecognition, we are still without a comprehensive long-term strategy either for undermining this giant's potential power or for helping her find a stable place in

[16] Speech, New York Council on Soviet Jewry, New York, N.Y., October 29, 1964.

[17] Address, Congregation Zichron Ephraim, January 17, 1965.

[18] Press release, March 30, 1966.

the community of nations. Given China's new-found nuclear punch, this vacuum in American policy hardly can be accepted as a satisfactory state of affairs.

Until recently Robert Kennedy had little more to offer on this matter than the State Department: he too had no policy of consequence; he too opposed Communist China's admission to the U.N. and proposals for a two-China policy.

On Red China I said she had indicated that she did not choose to live in peace and so, with the majority of the countries of the world, we were opposed to her admission to the United Nations.[19]

QUESTION: Mr. Attorney General, do you feel that a two-China policy is in the United States' interests at this time?
RFK: No. But I leave those questions to Ambassador Stevenson.
QUESTION: Did I understand you to say that you do not think that a two-China policy is desirable?
RFK: This is correct.
QUESTION: Would you like to amplify that?
RFK: No.[20]

He went through the motions of comparing prosperous capitalist Japan with impoverished collectivist China.

Yet today Japan, as I have had the privilege of seeing for myself, has a thriving economy. Her standard of living is higher than that of any nation in the Far East. . . . Communist China, on the other hand, suffers her ninth year of hunger. The tragic "commune" experiment has collapsed. Industrial production has slowed down. Poverty and disease stalk the land. Even worse, thousands of innocent people have been imprisoned and killed, and the more fortunate have fled to other lands, more than a million to Hong Kong alone.[21]

[19] Kennedy, *Just Friends and Brave Enemies*, p. 91.
[20] Press conference, U.N. Headquarters, New York, N.Y., January 28, 1964.
[21] Kennedy, *The Pursuit of Justice*, p. 110.

In the fall of 1965, Kennedy finally showed some initiative, suggesting that the United States had nothing to lose by inviting the Chinese to the Geneva disarmament talks.

If the Chinese refuse, we will have lost nothing; we will have opened another door to peace and the Chinese will show to the world that they are not interested.[22]

And when six months later he discovered that the State Department had rejected a Peking offer to conclude a nuclear nonaggression pact, he was openly upset.

It was stated yesterday by Chou En-Lai that the Chinese had offered a pact with the United States which would outlaw the use of nuclear weapons between our two countries. He went on to say that our rejection of that treaty made it imperative for them to resume the testing. A spokesman for the State Department has revealed that the Department did in fact reject this overture from the Chinese, on the basis that they were not sincere and that there were no adequate safeguards. Although our position seems well founded in fact and experience, I question whether this will be well understood in the rest of the world, unless we now take further open and affirmative steps to make clear our desire to reach effective control over nuclear weapons with the Communist Chinese.

This problem is compounded by the fact, as the State Department spokesman also revealed, that we have not yet invited Red China to the disarmament meeting in Geneva. . . .

The third Chinese nuclear explosion must be a matter of serious concern. The Albanian Premier is reported as saying at a banquet in Peking that the Chinese nuclear weapons will throw their enemy "into panic." Obviously this is not true, as was demonstrated in the firm remarks of President Johnson and the leaders of other countries of Asia.

However, this action by the Chinese must cause concern, in part as to the course of action that other nations in Asia will follow; newspaper reports today reveal that pressure by high Indian officials to develop nuclear weapons has increased, and that there is great concern also in Japan. More important,

[22] *Newsweek*, October 25, 1965.

there must be great concern as to the course of the Communist Chinese themselves—in their relations with their neighbors, and, as Prime Minister Pearson [of Canada] stated yesterday, as to the increased danger of miscalculation on their part, which could lead to a major war. Therefore, it seems to me all the more necessary to open wider discussions and negotiations with the Communist Chinese.[23]

However, it was not until the Senator appeared at the China Conference, sponsored by the University of Chicago in February of 1967 (a gathering of China scholars, diplomats and interested politicians), that he took the time to outline his views on China and discuss American policy in the Far East. Although his speech hardly constitutes a Kennedy "China policy," it is his only extended pronouncement so far dealing with U.S.-Chinese relations. Here are excerpts from that address:

It is safe to say that there is no aspect of American foreign policy so important and yet uncertain—no country so seemingly menacing about which we know so little—as China. . . .

What is most troublesome is not what we do not know about China; it is what we do not know about ourselves—about our own goals, our own policies, our own conception of our national interest in Asia. . . . Yet for many years we have disposed our forces, made commitments, and conducted our enterprises, virtually without conscious policy and direction, unaware of what we seek and the price we are prepared to pay.

We have striven to isolate China from the world and treated it with unremitting hostility. That, however, is not a policy. It is an attitude founded upon fear and passion and wishful hopes. In Korea, the Formosa Straits, and India we responded to immediate situations of danger; those actions were necessary, but they were designed to protect the present rather than to prepare for the future.[24]

Kennedy argued that, after nearly twenty years of

[23] Statement, May 12, 1966.
[24] Address, China Conference, University of Chicago, Chicago, Ill., February 8, 1967.

stumbling and reacting, it was high time this nation developed a coherent set of goals with regard to China.

The first need is a policy. And the time to at least begin to develop one is now. Political passions have dimmed, understanding and concern are rising, as you are demonstrating in such an important way. The cold war in the West is calmed, allowing us to divert some energy and thought to this part of the world. Most importantly, as danger grows and the war in Vietnam unveils the tragic possibility of recurring and draining conflict, necessity—the midwife of foreign policy—crowds in upon us. . . .

The first and overriding consideration is that this is a time of unique opportunity. The Great Proletarian Cultural Revolution, whatever else it has done, insures that China will wish to focus her attention on internal affairs for at least the immediate future. As is apparent from her diplomacy—or lack of it —all over the world, China seems to have little present wish for contact or change in her foreign policy. For us, therefore, this is a chance above all to *think*—to review the past, to analyze the present, to plan for the future course of relations between our nations. This is a chance which rarely comes to scholars or statesmen or nations in time of constant challenge and swirling change. We could do no better than to begin that assessment now.[25]

He informed his audience what a policy was not:

A policy is not fear or hostility or wish. Policy is the establishment of goals and of a course of action rationally calculated to achieve those goals. It must be ready to yield to the overriding logic of events, yet striving to shape circumstances rather than belatedly reacting to them. We do not have such a policy toward China.

First, a position which pleases us without a reasonable chance of acceptance or accomplishment is not a policy. Thus the liberation of the mainland by the Nationalist Chinese was at best empty rhetoric and at worst a dangerous illusion.

Second, faith in the ultimate goodness of human nature or the ameliorating impact of progress is not a policy. We cannot

[25] *Ibid.*

await with confidence the day when material wealth and a better understanding of economic reality will "bring China (or a new generation of Chinese leaders) to their senses." The history of our time gives ample proof that advanced, cultured and self-confident nations are fully capable of dark disorder, violence, and aggression. It was not Stalin, but Khrushchev who, in the fortieth year of the Russian Revolution, crushed Hungary, and seven years later came to the brink of nuclear war in his Cuban adventure. It was a Germany "advanced" far beyond the distant goals of China which half destroyed a continent and slaughtered millions. Moreover, nuclear weapons today can give a country a capacity to destroy far greater than its real power or wealth. . . .

Third, the desire for reconciliation or the hope of friendship is not a policy. Hostility springs from the clash of interests and ambitions, and their resolution or compromise is at the heart of accommodation. This mutual acceptance of legitimate claims and interests must precede reconciliation. Thus policy is the determination of terms on which reconciliation can and will be carried out.

Fourth, faith in the certainty of our historical judgment is not a policy. We cannot act as if we know China will certainly try to expand by force or that it will never try. We cannot assume that Communist expansion in Asia would inevitably be swallowed up by the nationalisms of Asian states; nor should we assume that all revolutions will be captured by Communists, or that all who call themselves Communists will come under the dominion and control of Peking. Rather, we must prepare for all contingencies which threaten the clear national interests of the United States.[26]

What did Kennedy want our China policy to look like? He proposed the following principles (with reference to the Vietnam situation as well):

Our policy must rest on the knowledge that we cannot predict the possibility of Chinese military expansion. Therefore, we must be prepared to help others defend themselves while refusing to base our actions and policies on the assumption that armed clash is inevitable. For we must realize that every

[26] *Ibid.*

extension of Chinese influence does not menace us. We must be able to discriminate between armed attack and internal revolution, between Chinese direction of revolutionary forces and Chinese exhortation. Where Chinese force is not directly involved or borders crossed, we must ask whether we should be willing to rely above all on the strength and vitality of the desire for national independence. After all, it is that powerful desire and not our military force which ousted the Chinese from central Africa and Algeria and Indonesia, and which is steadily eroding the Soviet empire.

Policy demands a conscious and open recognition that we live in the same world and move in the same continent with China—with its dangers and possibilities, strengths and terrible frustrations. Only when we accept this reality can we work toward our central task—to bring about Chinese acceptance of the fact that it too must live with us and the other nations of the world. These are, admittedly, general considerations, rather than guides to specific action. Yet it will make a great difference to our acts and policies if we treat China as a potential danger and a possible opportunity rather than as a certain enemy and a lost cause. . . .

China policy must be formed against the probability that when present convulsions subside we will still face a hostile China. We still have to refuse the temptation of assuming that any acts or gestures on our part will significantly improve relations. Yet hostile words and proclamations are not wars. They do not prevent us from having contact, or from reaching agreements on matters of mutual interest. They do not prevent us from having contacts which could lead us to know more about China and they about us and thus prevent the miscalculations of intentions which could lead to a worldwide holocaust.

We should not discourage contact of any kind, by ourselves or nations, whether economic or diplomatic—even tourism— for a rational or informed China will be far easier to deal with than an irrational and ignorant one.[27]

He recommended a Marshall Plan for Asia, though he left the details for others to develop.

[27] *Ibid.*

Although it is not precisely analogous, it must be remembered that it was the Marshall Plan which served more to contain Soviet expansion than the troops on her border. This group could surely apply your experiences and knowledge of Asia to develop and recommend this kind of program and policy.[28]

Drawing on happier days in the history of Chinese-American relations, he concluded with his hope for the future.

All our intentions and labor may ultimately dissolve in violence and bloodshed. But there is another possibility. Perhaps someday an American diplomat may go to China, carrying with him the same instructions Daniel Webster gave to Caleb Cushing in 1813 to tell the people of China "that your mission is entirely pacific . . . that you are a messenger of peace, sent from the greatest power in America to the greatest in Asia, to offer respect and good will and to establish the means of friendly intercourse.[29]

Cuba, Our Finest Hour . . . And Our Worst

Cuba provided John Kennedy with both his biggest diplomatic failure and his greatest success, the Bay of Pigs and the Cuban missile crisis, during his thousand days in the White House. That Cuba should figure prominently in our international relations at all during this period, much less become an object of major policy consideration, is difficult to explain. Though a self-confessed Communist state with strong Soviet ties, this former American satellite of six million people certainly poses no military or economic threat to our security.

Then why this often anxious concern in the United States over the fate of this small, impoverished island? The reasons appear to be principally geographic and psychological. To begin with, it is frequently pointed out with alarm that Cuba is a "mere ninety miles off our

[28] *Ibid.*
[29] *Ibid.*

shores" (of course, the Soviet Union, which is capable of devastating us, is a scant one mile away across the Bering Straits, but this doesn't seem to disturb Americans as much). In addition, many militant anti-Communists and some cold-war liberals complain that it is a humiliating affront to the most powerful nation in history to have a small-time Communist dictator (with a beard, no less) hurling insults at us "a stone's throw from Florida." It's an intolerable situation, they contend (though we have tolerated Castro's Cuba without too much difficulty since 1959).

Finally, many diplomats and congressmen view Cuba as a considerable psychological victory for the Soviets in the cold war and as a threat by example and active subversion to the pro-American governments of Latin America. Thus, in the eyes of some, the stability and security of the Western Hemisphere are at stake.

Less than a decade ago it appeared that the United States and Cuba might be able to reach a mutually acceptable understanding. When Fidel Castro toppled the Batista regime on New Year's Day, 1959—a dictatorship the U.S. had supported with military and economic aid to the day it fell—much of America was in sympathy with the bearded, baseball-playing revolutionary. The Eisenhower Administration, in characteristic fashion, was uncertain what its reaction ought to be—a position which at least implied flexibility.

However, as Castro began to bait the United States for its long history of military intervention and economic exploitation in Cuba, and as he accelerated his campaign to nationalize numerous American-controlled businesses on the island, American official and public opinion grew hostile. At last, in January 1961, the United States severed diplomatic relations with the Cuban government. And this was the state of affairs when Robert Kennedy entered the Cabinet as a member of the "New Frontier."

What the Kennedys discovered upon assuming office was that they had not inherited a Cuba policy from their predecessors, but a plot. It called for U.S. support of an attempt by a small force of Cuban exiles to land on the island and overthrow Castro. Hesitant at first to engage in what appeared a risky adventure, John Kennedy finally consented to carry out the plan after being reassured of its certain success by CIA and Defense Department intelligence reports. When the 1,400 exiles landed at the Bay of Pigs in the dawn of April 17, 1961, they were quickly and completely crushed by Castro's army. In retrospect, it is evident this scheme never had a chance, based as it was on wishful thinking that had been passed along as fact to the President by his military advisors. Following as it did a stirring inaugural address in which he had promised new vision and effectiveness for American foreign policy, the Bay of Pigs fiasco was a disillusioning setback for the new President.

Having shared in that ill-fated decision, Robert Kennedy was naturally questioned about it. At first he was reluctant to say anything.

MR. WILSON: Mr. Attorney General, I believe you have studied the Cuban problem, at least what happened during the invasion. In retrospect, do you think it was a wise course to have denied the Cuban nationals air cover for their invasion of Cuba?

RFK: Again we made a study of that—you are making a statement of fact which I am not sure that I could agree with—we made a study of that situation, and a report on that went to the President. He has already stated that he takes full responsibility for the failure of that operation and feels that it is within the national interest not to try to find any other scapegoats. The responsibility is where it should be, which is in the President of the United States.

MR. WILSON: I wouldn't suggest that this was a case of finding scapegoats. I would suggest that it is a case where the public might feel it is entitled to know what happened in connection with the Cuban invasion.

RFK: We made a report to the President. I would agree very strongly with the decision that it would not be within the national interest to make that study or report public. I don't think that it would be helpful at all at this time.[30]

Later he opened up slightly:

[30] "Meet the Press" (NBC-TV), September 24, 1961.

I felt, based on the facts that were presented to the President, that it was a worthwhile venture. And, I dare say, if the same facts were presented to him again, he would reach the same conclusion. Any reasonable man would make the same decision. You make a decision based on fact.[31]

When, after the United States had broken off relations with him, Castro announced that he was now and always had been a Communist, Kennedy was asked whether he had any comments. He replied curtly:

No, other than it is not the big surprise of the year.[32]

In his book dealing with foreign policy, *Just Friends and Brave Enemies,* Bobby painted a bleak picture of political conditions in Cuba.

Now, as far as Cuba is concerned, Castro was supported, initially, by a vast majority of the American people. He promised to institute a democratic system and allow elections. Since then you had these thousands of refugees that have flowed out of Cuba. They and objective reporters within Cuba say that it has become a complete police state. If you disagree with the government, you are imprisoned or shot. There is no freedom of speech, there is no freedom of the press. Any thought of having free elections has been abandoned.[33]

Later that same year, before the missile crisis, he outlined the Kennedy Administration's policy toward Castro in rather militant terms, before the American Legion.

In Cuba the last chapter of that sad story remains to be written. Our aim is to isolate the Cuban regime and rid South and Central America of Soviet Communist influence. We will not permit the Cuban regime to export its aggressive purposes by force or by threat of force. We are prepared to take whatever steps necessary to prevent the Cuban regime from taking

[31] R. E. Thompson and H. Meyers, *Robert F. Kennedy: The Brother Within* (New York: Macmillan, 1962), p. 36.
[32] Press conference, Cleveland, Ohio, December 5, 1961.
[33] Kennedy, *Just Friends and Brave Enemies,* p. 91.

action against its neighbors. The President has stated ver
plainly that if at any time the Communist buildup in Cub
endangers or threatens our security in any way, we will d
what is necessary to protect our own security and that of ou
allies.[34]

At a Washington news conference Kennedy was aske
to comment on Senator Morse's proposal that the U.S
Neutrality Act be enforced against exiles raiding Cub
from the Florida coast by denying them re-entry into thi
country. He was obviously not enthusiastic about th
proposal.

Well, those matters are being studied. I would say that, lik
all American citizens, we have a great deal of sympathy fo
the efforts of those who are carrying the fight against Castr
to return Cuba to its people, and so we are examining all c
these matters most carefully. The fact that an individual or
group of individuals want to take the step of risking the
lives to carry on this fight must evoke sympathy from u
which it does, and so whatever action we take—because it ir
volves the United States and our security—whatever actio
we take to try to protect that, we also take with well in min
the bravery of the particular individuals who are participatin
in these activities.[35]

The following year he hinted at what he thought th
ultimate outcome of the Cuban situation would be in
question-and-answer session after a speech.

QUESTION: Is there any truth to the rumor that there is anothe
proposed invasion of Cuba by the Cuban refugees?
RFK: I know nothing about it. I think there's a good deal c
interest by various Cuban groups outside of Cuba to go bac
into Cuba, and I think that eventually they will, someday the
will, but I don't know of any invasion that's being planned a
the present time.[36]

[34] Speech, American Legion Convention, Las Vegas, Nev., Octo
ber 9, 1962.
[35] Press conference, Washington, D.C., April 2, 1963.
[36] Speech, West Georgia College, Carrollton, Ga., May 26, 196

After that time Robert Kennedy had little to say on the topics of Castro and Cuba. Either he no longer believed Fidel constituted a threat to United States and Latin-American security, or perhaps he was satisfied with our policy of diplomatic and economic isolation of the island. However, in a major Senate speech on the Alliance for Progress, for the first time he placed some of the blame for Cuba's recent history on shortsighted American diplomacy.

In the late 1950s the failure of this policy, or lack of policy, erupted into anti-Americanism and the growth of communism. Our Vice-President was mobbed and stoned in Caracas. Communist revolution—caused less by Castro and his band in the Sierra Maestra than by the bloody and corrupt tyranny of Batista which we supported to the moment of its collapse— took power in Cuba; and his defiance of the United States received the secret admiration of many who hated communism, but rejoiced to see the discomfort of the huge and seemingly callous giant to the north.[37]

[37] Speech, U.S. Senate, May 4, 1966.

Chapter 21

Europe and the Berlin Question

Developments in Europe since V-E Day have been of immense consequence to both America and the world. Soviet control of the East, the Berlin blockade, the Marshall Plan, NATO, the European Common Market, cold-war tensions over a divided Germany, and, most recently, the growing independence from the United States and the U.S.S.R. of the nations of Western and Eastern Europe respectively, are matters directly affecting our security.

For the most part, these matters are exceedingly complex, but since our exclusive purpose is the examination of Robert Kennedy's views, we will be spared the task of sorting through the entire tangle of politics and economics that is Europe. This was an aspect of American foreign policy which RFK seemed not to have mastered in any detail or depth, and most of his statements in this area were platitudinous or vague. They are presented here more for what they do not say than for what they do say.

Toward Unity

European unity generally was Kennedy's dominant theme. In *Just Friends and Brave Enemies* he wrote enthusiastically about the prospect of a politically and economically integrated Europe.

One cannot foretell today the exact shape and structure of the political community of the new Europe. But no one can doubt that the will to a greater measure of political unity exists in Europe, and no one can doubt that in the end this will find its fulfillment in the creation of common political institutions.

The potentiality of this new Europe is enormous. In population, in productive power, in the skills and talents of its people, in the wealth of its natural resources, in intellectual and cultural achievement and influence, the new Europe equals or surpasses even so great a power as the Soviet Union. . . .[1]

The most dynamic force operating in Asia today is the new nationalism, of which I saw something in Indonesia. But in the Western world the most dynamic development of the postwar years is the Common Market.

This economic agreement among countries previously split by petty jealousies and historical boundaries promises to bring new wealth and economic stability to the participating nations and could indeed improve the condition of nations all around the world.[2]

By 1964, in keeping with the Kennedy-Johnson policy of "building bridges" between the West and the restive Soviet satellites, RFK's vision of a new Europe had come to include the eastern half of the continent.

Our objective is clear. It is to facilitate the reconciliation of Eastern and Western Europe in association with the United States. This is the only sure guarantee against nuclear war whether by design or by accident. It is also the surest means of fostering in our common prosperity.

The task is not easy. Among many problems, Europe is now divided by a deep and unnatural division—the division of Germany. That division is reinforced by a legacy of old hatreds. It is further reinforced by inertia born of uncertainty, for no one now sees clearly the path ahead.[3]

In a statement on the 185th anniversary of the death of Casimir Pulaski, the Polish hero of American independence, he said:

[1] Robert F. Kennedy, *Just Friends and Brave Enemies* (New York: Harper & Row, 1962), p. 174.

[2] *Ibid.*, pp. 171-172.

[3] Statement, Warsaw, Poland, July 1, 1964.

I know the possibilities of increased national independence that exist in all the nations of Eastern Europe. The purpose of American foreign policy in this area should be to encourage conditions of freedom and to create new bridges wherever possible between the people of Eastern Europe and the people of the United States.

I support and I will help pursue in the Senate every possible policy which holds eventual promise of freedom for people who live behind the iron curtain. Specifically I recommend:

1. We believe in freedom, self-determination, and national independence as an international objective, and this is true for the nations of Eastern Europe. Soviet domination is not a permanent fact of life.

2. We will use every opportunity to negotiate arrangements which will strengthen the freedom and independence of the peoples of the Eastern European nations, including trade and economic relations that have a specific and identifiable impact on the lives of the citizens of those countries. Surplus food trade is such a program in my judgment. We should also allow relatives and friends to be able to send food packages and private remittances directly to their families whenever possible.[4]

In Los Angeles he spelled out what he hoped increasing cooperation and unity would lead to.

But military arrangements are only a part—the lesser part —of an answer to the European security problem. It was President Kennedy's hope that progress toward West European unity would lessen emphasis on armaments in general and nuclear weapons in particular. The progress he sought was of two kinds. First, it was hoped that integration of Western Europe would make for a stronger Europe, an arena in which the brave, able and industrious people of West Germany could find ample scope for the exercise of their talents and energy. In a Europe in which all the nations of NATO were closely bound as partners, there would be neither need nor room for competition by the building of national nuclear forces. The nations of Europe

[4] Campaign press release, October 11, 1964.

must lead the way toward making this ideal a reality. It is too important and vital to be abandoned.

It was further hoped that this effort in Western Europe, with the tremendous economic and security advantages that would result, would in time bring an easing of tensions with the nations of Eastern Europe, and that closer relationships between the two Europes would follow. Within a context of general relaxation, and with West Germany looking to Western Europe as her major area of action, it might be that the Soviet Union and the East German government would relax the degree of Soviet control in, and the repressive character of, that regime. And a better and a freer life for East Germany could lead in turn to lower tensions and antagonisms between the Soviet Union and West Germany, toward less military and militant postures on both sides, and gradually toward reunification.[5]

Of two of Europe's principal political leaders, Charles De Gaulle and Willy Brandt, he had this to say:

I was impressed with De Gaulle's great vigor and determination. He made clear from the way he acted and the way he looked that he intended to be around for a long time to lead France to what he felt was her proper role in world affairs. . . .[6]

Willy Brandt is a courageous leader. He has a firm will, a tenacious spirit, an alert mind and—a necessary asset for any politician—a strong voice. When he speaks, one has the feeling he truly represents the strength that has molded the character of this city.

The image of Willy Brandt has become the image of Free Berlin all around the globe.[7]

[5] Address, Los Angeles, Calif., January 5, 1965.
[6] Kennedy, *op. cit.*, p. 186.
[7] *Ibid.*, p. 146.

The Wall That Divides

Kennedy spoke often of the problems posed by a divided Germany and Berlin. He put himself on record in
favor of a reunited Germany.

And while today Berlin is divided, as Germany is divided,
by the decision of the Communists, in the end all Berlin
and all Germany are one. The United States shares with all
Germans the peaceful but persistent purpose that Germans
shall one day find themselves reunited. This is the true path
toward lowered tensions and to lessened dangers. We shall
continue to hope that as policies of repression fail, and as
fears of "revenge" prove unfounded, the Soviet government
in its own true interest, will come to share this purpose and
to cooperate in its realization.[8]

But he vowed the United States would never permit
the Soviets to alter unilaterally the rights of the Western
Allies in Berlin. When Khrushchev threatened to do so by
signing a peace treaty with the East German government, Kennedy commented:

Certainly the Soviets can sign a peace treaty with East
Germany. That's their business. But we received certain
guarantees and rights after the Second World War. These
included rights of access to Berlin. They will not be abandoned.
We don't lose those because of an act of the Soviet Union and
East Germany. Of course, if the West Berliners decide they
don't want to have anything more to do with us, that is
something else again—although they took a plebiscite there
some time ago and it showed some 97 or 98 percent in
favor of the West staying in Berlin. I might say that we'd
welcome a vote in East Berlin or East Germany, which the
Soviet Union has never permitted.[9]

Returning from a good-will mission to Berlin on behalf of his brother in February of 1962, he sought to

[8] Robert F. Kennedy, *The Pursuit of Justice* (New York: Harper
& Row, 1965), p. 107.
[9] Kennedy, *Just Friends and Brave Enemies,* p. 89.

convince his countrymen of the extent to which the citizens of Berlin depended upon the United States.

Never have I been so moved by crowds as I was in Berlin. The welcome we received in that city affected by so much suffering and so much anguish is something we can never forget. It was not merely that by turning out in large numbers they demonstrated affection and trust, nor was their waving merely a gesture of greeting. It was all this, but it was more. Through their numbers, through their waving, through their tears, they wanted to tell American people, through us, that they depended on the United States—not on the French, not on the English, but on the United States—and that without the United States they felt they were dead and West Berlin was dead. This was the message.[10]

He regarded the construction of the Berlin Wall as a historic Communist defeat. As he told a huge audience from the steps of the Berlin City Hall:

I have seen the contrast between this city in the west part and in the Communist part as many hundreds of thousands of people have seen that contrast. And that is why Herr Ulbricht had to erect the wall. Because it was a contrast that he could not tolerate.

That is the true meaning of the wall that lies like a snake across the heart of your city. Mr. Ulbricht and the Communists cannot have the contrast. . . .

He cannot tolerate the contrast between freedom here and communism over there so that everyone can see it. He has to do that. We are aware of the heartbreak and anguish this wall has caused to the people of Berlin. But I would also ask you to look at the other side and see what an impression it has made all across the rest of the globe. Because this wall is an admission of failure by communism, it is an attempt for the first time in the history of mankind to erect a wall not to keep marauders or bandits out, but to keep their people in.[11]

He discussed what he felt the Communists were at-

[10] *Ibid.*, p. 140.
[11] Speech, Berlin, Germany, February 22, 1962.

tempting to accomplish with this stone and barbed-wire barrier.

The wall is more than a demonstration of Communist failure in the struggle for men's faith and hope; it is equally a desperate effort to stem the tide of unification in democratic Europe. By attempting to isolate West Berlin, the Communists hope to subtract West Berlin from West Germany and then to separate West Germany from Western Europe; and, by subtracting West Germany from Western Europe, they hope to defeat and wreck the great cooperative instrumentalities of the regathering of democratic strength, the Common Market, OECD and NATO.[12]

But, he concluded, the rest of mankind would not be deceived.

For the people of Berlin, the erection of the wall was of course an affront and a source of anguish. But I judge from peoples around the world, from my travels throughout the world, that the Berlin Wall is regarded everywhere as a proof of Communist bankruptcy, a symbol of Communist failure.[13]

[12] Kennedy, *The Pursuit of Justice*, p. 106.
[13] *Ibid.*, pp. 105-106.

Chapter 22

The Underdeveloped Nations

We recognize that the transition of so many peoples from dependencies to nations is not easy. At best it is difficult to fashion overnight the necessary system and structure of government.

The release of vast territories of this world from a system whose purpose was frequently to further the economic interests of the acquiring power with little or no interest in the people of the dependency has caused and is causing a monumental upheaval around the globe.[1]

Four areas in the world are at present or potentially major power centers: the United States, the Soviet Union, Western Europe, and Communist China. In all four, productivity is on the increase, and the political system performs relatively well its integrating and decision-making functions. Despite major differences among them . . . these four areas are likely to be in a position to play major roles in political, economic, and cultural international affairs in the coming decade. In contrast, the Middle East, Southeast Asia, tropical Africa, and Latin America are apt to remain power vacuums during this period, owing to their lack of unity, political instability, economic stagnation, and cultural heterogeneity. It seems improbable that ten years from now any of the areas mentioned above will cease to be, respectively, a power center or a power vacuum.[2]

[1] Speech, University of Gadja Mada, Jogjakarta, Indonesia, February 15, 1962.

[2] John Spanier, *American Foreign Policy since World War II* (New York: Praeger, 1962).

Given the stability and relative invulnerability of the United States, the Soviet Union, Western Europe, and China, the creation of a favorable world balance of power as far as each of the four power centers is concerned appears increasingly to depend on their respective abilities to acquire control or influence in the existing power vacuums. Thus the principal theater of conflicts for the great powers over the past decade—whether it is labeled the "cold war" or something else—has been the underdeveloped world.

Throughout this period it has been the consensus of U.S. policy makers that American security would be severely jeopardized if the nations of Asia, Africa, and Latin America were to come under effective Soviet or Chinese domination; that this would leave America isolated in an overwhelmingly hostile world. The question has been how best to avoid this eventuality.

Any American policy must begin with the recognition of two characteristics shared by most of the underdeveloped nations. First, these nations—with the exception of the Latin American ones—have emerged from Western imperialism or colonialism since World War II. The vehicles of independence have usually been aggressive nationalist movements which, owing to their anticolonialist origins, have been strongly anti-Western.

Second, these nations are characterized by the extreme poverty, illiteracy, and malnutrition of their peoples, who constitute two-thirds of the world's population. Annual per capita income in these nations seldom reaches the $100 level—compared with more than $1,500 in the U.S.—and the economic growth they do achieve is too often vitiated by their exploding populations.

From America's point of view, these two fundamental characteristics constitute a liability and an asset, respectively. The anti-Western predisposition of the majority of the underdeveloped states makes it more difficult for the United States to gain their good will and trust in competition with the Soviets and, particularly, the Chinese. On the other hand the United States is in the best position of the major powers to provide these impoverished nations with the economic assistance they require to attain their immediate goals of industrialization and a higher standard of living.

Unfortunately, these factors have frequently been forgotten or ignored in the formulation of our policy with regard to these nations. John Foster Dulles, Secretary of State during the Eisenhower Administration, believing as he did that the cold war was a historic battle between good and evil, disregarded the anti-Western feelings of the new nations and demanded that they commit themselves either for or against us. Indeed, our foreign aid was often conditional on receiving the "right" answer. This presumption and pressure were greatly resented in the capitals of Asia, Africa, and Latin America and cost the U.S. much prestige and influence in the Third World.

John Kennedy attempted to redefine our objectives and tactics in the underdeveloped nations along what he considered more realistic lines. Our goal, he declared, was not a multitude of American satellites, but the establishment of stable governments in the Third World which were responsive to the needs of their people and strong enough to resist *all* outside pressures, whether American, Soviet, or Chinese. The United States, he pledged, was ready to defend any neutral against outside aggression but would keep its fingers out of other nations' internal affairs. Foreign aid would be available to all governments —regardless of ideological bent—provided we had assurances that our assistance would benefit the people as a whole and not simply a small entrenched minority. The Alliance for Progress with Latin America was the first attempt to implement this new Kennedy policy.

Robert Kennedy was greatly influenced by his brother's approach to the underdeveloped nations, and he continued to champion it. It was Bobby's contention that a profound revolution was sweeping the Third World which America could influence only if it came to understand the nature of this upheaval.

Around the world—from the Straits of Magellan to the Straits of Malacca, from the Nile Delta to the Amazon basin, in Jaipur and Johannesburg—the dispossessed people of the world are demanding their place in the sun. For uncounted centuries, they have lived with hardships, with hunger and disease and fear. For the last four centuries, they have lived under the political, economic, and military domination of the West. We have shown them that a better life is possible. We have not done enough to make it a reality.

A revolution is now in progress. It is a revolution for individual dignity, in societies where the individual has been submerged in a desperate mass. It is a revolution for self-sufficiency, in societies which have been forced to rely on more fortunate nations for their manufactured goods and their education, cotton textiles and calculus texts. It is a revolution to bring hope to their children, in societies where 40 percent of all children die before reaching the age of five.

This revolution is directed against *us*—against the one-third of the world that diets while others starve; against a nation that buys 8 million new cars a year while most of the world goes without shoes; against developed nations which spend over 100 billion dollars on armaments while the poor countries cannot obtain the 10 to 15 billion dollars of investment capital they need just to keep pace with their expanding populations.

It is of the utmost importance that we come to recognize the magnitude and significance of this revolution, that we come not only to understand it but to identify with it—and with the new order which it seeks to establish, with the pattern of change which is its essence.

It is a revolution not just for economic well-being, but for social reform and political freedom, for internal justice and international independence.

We should understand the legitimacy of these ideals—for they are only what our forefathers sought. We should recognize their power—for they have sustained us throughout our history.

But in most of the world today, these are subversive ideals—subversive of the established order of power and privilege. So it may be difficult for us to understand, or to support, the changes that these ideals demand—or the men who act in their name.

The status quo, after all, seems comfortable. The established order seems safe. And the opponents of change too often call themselves our stoutest supporters—and hasten to brand *their* enemies as *our* enemies.[3]

To those who clung to the hope that change could be suppressed, the status quo maintained, Kennedy said:

We must recognize that the young in many areas of the world today are in the midst of a revolution against the status quo. They are not going to accept platitudes and generalities. Their anger has been turned on the systems which have allowed poverty, illiteracy and oppression to flourish for centuries.

And we must recognize one simple fact: they will prevail. They will achieve their idealistic goals one way or the other.

If they have to pull governments tumbling down over their heads, they will do it. But they are going to win their share of a better and cleaner world.

This affects us, Canada and the United States, you and me. Our future is tied up with what they think. Like it or not, what they are going to do will have a direct impact on all of us in this room.

We, in turn, are a part of their revolution. At least we should be, and I believe that we must encourage them in their efforts to bring about improvements. They will not be like Ireland was when Owen Row O'Neill died, "sheep without a shepherd, when the snow shuts out the sky."

Someone will share their aspirations and their leadership. If not the West, then some other system will make common cause with them to achieve their immediate goals.[4]

Nationalism was part of this revolution, too, he told an Indonesian student audience.

The outstanding spirit abroad in the world today is nationalism—nationalism linked closely with anticolonialism. Nationalism, itself, of course is nothing new.

This self-determination performs the essential function of

[3] Address, Queens College commencement exercises, Queens, N.Y., June 15, 1965.
[4] Speech, Canadian Press, Toronto, Canada, April 14, 1964.

giving people an identity with their country and with each other. . . .

This nationalism has taken the form of "nonconquest," of disengagement from former economic and political ties.

It is re-creating in many parts of the world a sense of identity and of national aims and aspirations that the old order has too often sought to stifle.[5]

In the same year, as if in an effort to assuage the fears of his countrymen, he pointed out the implicit American roots of this worldwide revolution.

In many aspects, of course, this world-in-the-making represents a rejection of Europe and America. Yet nothing has impressed me more in recent weeks than the extent to which this passion for independence and progress reflects Western purposes.

If the new nations have repudiated European rule, they have done so for European reasons. They are fighting for their new societies in terms of European ideals of nationalism and democracy.

It is their commitment to European doctrine which has led them to reject European dominion. The ghosts of Locke and Rousseau—and, if I may say so, Jefferson and Lincoln— preside over the awakening of the East.[6]

In much the same way he argued that the gap between the affluent and the impoverished in America could no longer be tolerated, he predicted international disaster if the chasm between the have and the have-not nations was not visibly reduced in the near future. This is a recurrent motif in his remarks about the underdeveloped nations.

It is in all our interests to narrow the frightening gap between the rich nations and the poor—between people living in affluence and comfort and people scratching to survive on less than one hundred dollars a year.

[5] Speech, University of Indonesia, Djakarta, Indonesia, February 14, 1962.

[6] Robert F. Kennedy, *Just Friends and Brave Enemies* (New York: Harper & Row, 1962), pp. 175-176.

A high standard of living cannot remain the exclusive possession of the West—and the sooner we can help other peoples to develop their resources, raise their living standards and strengthen their national independence, the safer the world will be for us all.

As President Kennedy said in his Inaugural Address a year ago: "If a free society cannot help the many who are poor, it cannot save the few who are rich." [7]

Two-thirds of the present world population—about two billion people—live in the so-called "developing nations" of Asia, Africa and Latin America. The "developing" refers to technology, for, as we all know, many of these countries had advanced civilizations when people in Europe and America were living in caves.

But these areas had fallen behind in the race for technological progress. Their problems today are the basic problems of population, and hunger and education, and it is these which demand and must receive worldwide attention and worldwide solution.

I believe that we recognize now—perhaps for the first time—that the gap between the developing and the developed nations of the world must be closed. And for this reason the attention of the world is turning to the problems which may engage your energies and your leadership talents tomorrrow. [8]

And of all these ends, none is more pressing and necessary than to bridge the gap which now yawns across the world, dividing all mankind—the gap between affluence and misery; between children of promise and hope, and children old and withered before their time; most simply, the gap between those who eat and those who starve. This gap is even now widening further as the undeveloped world is less and less able to feed its expanding population. It will be with us long after Vietnam is over, and will affect the lives of all of us. Even if we are successful in Southeast Asia and accomplish our immediate aims, the affluent part of the world will have a grave responsibility to meet the continuing and deepening

[7] Speech, Bonn, Germany, February 24, 1962.
[8] Speech, Fifth General Assembly, World Assembly of Youth, University of Massachusetts, Amherst, Mass., August 7, 1964.

crisis of starvation. And if we do not, chaos, catastrophe and bloodshed will be our future. And for us—for the world we live in, for the human race to which we belong—time is running short.[9]

He acknowledged the tremendous burden population growth places on the efforts of the developing nations to realize per capita economic gains, though he stopped short, perhaps because of his Catholicism, of direct recommendations for birth-control programs.

And the problems of developing nations are accentuated because they get such a high percentage of world population growth—about 80 percent of the increase over the last decade, for example. It is estimated that at present growth rates North America will go from 200 to 300 million by the end of this century, but Latin America will go from 200 to 600 million during this same period.

This is clearly a basic area in which world progress must be made in the coming years. There must be much better knowledge of population trends, particularly as they relate to economic and social progress. There must be medical and social research, to extend the boundaries of our knowledge. The wisest leadership and calm judgment will be required to reconcile conflicting views.[10]

He pointed to the related Malthusian problem of inadequate food supplies.

The Food and Agriculture Organization of the United Nations tells us that for all the people of the world to have a minimum adequate diet, world food supplies must quadruple in the next thirty-five years. But we are not making progress. We are falling behind. Food output in the less developed world is dropping, and more and more grain and other foods are shipped in, largely from the United States. And even as food production abroad is not keeping pace, our

[9] Remarks, dinner for Senator Gaylord Nelson, Milwaukee, Wis., October 28, 1967.

[10] Speech, Fifth General Assembly, World Assembly of Youth, University of Massachusetts, Amherst, Mass., August 7, 1964.

aid—and the aid provided by the rest of the developed world —is decreasing.[11]

What does all this—the poverty, the swelling populations, the starvation, the revolution of rising expectations —mean for American foreign policy? First, to Kennedy, it meant that we must put a stop to our alliances of convenience which find us linked with dictators who are on the wrong end of this revolution and who have somehow convinced us that stability is more to be valued than freedom and social justice.

We have made some progress in reaching the peoples of other countries. The aid and information programs, the Peace Corps, presidential trips abroad, all are ways of getting beyond mere government-to-government contact. But the critical moves, the moves that will determine our success, are the kinds of political choices this country makes in picking its friends abroad—and its enemies.

Far too often, for narrow, tactical reasons, this country has associated itself with tyrannical and unpopular regimes that had no following and no future. Over the past twenty years we have paid dearly because of support to colonial rulers, cruel dictators or ruling cliques void of social purpose. This was one of President Kennedy's gravest concerns.

By achieving harmony with broadly based governments concerned with their own peoples, we do more than make our way easier for a year or two. We create for this country the opening to the future that is so essential.[12]

The greatest enemy of freedom today, of course, is communism, a tyranny that holds its captives in viselike subjugation on a global scale. For nearly twenty years we and our allies have striven to halt the Communist advance. But one of the weaknesses in our common front has been the restraint on freedom sponsored by our allies and accepted by ourselves.

The conduct of our foreign affairs should be consistently

[11] Remarks, dinner for Senator Gaylord Nelson, Milwaukee, Wis., October 28, 1967.

[12] Robert F. Kennedy, *The Pursuit of Justice* (New York: Harper & Row, 1965), p. 136.

based on our recognition of every man's right to be economically and politically free. This is in the American tradition. We were, after all, the victor in our own war for independence. We promulgated the Monroe Doctrine and the "open door" policy with their clear warnings to the colonial powers of Europe.

We gave self-determination to our own dependencies; and for more than a century we opposed colonial exploitation elsewhere. But throughout all this we were still living largely in splendid isolation, removed from a direct control of world destiny.

This was changed by World War II. The frontiers of our national security became the frontiers of the world. We found ourselves obliged to deal with the harsh facts of existence on a global basis.

For the sake of our own security, we found our destiny to be closely linked with that of nations that maintained large colonial empires on which they felt their ultimate security depended. In some of the underdeveloped countries we have found our destiny linked with ruling powers or classes which hold the vast majority of their people in economic or military subjugation.

It is easy for us to believe that the imperialism of the West was infinitely preferable to the tyranny of communism. But the sullen hostility of the African and Asian colonial nations has shown us that not all hold the same view. The bloody struggles for liberty from the sands of Algeria to the steaming jungles of Indonesia and Vietnam proved that others would make the same sacrifices to throw off the yoke of imperialism today that the Irish did more than a half-century ago.

And we have a longer way to go in helping the people of some other nations to free themselves from economic domination. This is a part of our national policy not only because it is humane but also because it is essential. Our future may depend on how well this is understood throughout the world—how well it is understood that we still champion the quality of freedom everywhere that Americans enjoy at home.[13]

More positively, in order to successfully identify our

[13] Speech, Friendly Sons of St. Patrick of Lackawanna County, Scranton, Pa., March 17, 1964.

purposes and values with those of the stirring masses of the Third World, he declared,

> We must if we seek not merely to lead but to lead greatly, act consistently with our belief in human freedom and equality. Those are the seminal values of our entire history. We realize that for many, liberty today is often a remote pursuit, lacking urgency to those enslaved by material want. Nor should we, even if we could, compel other countries to adopt our principles. Yet there should be no doubt that we stand—in Africa, or Asia or in Latin America, and in the United States itself—on the side of equality and increasing freedom; never yielding that position to the demands of temporary expediency or short-run realism. For if we allow immediate considerations, one by one, to chip away proclaimed ideals and values, then we soon stand for nothing at all, except ourselves.[14]

To discover how Kennedy translated this general principle into the specific proposal and decisions that constitute an operational foreign policy, let us turn to his statements dealing with the actual situations the United States encounters in its relations with the various underdeveloped nations. (The Middle East will be discussed in Chapter 23 and Southeast Asia in Chapter 26. Here we will quote the Kennedy record on Latin America, Africa, and principles of foreign aid.)

Latin America, the Inevitable Revolution

Latin America provides us with an excellent case study, for the Senator discussed our relations with the rest of the hemisphere in detail and depth. It is a part of the world which, because of its relative military weakness and its geographic proximity to the United States, has been regarded as within America's "sphere of influence." As a result of numerous direct military interventions by the United States over the past seventy-five years, and of the continued use of "dollar diplomacy" to control the in-

[14] Address, Columbus Day Dinner, New York, N.Y., October 11, 1966.

ternal affairs of South America, Central America, and the Caribbean, a durable heritage of "anti-Yankee" sentiment has been inculcated in the people of these areas. This sentiment has been further strengthened by Washington's persistent support of reactionary military dictatorships which serve the interests of the small, wealthy land-owning classes at the expense of the peasants and urban laborers.

When John Kennedy entered the White House, he resolved to change both the appearance and the reality of America's policy toward her neighbors to the south. His answer—one of the major innovations of his abbreviated administration—was the Alliance for Progress. Stating that he recognized the imminence of revolutions in Latin America which neither the United States nor anyone else could hope to prevent, Kennedy tried to demonstrate to the people of Central and South America that their demands for political reform and a more just distribution of the wealth could be realized without resorting to the violence of a Marxist solution. The President promised substantial financial and technical aid, through the Alliance, to those governments willing to undertake needed reforms and to channel the benefits of this aid to their impoverished and increasingly restive majorities.

RFK was obviously won over to the President's approach, for he continued to champion the Alliance vigorously. On numerous occasions he made it clear that revolution in Latin America is in the cards, and that we had better be prepared to lead it when it comes.

The responsibility of our time is nothing less than to lead a revolution. A revolution which will be peaceful if we are wise enough, human if we care, successful if we are fortunate enough, but a revolution which will come whether we will it or not.[15]

A revolution is coming whether we will it or not . . . the question is how the revolution is to be made and guided.[16]

[15] *Newsweek*, November 22, 1965.
[16] *Commonweal*, June 3, 1966.

The time for caution is past, he declared. We must align ourselves quickly with the forces of progress and justice.

I think we should become associated with the more progressive elements in the hemisphere, rather than being momentarily safe and, in the long run, sorry.[17]

A better life for the people of Latin America can only come out of the progress toward a better, more democratic political and social structure.

If we allow ourselves to become allied with those to whom the cry of "communism" is only an excuse for the perpetuation of privilege, if we assist, with military materials and other aid, governments which use that aid to prevent reform for the people, then we will give Communists a strength which they cannot attain by anything they themselves might do.[18]

On a private trip through Latin America in November of 1965, Kennedy tried, if somewhat unconvincingly, to identify America's revolutionary traditions with the movements for change that were gaining momentum in the Southern Hemisphere. As he told a student audience in Santiago, Chile:

We have had other revolutions since our independence, for mine is a revolutionary country: in the 1820s to open political life to all regardless of birth or property; in the 1860s to abolish the great plantations and the slavery which supported them; in the 1870s to end our dependence on raw material exports; in the early twentieth century to break and control the power of the great corporations.

But it was the revolution of the New Deal that showed the power of affirmative free government—of government which joins the ideal of social justice to the ideals of liberty.[19]

He challenged his youthful listeners in Rio de Janeiro to join with their fellow students across the continent to lead a democratic revolution.

[17] *Newsweek,* December 6, 1965.
[18] *Commonweal,* June 3, 1966.
[19] Address, Estadio National, Santiago, Chile, November 1965.

And what I have asked students in Lima and Mendoza, in Santiago and Recife, I now ask you: what leadership will you give to the great question of our time—whether the traditions of freedom can survive in an era of unprecedented change; whether man's great unsatisfied yearning for economic progress and social justice can be answered by free men within a framework of democratic institutions; whether, in the words of the great Mexican patriot Benito Juárez, "Democracy is the destiny of future humanity." [20]

For Venezuelan labor leaders he painted a picture of a united Latin America playing an independent and influential role in future world affairs.

Latin America can and should take independent initiatives in the councils of the world, not only on matters of special interest to this continent, or to developing countries, but on worldwide concerns from disarmament to the peaceful settlement of disputes of Asia and Africa. Latin America can, for example, take the lead in assuring fair treatment in world trade for the developing nations. And as nations one step removed from the confrontations of the great powers, Latin American actions and proposals add substantially to hopes for settlement of conflicts.

The first concrete step that can be taken toward world leadership in this most vital area is the formation of a nuclear-free zone in Latin America. That alone could show the way for dozens of nations on two other continents and it could lead the way toward conventional arms reductions as well. . . .

Efforts to draw the countries of Latin America closer together should increase—not only for their own progress, but also to add force and weight to their acts in the world arena. This will involve not only economic integration, but the imaginative creation of new inter-American institutions. There could be, for example, an inter-American Assembly similar to the Western European Union, hemisphere-wide universities, joint projects in tropical agriculture, and a vastly increased flow of ideas, men, and artistic achievement from country to country in the hemisphere. . . .

[20] Remarks, Catholic University, Rio de Janeiro, Brazil, November 25, 1965.

The Latin American nations should increasingly share in the councils of the West—not after a decision has been made, but in a sincere and determined effort to draw upon their wisdom in advance of crisis and action. This effort is the mutual responsibility of Latin America, the nations of Europe, and the United States. Regular channels of communication and consultation should be established for continuing discussion of the great challengers to peace—from Southeast Asia to Berlin. This should not be an effort to bind any country to the policies of any other country; rather it should be to draw upon Latin American ideas and imagination, and to insure this continent that place of partnership which its history and the limitless prospects of its future demand.[21]

Upon his return to the States, Kennedy began to explain to Americans what he had seen and how Latin Americans had come to regard the "colossus to the north." He warned a student audience not to be misled into believing suspicion of our actions and intentions could be dispelled overnight.

Knowing virtually nothing about U.S. politics or economy, for example, most are deeply suspicious of "capitalism," which they identify only with the rapacious colonial economy of their history. They identify themselves, more than anything else, as "socialists"—though their "socialism" is in fact usually less daring than the platform of the Democratic party of the United States. So the fact of what the United States is, and does, is unknown; our self-description of capitalist means to them something like what fascist might mean to us; our standing among these leaders of their countries is determined by their response to a meaningless slogan. Further, standing here in New York, it is almost impossible to appreciate how large the U.S. looms in Latin America. But from there, we seem a colossus which blocks out the light—a colossus which determines, with only the slightest move, every event of any significance in Latin America. Everywhere I went in Latin America, students—and newsmen and government officials—raised the same points—asked me the same questions. They were usually asked in the form of declarations: The U.S. intervened in the

---

[21] Remarks to Venezuelan labor leaders, Venezuela, 1965.

Dominican Republic to deliberately crush a popular democracy; the foreign policy of the U.S. is determined by Wall Street; U.S. companies bleed the economies of sorely needed capital; the internal economic policies of Latin American governments are determined by Wall Street; the Pentagon controls the Latin American military and overthrows governments which disobey Washington.[22]

He sought to convey the feelings and ideas that were turning the sons of the wealthy in Latin America into radicals and revolutionaries.

What is behind such radicalism among the sons of a class which has been privileged for 300 years? Partly, I think, it is simple nationalism. For most of their history, the upper classes of Latin America have neglected their own nations—preferring to share the benefits of a cosmopolitan European culture. But the post-World War II period has seen a resurgence of national feeling all over the globe, and the birth of dozens of new nations from the former colonies of the great powers. It is not so easy, now, to be without a nation in which to take pride. The Latin American countries are weak and poor and "not modern"; they suffer badly, in the eyes of their young men, by comparison with the United States; to build up these nations is to rebuild their own pride. A second reason is the obvious demand of justice. No man is insensitive, and young people are particularly sensitive, to justice; to the demands of the landless and the sick and the untaught.

But more than anything else, I think, they act out of a desire "not only to equal or resemble, but to excel"; the desire which John Adams said "next to self-preservation will forever be the great spring of human actions." The students I saw seem to have sensed that their societies, as presently constituted, have not enough room for achievement; there is no way to pursue the ideal of happiness as defined by the Greeks for all men—"the exercise of vital powers along lines of excellence in life affording them scope.[23]

[22] Speech, Annual West Side Community Conference, Columbia University, New York, N.Y., March 12, 1966.
[23] *Ibid.*

When Lyndon Johnson decided to send the Marines into the Dominican Republic in 1964 to prevent what he feared might be a Communist takeover, Kennedy criticized the move.

Bobby's remarks on the revolution in the Dominican Republic, however, all but amounted to a break with administration policy. He agreed with President Johnson's determination to keep Communism out of this hemisphere. "But this cannot mean," said Bobby, "that we plan to act on our own without regard to our friends and allies in the Organization of American States." Thus he criticized the unilateral character of U.S. intervention and praised the OAS for its role in the cease-fire negotiations in the Dominican Republic. "This seems to be a record deserving commendation, not criticism," Bobby noted. And he lectured about our future course in Latin America: "Our determination to stop Communist revolution in the hemisphere must not be construed as opposition to popular uprisings against injustice and oppression just because the targets of such popular uprisings say there are Communists taking part in them."

In the case of the Dominican Republic, Kennedy acknowledged the presence of professional Communist operators, but asked that the matter be kept in perspective and reminded his audience that "the revolutionary forces include also many non-Communist democrats." [24]

In his analysis of the revolution being born in Latin America, he cited two key problem areas.

At the heart of the revolution, underlying all hope for economic progress and social justice, are two great resistant problems—education and land reform. Both education and land reform are needed for economic growth. No amount of capital, no purely economic measures, can bring progress unless each nation has the trained and skilled people to do the work of modernization and change. Nor can any industrial economy be built on a failing, inadequate and obsolete sys-

[24] Nick Thimmisch and William Johnson, *R. F. K. at 40* (Boston: W. W. Norton, 1965), p. 268.

tem of agricultural production. But these are far more than economic measures. No matter how rich or powerful a nation may grow, children condemned to ignorance, families enslaved to land they cannot hope to own, are denied this dignity—the fulfillment of talent and hope—which is the purpose of economic progress. Progress without justice is false progress—and a false hope. Thus education and land reform must be at the heart of our concern for change in Latin America; and among the highest priorities of Latin American governments themselves.[25]

In a lengthy speech delivered to the Senate on May 9 and 10, 1966, Kennedy outlined his views on the performance and prospects of the Alliance for Progress. He began with a brief recapitulation of U.S.-Latin relations.

In the past, the United States had acted as "protector" of hemispheric stability—intervening militarily in Latin American nations twenty-one times just in the period 1898 to 1924. And too often our great strength was used, not to advance the freedom and aspirations of the Latin American people, but in the name of stability, to protect our short-range economic interests.

Military intervention ended with the Good Neighbor policy; the last Marines left the Caribbean in the 1930s, and relations improved through inter-American cooperation in World War II.

In the fifteen years after the war, we provided $30 billion to Europe; $15 billion to Asia; but only $2.5 billion to our own hemisphere, to help the declining economies of an entire underdeveloped continent. We were content to accept, and even support, whatever governments were in power, asking only that they did not disturb the surface calm of the hemisphere. We gave medals to dictators; praised backward regimes; and became steadily identified with institutions and men who held their lands in poverty and fear.[26]

[25] Address, Society of Friends of Puerto Rico, New York, N.Y., May 13, 1966.
[26] Speech, U.S. Senate, May 9 and 10, 1966.

He contended that the Alliance could not achieve its
objectives without the aid of a successful revolution.

For there cannot be steady jobs and housing and economic
security; there cannot be schools for all the children; and there
can be no democracy, or justice, or individual dignity without
revolutionary changes in the economic, social, and political
systems of every Latin American nation. . . .
These people will not accept this kind of existence for the
next generation. We would not; they will not. There will be
changes.
So a revolution is coming—a revolution which will be
peaceful if we are wise enough; compassionate if we care
enough; successful if we are fortunate enough—but a revolution which is coming whether we will it or not. We can affect
its character; we cannot alter its inevitability.
At the heart of the revolution, underlying all hope for
economic progress and social justice, are two great and
resistant problems—education and land reform. Both education and land reform are needed for economic growth. No
amount of capital, no purely economic measures, can bring
progress unless each nation has the trained and skilled people
to do the work of modernization and change. Nor can any
industrial economy be built on a failing, inadequate and obsolete system of agricultural production.[27]

He placed a great deal of emphasis on the need for
meaningful land reform, but warned that redistribution
would entail widespread political and social change.

First, land must be redistributed. Many Latin American
farmers are really laborers who own no land at all; they have
neither the incentive nor the means to increase production.
Of those who do own land, the great majority farm less than
ten acres, which are likely to be of poor quality. Throughout
Latin America, it is estimated that more than 70 percent of
the landowners control less than 4 percent of the land. Ninety
percent of all land is controlled by less than 10 percent of the
landholders; and there are nations in which less than 1 percent

[27] *Ibid.*

of all landholders control nearly 70 percent of the land. . . . Most owners are absent. Their workers are uneducated and underpaid, with little incentive. The very size of the estates has allowed their owners to become wealthy without substantial capital investment to increase productivity.

It was recognized also [in the Alliance Charter] that redistribution of land is essential for the dignity and freedom of the man who lives on it. Like the framers of our own Constitution, the framers of the Alliance believed that an independent, propertied yeomanry would be the surest foundation of democracy and political stability. . . .

But these efforts [economic] are only part of what is required. Land reform requires a great political effort; for it is, at the root, a political question: of the will and determination to reform the basic social and political system of a nation.

Land is the principal form of wealth in Latin America; its possessors, while by no means all-powerful, still are highly influential everywhere, and naturally resistant to reform. Large-scale land redistribution necessarily implies major changes in the internal political balance of many Latin American countries—away from oligarchy and privilege, toward more popular government.

Improvements in the educational system, also vital to comprehensive land reform, would also work great changes in the political balance. Representation of any area in the Brazilian Congress, for example, is based on total population. But illiterates are ineligible to vote; and in some areas, dominated by large landowners, up to 80 percent of the people are illiterate. This illiteracy gives to the established groups in these areas great leverage in the Congress; there is a vested interest against educational improvement.[28]

He went on to discuss the spiritual preconditions of material progress.

But we must realize that the demands of the spirit—the demands for justice and a sense of participation in the life of one's country—are the essential precondition to material progress. The dispossessed and the landless will not strive

[28] *Ibid.*

and sacrifice to improve land they do not own, in whose proceeds they do not share. Parents will not sacrifice to insure education for their children, the children themselves will not study, if the schools to which they go end in the third grade, and if they are considered unfit for admission to higher grades. Individual entrepreneurs will not flourish in a closed society, a society which reserves all wealth and power and privilege for the same classes, the same families, which have held that wealth and power for the last 300 years. . . .

Without this spirit, the Alliance for Progress, the Peace Corps, all our efforts will be useless.

With this spirit, no matter what the obstacles, any material poverty can be overcome.[29]

Unfortunately, he continued, there are too many in the hemisphere who have not yet been moved by this spirit of reform.

As President Kennedy saw, the Alliance was not and could not be a program of U.S. assistance, but a cooperative effort among all the nations of the Americas. It embraced not simply economic progress, but social justice, political freedom, and democratic government. It was an attack not just on poverty, but on the oppression and exploitation of man by man which had too long been the ruling pattern in the hemisphere.

This was a pledge of revolutionary change, for Latin America as well as for the United States. But the need for change was not universally accepted, either in Latin America or in the United States; nor, despite President Johnson's efforts, is it universally accepted today.

There are still those who believe that stability can be maintained, and communism defeated, by force of arms; that those who have waited three centuries for justice can wait another so that old privileges may be preserved; that the economic machinery of the twentieth century can be developed and managed by social structures which were outmoded in the eighteenth.

But there can be no preservation of the status quo in Latin America. The central question before us is not whether we

[29] *Ibid.*

can prevent change, but, as President Kennedy put it, whether "man's unsatisfied aspiration for economic progress and social justice can best be achieved by freemen, working with a framework of democratic institutions." [30]

In addition to making available its economic and technical resources, what can the United States do to promote peaceful revolutions which will fulfill the rising expectations of the peoples of Latin America? In closing, Bobby recommended the following:

> . . . we can help Latin Americans meet the political challenges of land reform—above all, by clearly identifying and associating ourselves with the forces of reform and social justice. In nearly every Latin American nation elections are fought on the basis of the Alliance and its ideals; the great partnership that is the Alliance gives substantial weight to the opinions and feelings of other men and governments in the hemisphere. Strong association of the United States with land reform will everywhere help its supporters, and make others more reluctant to oppose it . . . we certainly can help by not extending our material and moral support to those who actively oppose necessary political, economic, and social change, including the comprehensive land reform which is at the heart of development efforts. [31]

The tone of this address had been essentially optimistic. At about the same time, however, other remarks about the Alliance sounded notes of doubt and pessimism.

> There are a lot of things we've ignored or let slide. . . . In total foreign aid, we're giving a third of what we gave fifteen years ago. I would do much more. People there work from six in the morning to six at night for $1.50 a week. The rich nations are getting richer, and the poor countries are getting poorer. . . . The question of land reform is complex. You can't just hand it over. . . . In the Alliance for Progress private investment has fallen off. There should be greater investment by private enterprise; businessmen should develop a code of

[30] *Ibid.*
[31] *Ibid.*

nvestment there for dealing with labor unions, stock owner-
hip, wages . . . all these questions that cause such bad
eelings.[32]

The Charter [establishing the Alliance for Progress] is no
recious talisman, to be taken from its case and exhibited
eriodically, it must be used. Its ideals must pervade every
spect of our policy. It must govern not only the necessarily
nfrequent acts of presidents—but the daily acts of every
nember and part of the United States government with
esponsibility to Latin America.[33]

He was visibly disappointed by the military overthrow
f President Illia of Argentina.

Senator Robert F. Kennedy (D-N.Y.) said today that the
verthrow of the elected government of Argentina by a mili-
ary junta is a grave setback to inter-American solidarity and
o the Alliance for Progress. "On my recent visit to Argentina,"
enator Kennedy said, "I was very impressed with the dedica-
ion shown by President Illia and his government and the
rogress he had made under serious pressure from both the
nilitary and the followers of Juan Peron." Senator Kennedy in-
licated his strong belief that "whenever a democratically
lected government is overthrown by the military, severe
lamage is done to the entire fabric of the inter-American
ystem. If real progress is to come in Latin America, it must
e with the democratic consent of the people." [34]

And he criticized the U.S. recognition proffered this
nilitary government two weeks later.

Senator Robert F. Kennedy described as premature today's
nnouncement by the Department of State that the United
tates had recognized the new military government of Ar-
entina. "I would have hoped," said the Senator, "that recogni-
ion would have been withheld until more positive assurances

[32] *The New Yorker*, May 14, 1966.
[33] *Commonweal*, June 3, 1966.
[34] Statement, June 28, 1966.

had been received from the present military leaders in Buenos
Aires with respect to an early return to democracy." Senator
Kennedy pointed out that in a similar situation four years ago
with respect to the military coup in Peru, "we withheld recog
nition until the military junta set a firm timetable for election
and a return to democracy." That timetable was kept, and
the military regime a transitional one. "Our commitment to
the Alliance for Progress," the Senator continued, "requires
firm support of democratic self-government throughout the
hemisphere." [35]

After mid-1966 Robert Kennedy said little about our
relations with our neighbors to the south. However, his
remarks at a dinner for Senator Nelson of Wisconsin re
veal that his views on the subject remained substantially
unchanged.

It requires all this—and it requires something more. Re
form and progress, the economy of the twentieth century, can
not and will not be planned and managed by leaders and
social structure that were outmoded in the eighteenth. Men
will not strive to learn, to improve lands they do not own, in
whose proceeds they do not share. They will not save and
sacrifice to develop a nation and an economy in which the
fruits of their labor are reserved for the privileged few. If
our assistance finds its way only to those who would perpetu
ate privilege, it will buy for us only contempt and hate which
will plague our children for generations to come. Justice can
not be a luxury for the rich—it must be the sustenance and
hope of the many; it is the only real way to progress. So the
task is difficult; for the needed changes can only be brough
about by the people of the countries themselves. But we can
help: at the very minimum, by not extending our help to
those who would hold their lands in tyranny and fear. Beyond
this, for those nations which are making the necessary com
mitments to justice and progress, there is much more we can
do—and there is real hope that the challenge can be met. [36]

[35] Press release, July 15, 1966.
[36] Remarks, dinner for Senator Gaylord Nelson, Milwaukee, Wis.
October 28, 1967.

Africa

Africa is the area of the underdeveloped world about which Robert Kennedy said the least and, presumably, about which he knew the least. Though the United States became embroiled in the Congo crisis in 1961, during the administration of John Kennedy, Bobby contributed none of his own thoughts on the matter to the public record. In fact, until he entered the U.S. Senate he all but ignored the world's second largest continent.

On one occasion, during a brief stay in the Ivory Coast, he was asked to comment on Assistant Secretary for African Affairs G. Mennen Williams' widely reported endorsement of the slogan, "Africa for the Africans."

QUESTION: Mr. Attorney General, what does the statement "Africa for the Africans" mean to you?

RFK: I think it probably means just what it says. If Africa is not for Africans, who is it for? [37]

Then, rather suddenly, in 1966, Bobby began to address some of his statements to United States policy in Africa.

If we do not do more in Africa to show that we are concerned, then we can expect Communism to fill the void. [38]

In an article published in the spring of 1966 he called for increased interest in African affairs, and for the first time he mentioned, though in rather mild terms, South Africa's racial policy of apartheid.

Africa is an ignored continent. There has to be greater interest, not only because of our moral responsibility but from our self-interest. They look to us for leadership, for education and for medical services they need so badly. We should show greater concern.

[37] Press conference, Ivory Coast, Africa, August 8, 1961.
[38] William V. Shannon, *The Heir Apparent* (New York: Macmillan, 1967), p. 292.

Vietnam is costing fifteen billion dollars a year. We spend about eight days of that amount in all Africa. . . .

But we should make an effort to keep a dialogue up, and to show there's no animosity toward people. We must criticize apartheid, but we want to talk to them. It's not a bright future, but it's worthwhile to try to make the effort.[39]

The following month, Kennedy journeyed to South Africa for a six-day whirlwind tour, at the invitation of the multiracial National Union of South African Students. To the surprise and dismay of the South African government, his arrival was sensationally received. Four thousand students mobbed him at the airport in Johannesburg and swept him triumphantly onto their shoulders and into the airport terminal. Similar displays of enthusiasm greeted him wherever he went; blacks as well as whites, Afrikaners as well as English hungered to see and hear him.

In his major address of the trip, before an overflow audience of fifteen thousand, he turned quickly to the key issue of racism.

We must recognize the full human equality of all our people—before God, before the law, and in the councils of government. We must do this, not because it is economically advantageous—although it is; not because the laws of God and man command it—although they do command it; not because people in other lands wish it so. We must do it for the single and fundamental reason that it is the right thing to do. And this must be our commitment outside our borders as it is within. . . .

Only earthbound man still clings to the dark and poisoning superstition that his world is bounded by the nearest hill, his universe ended at river shore, his common humanity enclosed in the tight circle of those who share his town and views and the color of his skin.

It is your job, the task of the young people of this world, to strip the last remnants of that ancient, cruel belief from the civilization of man. . . .[40]

[39] *The New Yorker,* May 14, 1966.

[40] Address, Cape Town University, Cape Town, South Africa, June 6, 1966.

He received a thunderous five-minute standing ovation. In Durban, where he spoke,

> . . . a white man boomed from the gallery, "Can you tell me what President of the United States said in 1885, 'There is an undeniable difference between the white man and black man'?"
> Kennedy shot back, "The one who was beaten in 1888."
> The audience roared with applause.[41]

He obtained permission to visit the Nobel Prize winner and former head of the outlawed African National Congress, Chief Albert Luthuli, who was kept under house arrest on a remote farm. After the brief meeting, Bobby described the chief as one of the most impressive men he had ever met.

> He has compassion and tolerance and harbors no bitterness against the whites.[42]

After this trip Kennedy seemed more aware of the explosiveness of the situation in South Africa.

The Senator predicted that unless South Africa modifies its policy of strict racial segregation, "there is going to be a major crisis not only in Africa, but throughout the world."[43]

Yet, rather surprisingly, Bobby expressed shock at the news of Prime Minister Verwoerd's assassination.

> I am deeply shocked by the assassination of Prime Minister Verwoerd. Violence is not an answer to problems that must be worked out between people, with compassion and understanding on both sides. Mrs. Kennedy and I extend our deepest sympathies to the Prime Minister's family.[44]

[41] Shannon, *op cit.*, p. 139.
[42] *Ibid.*, p. 141.
[43] *U.S. News & World Report,* June 20, 1966.
[44] Statement, September 6, 1966.

In general, he seemed to settle on a policy of no direc involvement in South Africa's affairs, leaving to the whit leadership of that nation the responsibility for elimina ing its inhumane and morally intolerable program a apartheid.

I stressed that it was up to South Africa to solve its raci problems, that all any outsider could do was to urge a con mon effort in our own countries and around the world an show that progress is possible.[45]

Foreign Aid: Investment or Give-away

A much-contested aspect of United States policy tc ward the underdeveloped world has been that of foreig aid. Many label the billions America has dispensed t Asia, Africa, the Middle East, and Latin America sinc the enunciation of President Truman's Point Four pr(gram in 1949 as a colossal "giveaway" which has bough us few friends. Aid supporters counter that the Marsha Plan proved what an adequate assistance program ca produce, and that we require a program of similar mag nitude to help the nations of the Third World out c poverty and on the road to economic self-reliance. Judg ing by the size of recent economic-assistance appropria tions by Congress, it would appear the opponents of for eign aid are carrying the day.

Like his brother, Robert Kennedy was an arden advocate of increased economic aid to underdevelope(countries. At an American Legion Convention in 1962 h sought to sell this militant anti-Communist organizatio1 on foreign aid by invoking a cold-war rationale.

As I traveled around the world earlier this year, I some times wondered what this world of 1962 would have bee like if we had had no foreign aid programs in the years sinc the war—no Marshall Plan—no Point Four—no economic o military assistance to Latin America or Asia or Africa.

[45] *Look*, August 23, 1966.

That world would now have been largely conquered by communism or chaos—and our own country, isolated and beleaguered, surrounded by poverty and hostility, would have been in terrible peril.[46]

After entering the Senate, he began to decry the growing gap between the have and have-not nations not only for diplomatic reasons but for humanitarian ones as well. He criticized America for doing less than she can and should.

The disparity between our wealth and that of the underdeveloped countries of the world is even greater. The United States GNP is over $600 billion per year. The dozen developed countries of Western Europe and Japan together have a gross national product of half that much. The more than a hundred remaining countries of the non-Communist world —the countries with which this bill is concerned—share a total gross national product of another $300 billion. This means that the income of the average Indian or African or Libyan is less than $75 a year. It means that the average citizen of Paraguay or Indonesia or Iran has an income of only a little over $100 a year.

At the same time, our gross national product per person is over $2,500 per year and is rising far faster than is production or income in the less developed countries. But as our wealth grows—as the gap between us and the rest of the world increases—we have been doing less, not more, to meet our responsibilities. Fifteen years ago, we contributed to economic development in the rest of the world fully 10 percent of our federal budget, nearly 2 percent of our gross national product. But to meet the challenges of the 1960s, we are spending only 3 percent of our federal budget—one-half of 1 percent of our gross national product—less than one-third the effort we made fifteen years ago.[47]

[46] Speech, National Commanders' Dinner, American Legion Convention, Las Vegas, Nev., October 9, 1962.
[47] Speech, U.S. Senate, June 14, 1965.

Without abandoning his commitment to a generous aid program, he called for a thorough re-examination of current foreign-aid programs and guidelines.

At times our aid has seemed to support governments unwilling to undertake the basic reforms essential to economic development and to the political and economic freedom of their people.

The foreign aid program has often achieved major successes. But at other times, political considerations have seemed to compel assistance which did not contribute to real economic progress. And results have sometimes appeared slow, so that the goals to which we have directed ourselves in certain countries seemed nearly as distant as they did fifteen years ago.

As a result, many Americans—and some senators—who are deeply committed to the principle that we should help the rest of the world are nevertheless severely critical of our actual foreign aid program.

Clearly, it is time that we take full stock of where we are going, and how we will get there.[48]

Yet only four months before he had argued for the continuance of aid to Egypt in order to preserve diplomatic ties, despite the actions of the Nasser government.

Mr. President, the issue today is not whether we approve of Mr. Nasser and the reprehensible acts that have occurred, but whether congressional action cutting off food-for-peace aid to Egypt advances our basic objective to preserve peace in the Middle East and protect the security and freedom of Israel. President Johnson believes that our policy of pursuing these goals could be furthered by not tying the administration's hands in this matter at this time. He has requested support from the Senate on this, his first foreign policy test of the session. I believe he deserves that support. Furthermore, I have been impressed by the fact that members of the Appropriations Committee and the Foreign Affairs Committee have changed their opinion after receiving classified information about what can be accomplished by supporting President

[48] *Ibid.*

Johnson on this issue. So, I vote today to support the President —not to express my feelings about Mr. Nasser—and I do so firmly believing that it is in the interest of the United States and in the interest of furthering our objective of preserving peace in the Middle East and preventing aggression against Israel.[49]

He also took the position of many liberals that the best way to free economic aid from the suspicions and manipulations of international politics is to disburse it through multinational agencies.

We may work more through institutions such as the World Bank; other multilateral approaches to foreign assistance loans and grants, as recommended by the Foreign Relations Committee, may prove more effective than bilateral assistance programs.[50]

However, the truest picture of Bobby's position on foreign aid can be seen in his Senate voting record.

KEY KENNEDY VOTES ON FOREIGN AID

Foreign Assistance Act of 1965 (S. 1837). Amendment to reduce the fiscal 1966 and 1967 authorizations for foreign military assistance by $115 million each year. Rejected 38-43, June 11, 1965. (D. 28-25; R. 10-18). Kennedy: AGAINST.

Foreign Assistance Act of 1966 (S. 3584). Amendment to provide that the interest rate on development loans and Alliance for Progress loans for the first 10-year grace period be raised from 1 percent to 2 percent. Accepted 51-38, July 20, 1966. (D. 25-34; R. 26-4). Kennedy: AGAINST.

Foreign Assistance Act of 1966 (S. 3584). Amendment to prohibit aid to any Latin American country with an annual defense expenditure expected to exceed 3.5 percent of the gross national product of that country. Rejected 11-78, July 26, 1966. (D. 11-49; R. 0-29). Kennedy: FOR.

Foreign Assistance Act of 1966 (S. 3584). Amendment stating the sense of Congress that the action of any government giv-

---

[49] Statement, U.S. Senate, February 3, 1965.
[50] Speech, U.S. Senate, June 14, 1965.

ing financial backing to an arrangement under which an international consortium in West Europe would supply steel plants to Communist China was a "grave blow to the common defense of the free world and the safety of American and allied troops in Vietnam." Accepted 56-33, July 26, 1966. (D. 35-25; R. 21-8). Kennedy: AGAINST.

Chapter 23

The Arab-Israeli Crisis

The people of the Arab world are largely illiterate, wracked by disease and poverty, without the education and organization to enrich their harsh desert lands. For decades, even the wealth of their oil fields has gone into palaces and Cadillacs, above all into the armaments and trappings of war. For decades, irresponsible leaders have turned their people's frustration outward—toward the West, and to that tiny outpost of Western culture and ideals which is the state of Israel. Three times in twenty years, Israel has had to fight for her very existence; and three times, her arms and courage have allowed this tiny nation, with less than the population of Queens, to defeat the armies of nations with total populations of tens of millions.

Our commitment to Israel is clear. This gallant democracy, this nation of survivors from history's greatest example of man's capacity for senseless cruelty to his fellow man, cannot be allowed to succumb to the threats and assaults of her neighbors. And while this period of danger continues—until a lasting peace settlement is achieved—we must maintain our vigilance in her behalf.[1]

Since the creation of the state of Israel in 1948, the Middle East has been the setting for three bloody wars linked by border skirmishes and verbal threats. These conflicts have been both the flame and the fuel of an

[1] Address, Fordham University, New York, N.Y., June 10, 1967.

intense level of chauvinism and hatred in the area. Covering the Israeli war of independence in 1948 as a reporter for the *Boston Globe,* twenty-three-year-old Robert Kennedy had an opportunity to observe this enmity between Arab and Jew.

The loathing and hatred between Arab and Jew was an all-consuming thing. It was impossible in those days to talk to any representative of either side without becoming immediately aware that every person on both sides had been caught up in the conflict. Men had lost their reason.[2]

How had such mutual hostility developed? The story goes back nearly two thousand years, to the expulsion of the Jews from Palestine by the Romans in the year 70 A.D. This Diaspora marked the birth of a dream harbored by Jews throughout the world that someday they would be able to return as a people to the Promised Land. At last, in 1917, their chance came. Britain consented to establish a "Jewish homeland" in Palestine.

However, the Jews who immigrated to Palestine in the twenties and thirties, to buy land and create a new state, were regarded as unwanted outsiders by many of the Arabs, who had been living in this barren land since the days of Christ. Under the yoke of foreign oppressors themselves for centuries, these Arabs dreamed too of an independent Palestine. Increasingly, growing Arab nationalism and Zionism clashed, often violently.

After World War II, under mounting Jewish pressure, the British proposed dividing Palestine into two states, one Arab and one Jewish. The Arabs protested that justice dictated nothing less than one Palestine under Arab control. It might be true, they argued, that the Jews had been persecuted terribly in Europe. But then let Europe bear the cost of solving its own conscience, not the Arab world.

Without first reconciling these grave differences, the United Nations adopted the British partition plan, and in

[2] Robert F. Kennedy, *The Enemy Within* (New York: Harper & Brothers, 1960), p. 274.

May 1948 Israel formally became a state. Outraged, the Arab armies attacked the new nation, vowing to drive the Jews into the sea. Reporter Kennedy predicted the Jews would win, though badly outnumbered:

. . . because they had much more spirit and zest and determination and discipline. They were tougher inwardly and outwardly than the Arabs.[3]

Israel did win the 1948 war, but peace in the Middle East was not secured. The Arab nations steadfastly refused to sign a peace treaty, for this would have amounted to an unpalatable concession—recognition of the state of Israel. Instead, they declared they would not rest until the Jewish state was destroyed.

In less than a decade the Middle East was ablaze again. Following Egyptian President Nasser's nationalization of the Suez Canal (at which time he barred the passage of all Israeli ships) in 1956, and his blockade of the Gulf of Aqaba—Israel's only remaining water outlet to the East—Britain, France, and Israel together invaded Egypt. Within a matter of days Israel had routed Nasser's armies and driven across the Sinai Peninsula to the Suez. But again victory did not result in a peace treaty. A cease-fire was arranged which called for Israel to withdraw her armies, and the situation remained as explosive as before.

During this period Kennedy was a Senate committee investigator, and his views on the matter drew no public attention. But by the mid-sixties this had changed, for he was then a national figure and a senator from a state with a large Jewish population that demanded he take a stand.

He began by deploring the accelerating arms race in the area, which found the Soviets equipping the Arab armies at an alarming rate.

The Egyptian Army continues to grow in power. The

[3] R. E. Thompson and H. Meyers, *Robert F. Kennedy: The Brother Within* (New York: Macmillan, 1962), p. 78.

Unified Arab Command has forced Jordan to double the size of its army. Sophisticated weapons—jets, guided missiles, submarines—continue to flow in from the Soviet bloc. A new round of arms increases is under way.

These arms are a threat to peace. They waste valuable development capital. They threaten the only Near Eastern state with traditions of democracy. And this new round of arms shipments is particularly unfortunate because other signs have shown that peace is possible. For the irresponsible and dangerous nature of the course chosen by Israel's enemies is becoming more clear to the world every day.[4]

He attacked the Eisenhower Administration for having encouraged Arab militarism.

For economic and military aid are useless if all around Israel the United States sustains unpopular, autocratic regimes that have to whip up foreign issues in order to make a demagogic appeal to their own peoples.

But under the Republican Administration that was the prevailing condition. The Republicans tried to impose a military pact in the Middle East. It is symbolic of their policy that the Republican Secretary of State [Dulles], when he went to Cairo, presented the military dictator with a pair of pistols. . . .

In contrast, the Democrats have moved to foster socially purposeful regimes in all the countries of the Middle East. The emphasis has been on beating swords into plowshares. There were no pistols given in Cairo. On the contrary, the symbol of the Democratic regime is that when Prime Minister Eshkol and President Johnson met in Washington, they signed an agreement to work on a system for converting salt water to pure water—an agreement that looks twenty, even thirty years to the future.[5]

However, so long as the Soviets continued to pour arms into the area, he maintained that the United States

[4] Address, B'nai Zion Award Dinner, New York, N.Y., February 6, 1966.

[5] Campaign statement, October 22, 1964.

must assist Israel, to preserve the Middle Eastern balance of power.

We should continue to assure a reasonable balance between Israel's arms and the arms of those who threaten her security. In courage, in determination, in alertness, Israel is equal to any challenge, as she has been in the past. Her arms must also always be equal to any challenge.[6]

He made no secret of where his sympathies lay in the struggle. During the 1964 Senate campaign, when Senator Keating, his Republican opponent, accused him of being pro-Nasser, Kennedy replied:

I intend to work for, and fight for, policies that will make sure that no dictator is allowed to engage in aggression; no canal is allowed to be blocked to ships of all nations; no boycott is allowed on American companies; and above all, that no avenue toward final and peaceful settlement in the Middle East is left unexplored.

There are people in this state who are trying to create, for political reasons, the false impression that because I am for peace, I am somehow for Nasser.

I want to make it clear that I am unalterably opposed to every aspect of Nasser's provocative policies toward Israel and I support every necessary measure to neutralize and defeat the expansionist anti-Israel policies of Nasser and his collaborators in the Middle East.[7]

Furthermore, he felt that the United States had a responsibility to ensure Israel's continued existence.

I believe that the United States and other peace-loving nations should exert every effort toward peace and stability in the Middle East. We should tell Syria and Egypt that their behavior and threats against their neighbors are contrary to the security of the whole free world. We should insist that

[6] Address, B'nai Zion Award Dinner, New York, N.Y., February 6, 1966.

[7] Campaign speech, Young Israel of Eastern Parkway, Brooklyn, N.Y., October 27, 1964.

Egypt stop inciting the Arab countries against Israel, and stop its costly arms build-up, particularly in the field of nuclear weapons.[8]

To meet this responsibility, he suggested the following steps:

1. The United States should give Israel whatever aid is necessary to prevent it from becoming the victim of a military imbalance.
2. The United States should continue its economic aid, and at the appropriate time help construct the desalting plants which offer so much hope to the Israeli economy.
3. We should make it abundantly clear to every nation that Israel has every right to use the waters of the Jordan River in accordance with the unified plan.
4. We should support the territorial integrity of Israel against whatever threat it faces, from any nation or combination of nations.
5. We should strictly enforce the laws that require the ending of foreign aid to countries engaged in aggression or preparation for aggression.
6. And finally we should try once again to bring about face-to-face negotiations between Israel and the Arab states.[9]

At the B'nai Zion Award Dinner he presented three reasons why the United States must be committed to Israel:

One is the fact that Israel is not the aggressor, but is trying to live in peace and harmony with her neighbors. It is in the national interest of the United States to protect and encourage such a policy.

A second reason is Israel's importance to the new nations around the globe. It is in the national interest of the United States to preserve the reservoir of talent and energy and intelligence that is Israel. The third reason is that the Jews

[8] Speech, Mizrachi Women's Organization, New York, N.Y., October 6, 1964.

[9] Statement, Amalgamated Clothing Workers Housing Project, Bronx, N.Y., September 27, 1964.

of Israel are survivors of the greatest example in history of man's capacity for senseless cruelty to his fellow man. What was done in Europe under Hitler can never be forgotten. What was done must never be repeated. Much less can anything like it be permitted to happen to the survivors of the first holocaust, or to their children, for that would be—in the deepest sense—against the national interest of the United States, our heritage as free men, and our basic morality.[10]

In the Middle East, conditions continued to deteriorate. Nasser ordered U.N. forces patroling the Israel-Egypt border to leave; Egypt, Syria, and Jordan mobilized their armies; and on May 23, 1967, Nasser once again blockaded the Gulf of Aqaba. That night Kennedy delivered the following statement:

We meet tonight in an hour of crisis. A third of a world away, the state of Israel stands surrounded by her enemies —the target of terrorism and menacing troop concentration— her borders and ports in the shadow of hostile armies—her very existence at hazard. I come here tonight, at this late hour, to join with you in assessing this dangerous situation; and to join also in a determination that we shall do all that is necessary to ensure that Israel shall not succumb to these threats—and that she shall continue to survive and prosper in independence and freedom and security. . . .[11]

Bobby quickly placed the blame for the crisis on the Arab governments.

In large part, we must realize, the current tension does not arise from a true clash of interests between Israel and the Arab states, as indeed several Arab nations have recognized. Rather the tension arises from the internal strains and conflicts within and between the nations of the Arab world. The current government of Egypt and Syria, after all, were born in revolutions brought on at least in part by their crushing

[10] Address, B'nai Zion Award Dinner, New York, N.Y., February 6, 1966.

[11] Address, B'nai B'rith, District Lodge No. 1, Kiamesha Lake, N.Y., May 23, 1967.

defeat at the hands of Israel in the War of Independence. Having come to power on a promise to avenge their humiliation, these governments have never wavered in their hostile propaganda and actions, for fear of being toppled by elements even more chauvinistic than themselves.[12]

He urged the following four steps on the United States government:

. . . to ensure that the peace and the rights of all nations are preserved in the Near East, I urge:

First, that the United States government must continue to make clear the consequences of conflict in the Near East, and our interest in the prevention of any aggression.

Second, that we continue to seek the concurrent and cooperative action of all other interested parties, such as Britain and France, the signers of the 1950 Tripartite Declaration, and including the Soviet Union, to impress on all nations the need of a peaceful solution.

Third, that we continue to seek a restoration of the United Nations presence in the area. There are serious difficulties in the way of stationing U.N. ground forces where neither party wishes them on its territory. But a U.N. naval presence could safeguard free passage through the Gulf of Aqaba, in recognized international waters. I urge therefore that we immediately explore the possibility of such a United Nations sea patrol. . . .

Fourth, even as we strive to defuse the present crisis, we must also admit, as the Secretary-General has said, that we have too long ignored the basic long-term issues in the area —especially the need for internal development of the Arab nations, so that the frustrations of poverty and misery do not endanger peace in the region and in the world. The more advanced Arab states have long since abandoned any overt hostility to Israel, and live in peace with their neighbors. That must be our aim for the entire Near East.[13]

However, tension in the area continued to build, and on June 5 war broke out. This time Israel's victories were

[12] *Ibid.*
[13] *Ibid.*

spectacular. In less than ninety hours the Jews had reached Suez and regained control of the Gulf of Aqaba. Bobby voiced his admiration.

We meet today in danger—but also in hope. The fighting is not over. The war still takes its awful toll. The Arab nations, save only Jordan, still defy the cease-fire. But Israel has passed from her hour of maximum danger. She has already won victories for the ages. Throughout this country—and all over the world—men are moved and impressed by the bravery of Israel's people—for the last four days—as for the twenty years before.[14]

By June 9 Israel had occupied 26,000 square miles of Arab territory, an area approximately three times its own size. The Sinai Desert, the west bank of the Jordan River, and the Gaza Strip were held by Israel, and the city of Jerusalem was united under Jewish rule for the first time since the year 70.

It was Kennedy's hope that out of this violence might come the lasting peace that had eluded the Middle East for so long.

Now the time has truly come, as Abba Eban has said, to look not backward to belligerency, but forward to peace. After all the sufferings of the Second World War; after the struggle for independence; after twenty years of crisis and threat, and after the third war in a generation—after all this, and out of this greatest of efforts, must come a genuine and secure peace, a just and lasting peace, for this brave nation of Israel.[15]

Of all the causes of the conflict, there is one which has been removed: the dangerous and self-destructive delusion that Israel could ever be eliminated. That impediment to peace, at least, is one which has been most convincingly shattered.[16]

[14] Press release, June 8, 1967.
[15] *Ibid.*
[16] Address, State of Israel Bonds Dinner, New York, N.Y., June 22, 1967.

But he did not let his hope cloud his reason.

The causes of this conflict are not gone. For tens of millions of Arabs, new humiliation has been piled upon old hostility. For some leaders the temptation to use Israel as a scapegoat for their own domestic failures has become a need to use Israel as a target for a rage which might otherwise turn inward against themselves. Israel still stands as an island of hope and prosperity in a resentful sea of poverty and human misery. And the world's great power rivalries still storm over the entire region. Thus there is still great danger.[17]

Kennedy called upon the United States to step in and help prevent future conflicts. After cessation of the hostilities, he declared:

. . . the United States should now pledge substantial and material support for regional development in the Near East: but only on a basis of peaceful cooperation among Israel and her Arab neighbors.[18]

He went on to list five basic requirements for a "just and secure peace" in the Middle East.

First. There must be an unequivocal recognition, on the part of all countries in the Near East, that Israel is a nation, and that she exists. Israel's borders and her commerce are equal in dignity to those of any country in the world. She has a permanent right to exist and grow and prosper. This is no longer open to doubt—and it can never again be open to question.

Second. Israel has earned the right to the final peace settlement which has been denied her for twenty years—not just a military armistice. In that final settlement with her neighbors, and through binding and enforceable arrangements with other nations—including the United States—Israel's borders must be guaranteed beyond doubt. There should be no room

[17] *Ibid.*

[18] Statement, Nassau County Meeting on the Near East Crisis, New York, N.Y., June 12, 1967.

for any to again miscalculate Israel's own strength and purpose—or our determination that Israel shall survive.

Third. Israel's access to all international waterways must also be guaranteed; not just for this year; not just after a war; but for next year and the year after, and as long as freedom of the seas lasts for any other nation. Israel has a right not only to use her port of Eilat—she also has a right to free transit through the Suez Canal.

Fourth. This period of trial is not yet ended. Until it is ended—until a final peace settlement is secured—we should supply Israel with whatever food or economic assistance she requires. I have urged the Secretary of State to furnish such assistance—and he has assured me that it will be provided.

Fifth. Let us also hold out our hand of friendship to the Arab people—so long living in poverty and disease and misery, so long the tools of irresponsible propaganda, so long the greatest losers from the military adventures of their leaders. Israel must live, after all, among many times her number of Arabs; within a few decades the Arab peoples will number 200 million. Thus lasting peace in the Near East— like lasting peace elsewhere—depends on mutual understanding across borders and between all the people of the region. If Israel, which has sacrificed so much, can still appeal to the Arab peoples, as General Dayan did yesterday—in a spirit of friendship and brotherhood, surely we who have suffered nothing in this war can generously do the same. This should be a time, not for recriminations, but for understanding; not for reprisals but for a new and expanded commitment to a better life for all the people of the Near East.[19]

Yet in spite of all the talk and proposals, the Middle East situation remains unresolved. Israel contends she will return the occupied Arab lands only in exchange for a formal peace settlement—i.e., for recognition of her right to exist by the Arab world. But this is a step which most of the Arab governments do not feel they can afford to take at this time. So the crisis continues. Arms are being poured into the area. The refugee problem worsens. And no one knows how soon it will be before Arab and Israeli armies clash again.

[19] Press release, June 8, 1967.

Were it for convenience or from conviction, Israel had a good friend in Robert Kennedy, one on whom she could have counted for support and encouragement. Said Kennedy:

Israel's creation, and her continuing progress in the face of continual adversity, have written a new chapter in the annals of freedom and courage—a story that my children and yours will tell their descendants to the end of time.[20]

[20] Speech, American Friends of the Hebrew University, New York, N.Y., October 25, 1965.

Chapter 24

National Defense

> I believe that, as long as the instruments of peace
> are available, war is madness. Government must be
> strong wherever madness threatens the peace.[1]

When Dwight Eisenhower announced his candidacy for
the Republican presidential nomination in 1952, much
of America already had become frustrated and fatigued
by the demands and pressures of the cold war. Truman's
policy of simply containing Communist expansion by
means of a nuclear deterrent and a capacity to fight limited wars struck many Americans as too passive and
too expensive. Containment seemed only to have mired
us in an international bog of unending crises with no
prospect of clear-cut victory in sight—Korea being a
premier case in point.

Historically, America's response to a threat to her
security was all-out war aimed at eliminating this diversion from "business as usual." Many people could not
understand why this Communist diversion was not handled in the same manner; they yearned for the days when
the nation's only concerns had been domestic and when
the crises, coups, and skirmishes that are forever breaking out in some obscure part of the globe could be rele-
gated to the back pages of the newspaper. In short, containment had been constructed upon an assumption of
American patience, and in less than five years that patience was found wanting.

[1] Robert F. Kennedy, *The Pursuit of Justice* (New York: Harper
& Row, 1965), p. 11.

465

Responding to this national mood of unrest and disillusionment, the Eisenhower Administration proposed a new defense strategy which was heralded as both more aggressive and less expensive. Known as "massive retaliation," this approach called for the United States to draw a clearly defined line around the Sino-Soviet bloc and then to warn Peking and Moscow that any incursions across that line—no matter how limited—would be met with the nuclear strike power of the Strategic Air Command.

"Massive retaliation" certainly sounded more dynamic than "containment," and it had one more essential difference. The containment policy had also relied upon air-atomic striking power to deter a total attack upon either the United States or its "first line of defense" in Europe. But in Asia, once the Communists had faced him with a limited aggression, Truman had met this challenge with local ground resistance. In other words, Truman's containment policy posited the need to be prepared to fight limited engagements as part of any effective strategy to deter Communist expansion. In contrast, the Eisenhower Administration believed that it would never be necessary to fight a limited war with an effective policy of massive retaliation. Informed in advance that we would regard any aggression, anywhere, as a direct threat to our security and that we would respond accordingly with nuclear weapons, the Soviets and Chinese would quickly realize that the cost of any adventure would overwhelmingly outweigh the benefits. The anticipated result of this policy: the elimination of the Communist threat.

Thus massive retaliation had the political advantage of reasserting the old American doctrine of either abstaining or fighting a total war. Furthermore, it was obviously considerably cheaper to concentrate military spending upon a one-weapon system (nuclear) than to build up and maintain large balanced forces to meet any contingency. Its only drawback was that it did not work.

Moscow and Peking simply did not believe we would initiate a nuclear holocaust that would destroy the world over a Chinese-backed guerrilla campaign in Southeast Asia or a Soviet-inspired coup in Latin America, and they were right. Our inaction in Indochina in 1954 proved it. So they avoided confronting us in North America or in Western Europe where they believed we might be willing to risk a nuclear exchange, and concentrated their activities in the underdeveloped world, always careful never to pose a direct military threat to us. As a result, we quickly found ourselves faced with a dilemma of suicide or surrender every time the Communists confronted us with a limited challenge, for we had dismantled our military machinery for coping with local ground wars as superfluous. And time and again throughout the fifties we were forced to take the only sane of these two unacceptable alternatives—surrender.

It was clear that our exclusive reliance on strategic air power—at a time when World War III was already a pseudonym for suicide—had seriously weakened our ability to contain communism. As John Spanier wrote, "Nuclear bombs were just *too* powerful; they were *too* enormously destructive to be used in any situation but the ultimate one. Our strategic power was—ironically—*so* great that it tended to paralyze our will to use it; it therefore paralyzed our diplomacy as well."

It was in the midst of this U.S. military and diplomatic paralysis that John F. Kennedy entered the White House. Though his presidential campaign had centered on the so-called "missile gap" between the Soviet Union and the United States—a gap which turned out to be mythical— the new President realized that America's Achilles' heel was her inability to respond effectively to limited military thrusts. Once in office, he and Secretary of Defense McNamara began the task of rebuilding and modernizing U.S. ground forces and developing techniques of antiguerrilla warfare and counterinsurgency.

"Balanced Deterrent"

Robert Kennedy's views on national defense first took shape, within this context. Reflecting the administration's position during the early sixties, he frequently stressed the importance of developing a balanced deterrent to Communist aggression:

. . . If the free world is to survive, it must accept the responsibility to resist aggression. And aggression in the contemporary world takes a multitude of forms. It therefore requires a variety of responses. It is our purpose to develop balanced military forces, capable of countering every form of attack, from the nuclear strike to a guerrilla attack, and then use the interval thus gained to work unceasingly toward disarmament and peace.[2]

For only through America's unquestioned capacity to wage war, he argued, could world peace be preserved.

With the irony of a paradoxical world, the surest guarantee of peace at present is the power to wage war. The United States has that power. It comes from our programs of strength and deterrence. Without this strength, we could not have achieved the truly momentous victory of the 1962 Cuban missile crisis. Without this strength we cannot reasonably expect to achieve other objectives even at the conference table in our constant pursuit of peace.

This is not really a controversial point. We are almost all agreed that American nuclear superiority is essential to unanimous nuclear restraint.[3]

The Need for a Nuclear Arsenal

All this talk of balanced deterrent and conventional ground forces quickly led some Americans to ask whether the Kennedy Administration possessed the "will" to employ nuclear weapons in a crisis. Kennedy assured them that his brother would push the button if the Soviets gave him no choice.

MR. SPIVAK: Mr. Kennedy, Senator Margaret Chase Smith said in the Senate the other day that the Kennedy Administration apparently lacked the will to use nuclear weapons. You know your brother better probably than almost anybody else. Do

[2] Speech, American Association of University Professors, University of South Carolina Chapter, Columbia, S.C., April 25, 1963.

[3] Kennedy, *op. cit.*, p. 130.

you think he has the will to use nuclear weapons if necessary?

RFK: I would say first that that is probably a matter that takes more of his time and more of his thoughts than anything else, because when we are talking about using nuclear weapons, we are talking about, almost, the destruction of the human race—at least a very large proportion of it. But on this question of whether when in a particular area, as we are in Berlin at the present time, there is no question that he is prepared to use nuclear weapons.

MR. SPIVAK: The United States has been building up its conventional forces in Europe, and this has confused a great many people. Isn't there danger, as some military men believe, that this serves to confirm in Mr. Khrushchev's mind that the United States would not use nuclear weapons?

RFK: I think we have built up our nuclear weapons force also. As Secretary of Defense McNamara has said, we spent more than $2 billion extra on nuclear weapons.

What we are talking about really is this tremendous destruction, and quick destruction, if we use nuclear weapons. The President doesn't want the decision to be one of surrender or the use of nuclear weapons. He wants to be able to have even a possibility of a third alternative, to at least explore a possibility, and maybe it is going to come to that, but at least if we have conventional forces as well as our nuclear forces, maybe in the last moment, in the last analysis, we are going to be able to preserve peace. I think we are going to have to take every calculation, make every effort to try to keep it out of nuclear warfare. If it comes to that, he is prepared to do it, but we would hope that it wouldn't come to that.[4]

The "missile gap" of the 1960 campaign having been miraculously transformed into "U.S. nuclear superiority" upon John Kennedy's election, his brother pledged that the United States would maintain that superiority at all costs.

We are committed to maintaining a nuclear force strong enough and impregnable enough to ride out any conceivable nuclear attack and retain enough striking power to annihilate

[4] "Meet the Press" (NBC-TV), September 24, 1961.

any conceivable attacker. We have such a force today and we are budgeting some $1.5 billion over the level proposed in January 1961 to see to it that we keep it that way.[5]

Well, any time you have a nuclear blast, there is no question that it increases the fallout in the atmosphere, and so the President and the National Security Council are making a study, and had a preliminary report last week and will have further reports over the period of the next month, on what can be done in this field and what should be done to insure what is really our primary interest—to insure that the lead over the Soviet Union in this field is kept and maintained. I think that everything else is secondary to that, because the only reason that we have—the only reason that we have relative peace in the world today is the fact that we have a nuclear capability. We have to continue to have that, and it has to continue to be superior to the Soviet Union. That is the President's intention and all of his efforts in this field over the period of the next two months are going to be aimed at maintaining that superiority.[6]

Guerrilla Warfare and Counterinsurgency

During this same period Robert Kennedy came to be regarded as "Mr. Counterinsurgency" in government circles. Assigned by the President to a special committee to review the abortive invasion of Cuba at the Bay of Pigs in April 1961, he emerged from that investigative venture a zealous convert to the doctrines of guerrilla warfare. He began to read and quote from the writings of Mao Tse-tung. As William Shannon says, "He became convinced that it is essential for the success of U.S. foreign policy to develop effective techniques to combat Communist use of terrorism, low-level violence, and brush-fire wars." Later that year, when John Kennedy designated a small group of high officials to supervise

[5] Speech, National Commanders' Dinner, American Legion Convention, Las Vegas, Nev., October 9, 1962.
[6] Answer to question following speech, Associated Press Managing Editors luncheon, Dallas, Tex., November 15, 1961.

U.S. counterinsurgency efforts, Bobby was reputedly its most active and committed member.

The urgent need for a strategy and tactics to counter "wars of national liberation" or insurgency, he contended, is clearly documented by the history of the past twenty years.

President Kennedy said in 1961, technology has made all-out war highly unlikely because if it comes it means the end of civilization as we know it. And we are faced instead, he said, with another kind of war—new in its intensity, ancient in its origin—war by guerrillas, subversives, insurgents, assassins, war by ambush instead of by combat; by infiltration instead of aggression, seeking victory by eroding and exhausting the enemy instead of engaging him.

This war has worn many faces.

It has been a war for independence from external domination, as in Algeria and Cyprus and Hungary.

It has been a war for regional or tribal identity, as in Burma or Iraq or in the Naga Hills of India.

And it has been a war for communism, as in Malaya or Venezuela or South Vietnam.

All these wars, of which there have been more than a score since World War II, offer us lessons for the future, for the decades of revolutionary war which are the challenge ahead.[7]

The struggle in Vietnam offered the Kennedy Administration its first real opportunity to test its reading of these "lessons for the future." American strategy was to prepare indigenous anti-Communist forces to defend themselves against insurgent movements; the U.S. would advise and equip, but not fight. With this in mind, a special force of Green Berets was created to train and inspire the regular army of South Vietnam to defeat the Viet Cong guerrillas and thus demonstrate to the world that Communist-backed "wars of liberation" would not be allowed to succeed.

However, when Robert Kennedy resigned from the

[7] Address, International Police Academy commencement, Washington, D.C., July 9, 1965.

Johnson Cabinet in August of 1964 to run for the Senate, it was already clear that our hopes were not being realized. The South Vietnamese army was being soundly beaten and the Saigon government was on the verge of collapse. The world was learning a lesson, but not the one we had sought to teach; a war of national liberation was definitely succeeding.

Looking back over three years of intensive effort in the field of counterinsurgency, Bobby tried to sound optimistic and unshaken. In fact, he had to be disappointed.

We have made a beginning. We have achieved some notable successes, but we have not mastered the art of counterinsurgency. More importantly, perhaps, in a practical sense, we have not perfected the technique of training foreign nationals to defend themselves against Communist terrorism and guerrilla penetration. This kind of warfare can be long-drawn-out and costly, but if communism is to be stopped, it is necessary. And we mean to see this job through to the finish.[8]

In 1964, one year before his book was published, RFK had already begun to shift away from a narrowly military approach to the problem of counterinsurgency.

Having an adequate defense against terrorism is only part of the answer, however. To the extent that guerrilla warfare and terrorism arise from the conditions of a desperate people, we know that they cannot be put down by force alone. The people themselves must have some hope for the future. There must be a realistic basis for faith in some alternative to communism.

It is for that reason that the United States must continue to expand its efforts to reach the peoples of other nations, particularly young people in the rapidly developing southern continents. Governments may come and go, but in the long run the future will be determined by the needs and aspirations of these young people.[9]

[8] Kennedy, *op cit.*, p. 132.
[9] *Ibid.*, pp. 133-134.

Once he went to the Senate, his emphasis increasingly became social-psychological and political. Before an audience of Green Berets at Fort Bragg he spoke of the complexities of maintaining friendly governments in the Third World.

This job requires the greatest of abilities; the ability to teach by example—the ability to teach without compulsion, to give without condescension, to share poverty and hardships with those you help—to serve as living proof that our aim for these people is not domination, but cooperation; not an American empire, but a world of free and independent states; not sterile anticommunism, but a better and a freer life for all the people of the world.

We know, and the world knows, that this will be the struggle of the coming decades. It is not like other wars.

We cannot hate our enemies—for they fight in the name of our own ideals.

We cannot win with mere military force—for guns cannot fill empty stomachs, napalm cannot cure the sick, and bombs cannot teach a child to read.

Neither can our air wings, or our divisions, give to the dispossessed people of the world a sense of individual dignity, or self-sufficiency, or a promise for their children's future.

For these things men will fight to the death; they will never stop fighting.[10]

In July of 1965, in an address at the International Police Academy commencement exercises in Washington, Kennedy delivered his most complete statement on the problems of successfully countering anti-American movements in Asia, Africa, and Latin America. He opened by confronting, if not exactly resolving, the sticky question of differentiating genuine popular revolutions from externally directed minority takeovers.

I am a citizen of a nation which itself was born in a war for national liberation. It would be against our deepest traditions to oppose any genuine popular revolution. But acts of aggression, masquerading as national revolutions, pose a

[10] Speech, Fort Bragg, N.C., May 29, 1965.

difficult problem. Revolutionary war carried on with the outside support of the Soviet Union, or of China, or of others
of their allies, offers the greatest threat to the world order of
free and independent states to which all nations pledged
themselves in the charter of the United Nations.

But if these conflicts are called wars, and have deep international consequences, they are at the same time not wars
—and their outcome is determined by internal factors. For
their essence is political—by an idea and a faith, by promise
and performance. Governments resist such challenges only
by being effective and responsive to the needs of their
people.[11]

He proceeded to warn against evaluating other governments and nations strictly in the light of their similarity
to the American system, and, in marked contrast to his
pre-Senate views, denigrated the primacy of military
considerations in existing counterinsurgency programs.

Effective and representative government can, of course,
take many forms. What is right for the United States may not
be right for your countries, and others would have still other
convictions on the precise form government should take—or
ownership and control of the means of production, on the
distribution of riches and the level of taxation, on the range
of domestic and international policy. These questions must
always be for each nation and people to decide for itself.
So long as their choice is their own, not imposed from outside or by dicatorship of left or right, it must be respected
by all others. If we wish to encourage the spread of democracy and freedom, primary reliance must be on the force of
our example: on the qualities of the societies we build in our
own countries—what we stand for at home and abroad.[12]

In the 1960s it should not be necessary to repeat that the
great struggle of the coming decades is one for the hearts and
minds of men. But too often, of late, we have heard instead
the language of gadgets—of force-ratios and oil blots, tech-

[11] Address, International Police Academy commencement, Washington, D.C., July 9, 1965.
[12] *Ibid.*

niques and technology—of bombs or grena
with special violence, of guns which shoc
of new uses for helicopters and special vehi

Men's allegiance, however, and this kinc
won by superior force, by the might of nu
sophistication of technology. On the tiny islan
British Army had 110 soldiers and policemen
ber of EOKA, which never numbered more th   ..w hundred terrorists; yet Britain had to surrender control of the
island within five years after the rebellion began. In the Philippines, by contrast, Ramón Magsaysay had an army of only
50,000 to fight 15,000 Huks who were at the gates of
Manila when he took office as Defense Minister. His forces
had no special modern armament; yet within four years the
Huk Rebellion was crushed and its leaders had surrendered.

But why are mere numbers, or the possession of advanced
weapons, not conclusive? And how can these conflicts be won
without such force, or modern technology.[13]

The following remarks, as he attempted to answer his
own questions, are of particular interest when applied to
the situation in Southeast Asia. Kennedy did not break
with the Johnson Administration over Vietnam until
seven months later, but the roots of that break with the
President are already emerging in this speech.

One answer lies in the character of military force itself.
Conventional military force—and all our advanced weapons
technology—are useful only to destroy. But a government
cannot make war on its own people, cannot destroy its own
country. To do so is to abandon its reason for existence—its
responsibility to its people—and its claim to their allegiance.
Suppose, for example, that a government force is fired upon
from a village, or that rebels have forced the village to fly
the insurgent flag. A government which attacks that village
from the air, or with heavy artillery, abandons the first duty
of any government worthy of the name. . . .

Guns and bombs cannot build—cannot fill empty stomachs
or educate children, cannot build homes or heal the sick. But
these are the ends for which men establish and obey govern-

[13] *Ibid.*

; they will give their allegiance only to government which meets these needs.

In the Philippines, for example, Magsaysay pursued the Huks vigorously. But he offered much more than conflict to the people. First, he ensured an honest election throughout the country; General Edward Lansdale has said that this election marked the turning point of the war. Second, a thorough land reform was begun; and it was enforced through such devices as special landlord-tenant courts which were held from jeeps so that the judges would be available to peasants in isolated rural areas. There followed many other reforms directed at the welfare of the people.

We all know the necessity for this political dimension to our action. Too often, however, it is not given the priority it demands, for we allow the military dimension to become more urgent and insistent. But reform, and the hope it brings, cannot be postponed. For insurgents of the modern variety continually institute at least a facsimile of such reforms in every area they control. In Vietnam, in China, in Cuba, to name but three, Communist insurgents have abolished landlordism, organized adult education classes, and established courts in all areas they occupied—even in many which they controlled only at night. They have thus entered into direct competition with the established government. When the defenders have ignored reform, the hopes of the people could only center on the insurgents. And when a victorious government army is followed by landlords collecting back rents from the peasants, we should not wonder that the insurgents often attract the allegiance of the peasants. It does little good to warn that the end result of communism will be dictatorship and exploitation; the deeds of today speak most loudly—if not most truly—on whose promises will be kept tomorrow.[14]

A second reason for the inadequacy of a predominantly military approach to counterinsurgency, he continued:

. . . is that it can give no hope. Force is neutral, it has no program. Every insurgent movement lives not primarily on force, but on a dream—of independence, of justice, of progress, of a better life for one's children. For such dreams

[14] *Ibid.*

men will undergo great hardship and sacrifice—as we have done for our dream, as you have done and are doing for your own. Without a vision of the future to offer, a government can demand no sacrifice, no resistance to insurgent terror or blandishments.

Not only is the military approach deficient in itself. More dangerously, it tends to obscure and prevent essential political action. In conventional war the aim is to kill the enemy. But the essence of successful counterinsurgency is not to kill, but to bring the insurgent back into the national life. In Malaya the British achieved great success by distributing photographs of prisoners—half-starved and ragged when captured, well-fed and smiling after internment. Bonuses were given for arms turned in to the government, with no questions asked; amnesty was offered to rebels who would surrender. Such devices were carried further in the Philippines; there Huks who surrendered were settled with families on newly cleared agricultural land of their own. George Marshall once said, "Let's not talk about this matter too much in military terms; to do so might make it a military problem." Too often we forget that wisdom.

Another central need of counterinsurgency effort is for adherence to fundamental rules of law and fair dealing. It may seem strange to assert that a legal government should bind itself by restrictions, such as the Geneva Convention, in the midst of an assault on its existence. But the government is competing with a rival administration, which often ruthlessly enforces its own rules of fair dealing with the people: no excessive taxation, no stealing (except from the rich), no physical maltreatment (except of those who aid the government). The government must match and overmatch the insurgents in this respect, punishing and rewarding wisely and consistently—as in Malaya, where villages were carefully graded on their help to the rebels, and food and equipment were distributed accordingly. Such a precise system of rewards and penalties is characteristic of civilian and political action—not of military force.[15]

How, then, are these conflicts to be won without recourse to force? Kennedy proposed a sort of policy, though

[15] Ibid.

in such general terms that it is questionable whether a government could act upon it.

It has also been said that an insurgency cannot be put down as long as it is supplied from, and can seek sanctuary in, a neighboring country. No matter what assistance they receive from outside, however, insurgents stand or fall on their political success. Without popular support, they become conventional invaders—and can be dealt with by conventional means.

I think the history of the last twenty years demonstrates beyond doubt that our approach to revolutionary war must be political—political first, political last, political always. Where the needs and grievances of the people begin to be met by the political process, insurgency loses its popular character and becomes a police problem—as it did in Venezuela and Colombia, in the Philippines and Malaya.

Military force of varying intensity will undoubtedly be a major component of a revolutionary war. I would like, in this connection, to make an important distinction. Just as mere military force cannot win political victories, so military aggression cannot be defeated by solely political means. If guerrillas are infiltrated into a country from outside, that aggression, like any invasion, must be met by armed force of sufficient power to defeat it. Where the threat is partly political and partly military, it must be met on its own grounds, with a response measured to its scope. To meet the political threat of revolutionary war, then, what are the essential forms of political action?

At the outset must be restated the need for effective and responsible government. Especially is this true in the rural areas in which live from 75 to 90 percent of the people of the developing nations. . . .

Most important, we must impart hope—hope for progress, fulfilled as quickly as circumstances permit. In many countries, land reform is the essential need of the vast majority of the people; it must receive central priority. Education is always vital—not just for the cities, not even only for children; but for every peasant who can learn to read, or drive a tractor, or even use a hoe instead of a forked stick.

We must also build all the other structures that help to make up a stable society—such as labor unions, and farmer cooperatives for those who work with their hands and their backs; student groups for the nation's new emerging leaders; political parties to give all men a voice in the councils of government. The political coloration of these groups is less important than the fact of their existence; simply by being organized, by being there, they add stability and permanence. Thus the British in Malaya did not attempt to break up the Communist labor union movement, so long as it did not engage in active subversion.[16]

In a statement on the activities of Communist guerrillas in Guatemala issued a year and a half after his International Police Academy speech, Kennedy was still making the same basic points.

As to the threat from the guerrillas, it is unfortunately apparent that our military aid program, over the years, has not sufficiently trained or motivated the Guatemalan Army to deal with them. The difficulties are not in any shortage of material equipment, but in poorly paid, unmotivated soldiers and an overmanned, wasteful, and indolent corps of officers. But beyond the military problem is the more fundamental question of whether the government is determined to meet the demands of its people for justice and hope for a better life. The people of Guatemala, like men and women throughout the hemisphere, have heard the message of our times. They want land and education and liberty and a share in decision, a stake in the government which asks their allegiance. President Mendez understands this fact, but years of promise have yielded little fulfillment. Unless the government is able to move quickly, with broad support, to meet these just demands, there will be no peace, security, or progress—only a desperate surge, sooner or later, to secure by force what has been too long denied.[17]

Most of Kennedy's later remarks on this aspect of national defense are interspersed throughout his statements on Vietnam. They tend to be consistent with the

[16] *Ibid.*
[17] Statement, December 3, 1966.

views expressed in the Police Academy address and can be found in Chapter 26.

The Space Race

Time and again, as we have witnessed throughout this examination of his public record, Robert Kennedy substantially altered his positions on major issues after leaving the Johnson Cabinet in 1964. His views on the space race with the Soviets—a competition motivated in part by national defense considerations—are no exception.

During his brother's tenure as President, Kennedy regarded the exploration of space as a contest between the world's two superpowers in which the United States must not come out second best.

We mean to lead the world in the exploration of space. We are determined to see that space is filled with instruments of knowledge and understanding, not weapons of war and mass destruction. We will be constantly alert against the hostile misuse of space as we stand today firmly against the hostile misuse of the land, sea or air. But it is our purpose to explore space without adding fuel to the fire of war. . . .

In some aspects of the space program we are behind. But we do not intend to stay behind. We intend to move ahead and we are making the effort to do so.[18]

When he entered the Senate his priorities shifted. He no longer regarded beating the Russians to the moon as a national objective which merited the resources being devoted to it. And in 1965, 1966, and 1967, Kennedy was one of a small group of senators who unsuccessfully sought to reduce the budget of the National Aeronautics and Space Administration by a quarter of a billion dollars.

[18] Speech, National Commanders' Dinner, American Legion Convention, Las Vegas, Nev., October 9, 1962.

The Draft and the G.I. Bill

On the question of the military draft, Robert Kennedy was as outspoken in his criticism as his brother, Senator Edward Kennedy of Massachusetts. Originally he was reluctant to either criticize the draft or call for major reform. Asked by a Rochester University student during the 1964 Senate campaign whether he would favor ending the draft, Kennedy cautiously replied:

I would be opposed to eliminating the draft at this time. There is a study being made by the Secretary of Defense in which some of these questions were raised. The study is going to be made available as to what the implications of it would be. Where are we going to get the manpower for the functions that we need to perform around the world? Until I have had a chance to examine that study, I would be opposed to eliminating the draft.[19]

However, by 1965 he was a vigorous supporter of brother Teddy's proposal to substitute a no-exemption lottery for the present selective service system. He began calling for the elimination of certain inequities in the draft. As he explained on the floor of the Senate:

[Those in the armed services] are special for yet another reason; they serve because they have less money than others, equally well qualified, who do not serve. By regulation, simply being in a college or university—for however many years, no matter the quality of the school or the importance of the course of study—guarantees a deferment.

As we all know, it is far more likely that as between two students of equal merit, the wealthier is far more likely to attend college. . . .

So our draft laws discriminate among our young men on the ground of wealth. And since most enlistments are undertaken by those who expect to be drafted, the net result is that our armed services are disproportionately made up of our less-fortunate young men.[20]

[19] Answer to question following speech, University of Rochester, Rochester, N.Y., September 29, 1964.
[20] Statement, U.S. Senate, July 16, 1965.

It was presumably because of the disproportionate number of the sons of the poor in the armed services that Kennedy took it upon himself in that speech to champion the Cold War G.I. Bill. He attacked Veterans' Administration opposition in no uncertain terms.

But the reward for this service has been only further disadvantage. They have lost two years of their lives—time which their more fortunate contemporaries have spent in school or on the job. The result is that veterans aged twenty to twenty-four have an unemployment rate of 9 percent as opposed to only 7.4 percent for nonveterans. . . .

We ask these young men to give up two or three or four years away from their homes and their families—often to serve in ports of danger and hardship—we do so on a discriminatory basis—and then we allow them to suffer greater unemployment, and work at lower-paying jobs, than those who do not serve.

I do not think that this country can so ill reward those who serve it.

For this intolerable situation, S. 9 is an excellent remedy.

This bill would make available to veterans educational benefits roughly comparable to those we gratefully gave the veterans of World War II and Korea.

Each day of service would entitle them to 1½ days of education or training, for a period of up to 36 months of study. For each month of full-time study the veterans would receive $110 if single, $135 with one dependent, $160 with two or more; lesser benefits would be provided for part-time study or training. This program is simple. It meets the needs of the veterans. And it is proved by experience. . . .

But the Veterans' Administration and the Department of Defense and the Bureau of the Budget do oppose it. How can they do so? Their witnesses came before the Subcommittee on Veterans' Affairs with opinions, not facts; with surmises instead of knowledge; with assertions unsupported by experience or logic. They asserted that in-service training is meeting the educational needs of servicemen—and none could say how many get such training, or what kinds are offered.

Among five representatives of the Veterans' Administration, not one could tell the committee even the age at which young men are being drafted. They made flat errors of important fact—for example, the VA said that present veterans serve for a relatively short time, when in fact the average term of service is now six months longer than it was during the Korean conflict. And they took positions that simply made no sense at all. Their arguments against the bill can be briefly stated and answered. They object to its cost; but this bill will pay for itself two or three times over. The VA also says that service is now more limited and less disruptive than under wartime conditions. But in fact it is of longer average duration, 28.2 months as against 22.6 months in Korea; the uncertainties of fighting in Vietnam or tension in Berlin or crisis over Cuba are as great as those of previous emergencies; and the veteran of today, with the reserve obligation which often follows active duty, is all too likely to be recalled to service—as many were in 1961. . . .

It has been proposed here that the benefits of this bill be applied only to those serving in "areas of hostilities." I think such a restriction harmful. First, it might cause designation of such areas at an unpropitious time or place from the standpoint of foreign affairs.

Second, it would add to the vagaries of the draft the further happenstance of military assignment.

Even in World War II, only a minority served in overseas fighting zones—but all who served made sacrifices, and all were eligible for the G.I. bill. That should be the case today.[21]

The Senator closed his speech as follows:

There is a poem on a sentry box at Gibraltar:

God and the soldier all men adore
In a time of trouble and no more.
For when war is over and all things righted,
God is neglected and the old soldier slighted.

I think we can do better than that in this country. I think we will.[22]

[21] *Ibid.*
[22] *Ibid.*

Chapter 25

The Bomb

> [We must] enlist the help of the U.N. and all other nations—including Communist China—to try to ban nuclear weapons.[1]

Since Hiroshima, almost a quarter-century ago, a race against time has been under way between the technological capability to destroy civilization and the political skill to save it. Up to now the politicians have been running a dangerously poor second.

Each year men of every nation mount the speaker's stand at the U.N. and eloquently warn the peoples of the world that unless nuclear weapons are effectively controlled or eliminated mankind will ultimately commit suicide. Yet they have done nothing of consequence to put off the day when the bombs will fall and obliterate civilization.

This inaction can only be judged by history as madness. For not even the diplomats who easily accept Clausewitz' definition of war as the continuation of politics by other means can rationally integrate the use of nuclear weapons into their international scheme of things. If contemporary diplomacy has one inviolable commitment, it is to the survival of the nation-state. And all-out nuclear war renders that commitment meaningless. Between 80 and 160 million Americans can expect to die within the first twenty-four hours of a full-scale nuclear exchange, and as Khrushchev put it, the living would envy the dead. All parties to such a conflict would be

[1] *U.S. News & World Report*, March 28, 1966

damaged beyond recognition. Given these consequences, no sane man can argue that any national interests would be served by such an exchange. Nonetheless, the issue of nuclear disarmament remains in a state of diplomatic deadlock, entangled in mutual distrust, fears of altering the balance of power, and unbridled chauvinism.

Test Bans

The deadlock appeared to give slightly in 1958, when the United States and the Soviet Union informally agreed to halt the testing of nuclear devices in the atmosphere. But, during the first year of the Kennedy Administration the Russians unexpectedly ended the moratorium with the detonation of a series of multimegaton hydrogen blasts over the Pacific. Apparently caught off guard, Washington did not respond immediately to this breach of good faith, though it was speculated that the United States would have no choice but to resume testing.

During this brief deliberation before the President decided to authorize American atmospheric nuclear tests, while on a good-will mission in the Far East, Robert Kennedy was asked by a group of anxious Japanese labor leaders whether the United States would also start testing.

The reason that testing will be resumed, if it is, is so that the United States and the Free World cannot be blackmailed into surrender by being weak . . .

He [President Kennedy] appeared before the United Nations and asked that it be turned over to them as far as inspection of bombs and atomic weapons is concerned. Some international authority could not only determine who was producing bombs, who was testing, but also as far as the transfer of atomic weapons.

Our government and the American people feel this is the most important issue facing mankind; and I can understand your own personal concern, having suffered in the war as you did.

All I can say is that the greatest effort is being made in

this area. Unfortunately, we do not live in a world in which we can just unilaterally disarm and expect to survive.

This lesson was brought home to us in Geneva. While we were discussing in good faith, they were making plans for testing. If it happened once, it certainly can happen again.[2]

On September 24, 1963, three of the five nuclear nations—the United States, the U.S.S.R., and Great Britain —entered into a formal treaty banning the testing of nuclear weapons in the atmosphere; France and Red China, feeling their national nuclear capabilities far from developed, refused to become parties to the agreement. Despite the limited effect of the test-ban treaty, Kennedy saw it as a meaningful step forward and attempted to draw some lessons in diplomacy from the circumstances that led to its conclusion.

The leaders of the world face no greater task than that of avoiding nuclear war. While preserving the cause of freedom we must seek abolition of war through programs of general and complete disarmament. The Test-Ban Treaty of 1963 represents a significant beginning in this immense undertaking.

We cannot pretend that such beginnings signal a millennium or an armistice in the cold war. They are modest steps. But they are steps *forward,* steps toward the ultimate goal of effective and reliable international controls over the destructive power of nations. Until such a goal can be achieved, however, we have no other choice to insure that we can defend our country and help other peoples who are willing to work for their own independence.

With the irony of a paradoxical world, the surest guarantee of peace at present is the power for war. The United States has that power. It comes from our programs of strength and deterrence—programs to which this institute has made such substantial contributions for so many years. Without this strength, we could not have achieved the truly momentous victory of the 1962 Cuban missile crisis. Without this strength

[2] Round table discussion with labor union representatives, Tokyo, Japan, February 9, 1962.

we cannot reasonably expect to achieve other objectives even at the conference table in our constant pursuit of peace.[3]

[3] Speech, California Institute of Technology, Pasadena, Calif., June 8, 1964.

The whole world has benefited by that treaty. The vicious circle of ever larger tests, of increasing poison in the air, has at last been broken.

That treaty is also a great lesson for Americans. Its signing followed the Cuban crisis of 1962, when the Soviet Union learned that we would exercise our great power, but would do so with responsibility and restraint. If we would preserve peace, if we would preserve the air we breathe and the health of our children and our children's children, we must continue to exercise our power with the same firm dignity and responsible calm.[4]

Nonproliferation

High on the list of nuclear-control priorities is the subject of proliferation. Five nations already possess nuclear weapons, and at least ten others have the resources and know-how to produce them. Obviously, the more nations that have such weapons, the more difficult effective control becomes.

During his campaign for the Senate in 1964, Kennedy raised the issue:

No nation has a legitimate interest in the spread of these awful weapons—and I want to say right now that I am strongly opposed to their spread. This is a critical matter for all of us at this moment—for our children and for our children's children. Nothing is more important over the next five years—if we are granted that much time—than to gain control over the spread of nuclear weapons. I will throw all my strength behind President Johnson's efforts to reach agreement on a nondissemination treaty.[5]

[4] Campaign statement, September 24, 1964.
[5] Campaign speech, St. John Fisher College, Rochester, N.Y., October 20, 1964.

Once elected, he came out with a six-step proposal for halting the spread of nuclear weapons.

First, we should initiate at once negotiations with the Soviet Union and other nations with nuclear capability or potential, looking toward a nonproliferation treaty. This treaty would bind the major nuclear powers not to transfer nuclear weapons or weapons capability to nations not now in possession of them, and it would pledge nations without nuclear arms . . . not to acquire or develop these weapons. . . . Second, we should immediately explore the creation of formal nuclear-free zones of the world. . . . Third, we should complete the partial test-ban agreement of 1963 by extending it to underground as well as above-ground tests. . . . Fourth, we should act to halt and reverse the growth of the nuclear capabilities of the United States and the Soviet Union, both as to fissionable material for military weapons purposes and as to the strategic devices to deliver such material. . . . Fifth, we should move to strengthen and support the International Atomic Energy Commission. . . . Sixth, it is vital that we continue present efforts to lessen our own reliance on nuclear weapons.[6]

And in a speech to newspaper editors, Kennedy said the United States

. . . must pledge to the world that we will not be the first to use nuclear weapons against a nation which itself does not possess them.[7]

In 1965 seventeen nations began meeting at Geneva to draft an effective nonproliferation treaty. This effort to close the "nuclear club" to new members has met with the expected diplomatic difficulties from all corners, though at this writing an agreement was reportedly in the making.

Kennedy had vigorously supported the Geneva Disarmament Conference in public speeches around the country.

[6] Press release, June 23, 1965.
[7] Speech, New York State Society of Newspaper Editors, February 7, 1966.

The service you do to your country, however, is in more than fulfilling an ancient idea. For now, as never before, we need the work of groups like yours, as we move to meet a challenge more serious than any in our history. The question we are now faced with is whether, in an age of unprecedented scientific advancement, our politics can grow up to our technology. The nuclear weapon, as Henry Stimson said, "constitutes merely a first step in a new control by man over the forces of nature too revolutionary and dangerous to fit into the old concepts—it really caps the climax of the race between man's growing technical power for destructiveness and his psychological power of self-control and group control—his moral power."

No task now before us is more important than to prevent any spread of "those terrible arms" which modern science has given us, the nuclear weapons which could, if unleashed, utterly destroy our societies—our lives—the world itself. As President Kennedy said to the United Nations four years ago: "Every man, woman, and child lives under a nuclear sword of Damocles hanging by the slenderest of threads, capable of being cut at any moment by accident or miscalculation or by madness. The weapons of war must be abolished before they abolish us. . . ."

We will need to reach agreement on a treaty to prevent nuclear spread. We will need to make that treaty more than a scrap of paper—to persuade other nations that it is in their direct interest to accede to and abide by it—to abstain from nuclear weapons development.

We will need to ban nuclear weapons entirely from certain areas of the world.

We will need to extend the limited Test-Ban Treaty to underground tests.

And we will need to enlist the help of the United Nations, and all other nations—including Communist China—in the effort to prevent nuclear catastrophe.[8]

The most obvious change, the greatest immediate threat, and the greatest need for further change, is in our concepts and methods of war. The United States is not a warlike nation; still armed combat has always been our last resort,

[8] Address, Town Hall, Los Angeles, Calif., November 5, 1965.

490 ROBERT F. KENNEDY: APOSTLE OF CHANGE

our last line of defense of our interests—and every generation of Americans has met its own test, made its sacrifice in battle. But now science has made war a threat to the very existence of man on this earth.

Already five nations possess the nuclear weapon, the weapon of ultimate destruction. A dozen nations now have the capacity to build nuclear arms: the cost of developing them is now well within the resources of many private business corporations. The danger is great that other nations will produce these awesome weapons—and that once produced, one day they will be used. And once nuclear war were to start, even between small, remote countries, it would be extremely difficult, perhaps impossible, to prevent a step-by-step progression of local war into general conflagration.

Eighty million Americans—and hundreds of millions of other people—would die within the first twenty-four hours of a full-scale nuclear exchange . . .

This is simply not an acceptable future—an acceptable world for our children. We must remove that sword of Damocles from the heads of the peoples of the world—from ourselves, our own families, our own children. The place to begin is by reaching an agreement which will at once prevent the further spread of nuclear weapons to any countries that do not now possess them, and then to control and eventually eliminate the weapons now in possession of the present nuclear powers.[9]

Nonproliferation and the MLF

He was quick to add, however, that the conclusion of such a treaty would be no simple matter. One obvious obstacle was the difficulty of reconciling Soviet fear of German rearmament with West Germany's demand for a significant voice in NATO's nuclear decisions through a multilateral force.

The complexity and the difficulty just of arriving at a treaty to prevent the spread of nuclear weapons should show us the magnitude of the task ahead. This summer the United

[9] Speech, Democratic State Committee Dinner, Columbus, Ohio, October 8, 1966.

States presented to the Geneva Disarmament Conference a draft of such a treaty. By this treaty nonnuclear powers would pledge not to acquire or develop nuclear weapons. The present nuclear powers would pledge "not to transfer nuclear weapons into the national control of any nonnuclear state, either directly or indirectly through a military alliance." The nuclear powers would also pledge not to increase the "number of states and other organizations having independent power to use nuclear weapons."

The Soviet Union, however, regards our treaty as potentially allowing West Germany a degree of control over nuclear weapons which is in the Soviet view unacceptable. Soviet Foreign Minister Gromyko stated to the United Nations that the Soviet Union is now ready to sign its own draft treaty—which seemingly would prohibit any direct West German participation in the use of nuclear weapons by the NATO allies. And he seemed to reject the United States draft so long as it contains any opening for a multilateral nuclear force.

It is quite clear from the Soviet draft that we have a similar objective—preventing nuclear weapons from spreading to the national control of any present nonnuclear power. This shared objective may be as important as our differences over an MLF. As our delegate William Foster said at Geneva, the fact that "[the Soviet] government can accept most of the language of the U.S. treaty concerning the obligations of nuclear and nonnuclear states to prevent the spread of nuclear weapons" indicates that "it should be possible to proceed with that draft as the basis for negotiations when we meet again. . . ."

But if the negotiations are to be fruitful, much more than persistence will be required. All concerned nations—the United States, the Soviet Union, West Germany, and the other nations of Europe—must be prepared to rethink their positions; to make compromises; and to place an overriding priority on the prevention of nuclear proliferation. . . .

We must seek for new answers to the problem of the military security of Western Europe, so that we can satisfy our allies' desire for security in a way which does not meet with Soviet objections. Both we and the Soviet Union must realize that we cannot simply abandon the MLF and then arrive at an agreement with the Soviet Union. There are legitimate and responsible questions being raised in Europe, and in West Germany, as to the role they will play in European defense.[10]

The Responsibilities of Nuclear and Nonnuclear Nations

Kennedy contended that America's responsibility in the arena of nuclear diplomacy was the largest because we were first to develop and use the atomic bomb.

This is not to say that my country and the other nuclear powers, are without responsibility. Our responsibility is the greatest; for we first unlocked the atom's mystery, so that all men must live in future with the power of complete self-destruction. We must attempt to reach agreement on a general nonproliferation treaty; we must attempt to destroy some of our own nuclear power, and lessen our own reliance on nuclear weapons; we must extend the limited test-ban treaty to underground tests; we must strengthen the International Atomic Energy Agency; we must move, as we have agreed with the Soviet Union in the United Nations, toward the goal of general disarmament under adequate inspection and control.[11]

However, in his travels around the world he had sought to convince the nonnuclear nations that they too had a responsibility to help stop the spread of nuclear weapons. In São Paulo he urged that Latin America become the world's first official nuclear-free zone.

In 1963 the world took the first step in the journey of a thousand miles toward peace. The nuclear test-ban treaty which was reached in Moscow was acclaimed—and agreed to—by almost every nation in the world. President Kennedy regarded it as the foremost accomplishment of his time in office.

But the world has not yet moved beyond the test-ban treaty,

[10] Address, Town Hall, Los Angeles, Calif., November 5, 1965.
[11] Address, Forum of the Americas, São Paulo, Brazil, November 1965.

has not yet moved to take the second step toward nuclear sanity and peace.

That second step can be taken by you—by the nations of Latin America.

And it must be taken. The benefits—for yourselves and for the world—will be almost incalculable. For Latin America, a nuclear-free zone means a much decreased danger of ever receiving the direct impact of a nuclear attack from within or without the continent.

And it also would mean that massive resources would not be invested in nuclear weapons development—resources that will be far better used for the benefit of the hungry and the homeless, the sick and untaught. There is no country in this hemisphere, including my own, so rich that further expenditures on arms will not seriously detract from our ability to meet the true challenges of our time—work and land, education and dignity.[12]

Disarmament: Possibility or Pipe Dream?

In the same speech the Senator also expressed the hope that the nations of Latin America would take the lead, in concert with the other Third World nations, in the campaign to secure worldwide disarmament, conventional as well as nuclear.

With the experience and the moral initiative which will come from such disarmament measures on this continent, I would hope that the nations of the Americas would play an even greater role in worldwide disarmament councils—the eighteen-nation conference at Geneva, the United Nations Disarmament Commission, and the United Nations itself. All too often these conferences stall on great-power deadlock, with neither side willing to make the first concession, with both sides frozen in the ice of old positions and old quarrels.[13]

He was very perturbed, however, when the policies of the United States government continued to encourage

[12] *Ibid.*
[13] *Ibid.*

an accelerated arms race in Latin America rather than the beginning of disarmament.

I believe we must act now to discontinue sales of these unnecessary arms to Latin America. And if they persist in seeking arms elsewhere, wasting their own resources and depriving their own people, then we should take account of this waste in determining the amount of our own economic aid to them. For there is no longer time or room for only thinking so much of the present, of the immediate problem, that we forget the future; only for a commitment so great to a better world that we will examine carefully every consequence of our actions, refusing to borrow against the future of all for the present ease of the path of least resistance.[14]

If our neighbors to the south persist in wasting their national resources on unnecessary armaments, Kennedy went on, then we should at least see to it that these weapons are not purchased from us or with our economic assistance.

The reported purchase by Venezuela of 74 Sabrejets from West Germany illustrates once again the folly of the present Latin American arms race. It seems all the more unfortunate if, as the report indicates, the Departments of State and Defense knew of the sale and had no objection. No country in Latin America is threatened by aggression of a type requiring the kinds of arms they are now seeking. Cruisers, aircraft carriers, submarines, tanks, and jet planes are useless at best, and at worst constitute both a heavy drain upon precarious economies and devices to overturn democratic regimes. While it is certainly advisable to furnish Latin American countries with the means to conduct vigorous counterinsurgency programs—such as jeeps, communication equipment, and construction material—we should be clear in our determination that reckless purchases of useless arms not detract from needed expenditures for development. If Latin American countries seek and obtain these arms elsewhere, as I have previously urged, we should consider reducing our economic assistance by corresponding amounts, and

[14] Statement, Portland, Me., October 30, 1966.

make it plain that rampant militarism is incompatible with the aims of the Alliance for Progress.[15]

Kennedy regarded China as a potential problem in any serious efforts to control the use and proliferation of nuclear weapons, though not as an intransigent problem, as many in the State Department contended. When China set off her first nuclear explosion in the fall of 1964, he did not see the immediate danger as a direct threat to American security.

The danger is that the Chinese explosion may tempt or frighten many smaller countries to divert their atomic-energy programs into nuclear weapons. In that way a dozen different states would suddenly seek to become nuclear powers.

The spread of nuclear weapons from such decisions would deal a grave blow to the prospects of a peaceful world. Such a spread would once more poison the atmosphere. It would inflame relations between most of the smaller nations, and might touch off a nuclear arms race among them.[16]

Kennedy considered it imperative that the United States find a way to bring Peking into the disarmament discussions at Geneva and elsewhere if the world was to survive. Thus he was predictably angry when the State Department admitted that it had rejected an offer from the Chinese to negotiate a treaty prohibiting the use of nuclear weapons between the two nations. In a speech on the Senate floor the following day he declared:

It was stated yesterday by Chou En-lai that the Chinese had offered a pact with the United States which would outlaw the use of nuclear weapons between our two countries. He went on to say that our rejection of that treaty made it imperative for them to resume the testing.

A spokesman for the State Department has revealed that the Department did in fact reject this overture from the

[15] Press release, November 19, 1966.
[16] Campaign speech, St. John Fisher College, Rochester, N.Y., October 20, 1964.

Chinese, on the basis that they were not sincere and that there were no adequate safeguards.

Although our position seems well founded in fact and experience, I question whether this will be well understood in the rest of the world, unless we now take further open and affirmative steps to make clear our desire to reach effective control over nuclear weapons with the Communist Chinese.

This problem is compounded by the fact, as the State Department spokesman also revealed, that we have not yet invited Red China to the disarmament meetings in Geneva.[17]

He then went on to say:

I emphasize, as I have before, that Communist China should in fact be invited to participate in the Geneva disarmament negotiations.

It seems to me also important to make clear that we are prepared to enter into direct high-level discussions for just this purpose anywhere in the world. Involved in these discussions must be an exploration with the Chinese of whether, as part of any agreement that might be reached, they would agree not to test in the atmosphere as they inferred publicly they were willing to do. I have serious reservations as to whether in fact they would make such an agreement. But it is nevertheless important that their position as well as our own be clearly understood throughout the world.[18]

In a statement issued by his office a week later, Kennedy reintroduced his proposal that China be invited to sit as a participating member of the Geneva Disarmament Conference.

We are, of course, engaged in negotiations with the Soviet Union and sixteen other nations at Geneva, but one of the world's five nuclear powers—Communist China—is not represented at that conference. [France agreed to participate] We know that China is a difficult and hostile power and that negotiations with China may be frustrating—and perhaps fruitless. But China exists. China is a nuclear power. And

[17] Statement, U.S. Senate, May 12, 1966.
[18] *Ibid.*

without China's cooperation, the proliferation of nuclear weapons may be beyond our capacity to control. It is therefore our responsibility to take the first step—to take every honorable step—to bring China to the table of discussion at Geneva, or to engage in bilateral discussions at a high level elsewhere. But this we have not done. I think the Senate—I think the American people—are mature enough and concerned enough about the problem of nuclear weapons to support such negotiations with Communist China. I think we understand, as President Kennedy told us in 1963, that world peace does not require that every man love his neighbor—that even between nations whose interests are fundamentally opposed there may be agreements, definite and limited in nature, which are in the interests of all. I therefore urge again that China be invited to Geneva. And I further urge, as I did last week, that we explore fully with China whether, as Chou En-lai indicated, they would be willing to suspend nuclear testing in the atmosphere and outlaw the use of nuclear weapons between our two countries.[19]

That invitation still has not been issued.

[19] Press release, May 17, 1966.

Chapter 26

The War in Vietnam

> We will win in Vietnam and we shall remain here
> until we do.[1]

> I believe there is a middle way, that an end to the
> fighting and a peaceful settlement can be achieved. . . .
> A negotiated settlement means that each side must
> concede matters that are important in order to preserve
> positions that are essential.[2]

Opposition to the war in Vietnam was the keystone of
Robert Kennedy's campaign to capture the Democratic
party and, ultimately, the White House. His critics contended that his outspoken attacks on the administration's
handling of the war—attacks, they pointed out, which coincided with Lyndon Johnson's election in November,
1964, and Kennedy's own drive to disassociate himself
generally from the President's policies—were the product
of shrewd calculation that growing anti-war sentiment
would eventually make the President vulnerable and provide Kennedy with his own political base. Supporters
argued that the Senator's opposition to the war reflected
his deeply held conviction that the war was wrong and
demonstrated his courage to speak out regardless of the
personal political risks involved. The reader will have to
decide this contention for himself.

One thing is clear: Robert Kennedy's views on Vietnam
altered radically during the last four years of his life.

[1] Press conference, Saigon, Vietnam, February, 1962.
[2] Speech, U.S. Senate, February 19, 1966.

A bitter critic of America's role in Vietnam toward the end of his career, he was an avid enough supporter of Lyndon Johnson's Southeast Asia policy in 1964 to reportedly ask for appointment to the ambassadorship of the Republic of South Vietnam, a request that LBJ allegedly politely refused.

The objective of this chapter is to trace carefully the evolution of Kennedy's position on the war from his hawkish stands as his late brother's vizier to his dovish pronouncements as a peace candidate for the presidency. Given the currency and importance of the Vietnam issue —one which some believe is pregnant with the possibilities of World War III—as much detail will be included as is consistent with our intention of avoiding the repetitious and the trivial.

RFK, the Hawk

It was during the Kennedy Administration that the United States first began to commit military personnel ("advisors," as they were euphemistically characterized) to aid the pro-Western government of South Vietnam in its struggle against the Viet Cong for control of that demi-nation. That the war in Vietnam did not dominate the headlines during John Kennedy's term in office as it does today was due primarily to the fact that the number of Americans in Vietnam prior to Johnson's accession never exceeded several thousand.

But there was much debate in the government and some discussion in the press during this period over the wisdom of United States involvement in the conflict and exactly what our goals ought to be. To Robert Kennedy, whose views on the matter mirrored those of his brother, Vietnam represented a crucial battle in the cold war. As he saw it, this was another test, like the pressure being exerted by the Soviets in Berlin, of America's resolve to defend freedom around the world. The loss of Vietnam to the Communists—which would lead via the "domino theory" to the loss of all Southeast Asia—would dangerously threaten the fragile international balance of power upon which Western security rested. We could, Bobby

500 ROBERT F. KENNEDY: APOSTLE OF CHANGE

believed, settle for nothing short of clear-cut victory.

He began expressing these views on behalf of the administration on an official visit to the Far East in February of 1962, just three months after his brother's decision to begin more active assistance to the government of South Vietnam. At a press conference in Hong Kong, Kennedy bluntly stated his government's intentions:

The solution there [in Vietnam] lies in our winning it. This is what the President intends to do.[3]

Several days later, during a brief stopover in Saigon, he explained:

Hanoi may deny its responsibility but the guilt is clear. In a flagrant violation of its signed pledge at Geneva in 1954, the North Vietnamese regime has launched on a course to destroy the Republic of Vietnam.[4]

Recalling those few hours in Saigon in his book, *Just Friends and Brave Enemies,* Kennedy wrote:

Far from home, they [United States military personnel] fully realized the possibility that Southeast Asia might explode in the near future. It was clear that they wondered if the people in the United States knew. In a brief statement to the press about the struggle under way in Vietnam, I made the point that this is a new kind of war. It is war in the very real sense of the word, yet it is a war fought not by massive divisions but secretly by terror, assassination, ambush and infiltration. I added that the President "has been extremely impressed with the courage and determination of the people of your country and he has pledged the United States to stand by the side of Vietnam through this very difficult and troublesome time. We will win in Vietnam and we shall remain here until we do."[5]

[3] Press conference, Hong Kong, China, February, 1962.

[4] Press conference, Saigon, Vietnam, February, 1962.

[5] Robert F. Kennedy, *Just Friends and Brave Enemies* (New York: Harper & Row, 1962), p. 10.

Back in the States, Kennedy participated in the campaign to explain America's expanded role in Vietnam to the electorate:

Thus, I am sure you understand more than most [i.e., as former soldiers] the conditions under which several thousand of our fellow Americans are serving in the undeclared war in South Vietnam.

They are there because last November a comprehensive program was initiated calling for many forms of American aid to reverse the trend in South Vietnam. This included military assistance to the friendly forces combatting the Communists, economic assistance to the villagers who were the Communists' principal targets, and administrative and technical assistance to bolster the Vietnam government. . . . You know that this kind of warfare can be long, drawn out and costly, but if Communism is to be stopped, it is necessary. And we mean to see this job through to the finish.[6]

And at the opening of an exhibit on the Emancipation Proclamation he declared:

And we must do more because nations which are free and peoples who would be free look to us for leadership—not merely in strength of arms but in strength of convictions. Americans are on duty today in South Vietnam, South Korea, at the Berlin Wall, and around the world because the freedoms which Lincoln lived and died for belong to all men.[7]

Occasionally, Kennedy was given to statements similar to those which Americans became so accustomed to in the 1965-1967 period that we had "turned the corner" in Vietnam and were approaching victory.

We have taken major steps in recent months to strengthen the frontiers of freedom. The proof of our progress is that the reservists who were called up last summer at a time of crisis

[6] Speech, National Commanders' Dinner, American Legion Convention, Las Vegas, Nev., October 9, 1962.

[7] Speech, The National Archives, Washington, D.C., January 4, 1963.

502   ROBERT F. KENNEDY: APOSTLE OF CHANGE

are now returning to their homes all across the country.
Where a year ago the situation in South Vietnam was dark,
the forces of national independence now have a fighting
chance.[8]

In a radio interview one week before the 1964 elections
in which both he and Lyndon Johnson were victorious,
Robert Kennedy was asked what advice he as a Senator
would give to the President (assuming they were both
elected) on what the United States should do in Vietnam.
Kennedy replied:

Well, I've given advice before as to what I think needs to be
done. I think that . . . [there] has to be the support of the people for the military effort that is being made, [and there] has
to be support of the people for the government. We've had
overturns of the government on three different occasions now
and I think it makes it difficult when the wars have been going on for 25 years so that the country lacks that kind of stability, and there is tremendous exhaustion by the people, and
the fact that you have this guerrilla warfare that goes on continuously . . . I think that the people have to feel that there is
political progress being made and that they can be protected
in their communities, protected in their villages, and I think
that once there is that confidence, then I think the war will be
won.[9]

I believe this statement, though somewhat muddled,
offered on the eve of the transition from the Kennedy-
Johnson Administration to the Johnson Administration,
still found Robert Kennedy in accord with the government's Vietnam policy. However, this statement was one
of the last of its kind.

1965: The Year of Indecision

It was during his first year in the Senate, 1965, that
Robert Kennedy took preliminary halting steps to disas-

[8] Speech, Seattle World's Fair, Seattle, Wash., August 7, 1962.
[9] "News Conference" (WINS), October 25, 1964.

sociate himself from the administration's position on the war. Certain aspects of the Johnson policy appeared to disturb Kennedy, but he seemed uncertain as to what his own position ought to be. Initially, he stressed the complexity of the situation in Southeast Asia, ostensibly to warn against the "simple solution," but also as a means of explaining his own inability at the time to offer alternatives.

It is not helpful—it is not honest—to protest the war in Vietnam as if it were a simple and easy question, as if any moral man could reach only one conclusion. Vietnam admits no simple solution. But the complexity and difficulty of any question should not keep you from speech or action.[10]

At times during this period of personal indecision and transition, Kennedy offered what appeared to be conflicting opinions about the war. For example, the following two statements were issued only one week apart:

At the moment, our most prominent problem is in Vietnam. We must realize, however, that Vietnam has become more and more an open military conflict, as well, in which military action on our part is essential just to allow the government to act politically.[11]

Victory in a revolutionary war is not won by escalation, but by de-escalation . . . air attacks by a government on its own villages are likely to be far more dangerous and costly to the people than is the individual and selective terrorism of an insurgent movement.[12]

Later in the year, Kennedy began making the point that the war in Vietnam should not be used as an excuse for failing to meet our domestic needs—a valid point but one which begged the question of whether or not the war was justified.

[10] Address, Queens College commencement exercises, Queens, N.Y., June 15, 1965.
[11] Address, International Police Academy commencement, Washington, D.C., July 9, 1965.
[12] *Time,* July 16, 1965.

The McCone Report warned that "the August riots may seem by comparison to be only a curtain raiser for what could blow up one day in the future," and that the result could be to "split our society irretrievably."

Certainly, the Senator said, the war in Vietnam will require great sums from the budget; certainly it will impose some strain on our resources; certainly our young men are entitled to all the support we can give them. And all this will require sacrifices on our part as well as theirs.

But to limit our efforts to the support of the war in Vietnam —to postpone action on our pressing domestic needs—would be a terrible mistake. To refuse to make the further efforts and the further sacrifices that justice and tranquility require at home would be to invite the very internal conflagration of which we have been warned—to invite a society so irretrievably split that no war will be worth fighting, and no war will be possible to fight.[13]

On November 5, 1965, he became the center of controversy when he asserted that giving blood to the North Vietnamese would be "in the oldest traditions of this country. I'm willing to give blood to anyone who needs it." He added, however, that he would approve of such donations only if they were administered by an international organization. The outcry against this statement was loud and vitriolic, with Barry Goldwater condemning Kennedy's remark as "close to treason."

Then on Christmas Eve of 1965, Kennedy's Senate office issued a significant release to the press. It called on the Johnson Administration to attempt to extend the Christmas cease-fire in Vietnam and put Kennedy on record as favoring a negotiated end to the conflict. Here is the text of that release:

There are two cease-fire periods now established in the Vietnamese conflict. One 12-hour period, announced unilaterally by the Viet Cong, will end at 7:00 A.M. Christmas Day (6:00 P.M. Eastern Standard Time, December 24, 1965). The United States and South Vietnam governments have

[13] Press release, December 16, 1965.

themselves ordered a more extended cease-fire period lasting 30 hours and ending midnight, Christmas Day (11:00 A.M., Eastern Standard Time, December 25, 1965).

It is my view that American and South Vietnamese troops should not be the first to attack if the Viet Cong substantially honors the additional hours of the truce period established by our side. In this way we would take further advantage of the cease-fire periods themselves in order to provide an avenue by which the conflict can be brought from the battlefield to the conference table. There should also be a restatement by the administration of its willingness to enter into unconditional discussions by all diplomatic means." [14]

RFK, the Dove

Seven weeks later, on February 19, 1966, in a speech to the Senate, Robert Kennedy broke dramatically and decisively with the Johnson Administration over the war in Vietnam. The speech placed Kennedy securely in the camp of the doves for the first time and set down the views that were to govern his remarks and actions regarding the war over the next two years.

He opened this historic address by defending the importance of honest dissent in a democracy, undoubtedly in anticipation of the cries of "un-Americanism" he believed would greet the critique he was about to deliver.

Shall we then debate with force and passion the issues of labor relations and housing and trade—while the great issues of peace and war are allowed to pass in silence? Shall we discuss the standard of living of our constituents—while policies which affect their very existence go undiscussed? To do so would be the gravest departure from our duties as representatives of the people of the American States. Full and informing debate rests upon moderation and mutual indulgence. Men must seek acceptance of their views through reason, and not through intimidation; through argument, and not through accusation. We are all patriots here. We are all defenders of freedom. We are all Americans. To attack the motives of those who express concern about our

[14] Press release, December 24, 1965.

present course—to challenge their very right to speak freely—
is to strike at the foundations of the democratic process which
our fellow citizens, even today, are dying in order to protect.

He explained why Vietnam demanded our urgent attention and sought to define the concerns the war had
created in this country.

All of us are concerned, as the American people are concerned, about the progress of the struggle in Vietnam. There
are several aspects to this concern. We are concerned at the
casualties, the death and suffering, of our young men in
South Vietnam. We are concerned over the effect of some
of our military action on the people of South Vietnam—
whether more cannot be done to lessen the death and
destruction of the innocent that comes with war. For a
military victory at the cost of a completely destroyed South
Vietnam would be a defeat for our larger purposes. We are
concerned whether the people of South Vietnam are being
offered something positive to live and fight for—something
beyond negative anti-Communism. . . . We are concerned
over our relationship with Communist China—not just concern to avoid a deadly war, but also concern lest the Vietnam
struggle make any reasonable accommodation with China
impossible in the future. . . . And we are concerned about
the effect of the war on our domestic efforts to conquer
ignorance and disease and unemployment—the problems of
the cities—problems which, warned the McCone Commission,
could split our society irretrievably. And this concern is
heightened by the way in which the war perpetuates discrimination—for the poor and the less fortunate serve in
Vietnam out of all proportion to their numbers in the United
States as a whole. But the central question before us now—
the area of greatest present concern for the Senate, and
what we must discuss at all levels of government—is our
political strategy in the war in Vietnam; not simply how to
move, but in what direction we wish to move.[16]

Kennedy then turned to the heart of his disagreement

[15] Speech, U.S. Senate, February 19, 1966.
[16] *Ibid.*

with the Johnson Administration, the matter of how the war ought to be settled. The President and his Secretary of State, Dean Rusk, had made it clear through their actions, if not by their rhetoric, that the United States was pursuing principally a military policy in Vietnam. They believed, given enough time and fortitude, we could decisively defeat the Viet Cong and North Vietnamese in the field, which would enable Washington to dictate the terms in any future negotiations. Kennedy rejected military victory as a realistic policy goal—as well as the immediate withdrawal of United States troops, which some doves were advocating—and counseled a "middle way" of unconditional negotiations in which both sides would be forced to compromise. The following statement, more clearly than any other, defines his position on the war.

At the outset, it must be realized that negotiations are not an ultimate goal. Negotiations or discussions are only a means by which ultimate goals may be reached. Our arrival at the bargaining table will not make the struggle disappear. Even if we arrive at the bargaining table, the real question is what goals we will seek there. Without clear goals in mind, negotiations are pointless. And without clear goals and realistic objectives, it is doubtful whether the bargaining table will ever be reached. What, then, are our goals in Vietnam? The Secretary of State and others have stated objectives in general terms. They are the independence of South Vietnam—or, at least, its independent right to determine its own future. They are to halt the aggression from the North and to prove to China that a policy of subversion in other lands will not work. These are worthy objectives. All are important. The question remains, however, under what realistic terms and conditions they can be advanced in Vietnam. There are three routes before us: military victory, a peaceful settlement, or withdrawal. The last is impossible for this country. For the United States to withdraw now, as I said last May, would be a repudiation of commitments undertaken and confirmed by three administrations. It would flatly betray those in Vietnam whom we have encouraged by our support to resist the forces of Hanoi and the Viet Cong. Unilateral withdrawal would injure, perhaps irreparably, the principle of collective security, and undermine the independence of small nations everywhere in the world. And it would offer no hope for a reasonable accommodation with China in the future. There are reasonable and responsible steps which we can take to raise the possibility of improved relations with China in the future. But unilateral withdrawal would only reward aggression and could offer China no inducement to reach accommodation in a peaceful world. I now turn to the open avenues—military victory or a peaceful settlement.

Military victory requires that we crush both our adversary's strength and his will to continue the battle; that the forces from the North be compelled to withdraw beyond the border; that much of Vietnam be destroyed and its people killed; that we continue to occupy South Vietnam as long as our presence is required to insure that hostilities, including insurgency, will not be resumed. And this will be a very long time indeed. I cannot say with certainty that such an outcome is beyond our reach. We do know, however, that it would mean rapidly increasing commitments of American forces. It would mean a growing risk of widening war—with North Vietnam, with China, even with the Soviet Union. It would lead, indeed already has led, thoughtless people to advocate the use of nuclear weapons. And it would involve all these things—commitment, risk, and spreading destruction—in pursuit of a goal which is at best uncertain, and at worst unattainable. Despite all these dangers, we may yet come to this course. The intransigence of our adversaries may leave us no alternative. There should be no misunderstanding or miscalculation of this point in either Hanoi or Peking. The American people possess the bravery and the will to follow such a course if others force it upon us. I also believe, however, that given the opportunity by our adversaries, we possess the wisdom and skill to avoid such a grim necessity. In this pursuit we have asked for unconditional discussions. This means simply that we will neither demand nor yield specific formal commitments before bargaining begins. In fact, both sides must come to any discussion with at least one basic condition; one irreducible demand; one point they will not yield. For the United States it must be that we will not turn South Vietnam over to the North. For North Vietnam it must be that they will not accept a settlement which leaves in the South a hostile government dedicated to the final physical destruction of all Communist elements, refusing any economic cooperation with the North, dependent upon the continued presence of American military power. These conditions, these minimum terms, can be breached only at sword's point; only by driving the adversary's forces from the field. For either side to yield its minimum conditions would be in fact to accept defeat. If we intend to deny these minimum conditions to our adversaries, then we must defeat them completely. If this is what we intend, we should understand it clearly and undertake it with resolution. But if negotiation is our aim, as we have so clearly said it is, we must seek a middle ground. A negotiated settlement means that each side must concede matters that are important in order to preserve positions that are essential. It may be that negotiation is not possible in this war because our political aims are irreconcilable; because one side, or both sides, are not willing to accept anything less than the fruits of victory. If that is so, then we must reluctantly let slip the hope of reasoned discussion and proceed to the uncertain, uncharted course of war. I believe there is a middle way, that an end to the fighting and a peaceful settlement can be achieved. It must be said, before all else, that the middle way—the way of negotiation—involves risks. An adversary who lives may perhaps fight another day. And a government which is not continuously sheltered by American military power may be again attacked or subverted or overthrown. These risks, I believe, we are courageous enough to undertake. They are risks, in fact, which we do take every day in a hundred countries in every corner of every continent.[17]

Next, Kennedy turned to the role that the National Liberation Front (the political arm of the Viet Cong) ought to be permitted to play in any meaningful settlement of the war. The State Department's position was that the NLF should never be recognized as a formal participant in any negotiations (we should talk only with Hanoi) or accepted into a coalition government in the South. Kennedy disagreed.

[17] *Ibid.*

Whatever the exact status of the National Liberation Front—puppet or partly independent—any negotiated settlement must accept the fact that there are discontented elements in South Vietnam, Communist and non-Communist, who desire to change the existing political and economic system of the country. There are three things you can do with such groups: kill or repress them, turn the country over to them, or admit them to a share of power and responsibility. The first two are now possible only through force of arms.

The last—to admit them to a share of power and responsibility—is at the heart of the hope for a negotiated settlement. It is not the easy way or the sure way; nor can the manner or the degree of participation now be described with any precision. It may come about through a single conference or many meetings, or by a slow, undramatic process of gradual accommodation. It will require enormous skill and political wisdom to find the point at which participation does not bring domination or internal conquest. It will take statesmanship willing to exploit the very real differences of ambition and intention and interest between Hanoi and Peking and the Soviet Union. It may mean a compromise government fully acceptable to neither side. It certainly means that we must take considerable risks in the expectation that social and economic success will weaken the appeal of Communism—and that sharing the burden and the satisfaction of helping to guide a nation will attract hostile elements toward a solution which will preserve both the independence of their country and their new-found share of power. And we must be willing to face the uncertainties of election, and the possibility of an eventual vote on reunification. We must be prepared to think about what kind of relationship such a reunified country would have to the United States, to Communist China, to the Soviet Union.[18]

Finally, Kennedy urged the administration to accept the risks inherent in any negotiated settlement.

If we are willing to accept these uncertainties and run the risks—and if our adversaries are willing to submit their cause to the same arbitration, the same peaceful choice—then

[18] *Ibid.*

a settlement may be possible; and the other hazards, the hazards of widening conflict and devastation, may be ended. Of course, such a road toward solution must be protected from sudden violent upheaval. There must be international guarantees to back up agreement, good faith, and mutual self-interest. Foreign forces must be withdrawn, by balanced and verified stages. And we must insist that the political process go forward under the rigorous supervision of a trusted international body.[19]

Negotiations, Bombing, and United States Objectives

For the next two-and-one-half years, Robert Kennedy adhered to the basic positions he had enumerated in his February 19, 1966, speech before the Senate. The remainder of 1966, 1967, and the campaign for the Democratic presidential nomination in 1968 found him reiterating and expanding these positions to meet the constantly shifting realities in Vietnam and the international community. Let us now review his statements during this period chronologically and in detail.

A few days after his February 19, 1966, Senate speech, Kennedy addressed the Jewish Theological Seminary and spelled out the objectives he believed most Americans shared about Vietnam. It was an attempt to soften the hostile reaction of many to his dissenting Senate speech by explaining that, while he might be critical of the President's means in Southeast Asia, they sought the same ends.

All of us who participate now must keep in our minds and hearts that there are good men on all sides of the debate, that most of us share the same objectives about Vietnam. I made my statement about Vietnam a week ago Saturday in furtherance of these shared objectives: to help us reach a just negotiated settlement which preserves our essential national interests and meets our essential commitment to the people of South Vietnam; to help bring the war to an early end; to thus save thousands of American lives;

[19] *Ibid.*

and to limit the destruction and devastation which war brings to the innocent people of South Vietnam.[20]

Two weeks later, in an interview in *U.S. News & World Report,* Kennedy attempted to clarify his earlier statements. He reasserted the need to maintain military pressure on the Viet Cong and North Vietnamese, justifying it as necessary to convince Hanoi and the NLF that negotiating would be "worth their while."

I favor continuing our military commitment with the objective of getting a settlement in Vietnam which would prevent North Vietnam and the National Liberation Front from taking over South Vietnam by force, free the people of South Vietnam of terror and intimidation and from the destruction of war, preserve our honor and our commitment, and end as quickly as possible the loss of American lives and the strain on our resources. . . . I'm convinced there is tremendous pressure on them [South Vietnamese Communists] from China not to come to the negotiating table. If they do come, they are going to impair their own relationships with Communist China. So I think, first, they have to be hurt enough to know that they aren't going to win and, second, they have to feel that there is enough reason for them to negotiate to make it worth their while.[21]

And he repeated his assertion that peace would come only if it were made clear that the Communists must be invited to share in the governing of South Vietnam.

Now, if they're [the Communists] going to share in the political processes of the country, we'll want them to concede some things, too—to lay down their arms and return the area and people now under their control to the central government, and to refrain from interfering with the freedom of the people of South Vietnam to determine their own destiny. But we can't get these concessions, and thereby shorten the war, without being prepared ourselves for a

[20] Address, Jewish Theological Seminary, Hollywood, Fla., February 28, 1966.
[21] *U.S. News & World Report,* March 14, 1966.

settlement that brings them into the governmental structure and society in South Vietnam.[22]

About this time, Kennedy also began to express concern over United States bombing of North Vietnam, which had been initiated in early 1965. In a Senate statement on April 27, 1966, he questioned whether this policy might not lead us into a dangerous confrontation with either the Soviet Union or China, or both.

The latest reports of clashes with advanced aircraft over North Vietnam must be viewed with the gravest concern.

The Soviet Union has made these high-performance aircraft available to North Vietnam. We do not know where the planes are based—whether in North Vietnam or across the border in China.

But the Secretary of State has said—and a State Department spokesman repeated yesterday—that there will be "no sanctuary." Our planes will pursue hostile aircraft to wherever they go—even over the border of China—and there is no sanctuary for Chinese bases.

What is occurring in North Vietnam is escalation of the war by them or by us—the fact is that we are both inexorably involved. That fact and its implications must be faced. What will be the Chinese response, if her territory is bombed or her airspace invaded? Will the Chinese seek to strike at our bases—in Vietnam, or Thailand, or aboard our aircraft carriers? And if they do, what then will our response be—further bombing? And if the scale of bombing increases, will China confine itself to air fighting—or will it send its troops to engage ours on the ground in South Vietnam?

Mr. James Reston reports today in the *New York Times* that our military planners are not concerned over the possible consequences of this escalation. They are said to feel that "China and the Soviet Union will tolerate military defeats the United States clearly would not tolerate itself."

Such assumptions are not a sound basis for policy. Similar assumptions about the Viet Cong and North Vietnam have been proven wrong time and again in this war.[23]

[22] *Ibid.*
[23] Statement, U.S. Senate, April 27, 1966.

When the President ordered an escalation of the bombing two months later to include the important North Vietnamese port of Haiphong, Kennedy was clearly disturbed and cautiously began to challenge the assumptions upon which the administration's bombing policy rested.

I am sure that all Americans are concerned at this expansion of the war in Vietnam. It seems to me that the major question to be answered with respect to the bombings is this: Will this step effectively prevent North Vietnam from supplying the Viet Cong in the South with sufficient men and material to enable them to continue the war at levels they desire?

Unfortunately, past escalations have often been accompanied by assurances and predictions that this would be the case. These hopes have not been fulfilled. Had these predictions been correct, the bombings announced today would not have been necessary. Indeed, on each occasion the effort from the North has either increased in spite of our efforts, or taken a different and more dangerous course.

I regret that it has seemed necessary to take this step. We must all hope that the predictions based on this latest heightening of the battle will prove to be realistic ones.[24]

Finally, to appease those who were arguing publicly that cessation of the bombing would be a major step toward inducing North Vietnam to the bargaining table, and perhaps in an honest attempt to see what would result, Lyndon Johnson ordered an indefinite halt to the bombing to coincide with the Vietnamese holiday truce in late December, 1966. After approximately six weeks, the President resumed the bombing, explaining that he had received no signs that Hanoi intended to reciprocate by de-escalating its military efforts. Kennedy apparently felt we had not done as much or waited as long as we should have.

I deeply regret that the bombing of North Vietnam has resumed. Beyond that, it is most unfortunate that the truce period has gone by without greater progress being made

[24] Press release, June 29, 1966.

by all of us on both sides toward a peaceful ending of this tragic war.[25]

In a thoughtful address before a group of Asian scholars and students at the University of Chicago that same day, Kennedy explored publicly for the first time some of the broader questions relating to United States involvement in Asia generally and Vietnam specifically. He began quite dramatically by challenging the cardinal assumption of United States policy in Southeast Asia that China is threatening the successful export of her Communist revolution to her neighbors, Vietnam in particular.

If our common understanding of Chinese capabilities has been exaggerated, so has our common understanding of her potential as a source of revolution elsewhere. China's revolutionary experience is unique; and it is clear also that the revolutionary credo which accompanied it is not readily transferable to other nations. In Cuba, in Indonesia, in Algeria, in Africa, men have made clear that they would design and control their own national revolutions. There are sometimes attempts to portray Vietnam as a Chinese-inspired conflict and China as assisting the North Vietnamese. But Vietnam's Communism is basically a native growth, with its own revolutionary tradition and dynamism. There is always a potential danger to which we must be alert, but as of now, not one example anywhere in the world of Chinese-inspired or directed revolution has had any lasting success; only the Malayan revolt had even the most minimal success, before being crushed, and that was carried out by ethnic Chinese, not Malayans.

The record of Chinese effort to export revolution has been one of consistent and dramatic failure. It is perhaps natural that China, whose principal word for foreigners is the approximate equivalent of "barbarians," should have a Foreign Minister capable of publicly calling for armed revolution in the presence of the African Head of State who was his host at the time.

All this is not to say that China is helpless—a "paper tiger" as her leaders once called the United States—or that China can be ignored as a force in the world. China's millions, now and in the future, can be expected to exert considerable power in Asia and to make efforts elsewhere.[26]

The implications of this statement were considerable. Kennedy seemed to be saying that the conflict in Vietnam should be regarded principally as an internal affair between local Communists and non-Communists, not as a serious effort by China to extend her power into Southeast Asia. Were this the case, it would be difficult to justify the large-scale commitment of men and resources to the Vietnamese war inaugurated by the Johnson Administration two years before.

Kennedy contended that we did not know how to distinguish external aggression from civil war in Asia, that we had no guidelines to govern our participation in Far Eastern affairs—in short, that we had no carefully constructed, comprehensive Asian policy.

It has been suggested, for example, that we are pursuing strategic interests in Asia; denying the control of other land and resources to Asian Communism. Yet less than two years ago we were quite prepared to accept the spread of Communism to Indonesia—a nation of one hundred million people, incomparably rich in resources, standing over the critical Straits of Malacca and flanking the Philippines. Of course, we want to prevent the expansion, the acquisition of vast new resources, by powers deeply hostile to the United States. That statement, however, is only the beginning of thought. How do we discriminate between Chinese expansion and autonomous revolt? Where and under what circumstances can we bring our power effectively to bear? Where and under what circumstances should we limit ourselves to helping others, without hazarding large-scale combat or major war? These are not easy questions to answer. But until we at least begin to discuss and debate them we will be unable to develop any kind of long-range planning, let alone policy. And let me add that even then the application of

[26] Address, China Conference, University of Chicago, Chicago, Ill., February 8, 1967.

that policy in any given situation may be painfully difficult.[27]

Then on March 2, 1967, Kennedy delivered his second major Senate speech on the war and United States policy in Southeast Asia. Largely consistent with his February effort of a year earlier, this speech contained a more thorough analysis of the international context in which the war in Vietnam was being waged and offered more specific suggestions on how we might extricate ourselves.

He opened his remarks by placing much of the blame for the failure to find peace in South Vietnam on the Viet Cong and North Vietnamese.

The fault for no peace rests largely with our adversary. He has pursued relentless and unyielding conquest with obdurate unconcern for mounting desolation. Now his victory has eluded him, replaced by a conflict where violence breeds only endless violence.

If our enemy will not accept peace, it cannot come. Yet, we must also look to ourselves. We must have no doubt that it is not our acts of failures which bar the way; that there is nothing we have left undone which we might have done. Our own course must be subject to a ceaseless and critical examination, not with certainty that change will bring success, but in order that our own people can take comfort and strength from the knowledge that America has taken every step, done every act, and performed every deed within its power to put an end to this distant and ferocious war.[28]

Kennedy reminded his listeners of the enormous damage to the people of South Vietnam and to their prospects of building a viable society inflicted on them by the continuous fighting.

We are now steadily widening the war in order, we are told, to increase the costs to Hanoi. Yet, in our concern with the price our adversary must pay, let us not omit our own costs from the war's account.

[27] *Ibid.*
[28] Speech, U.S. Senate, March 2, 1967.

The mounting devastation of South Vietnam—the destruction of villages and burning of the countryside—is steadily eroding the fabric of that society; making the ultimate reconstruction of South Vietnam more remote and difficult. Yet lasting peace depends upon the strength of the nation we leave behind. The war has also made far more difficult the hopeful pursuit of fresh understanding and diminishing tension between the two great nuclear powers: The United States and Russia. It has absorbed some of the energies needed if we are to exercise our full weight and responsibility in the Western Alliance. It is diverting resources which might have been used to help eliminate American poverty, improve the education of our children and enhance the quality of our national life.

Of course we are willing—we must be willing—to pay all these costs if the alternative is surrender or defeat. We cannot dishonor our commitments, nor yield the lawful interests of the nation at any price. But neither should we deceive ourselves into thinking these are not massive and difficult debts which other generations will have to discharge.[29]

He implied that circumstances had created a potential turning point which could lead to negotiations if we were alert to our opportunities and prepared to seize them.

For years, President Johnson has dedicated his energies in an effort to achieve an honorable peace.

However, we are now at a critical turning point in pursuit of our stated limited objectives: balanced between the rising prospects of peace and surely rising war, between the promise of negotiations and the perils of spreading conflict. For our attacks are mounting in intensity, just as the evidence mounts that a new and more hopeful moment of opportunity for settlement has been at hand.

Before reawakened hope is lost in renewed and evermore far-reaching assault, we should test this moment with new initiatives and acts in pursuit of peaceful settlement. Whatever the disappointments of an effort which fails, the costs

[29] *Ibid.*

of continued war are certain. As our objectives are limited they may well be secured at the conference table without further months or years of war. If our effort fails, then the conflict will continue.

Therefore, agony and interest, the limited nature of our goals and the formidable consequences of rising war combine now to compel us to embrace any initiative that may resolve this conflict—honorably, justly, consistent with our aims and in peace.[30]

Kennedy warned that we must not let either fear or pride bar our way to the conference table. Initiative and cooperation with all who might lend a hand in resolving the war, he seemed to be saying, must be the order of the day.

We need not wait timidly for a certain outcome and sure guarantees, fearful for our dignity and anxious for our prestige. This enormous country, a nation which commands half the wealth and power of the globe, need not be fearful of North Vietnam. Viet Cong guerrillas, even with their Northern allies, will not drive from the battlefield an American army, backed by endless funds and towering resources. No one is going to defeat us, or slaughter our troops, or destroy our prestige because we dare take initiatives for peace. If Pope Paul or U Thant or Prime Minister Wilson or Premier Kosygin believe they have the key to peace, let us welcome their efforts and continuously ask their help. If any among us can suggest any act which offers hope of peace, let his counsel be welcomed. "Where no counsel is," the Bible says, "the people fall: but in the multitude of counselors there is safety."[31]

He then came to the primary purpose of his speech: a call for the unconditional cessation of the bombing of North Vietnam by the United States.

Our government has unequivocally said that our objective in Vietnam is a negotiated settlement with the Communists.

[30] *Ibid.*
[31] *Ibid.*

"The only path for reasonable men," President Johnson said at Johns Hopkins, "is the path of peaceful settlement." I am sure most Americans share this conviction. The question is whether we are doing everything possible to reach that goal. It is the most important and urgent question of the American nation.

The steps I am suggesting are intimately related. They stand together, each dependent on the other. It will do little good to go to the conference table if discussions are simply used to mask continued escalation of the war. Nor will negotiations be fruitful unless they lead to a reasonable and honorable settlement with some hope of lasting peace. Therefore, I propose that we test the sincerity of the statements by Premier Kosygin [of the Soviet Union] and others asserting that if the bombardment of the North is halted, negotiations would begin—by halting the bombardment and saying we are ready to negotiate within the week; making it clear that discussions cannot continue for a prolonged period without an agreement that neither side will substantially increase the size of the war in South Vietnam—by infiltration or reinforcement. An international group should be asked to inspect the borders and ports of the country to report any further escalation. And under the direction of the United Nations, and with an international presence gradually replacing American forces, we should move toward a final settlement which allows all major political elements in South Vietnam to participate in the choice of leadership and shape their future direction as a people.

If we can follow this course, we cannot be certain that negotiations will take place, or that they will be productive. No one can give such a guarantee. But measures such as these will enhance the chances of peace while the risks are comparatively slight. Certainly they will help us to know we have done everything within our power to reach a settlement. Therefore they should be pursued. . . .

We were willing to do this [halt the bombing] a year ago, even without the evidence we now have that an end to bombing attacks on the North may well bring negotiations. A year ago it was our adversaries who publicly laid down conditions for negotiations—acceptance of the Four Points or withdrawal of American troops. Now Mr. Kosygin and Mr. Podgorny have said negotiations can begin on terms we clearly would have accepted then. Why then do we not try again in this far more hopeful moment? [32]

Kennedy then added, anticipating his critics:

If the passage of substantial time and events proves that our adversaries do not sincerely seek a negotiated solution, if discussions are used only as a pretext to enlarge the conflict in the South, then we can re-examine our entire military strategy—including the bombing or the possible erection of a physical barrier to block infiltration—in light of the changing nature of the war. Our actions at that time, after such a dedicated effort to secure peace, would have the increased understanding and support of our allies and of our own people. We should be generous in our search for peace, but I am also aware of the precedent of Panmunjon. [33]

It was not only because the continued bombardment of the North might delay or prevent negotiations that Kennedy demanded a halt. He implied that morally we had no right to punish the people of North Vietnam in this manner.

If our adversary has seen his hopes for victory destroyed, it is primarily because of the skill and bravery of our forces on the ground. Moreover, there is every sign that the bombing itself is now an insuperable obstacle to negotiations and that the North Vietnamese feel it impossible to discuss peace while bombs are falling on their country; just as the bombing of Britain only united resistance; just as we would join in unyielding determination if bombs were falling on Detroit or Chicago. . . .

Certainly the bombing of the North makes the war more costly and difficult and painful for North Vietnam. It is a harsh punishment indeed. But we are not in Vietnam to play the part of an avenging angel pouring death and destruction on the roads and factories and homes of a guilty land. We are there to assure the self-determination of South Vietnam, to fight the war effectively, and to protect as many lives as

[32] *Ibid.*
[33] *Ibid.*

we can. It should be clear by now that the bombing of the North cannot bring an end to the war in the South: that, indeed, it may well be prolonging that war. None of those who have advocated a cessation of bombing—men like General Gavin, or Ambassadors Kennan, and Reischauer—would contemplate a step which might unnecessarily endanger the lives of many Americans. Our troops are being killed by the bullets and the mines of forces in the South. If by ending the bombing of the North we bring peace in South Vietnam nearer, then we will save the lives of thousands of our young men and thousands of Vietnamese.[34]

If the bombing is stopped, the next logical question is how best to proceed to negotiations. The Senator offered a three-part plan in the next section of his speech.

As soon as we halt the bombing of the North—international teams under the United Nations or, perhaps, a strengthened International Control Commission, should be asked to provide detached and objective information to the world about any large buildup of troops or supplies by our adversaries.

They would patrol the borders, ports and roads of Vietnam. Equipment which we now use to watch and monitor enemy movements—such as reconnaissance planes and other intelligence facilities—can be placed at their disposal.

Our next step should be to seek an understanding with our adversaries that neither side will substantially increase the rate of infiltration and reinforcements during negotiations.

For even though we begin negotiations it is not likely that peace can be discussed effectively or with confidence while the other side is preparing for a larger war. It is unrealistic to think we would sit through prolonged and fruitless negotiations while casualties mount and the war gets bigger. Thus, even if hostilities continue it will be necessary for both sides to refrain from escalating the war on the ground and trying to change the military balance.

Therefore, whether or not we are able to reach a specific agreement on this subject, the international inspection team which, hopefully, was established as soon as the bombing halted, would report any effort, by either side, to increase

[34] *Ibid.*

its strength while peace talks proceed. They would also monitor any agreement reached during the course of negotiations on suspension of military activity, including, hopefully, a cease-fire. Thus the detached and objective testimony of the international community would be witness to our sincerity, and to any attempt by North Vietnam substantially to step up its help to the NLF under cover of negotiations. And if the failure of negotiations, coupled with the actions of our adversary, makes it necessary for us to re-examine our position, we would act with far clearer international understanding of our motives and necessities. . . .

It will not be easy to devise a workable system of international inspection in a situation so charged with complexity, conflict and clashing interests. We do know, however, that the participation of other nations can both help sustain the good faith necessary to successful talks and make a satisfactory final settlement possible. These suggestions may contribute to that necessary end.

Third, we must know and clearly state what kind of Vietnam we would like to see emerge from negotiations, and how we propose these general objectives could be best achieved. Negotiations are not the end of the road. They are the bridge of the future of South Vietnam. That future must include the right of the people of South Vietnam to self-determination. How to accomplish this is at the heart of the problem of peaceful settlement.

To speak of our objectives in advance of our negotiations does not yield advantage to our adversary by "showing our cards." Discussions of peace and war are not poker games. They are decided by power and interest, reason and the knowledge, as Franklin Roosevelt said, that "no nation ever loses its dignity or its good standing by conciliating its differences." Understanding of our aims will speed, not retard, the course of settlement. And since they are worthy and honorable goals they will help win us the support and sympathy of others.[35]

Then the issue of what is to be negotiated and how peace talks ought to be conducted arises. Again, Kennedy had a tentative blueprint.

[35] *Ibid.*

The first task for the negotiators will be to dismantle the war. They will have to establish procedures for a cease-fire, for the laying down of arms and for the gradual withdrawal of foreign forces from the country. This must be accompanied by the political steps necessary to protect the safety of all sides while the war is being dismantled. The President has clearly stated to the world that for our part we neither want nor intend to keep our forces or bases in South Vietnam once peace is secure.

More difficult and intricate is the resolution of South Vietnam's tangled politics.

As I said a year ago, a negotiated settlement is a compromise. One must either defeat an enemy and compel his surrender or else settle on terms in which both sides can find some degree of satisfaction. We have not defeated the Viet Cong, nor, as President Johnson said in his State of the Union Message, is a military victory in sight. We must, therefore, find—and I think we can find—an agreed solution which, however imperfect, protects our basic interest in Vietnam: The self-determination of the people of South Vietnam.

All the people of South Vietnam, Communist and non-Communist, Buddhist and Christian, should be able to choose their leaders, and seek office through peaceful processes, free from external coercion and internal violence. All should have the opportunity to seek peacefully a share of power and responsibility through free elections. They should determine their future and the nature of their system and resolve the question of Vietnamese reunification.

We might begin moving toward this future by encouraging the South Vietnamese government, including the present Constituent Assembly, to begin its own discussion with the National Liberation Front. Other political elements, not now represented in the government, should share in this effort. For many years the people of South Vietnam have been divided in fierce and hostile combat. If they are to settle their own future they must at least begin to talk to each other, try to eliminate unnecessary conflicts, and search out areas of possible agreement.

And as a major combatant, we must also be ready to talk

directly to all parties—North and South, Communist and non-Communist alike. . . .

Finally, a lasting settlement of the war will be extremely difficult unless all parties to the present conflict are secure in the knowledge that free elections open to all will ultimately be held, and that those who win them will take office. This confidence will depend on the structure of government be-tween the end of hostilities and elections. This may be a prolonged period. It will certainly be a period of great importance. Therefore, the rights of all major political elements must be protected by any interim governing assembly.

That, however, is not enough; suspicion and fear are now too deeply ingrained. The Communists would fear a takeover by the military, just as we might fear a Communist coup. Therefore it will be necessary to phase out the withdrawal of American and North Vietnamese forces over a period of time and, as our forces depart, to replace them by international forces to police the cease-fire, guard against violence and coercion, and supervise the elections. In this we can create the confidence necessary to agreement.

Moreover, it is both wise and right for other countries to play a part in keeping the peace in Asia. As all are menaced by conflict, all should help bear the burden of peace. There is no reason why the United States should expend its resources and the lives of its men while others await the result. Statements by U Thant and many other leaders prove there is intense world concern about Southeast Asia. This is an opportunity to encourage those concerned to share responsibility and decision.[36]

But after negotiations and the withdrawal of American troops, what guarantees would we have that South Vietnam would not be quickly taken over by the Communists? Kennedy attempted to head off this criticism of his proposal in the following fashion:

Once a civilian government has been freely chosen, South Vietnam will be in the hands of its own people; subject to the uncertainties, risks and promise of the political process

[36] *Ibid.*

in a turbulent land. We can be hopeful that it will re-establish friendly relations and commerce with the other countries with whom it shares Southeast Asia. Indeed, its relationship with North Vietnam, and that of the North with other countries, is critical to any lasting settlement of the conflicts in that volatile area.

For even though the war in Vietnam has its unique difficulties and dangers, its resolution must be viewed against the shifting nature of world Communism. In the forties and fifties Communism everywhere was guided from a single center. Communist parties in every land took their orders from Moscow. A Communist victory anywhere meant an automatic extension of the influence and power of the Soviet Union.

There is still grave danger, but the monolithic Communist system is forever shattered. The increasing independence of eastern Europe, the death of Stalin, the bitter quarrel between China and Russia, and the failures of Communism in the developing world have all combined to increase the freedom of Communist states to pursue their own national interests. A Communist state can no longer be assumed to be the automatically obedient instrument of expanding Russian or Chinese power. North Vietnam, like North Korea, Rumania, Yugoslavia, and others can be encouraged to assert its own independence.

We should, therefore, help to demonstrate the rich possibilities open to all Vietnam and, indeed, to all of Southeast Asia once steps are taken down the road to peace. In particular, we must show that peace can lead immediately to an increase in trade and communications between North Vietnam and its neighbors. We must show, perhaps in conjunction with the Soviet Union, that the security and economic welfare of North Vietnam is not in danger. And of great significance, it may be that in such a context North Vietnam will be better able to increase its independence of China, as it has struggled to do throughout much of its history.

In this way, the settlement in South Vietnam may become a bridge to a solution for all Southeast Asia. And perhaps from today's terrible violence can come not only an end to conflict, but also a decisive movement toward that liberation from misery and fear which is necessary to bring fruitful tranquility to the nations and people of Southeast Asia.[37]

Finally, he closed this Senate address with an eloquent restatement of his opening plea for a de-escalation of the war in the hope that negotiations might follow.

Here let me reiterate: I do not think the expansion of this war—whether by an increase of North Vietnamese infiltration into the South, or by a widening of our efforts against the North—will bring the kind of peace we seek. The acts or obduracy of our adversaries may bring a wider war upon us, but it should not be of our doing. And even those, on either side, who think greater force the road to peace should realize that it costs little to try negotiations now, before the war widens further. We address our adversaries, but also ourselves, when we remember the words of Edmund Burke: "Conciliation failing, force remains; but, force failing, no further hope of reconciliation is left." And death—Vietnamese or American—is irrevocable.[38]

However, the Johnson Administration did not accept Kennedy's advice to de-escalate the conflict in Vietnam; indeed, we continued to send more men and munitions. It was in this context that the Senator was asked late in 1967 whether he found credible the official government predictions that victory was in sight.

MR. AGRONSKY: Do you disagree with the current evaluation that has just been given us by General Westmoreland, Commander in South Vietnam, and by Ambassador Bunker, that the end of the war may be in view, that within two years we may be able to bring troops home from Vietnam?
SENATOR KENNEDY: Well, what he said, of course, was that if North Vietnam doesn't escalate, that we continue to do what we are doing, that we continue to bomb the North and that they don't escalate, that is one part of it. And the second is that the South Vietnamese begin to do more. Well, I think the history of the period of the last two years is

[37] *Ibid.*
[38] *Ibid.*

that they are going to continue to escalate. They escalate in a different way, as I point out in my book, than we escalate. They don't bomb Detroit and they don't bomb Chicago and they don't bomb Los Angeles. But the Russians send them more sophisticated weapons. They send more men into the South, and the casualties go up. The casualties have gone up over the period of the last 18 months steadily. So they are going to kill more Americans. I don't see how we can anticipate that they are going to stand still as we escalate on our side. The history of the war hasn't been that. The second part of this question was that the South Vietnamese would do more. But the South Vietnamese, in fact, over the period of the last year, have done less, far less. Our casualties are greater than the casualties of the South Vietnamese now. We are carrying the burden of the fighting. We are carrying the burden of the war. I have always said that it is their war and we are over there to help them, that we cannot win. Now they have had corruption, they have had a lack of land reform, they have failed to put in the democratic procedures that I think we should have, and the democratic processes. Unless they change, unless there is a drastic change, the people of South Vietnam are not going to feel loyalty to Saigon, rather to the Viet Cong and feel that it is worthwhile—they are making the sacrifice, they are making the effort. The South Vietnamese army has really pulled out. Why isn't, for instance in the battle of Dak To, why hasn't it been the South Vietnamese army that has gone up that hill? Why hasn't it been the South Vietnamese army that has been on the demilitarized zone and stayed there? Why does it always have to be the Americans? I think they should do it. They should carry the burden. If they are going to do more of that, and the North Vietnamese will not escalate—which I expect that they will, and the Russians can send them far more sophisticated weapons than they have already—if all of those things come true, then I think that we will be well on our way to winning the war. But I think there has to be a complete 180-degree turn for the South Vietnamese and there has to be a complete change of policy in North Vietnam. I have not seen any indication of that up to the present time. I would like to see the South Vietnamese do more. I would like to see them carrying this burden. Let's see them doing the fighting and not just Americans, because

I don't think there is any alternative to that. We are not going to win unless the South Vietnamese begin to do more, make more of an effort. And it should not be just the United States and Americans doing it. That is what I resent. And, as I say, I think that when we talk about it, there is nothing about this really being said within the Republican party or what we should do within our own country. And that is why I think that people, when we talk about the violence and the people walking out and the lawlessness, there is no way for people to express their point of view, and I think that this is most unfortunate in this country. There is an unhappiness and an uneasiness within the United States at the moment, and there has to be an outlet for them. I think that this poses a very, very important problem and the Republican party offers nothing and we have to do something within the Democratic party.[39]

During the same program he was asked whether he still thought it possible for President Johnson to bring about peace in Vietnam.

MR. AGRONSKY: Let us return to the war and politics in a different way. Do you think that this administration, the administration of President Johnson, can conclude a peace in Vietnam?

SENATOR KENNEDY: Yes, I think it is possible.

MR. MUDD: When? Could it be during this election year?

SENATOR KENNEDY: Well, I think it is more difficult. I think that it is possible to do. I think that the indications over the period of the last few weeks are that we are just going to go in the military field and that we are not going to go to the negotiating table. I think that, under those circumstances, we will continue with the military effort and I think that is going to get—the casualties will continue to rise on both sides, in my judgment.

MR. MUDD: Using the Truman-Eisenhower analogy, if one exists, do you believe that it will take a new President to negotiate a settlement?

SENATOR KENNEDY: No, I think that President Johnson could

[39] "Face the Nation" (CBS-TV), November 26, 1967.

negotiate a settlement. I happen to disagree with the way we are going about it, but I think it could be done.[40]

Two days later, in a major article published under his name in *Look* Magazine, Kennedy summed up his views on the manner in which the administration had been handling the war over the past year. On balance, his outlook was gloomy. He did nothing to mask his feeling that the President had thrown away—possibly irrevocably— several excellent opportunities to initiate negotiations with the enemy.

We can invade the North—and thereby engage another quarter of a million of the enemy in combat: somewhat as if a man afflicted with one migraine were to request another head in which to have a second. We can settle into a "war of attrition" on the Asian mainland, where our adversary has a strategic reserve of 700 million Chinese. In 1964, a former chief of the Strategic Air Command told us that an ultimatum, coupled with the bombing of selected military depots, would bring Vietnam to its knees "within a few days": another of the promises of easy and imminent victory that have not ceased since the French began them in 1946. It is perhaps too much to expect that these promises will no longer be made. It would be incredible if they would any longer be made. It would be incredible if they would any longer be believed.

The third alternative is a negotiated settlement—as we have known for more than two years, the only satisfactory solution to the war. This course is our stated government policy. This is the course that I favor. Only negotiations could allow us to end the fighting without precipitate withdrawal, to avoid the progressive destruction and weakening of South Vietnam and end the drain on our own energies and resources, without great damage to our position in Asia and the world.

Throughout 1966, the chances for such negotiations were present. They reached their height in the winter of 1966-1967. At that point, with a false scent of victory leading us on, the United States cast away what may well have been the last

[40] *Ibid.*

best chance to go to the negotiating table, on terms we clearly would have accepted before. The months of war that have followed have been as destructive, to our own forces and to North Vietnam, as all the years of war before 1967. The damage, and hardening attitudes, may make a negotiated peace impossible for some time to come. An effort for negotiation now may well be rejected.[41]

He even accused the President of some duplicity:

Without further support of any kind, Hanoi's 50,000 regular troops in the South would be hard pressed and at a significant military disadvantage before the 400,000 Americans already there, especially since our great superiority of firepower could be indefinitely maintained by ship and plane. Thus, our February, 1967, terms, still our official position, were in effect a demand for the North Vietnamese to withdraw their forces, to abandon the Viet Cong in the South. This was quite clearly understood in the highest circles of our government at the time. In the winter of 1966-1967, important United States officials felt we were on the brink of a military victory, that our position was considerably stronger and that of our adversaries considerably weaker than had been true a year before. Therefore, they thought, we could afford to stiffen our position. And we did.

Our public pronouncements at this time were very different; publicly, we wanted "just almost any step" in return for a bombing halt. If such a small step is at issue, should it be allowed to determine such a weighty matter? In fact, as was apparent from the President's letter when it was released in March, our actual demands have been much more serious than our public statements have indicated.[42]

Still, Kennedy held out some hope for a negotiated settlement if we would only stop the bombing and if both sides would accept the need for compromise inherent in any meaningful negotiations:

Objective assessment of the prospects for a negotiated

[41] *Look,* November 28, 1967.
[42] *Ibid.*

settlement rests on clear analysis of the minimum goals of both sides, our adversaries' as well as our own. To say that North Vietnam "cannot" negotiate while bombs are falling on Hanoi is not an approbation of its refusal to come to the conference table but merely a prediction that as long as the bombs fall, the war will go on. And to say that the bombing will not cease until we are "assured that infiltration into South Vietnam by land and by sea has stopped" is only to insure that bombing and infiltration will continue, that there will be no negotiations, and that the war will go on.

It was for these reasons—because I felt that the bombing of the North was a major obstacle to negotiations, that it could have been halted at a relatively small risk to ourselves, and that a halt would have demonstrated, to our own people and the world, our interest in a peaceful solution—that I urged in the winter of 1966-1967 that we test the sincerity of the statements by Premier Kosygin and the others by halting the bombing and stating our immediate readiness to negotiate. I said then, as I continue to believe, that "the bombing of the North cannot bring an end to the war in the South; rather that it may well be prolonging the war." And while I feel the possibilities of fruitful negotiations to be significantly less than existed in the winter and spring of 1967, I still feel the effort to reach them should be made.[43]

Of the general elections held in South Vietnam on September 3 of that year—elections Kennedy had enthusiastically welcomed when they had first been proposed—he said merely,

With all the advantages of incumbency, with the support and votes of the armed forces, with their strongest rivals excluded from the contest, running against candidates who themselves did not represent social change or identification with the peasantry—with all this, the military ticket could still win only 34 percent of the vote of three-fifths of the nation.[44]

Yet despite all of this and his loss of faith in the "dom-

[43] *Ibid.*
[44] *Ibid.*

ino theory" (the theory that if Vietnam is allowed to fall to the Communists, the rest of the nations in Southeast Asia will be toppled one after another), Kennedy refused to embrace the belief of many doves that we should simply withdraw our forces unilaterally.

Withdrawal is now impossible. American intervention has created its own reality. All the years of war have profoundly affected our friends and adversaries alike, in ways we cannot measure and perhaps cannot know. Moreover, tens of thousands of individual Vietnamese have staked their lives and fortunes on our presence and protection, and cannot suddenly be abandoned to the forcible conquest of a minority.

Beyond this is the more general question of the American commitment and the effect of withdrawal on our position around the world. Without doubt, the so-called "domino theory," by itself, is a vast oversimplification of international politics. In Asia, China is the biggest of all possible dominoes; yet its fall to the Communists in 1949 did not cause Communist take-overs in its neighbors (though it participated in the Korean War and aided the cause of the Vietminh rebellion already under way). Burma, which refused military and economic assistance from the United States, repressed two Communist insurgencies without interference or disturbance by the Chinese. The Cuban domino did not lead, for all Castro's efforts, to Communist take-overs elsewhere in Latin America. Vietnam's neighbors do not share its combination of government weakness and nationalist revolutionary strength; if they did, surely we would expect that they would long ago have erupted in insurgency while the United States is so heavily engaged in Vietnam.

If the domino theory is an unsatisfactory metaphor, still it contains a grain of truth. A great power does not cease to be that because it suffers a defeat peripheral to its central interests. The Soviet Union is still a great power, notwithstanding the collapse of its Cuban adventure in 1962. But in some degree, the aftermath of Cuba was a perceptible lessening of Russian prestige and ability to influence events in many parts of the world. So, I believe, would defeat or precipitous withdrawal in Vietnam damage us. We would not suddenly collapse; Communist fleets would not appear in the harbor of Honolulu and San Francisco Bay. But there would be serious effects: increased Communist influence—at least—especially in Southeast Asia itself. That is not to say, however, that Chinese expansion would thereby be strengthened. North Vietnam has its own interests and dynamism, and the most constant thread of Vietnamese history and present nationalism seems to be hatred and fear of China.[45]

Finally, the Senator warned that we are making this our war, whereas it must be that of the Saigon government. He also bluntly criticized the military leaders of the South for their unwillingness to institute reform and questioned the wisdom of continuing to support them.

The worst danger of making this our war is that our stake in it becomes greater than that of the Saigon government. But, it is their war, and they must understand that refusing the necessary reforms will have direct and severe consequences. President Kennedy said in 1963: "It is their war. They are the ones who have to win it or lose it. We can help them, we can give them equipment, we can send our men out there as advisers, but they have to win it, the people of Vietnam, against the Communists." Similarly, when President Eisenhower sent American troops to Lebanon in 1958, he ordered them to occupy only the capital and the main airport. "If the Lebanese army were unable to subdue the rebels when we had secured their capital and protected their government," he has written, "we were backing up a government with so little popular support that we probably should not be there."

Continued support of a government that, after this long history and our patient effort, still refuses reform is not pragmatic or tough-minded. It is ideological self-deception and a surrender of American interests to a government that without our support would not survive a month. Moreover, these reforms will be necessary whether or not negotiations take place. In fact, it is only genuine progress in the South, beginning at last to attract the support of the people—and not greater destruction in the North—that offers a real prospect of convincing our adversaries that an early settlement is prudent.[46]

[45] *Ibid.*
[46] *Ibid.*

The Immorality of Vietnam

As you have seen, Robert Kennedy's beliefs about the war in Vietnam underwent enormous change after he entered the Senate. An advocate, as late as 1964, of military victory in South Vietnam as imperative to the preservation of American security, by 1966 he was condemning our escalation of the conflict as contrary to the national interest. It was not until 1967, however, that he began to measure our involvement in the war in moral terms as well.

The emotional elements of his moral doubts about the war were eloquently unveiled by Kennedy in a moving speech on the Senate floor.

Few of us are directly involved while the rest of us continue our lives and pursue our ambitions undisturbed by the sounds and fears of battle. To the Vietnamese, however, it must often seem the fulfillment of the prophecy of Saint John the Divine: "And I looked, and beheld a pale horse: and his name that sat on him was Death, and hell followed with him. And power was given unto them over the fourth part of the earth, to kill with sword, and with hunger, and with death. . . ."

Let us reflect for a moment not on the wisdom and necessity of our causes nor on the valor of the South Vietnamese, but on the horror. For although the world's imperfections may call forth the acts of war, righteousness cannot obscure the agony and pain those acts bring to a single child. The Vietnamese war is an event of historic moment, summoning the grandeur and concern of many nations. But it also is the vacant moment of amazed fear as a mother and child watch death by fire fall from the improbable machine sent by a country they barely comprehend. It is the sudden terror of the official or the civil guard absorbed in the work of his village as he realizes the assassin is taking his life. It is the refugees wandering homeless from villages now obliterated, leaving behind only those who did not live to flee. It is the young men, Vietnamese and American, who in an instant sense the night of death destroying yesterday's promise of family and land and home.

It is a country where young men have never lived a day in

peace and where families have never known a time when it was not necessary to be afraid. It is a land deafened by the unending crescendo of violence, hatred and savage fury; where the absorbing goal for millions is not to live well or to improve their lives, but simply to survive.

It is a country where hundreds of thousands fight, but millions more are the innocent, bewildered victims of brutal passions and beliefs they barely understand. To them peace is not an abstract term describing one of those infrequent intervals when men are not killing each other. It is a day without terror and the fall of bombs. It is a family and the familiar life of their village. It is food and a school and life itself.

All we say and all we do must be informed by our awareness that this horror is partly our responsibility; not just a nation's responsibility, but yours and mine. It is we who live in abundance and send our young men out to die. It is our chemicals that scorch the children and our bombs that level the villages. We are all participants. To know this and to feel the burden of this responsibility is not to ignore important interests, nor to forget that freedom and security must, at times, be paid for in blood. Still even though we must know as a nation what it is necessary to do, we must also feel as men the anguish of what it is we are doing.[47]

On the television show, "Issues and Answers," several months later, Kennedy explained in more intellectual tones why he thought our moral position in the war had been badly undermined. Senator Kennedy was responding to questions put forward by reporters on the show.

SENATOR KENNEDY: Could I answer the first—Mr. Wicker's question, because I think this really is extremely important for us. First we were making the effort there so that people would have their own right to decide their own future and could select their own form of government, and it wasn't going to be imposed on them by the North Vietnamese, and we had the support of the people of South Vietnam. I think that is why we were involved in that struggle. That is certainly the way I looked at it when I was in President Kennedy's administration and when I was with President Johnson. Now

[47] Speech, U.S. Senate, March 2, 1967.

we turned, when we found that the South Vietnamese haven't given the support and are not making the effort; now we are saying we are going to fight there so that we don't have to fight in Thailand, so that we don't have to fight on the West Coast of the United States, so that they won't move across the Rockies. But do we; our whole moral position, it seems to me, changes tremendously. One, we're in there, we're helping people. We're working with them. We're fighting for their independence. Second, we're killing the enemy and we're also killing many civilians, but we're doing it because they want it. Now we've changed and we've switched. Maybe they don't want it but we want it, so we're going in there and we're killing South Vietnamese, we're killing children, we're killing women, we're killing innocent people because we don't want to have the war fought on American soil, or because they're 12,000 miles away and they might get to be 11,000 miles away. Our whole moral position changes, it seems to me, tremendously. Do we have the right here in the United States to say that we're going to kill tens of thousands, make millions of people, as we have, refugees, kill women and children, as we have? There are 35,000 people without limbs in South Vietnam. There are 150,000 civilian casualties every year, thousands of children are killed because of our efforts. Do we have that right here in the United States to perform these acts because we want to protect ourselves, so that we don't have —it is not a greater problem for us here in the United States. I very seriously question whether we have that right and I think other people are fighting it. Other people are carrying the burden. But this is also our war. Those of us who stay here in the United States, we must feel it when we use na- palm, when a village is destroyed and civilians are killed. This is also our responsibility. This is a moral obligation and a moral responsibility for us here in the United States. And I think we have forgotten about that. And when we switched from one point of view to another, I think we have forgotten about that. And I think that it should be discussed and all of us should examine our own conscience of what we are doing in South Vietnam. It is not just the fact that we are killing North Vietnamese soldiers or Viet Cong; we are also responsible for tens and tens of thousands of innocent civilian casualties, and I think we are going to have a difficult time explaining this to ourselves.

MARTIN AGRONSKY: You feel that our moral position, then, is not really defensible, that it can't be?

SENATOR KENNEDY: Well, I think it has been badly undermined and I think it should trouble us. I think that the picture in the paper of a child drowning should trouble us more than it does, or the picture last week of a paratrooper holding a rifle to a woman's head, it must trouble us more than it does. All acts of aggression, death, and destruction occur in war and—sometimes wars are essential, are necessary, are going to occur. But we should also consider the price that we are paying. It is not just the Americans that are being wounded and the price that we are paying so that we can't do the kinds of things that we should, but we have a moral position around the world. We stand for anything that is different from the Communists. We have a moral position around the world. But we can't lose that, as it appears to be that we are doing in Vietnam. Why can't the President of the United States or the Vice-President of the United States travel freely around the world anymore? It is because of Vietnam. Why can't they go through Latin America? Why can't they travel through Europe? Why can't they even travel freely through our own country? . . .

We should look at it in an objective way, of what we are doing, what we are trying to do, and what this country stands for, both within our—internally within the United States, and what we have to stand for around the rest of the globe. If this country is going to mean anything—when we say we love our country, we love our country for what it can be and for the justice it stands for and what we are going to mean to the next generation. It is not just the land, it is not just the mountains, it is for what this country stands for. And that is what I think is being seriously undermined in Vietnam and the effect of it has to be felt by our people.[18]

And on March 16, 1968, when he threw his hat into the primary race against Lyndon Johnson and Eugene McCarthy, Kennedy's credentials as a vigorous opponent of the war in Vietnam were undeniable. No one could doubt that Robert Francis Kennedy was a peace candidate for the presidency of the United States.

[18] "Issues and Answers" (ABC-TV), June 17, 1962.

Appendix

Your Eminences, Your Excellencies, Mr. President. In behalf of Mrs. Kennedy, her children, the parents and sisters of Robert Kennedy, I want to express what we feel to those who mourn with us today in this cathedral and around the world.

We loved him as a brother and as a father and as a son. From his parents and from his older brothers and sisters, Joe and Kathleen and Jack, he received an inspiration which he passed on to all of us.

He gave us strength in time of trouble, wisdom in time of uncertainty and sharing in time of happiness. He will always be by our side.

Love is not an easy feeling to put into words. Nor is loyalty or trust or joy. But he was all of these. He loved life completely and he lived it intensely.

A few years back Robert Kennedy wrote some words about his own father which expresses the way we in his family felt about him. He said of what his father meant to him, and I quote:

"What it really all adds up to is love. Not love as it is described with such facility in popular magazines, but the kind of love that is affection and respect, order and encouragement and support.

"Our awareness of this was an incalculable source of strength. And because real love is something unselfish and involves sacrifice and giving, we could not help but profit from it."

And he continued:

"Beneath it all he has tried to engender a social conscience. There were wrongs which needed attention, there were people who were poor and needed help, and we have a responsibility to them and this country.

"Through no virtues and accomplishments of our own, we have been fortunate enough to be born in the United States under the most comfortable condition. We therefore have a responsibility to others who are less well off."

That is what Robert Kennedy was given.

What he leaves to us is what he said, what he did and what he stood for.

A speech he made for the young people of South Africa on their day of affirmation in 1966 sums it up the best, and I would like to read it now.

"There is discrimination in this world and slavery and slaughter and starvation. Governments repress their people. Millions are trapped in poverty, while the nation grows rich and wealth is lavished on armaments everywhere.

"These are differing evils, but they are the common works of man. They reflect the imperfection of human justice, the inadequacy of human compassion, our lack of sensibility towards the suffering of our fellows.

"But we can perhaps remember, even if only for a time, that those who live with us are our brothers, that they share with us the same short moment of life, that they seek as we do nothing but the chance to live out their lives in purpose and happiness, winning what satisfaction and fulfillment they can.

"Surely this bond of common faith, this bond of common goals, can begin to teach us something. Surely we can learn at least to look at those around us as fellow men. And surely we can begin to work a little harder to bind up the wounds among us and to become in our own hearts brothers and countrymen once again.

"The answer is to rely on youth, not a time of life but a state of mind, a temper of the will, a quality of imagination, a predominance of courage over timidity, of the appetite for adventure over the love of ease. The cruelties and obstacles of this swiftly changing planet will not yield to the obsolete dogmas and outworn slogans; they cannot be moved by those who cling to a present that is already dying, who prefer the illusion of security to the excitement and danger that come with even the most peaceful progress.

"It is a revolutionary world which we live in, and

this generation at home and around the world has had thrust upon it a greater burden of responsibility than any generation that has ever lived. Some believe there is nothing one man or one woman can do against the enormous array of the world's ills. Yet many of the world's great movements of thought and action have flowed from the work of a single man.

"A young monk began the Protestant Reformation. A young general extended an empire from Macedonia to the borders of the earth. A young woman reclaimed the territory of France, and it was a young Italian explorer who discovered the New World, and the thirty-two-year-old Thomas Jefferson who explained that all men are created equal.

"These men moved the world, and so can we all. Few will have the greatness to bend history itself, but each of us can work to change a small portion of events, and in the total of all those acts will be written the history of this generation.

"Each time a man stands for an ideal, or acts to improve the lot of others, or strikes out against injustice, he sends forth a tiny ripple of hope.

"And crossing each other from a million different centers of energy and daring, those ripples build a current will ultimately be judged and as the years pass, we will surely judge ourselves, on the effort we have contributed to building a new world society and the extent to which our ideals and goals have shaped that event.

"Our future may lie beyond our vision, but it is not completely beyond our control. It is the shaping impulse of America that neither faith nor nature nor the irresistible tides of history but the work of our own hands matched to reason and principle will determine our destiny."

There is pride in that, even arrogance, but there is also experience and truth, and in any event it is the only way we can live. That is the way he lived. That is what he leaves us.

My brother need not be idealized or enlarged in death beyond what he was in life. He should be remembered simply as a good and decent man who saw wrong and tried to right it, saw suffering and tried to heal it, saw war and tried to stop it.

Those of us who loved him and who take him to his rest today pray that what he was to us, and what he wished for others, will someday come to pass for all the world.

As he said many times, in many parts of this nation

For Release: AM's
Sunday, May 12, 1968

Statement of Senator Robert F. Kennedy

A Program for a Sound Economy

The inner strength of the American economy pushes the nation's output and employment upward to new levels, but inflationary pressures and the balance of payments problem could create an economic crisis of major proportions within the next year. Three obstacles to our prosperity are of considerable importance:

1. Inflation and the Budget Deficit
2. Balance of Payments Deficit
3. Declining ratio of productivity to labor costs

We must have an economic program that will avoid the grave risks to our prosperity inherent in each of these areas. The objectives of that sound economic program are shared by all:

~~bravery in battle or great i~~ ~~context of~~ greater price essential vital quality for those who seek to change a world that yields most painfully to change.

"And I believe that in this generation those with the courage to enter the moral conflict will find themselves with companions in every corner of the globe.

"For the fortunate among us there is the temptation to follow the easy and familiar paths of personal ambition and financial success so grandly spread before those who enjoy the privilege of education. But that is not the road history has marked out for us.

"Like it or not, we live in times of danger and uncertainty. But they are also more open to the creative energy of men than any other time in history. All of us

      —increases in expenditures for domestic programs of benefit to our people
      —an easing of monetary policy, with lower interest rates

Our economic policy must reflect our social goals—the prosperity we build must be shared by all Americans. This is a program to make our economy sound, strong and able to meet the needs of all our citizens:

First, maintain full employment without inflation by coordinating fiscal, monetary and foreign policies. This means prompt action to moderate the pace of the economy by:

      —a moderate increase in individual and corporate income tax—insuring that this tax rise does not bear too hard on families with modest incomes or on small businesses.

      —controls on expenditures in non-essential defense, in space, in SST development, in those public works and highway projects which involve site acquisition and other special costs out of all proportion to their employment benefit—but no reduction of expenditures for education, health, housing, urban development and job programs.

      —an expectation that the Federal Reserve Board would respond by easing monetary policy and a readiness to make special provisions to ensure a steady supply of money for home financing.

      —a willingness to withdraw the tax increase if it exerts too much restraint on the economy or if we are successful in our efforts to end the war in Vietnam. In passing a tax increase Congress should give the President standby power to make this adjustment in fiscal policy—subject to approval or rejection by the Congress. President Kennedy made such a proposal for a more flexible fiscal policy in 1962—Congress ought to adopt it now.

At the same time greater emphasis must be placed on long-term policies to stabilize the economy:

—the government must adjust its own policies to exert a stabilizing influence on the economy: to insure that minimum wage increases are consistent with a policy of full employment; to insure that wage increases for public employees are not self-defeating in their inflationary effect: to insure that procurement practices encourage pricing that is not inflationary.

—business and labor must work out their own wage and price levels, but show statesmanship—so that excessive demands or efforts to get the last bit of profit out of an overheated economy do not fuel the wage-price spiral.

—our policies must recognize the importance of increasing productivity as a cost reducing program. In 1967 output per man hour increased only 40% as much as the average annual gain from 1960-1966, and new investment rose only 1½% compared to gains of 14% in 1965 and 18% in 1966. Private industry must be stimulated to develop new products and new methods of production through technological research. Government should undertake a thoroughgoing review of its contracting policies in order to encourage modernization as a means of reducing prices and increasing profits.

—we must promote labor mobility—from one skill level to another in order to allow realization of the benefits of new technology and open new job opportunities for the unemployed and the under-employed; and from one part of the country to another in order to insure that spot shortages and surpluses of labor—now prevalent—are avoided. Realization of these goals involves assisting workers to improve their skills and get a better job; breaking down barriers to entry into all trades and all professions; modernizing placement services to provide instant information and recruitment for job openings in different parts of the country; and exploring ways to insure that pension rights are not sacrificed as a consequence of accepting a better job.

—our policies must promote competition in order to pass on the benefits of productivity to consumers.

—the government must do more to provide full information on economic developments and trends in order to facilitate business planning and movements of labor and capital.

Second, reduce the balance of payments deficit and act to reform the international monetary system:

—by pressing for multilateral action to create a reserve currency that can grow with expanding world trade. This is essential if speculation against the dollar is to be controlled; and if there is to be an international monetary system which is able to make allowances for deficits and surpluses. World trade has increased from $50 billion in 1950 to $200 in 1967, and continues to grow by 5-7% each year. The world supply of gold increases only 2% a year and the demands of private industrial consumers have prevented any increase in gold reserve. The implementation of Special Drawing Rights is a constructive step toward reform of international money and the Congress should give prompt approval to SDR's—but we should not stop there. Trade is so important that the nations of the world can no longer rely on a single commodity whose value is determined by supply and demand. We must have a reserve currency responsive to the requirements of orderly world economic development.

—reform of the international monetary system is an important step, but it will not cure America's balance of payments problem. It is important, too, that we end the war in Vietnam—which accounts for nearly $2 billion of last year's $3.7 billion deficit—although that will not end the payments deficit. In the last 10 years the United States has accumulated deficits amounting to $25-$30 billion. And the dollar holdings of foreign banks have increased correspondingly. They are less and less willing to continue to increase their dollar holdings and are more likely to demand gold instead—a situation which could cause us great difficulty. We must reduce the imbalance by action to:

1. Eliminate unnecessary military expenditures abroad, not just by pressing our effort to de-escalate the war in Vietnam, but by reassessing our troop commitments in other parts of the globe. Press for mutual action with the Soviet Union to reduce the number of troops in Europe.

2. Promote American exports abroad by further multilateral action to remove existing barriers to trade. From 1962-1967 imports rose 63.6% and the value of exports increased only 47.5%. In the first three months of this year, imports rose in value by 20.5% over the first quarter of 1967, while exports rose less than 5%—and in March the three-month figures showed a trade deficit of $158 million, the first in five years. We have consistently run a trade surplus of from $5 to $8 billion, and we need to restore that surplus to offset deficits in other accounts including lending and investment abroad, travel, military expenditures and foreign aid.

3. Stimulate foreign travel in the United States; restrictions on Americans traveling abroad are neither economically sound nor socially desirable.

4. Avoid undue and short-sighted restrictions on the flow of private capital abroad, because productive investment eventually returns substantial income to the United States. An effort should be made to encourage investment in the less developed countries of the world—investment that benefits the economic development of the host country rather than simply extracts its natural resources.

5. Make our products competitive in world markets by controlling inflation at home, stimulating investment in research and development that can increase productivity and reduce prices.

Third, we must undertake major reform of our tax laws to assure that all Americans share equitably in the cost of government, and to assist in raising the revenues necessary to meet the challenges which confront America.

We must reexamine those provisions that permit many Americans to escape their fair share of the tax burden, including:

—the oil depletion allowance and immediate write-off of intangible drilling costs which cost the Treasury $2 billion a year.

—the exemption of income on state and local bonds—
for two-thirds of these securities are held by persons
with income in the top 1% of all taxpayers; the tax exemption costs twice as much as a direct subsidy to local governments to meet the added cost of marketing taxable
securities; and the exemption reduces tax revenue about
$1.8 billion a year.

—the failure of the law to impose a tax on the appre-
ciation in property—passed at death—an omission that
costs the government an additional $3 billion a year.

This effort at reform is complex and difficult, and will
take time. But there is at least one matter of reform
which is relatively simple and would end the flagrant
situations of tax avoidance.

That is a *minimum income tax*, a minimum percentage
which would prevent the wealthy from continuing to escape taxation completely. We might, for example, require
all who earn over $50,000—in ordinary income, in tax
exempt interest on capital gains and so on—to pay at
least 20% of that income in taxes. This is not a complex
proposal. It is just and fair. It should be enacted now. At
the same time we can begin to work for a general tax
reform—so our tax system is equitable and efficient, and
capable of producing the revenue required to meet our
needs.

Fourth, the resources of private enterprise must be
enlisted in the effort to meet the needs of 29 million
Americans living in poverty:

—by granting tax benefits to companies that provide
jobs for men without work, so that the economy can take
advantage of the productive potential of more than 5 million unemployed and underemployed.

—by granting tax benefits to those who will build housing where it is most needed.

—by providing credit for businesses, locating facilities
in or near poverty areas.

—by assisting private enterprise in securing adequate
insurance for their plants and equipment.

Fifth, we must institute a simple technique to supplement federal grant-in-aid programs and return a portion of federal tax revenues to local communities so that needed services in fields like education, health, and job development and training can be provided without undue federal red tape and necessary decisions made to a greater extent at the local level. We can begin to do this by taking 1% of taxable personal income and returning it to local communities according to a formula based on population and state-local tax effort. The federal government should set guidelines for the use of these funds—not detailed regulations, as under present grant-in-aid programs, but over-all policy goals. The federal government should retain general supervisory power over plans for the use of the money, but the local communities must have control in deciding how to develop the facilities and services needed by all of their citizens.

The Economy After Vietnam

Peace in Vietnam will bring great economic opportunity at home. But we must be prepared to make the adjustments necessary in our economic policy:

—over eighteen months arms spending can probably be reduced by $15-$20 billion. A recent study suggested this will mean a loss of 1.5 million jobs, but the same study suggests that we can create 1.7 million new jobs by appropriate public policy decisions. This should involve a two-fold program: stimulate demand by a tax reduction, thereby creating employment; and at the same time increase spending on programs of social benefits, which also stimulates economic growth and creates jobs.

—the great resources which have been devoted to Vietnam—public and private—must be directed to meet the pressing needs of our people for jobs, for quality educations, for better housing and adequate food; funds should be allocated in greater proportion to improve our environment by attacking pollution in the air and water, restoring the beauty of open spaces, improving the comfort and efficiency of transportation systems. The resources of government and private enterprise must be mobilized for peace.

—to improve the lives of all people.

—we should expect an easing of monetary policy with lower interest rates. In this way, housing construction and industrial investment in new products can be stimulated in order to meet the demand created by the return of 900,000 servicemen to civilian life. This demand will help the economy adjust to the post-war period without a decline in prosperity.

—we should be prepared to expand programs of job retraining, relocation, and low interest loans to assist adjustment in areas dependent on defense spending. Workers will need assistance to find new jobs; and industry will need help in switching its resources from war production to the products necessary to rebuild American communities. We should begin now to inform industry and labor of their opportunities to invest in consumer areas.

—we must re-examine all of the government programs which transfer resources to the less fortunate to determine whether our investment is being administered as efficiently as it might be and whether it is bringing the greatest return in human dignity and productivity and the greatest contribution to the nation's economy. Our review of transfer payments should be guided by some basic principles: that the availability of productive employment is the most dignified and most economic means of assisting those in need; that need alone should be a sufficient reason for assistance regardless of whether the assistance takes the form of employment or any kind of transfer payments; that minimal standards should be established nationwide to assure that no individual or family falls below the poverty line; that any assistance plan must provide incentives to work, to increase earning capacity of the family. For our fundamental goal must be to insure that all Americans share in our increasing prosperity.

We should be aware that with cooperative effort, the transition can be made without the jarring economic effects that have followed other wars.

May 19, 1968

Statement of Senator Robert F. Kennedy

Solutions to the Problems of Welfare

Perhaps the area of our greatest domestic failure is in the system of welfare—public assistance to those in need. There is a deep sense of dissatisfaction—among recipient and government alike—about what welfare has become over the last 30 years, and where it seems to be going.

Welfare is many things to many people. To the recipient it may be the difference between life and starvation, between a house and homelessness, between the cold wind and a child's coat. To the tax payer, facing inflation in the cost of living, paying for his home and educating his children, welfare may be an unwarranted imposition on an already overburdened tax bill. To certain politicians, willing to oversimplify and confuse the issue, it may be a means to easy popularity.

What really is welfare?

There are about 29 million Americans in poverty. About one fourth of them receive some sort of public assistance; the others must fend for themselves. The average person on welfare receives $89 if blind and $80 if disabled. Dependent children receive $89 a month on a national average; but that average means that children receive $60 a month in New York—and $8.35 a month in Mississippi. No state provides welfare payments which add up to recognized subsistence levels.

Even at these minimal levels, however, the bill for public assistance has been spiralling upward at an increasingly rapid rate.

At the beginning of this fiscal year, there were about 4.5 million people receiving federal aid to dependent children. There are now well over 5.2 million—an increase of nearly 700,000 or 13 per cent in just a few months. In New York City, with over half a million names already on the ADC rolls, 7 to 10 thousand more are added every month. In California, over 65 per cent of the 1.2 million welfare recipients are ADC families.

During fiscal 1967—the last year for which complete

figures are available—the national bill for public assistance was near $5.5 billion: over $3 billion from the federal government and nearly $2.5 billion from state and local governments, and the bill has risen since.

Of the nation's total welfare budget, $1 billion is spent in New York and an equal amount in California. And these totals will rise again as more and more poor people leave farms and dying small towns all over the country.

The bill is rising further every day.

With all this enormous expenditure might we not expect that the recipient would be satisfied? Yet the fact is that they are not. They are as dissatisfied with the welfare system as is anyone in the U.S. They organize and protest and sit-in at welfare offices. Is this rank ingratitude—or is it an indication of how the welfare system has failed? For what are we to make of a system which seems to satisfy neither giver nor recipient—which embitters all those who come in contact with it?

The worst problem is in our very concept of welfare. Welfare began as a necessary program of assistance for those unable to work. But we have tried as well to make it the easy answer to the complex, but by no means insurmountable, problem of unemployment. Our society is full of men without work: two and a half million officially counted as unemployed; over a million and a half who can find only part time or occasional jobs; over half a million more who have become so discouraged that they no longer even look for work; and—especially in the black ghettos of the great cities—hundreds of thousands who have dropped from sight, without homes or families, unseen by all the computers and agencies of government.

These are men like other men. They marry and have children; or they do not marry, but have children just the same. In either case, they often leave home under the strain of joblessness and poverty. We have dealt with the resulting female-headed families not by putting the men to work but by giving the mothers and children welfare. They might have wanted fathers and husbands; we have given them checks. In fact, the welfare system itself has created many of these fatherless families—by requiring the absence of a father as a condition for receiving aid; no one will ever know how many men left their families to let them qualify for assistance so that they might eat, or find a place to live.

More basically, welfare itself has done much to divide our people—to alienate us one from the other. Partly this separation comes from the understandable resentment of the taxpayer, helplessly watching your welfare rolls and your property taxes rise. But there is greater resentment among the poor, the recipient of our charity. Some of it comes from the brutality of the welfare system itself: from the prying bureaucrat, the all-powerful administrator deciding at his desk who is deserving and who is not, who shall live another month and who may starve next week.

But the root problem is in the fact of dependency and uselessness itself. Unemployment means having nothing to do—which means nothing to do with the rest of us. To be without work, to be without use, to one's fellow citizens, is to be in truth the "invisible man" of whom Ralph Ellison wrote; as John Adams said a century and a half ago, "the poor man's conscience is clear; yet he is ashamed. . . . He feels himself out of the sight of others, groping in the dark. Mankind takes no notice of him. He rambles and wanders unheeded. In the midst of a crowd, at church, in the market . . . he is in as much obscurity as he would be in a garret or a cellar. He is not disapproved, censured, or reproached; he is only not seen." Well might we conclude with Adams that: "To be wholly overlooked, and to know it, is intolerable": So we have seen all over the country.

We often quote Lincoln's warning that America could not survive half slave and half free. Nor can it survive while millions of our people are slaves to dependency and poverty, waiting on the favor of their fellow citizens to write them checks. Fellowship, community, shared patriotism—these essential values of our civilization do not come from just buying and consuming goods together. They come from a shared sense of individual independence and personal effort.

They come from working together to build a country and that is the answer to the welfare crisis.

The answer to the welfare crisis is work, jobs, self-sufficiency, and family integrity; not a massive new extension of welfare; not a great new outpouring of guid-ance counselors to give the poor more advice. We need jobs, dignified employment at decent pay; the kind of employment that lets a man say to his community, to his family, to the country, and most important, to himself—"I helped to build this country. I am a participant in its great public ventures. I am a man." For this reason, the first domestic task of any administration must be, and the first priority of my administration will be to create jobs and put men to work: to take new steps, including the provision of tax incentives, to encourage private industry to hire the jobless, and to make the government the employer of last resort.

But if we are to take the necessary action, we must first rid ourselves of certain prevalent myths.

First is the myth that the creation of jobs would not reduce the growth of welfare rolls.

I am aware, of course, that some government officials have contended that of the approximately 8 million wel-fare recipients only 50 thousand plus are able-bodied and employable men. The point, no doubt, was to show, and properly so, that welfare recipients are not simply idlers feeding at the public trough and that the vast majority of welfare recipients need help to survive. An-other 4 million of the 8 million recipients are children, and 1 million are the mothers of these households. The children have a father somewhere; he is not counted in the welfare statistics because in most states he does not qualify for aid, and his family can qualify—and thus be included in the statistics—only if the father does leave home. So it is in no sense inevitable that those 4 million ADC children with their 1 million mothers—well over half the welfare rolls—should have ended up costing us what they do. If those fathers had had jobs, many might never have left their families. And if we provide jobs today, we can help keep hundreds of thousands of fam-ilies from breaking up in the future. We can check—and perhaps even reverse—the disastrous present growth of the welfare system with its burdens on local property taxes and the lives of millions.

Second is the myth that the poor and unemployed do not want to work. All disinterested investigations—most recently the President's Riot Commission—have found that the unemployed do want to work. I myself have met and spoken with these men, white and Negro, from Watts to Eastern Kentucky, from Harlem to Atlanta; and without exception they have said, "No more welfare. Give us work." In California, in Oakland, there was a job fair about a year ago. Fifteen thousand men and youths came looking for jobs; there were jobs for 250. Of course there are those in America who do not want to work. But they are, I think, far more likely to be children of favored families than they are to be men and youths of the poor.

Third is the myth that the problems of welfare can be solved by slogans—by getting tough or cutting back, by making the system even more harsh and punitive than it now is. This is the myth that led the Congress, last year, to adopt amendments, for example, restricting help to families which stay together, allowing states to force mothers to leave their children and placing an absolute limit on federal welfare payments. It helps nothing and no one to rail at and condemn welfare recipients, if there are no jobs for them to take. It will only leave a greater social problem to our own children, if we force millions of other children to grow up without fathers.

Fourth is the myth that all the problems of poverty can be solved by the ultimate extension of the welfare system to guarantee to all, regardless of their circumstances, a certain income paid for by the federal government. Any such scheme, taken alone, simply cannot provide the sense of self sufficiency, of participation in the life of the community, that is essential for citizens of a democracy. At this time, it would have to be maintained at a very low level which would only make dependency and separation between our people more permanent. Indeed, there are some who not only explicitly advocate a guaranteed minimum income at an unlivably low level, but would cut other welfare assistance as well. Most of all, however, primary emphasis on a minimum income guarantee would postpone, perhaps until too late, a massive effort to create new jobs—an effort that we know is the only real solution to this problem. The McCone Commission—Kenneth Clark's pioneering HARYOU study, the White House Conference on Civil Rights, The National Commission on Automation and Technology and most recently the President's Advisory Commission on Civil Disorders all have said that employment is "the major problem." Certainly, all the proposals for various systems for income maintenance deserve careful study. But if there is anything we have learned in the last three years, it is that we cannot do everything at once —that we must understand, establish, and adhere to a clear sense of national priorities. The priority here is jobs. To give priority to income payments would be to admit defeat on the critical battle front. And the worst thing we could do would be to pretend to the poor or to ourselves that we could give them a pittance to leave us alone.

Moreover, putting our primary emphasis on the guaranteed annual income would also be tremendously wasteful. Virtually every man represents potential labor that can make a real contribution to our society. With all the dilapidated housing in America, with the ravaged parklands and inadequate school buildings, with all this work to be done, how can we pay men to sit at home? Government transfer payments help those who receive them, with indirect benefits for the rest of us. But putting men to work is of immense direct benefit to themselves and to the entire country. A million unemployed men represent an investment in their feeding and care and education—just through their eighteenth year—of at least $30 billion. Maintaining them and their families would mean another $3 billion each year. If they do not work, all that investment is lost to us. But the employment of even half of them, at minimal levels of productivity, would return $2 billion to society each year, and more as time goes on. It would build up equities in social security, union pension funds and insurance programs. It would, in short, help to build the nation. We need the productivity of these men—for themselves and for others.

Once, however, that we have begun to move toward real employment, it will be imperative to move toward an adequate system of assistance for those who truly cannot work to enable them to lead decent lives. The system should have these characteristics, among others:

—It must be automatic, without the complex and complicated bureaucratic structure that now bedevils the welfare system—and which eats up as much as one-fifth of every welfare dollar.
—It must be based on one criterion: need.
—It must have national standards, and not the state by state variations which now allow Mississippi to pay $55 welfare a month to a family of six.
—It must contain substantial incentives for people to work if they can, rather than the present welfare system which virtually penalizes work.
—The social services offered in association with it should not be segregated, but should also be available for an appropriate fee to people able to pay.

Meanwhile, it is urgently necessary to reform certain features of the present welfare system, as follows:

One, repeal the restrictive 1967 welfare amendments:

a) the freeze of federal aid for dependent children;
b) the requirement that mothers with small children leave home and go to work;
c) the restrictions on the program of aid to dependent children of unemployed fathers.

Two, enact a mandatory program of aid to dependent children whose fathers are unemployed and living at home (now implemented in only 22 states) and thereby repeal the man-in-the-house rule which has caused family after family to break up so that children can obtain assistance.

Three, enact federal minimum standards for welfare assistance to assure a floor of security for every citizen in need.

Four, raise the earnings incentive enacted last year so wages do more than essentially replace welfare payments and more welfare recipients will thereby be encouraged to go to work.

Five, make assistance available to men who work but do not earn even subsistence pay.

Six, assure a full and fair hearing before welfare assistance is cut off or refused, and assure that all rights to assistance are clear and enforceable.

Seven, simplify the process of applying for welfare to minimize degrading interrogations and investigations, and insure that recipients are treated with simple elementary dignity.

Eight, encourage the formation of client and advisory councils to assist in making the system responsive to recipients' needs and concerns.

Nine, provide simplified handbooks for welfare recipients so they know what services the law entitles them to.

Ten, employ more recipients and neighborhood residents as case aides and expeditors to help obtain assistance and service.

Eleven, encourage decentralization of administration in large cities and sparsely populated rural areas so help and assistance are easily available through neighborhood or area centers to those in need.

Twelve, expand day care centers so mothers who want to work can obtain care for their children, and employ neighborhood residents in the centers.

Nevertheless, the first priority is and must be jobs. Work is a mundane and unglamorous word. Yet it is, in a real sense, the meaning of what this country is all about—for those of us who live in affluent suburbs and for our children no less than for the children in the ghetto. Human beings need a purpose. We need it as individuals; we need to sense it in our fellow citizens; and we need it as a society and as a people.

We can achieve that purpose if we develop a system where there are jobs at decent pay for all who are able to work, and adequate assistance provided in a dignified way for those who are unable to work.

For Release:
Sunday, May 26, 1968

A Business Development Program for Our Poverty Areas

May 26, 1968

No single problem underlies the poverty of our urban centers and rural backwaters. Poverty means inadequate educational systems which result in high-school drop-out rates often reaching nearly 70 percent. Poverty means inadequate health conditions which doom thousands of children before they even reach school age. Poverty means broken families and high crime rates. It means inadequate housing and inadequate social services. And it means going to school on an empty stomach and going to bed hungry.

But above all else, poverty means a lack of jobs. For a young man, it means being cut off from the ability to sustain himself and his family—from contributing to his community and his Nation. It means living without the dignity and pride that comes from working at a meaningful job paying a meaningful wage.

During the last 6 years, we have tried to solve this terrible problem. Almost every Congress has enacted another bill designed to put people to work: the Area Redevelopment Act, the Manpower Development and Training Act, the Investment Credit Act, the Economic Development Act, and the Economic Opportunity Act. But despite all these efforts and despite the uninterrupted rise in prosperity experienced by the rest of the Nation:

—more than 11 million working age Americans are either unemployed or have jobs which pay less than a living wage;
—more than 4 million of our citizens cannot find jobs at all today, 750,000 of whom have given up looking;
—for 2 million of these unemployed no jobs exist no matter what their qualifications and new jobs must be created for them;

—in our urban slums unemployment is two and three times higher than in surrounding communities and the subemployment rate is as high as 45%;

—in rural areas, where 14 million of our 29.7 million poor live, 800,000 Americans cannot find jobs.

But these dismal figures measure only the shortage of jobs. They fail to reveal the fact that to millions of Americans who sit in idleness and despair, participation in the *economic* life of their country, their state and their community is denied. It is not simply jobs that our unemployed lack. They also lack what the Kerner Commission called "a stake in the economic community"—the opportunity to own or manage a business. And this is especially true for minority groups:

—Negroes own only 50,000, in terms of population, one tenth their proportionate share of businesses across the country.

—In cities like Newark, with a majority of its population Negro, only 10% of the businesses are owned or managed by Negroes.

—In Washington, D.C., where the population is 63% Negro, only 13% of the businesses are owned by Negroes.

—One large corporation has reported that not one of its 7000 subcontractors is Negro-owned or managed.

—Most Negro businesses, except for a few moderate-sized banks, insurance companies and publishing houses are marginal enterprises—small retail groceries, lunch counters, and small contractors which provide little income to their owners and have no opportunity to expand.

Similar problems exist for low and moderate income white residents of poverty areas.

Clearly then, our main focus must be on providing employment opportunities which will enable the residents of poverty areas to participate in the economic life of their community—a task which we have not yet begun nationwide, but which has already been demonstrated in one community.

In 1966 I helped organize in New York City's Bedford-Stuyvesant area, a new joint venture between residents and the business community, with the support and assistance of local and state public officials from both parties. We have demonstrated there that meaningful social and economic change can be made in the country's most populous black community. *Newsweek* Magazine has called the Bedford-Stuyvesant project "the most sweeping and comprehensive rehabilitation effort ever brought to bear on a single American community."

Some of the accomplishments in Bedford-Stuyvesant to date illustrate the major changes that are taking place:

—Community residents have worked out their own programs for jobs, housing rehabilitation, and educational advancement with financial help furnished by the government and by some of America's largest corporations.

—Two community corporations, the Restoration Corporation and the Development and Services Corporation, one controlled by residents and the other by some of the leading businessmen in the Nation, are working together on all phases of the project. They are developing, for example, local Negro-owned businesses and they have succeeded with assistance from the Federal Special Impact program in getting local franchises from community residents from national firms.

—A $100 million commitment has been made by more than 80 banks and insurance companies to provide long term mortgage money which will reduce residents' monthly payments by as much as one-third.

—A major corporation has announced plans to build a plant in the area to create 300 new jobs.

—Labor unions have cooperated in training young men to work on housing rehabilitation projects.

—A new community college will be established.

—The community has its own television program—in effect, a community newspaper—twice a week.

All these efforts, and others in Bedford-Stuyvesant have

demonstrated that our slum areas can be rebuilt through local ownership, self determination and cooperation.

But new programs are needed—programs which will create new jobs, which will enable the hard core unemployed to fill existing job vacancies, and which will open new opportunities in private enterprise.

We must make it possible for urban ghetto residents to move out of the ghetto if they so choose. Jobs must be made available throughout our metropolitan areas and transportation assistance must be given to enable ghetto residents to travel to those jobs.

We must have an immediate emergency employment program, a program that I have co-sponsored in the Senate, providing jobs in public service with built-in training so that those on the job can move up career ladders. Public service employment is growing at nearly 4 or 5 times the rate of private employment. Major contributions can be made by community residents to meet the need for constructing and maintaining new community facilities and for improving our schools, libraries, hospitals and police forces.

We must also promote on-the-job training in existing private industry. This is now being undertaken with increased emphasis on the hard core. But direct subsidies of employee training costs, while helpful, are of limited value since, alone, on-the-job training will not create new jobs. Unless private businesses can also expand existing establishments or build new facilities, the hard core and the unskilled person will simply replace another more qualified worker who might have filled a vacant job.

We must, if we are to solve the employment problems of the poor, provide new jobs in our poverty areas. We must create an economic climate in which businesses, especially those owned and managed by members of minority groups and residents of poverty areas, will be willing to establish new facilities and expand existing facilities in the centers of our cities and in the midst of our rural poverty areas.

But the role of private enterprise can only complement other community efforts. There must be new community-based institutions such as Community Development Corporations, controlled by local residents, through which their wishes will be made known. This is central to the success already demonstrated in Bedford-Stuyvesant. It is essential that indigenous resident participation be coupled with economic development programs.

We must make these efforts for these reasons:

First, we must begin to stem the tide of migration from our farms and rural villages. Without a viable economic base for rural America, a base which can support the men, women and children of these areas at more than a bare subsistence level, millions of poor people will continue to pour into our cities, straining their resources to the breaking point.

Second, we know that at the present time, large numbers of the urban poor cannot be induced to take jobs far away from the areas in which they live. As the Secretary of Labor told the Senate Executive Reorganization Subcommittee, "most of the unemployed in the slums" are so "conditioned by a century of insecurity" that even distances of "more than six or eight blocks away from where they live" create a severe problem. Most new job openings are, of course, much more than a few blocks outside poverty areas.

Third, most cities lack the mass transportation facilities to take them to and from their place of work at a price they can afford to pay. The Department of Labor has found that "present transportation systems are both inadequate and too expensive to bring the slum residents to these jobs."

Fourth, location of new industrial facilities in or near poverty areas will have an important "multiplier" effect on the creation of jobs. New auxiliary businesses will be spun off in the same area to service the needs of the primary facility. New retail and service facilities—restaurants and food stores, barbershops, dry cleaners, and clothing stores—will be required to satisfy the demands of the workers at the primary establishment. Most of these derivative jobs and entrepreneurial opportunities will be open to poverty area residents.

Fifth, location of investment and jobs in or near poverty areas is important for its own sake. Partly, it is important to end these areas' isolation—to bring not just individual residents, but the entire community, back into contact with the mainstream of American life. It is important that children and young people see change and development take place through the work of their own fathers and brothers—providing concrete hope through living example. And, it is vital that poverty areas, like other communities, be able to develop a sense of joint community achievement and purpose.

But merely to reach the conclusion that it is necessary for new businesses to establish facilities in and near urban and rural poverty areas will not suffice. For the simple fact is that businesses are not presently making any efforts to establish such facilities in these areas.

Private corporations are, of course, responsible to their stockholders. Large-scale investment in poverty areas will certainly be more costly and difficult than investment elsewhere. Land, transportation, procurement of supplies, training of workers, extra supervision—all these are so costly in poverty areas as to make investment there, under present conditions, uneconomical. If private enterprise is to play its full part in relation to poverty areas, therefore, it must have the support of government to help make up for increased costs.

I have already proposed the first step in this effort. Last July I introduced legislation to provide this support to certain businesses locating facilities in the poorest urban and rural areas. That bill is designed to provide such businesses with tax credits and excess deductions which they can offset against income derived directly from the new facility or against income derived from another source.

In brief, this tax incentive program would work as follows:

First, it would apply only to companies constructing new facilities or expanding existing ones in poverty areas.

Second, full consultation with the residents of the poverty area affected would have to take place before any industrial facility was constructed.

Third, any qualifying business would have to meet certain hiring requirements—both as to number and percentage of low-income, unemployed persons.

Fourth, job training would be undertaken to prepare men for specific roles in clearly designated and available jobs.

Fifth, any qualifying business would receive the following tax incentives during the ten years immediately following the time that it began operations:

—a 10 percent credit on machinery and equipment in lieu of the normal maximum 7 percent credit.
—a 7 percent credit on expenditures for constructing an industrial facility or for leasing space for a qualifying business.
—a credit carryback of 3 taxable years and a carryover of 10 taxable years.
—a useful life, for purposes of depreciation, of 66⅔ percent of the normal useful life.
—a special deduction of an additional 25 percent of the salaries paid to all workers hired to meet the requirements of this act.

That the use of tax incentives to encourage industrial development in this nation's poverty areas is both a necessary and appropriate step has received growing recognition. In its recent report, the President's Advisory Committee on Rural Poverty concluded that for firms locating in poverty areas, tax incentives in the form of "liberalized investment . . . credits, accelerated depreciation . . . and broader carry forward-carry backward provisions [should] be given." This conclusion was strongly seconded by the National Advisory Commission on Civil Disorders. In a special report to the commission by a businessmen's group headed by Charles Thornton, Chairman of Litton Industries, tax incentives in the form of credits, accelerated depreciation and excess salary deductions were recommended.

Thus, the most extensive studies done on the problems of inducing private enterprise to come into this nation's poverty areas have concluded with one basic recommendation. They have found that tax incentives must be utilized if new facilities are to be built in these areas.

Clearly, the time has come for the Administration to support and the Congress to act on these recommendations.

But while enactment of a system of tax incentives

would constitute a major achievement in bringing jobs to those who most need them, it is only a first step.

Businesses can only utilize tax incentives after they have opened new plants. They cannot use them to raise capital.

For all but our largest public companies, the task of obtaining capital to open a new facility—especially one that is in a poverty area—is an insurmountable obstacle. The present tight money market and increased fears of loss due to riots, crime and vandalism have made financing particularly difficult for businesses seeking to begin operations in economically distressed areas.

Present federal economic development programs have proved inadequate. The Economic Development Administration has moved too slowly and cautiously. In 1967, its disbursements totaled only $34 million—a fraction of the money which should have been made available for the financing of new businesses. Although Congress gave EDA authority in 1967 to operate in urban poverty areas—it had previously been confined almost entirely to rural areas—this authority has still not even begun to be implemented. Even when EDA does begin to make urban loans, its interest rate and loan period authority is still too restricted to provide any substantial stimulus to business to open new facilities in urban or rural poverty areas. The tools available to the Small Business Administration are similarly inadequate.

A new capital creation program is clearly needed. We must provide a mechanism which will break the cycle that turns capital away from businesses seeking to establish facilities in poverty areas. In short, we must provide a flow of short term and long term loans to those businesses which will open and expand badly needed industrial and commercial facilities and help turn these economic wastelands into areas of hope and opportunity.

With these needs in mind, I propose two new programs which will directly attack the problem of increasing the flow of capital into poverty areas. Both are designed to create new jobs for the unemployed and underemployed.

The first proposal would make long and short term credit available to any industrial or commercial enterprise, including those owned by members of minority groups and poverty area residents, opening a new business or expanding an existing facility having nine or more employees, two-thirds of whom are poverty area residents. Loans would be made available from private lenders and the federal government, with federal interest subsidies and repayment guarantees up to 50 percent of the total loan. Short term loans would be subsidized up to 3 percent below the marked rate for short term credit; long term loans at a rate of 1 percent below federal borrowing costs.

The second proposal, supplementing the first, is designed to promote the ownership of retail, commercial and industrial enterprise by members of disadvantaged minority groups and residents of poverty areas. Any new or expanding business, at least 30% of which is owned by such persons and which employs six or more persons, two-thirds of whom are poverty area residents, would be eligible for special loan and technical assistance and would have first priority for direct federal loans. Federal loan guarantees would cover 90% instead of 50% of the total loan.

Loan assistance to minority and resident owned business would be coupled with a technical assistance program which would help open up new business opportunities, seek out capital and provide counseling and management training to eligible borrowers and other poverty area businessmen.

Long term credit will be provided through a New Fund administered by the Secretary of Commerce and coordinated with the Administrator of the Small Business Administration and the Secretary of Labor. The proposed New Fund will have a first year appropriation of $400 million which will be increased by $150 million each year thereafter, reaching a maximum authorization of $1 billion.

Short term credit will be provided from Treasury Tax and Loan Accounts—tax and bond purchase payments made to the federal government which are then deposited in commercial banks throughout the country.

The principal features of these two programs are explained briefly below:

Capital Loans for Poverty Area Businesses

First, Eligible Areas—The areas at which this proposal
is directed are:

> —the 193 poverty areas which are located in our ma-
> jor metropolitan centers,
> —this nation's worst rural poverty areas, and
> —Indian reservations.

Second, Eligible Businesses—Virtually any type of industrial or commercial enterprise that can be conducted
in or near an urban or rural poverty area, will be eligible
for assistance under this bill. Thus, manufacturing enterprises as well as service establishments dealing with other
business enterprises will be permitted to obtain financing.
Safeguards will be provided to assure that loans are not
available merely for the purpose of moving an enterprise
from one area to another.

Third, Employment Criteria—The facility must employ
at least nine persons. Of these, at least two-thirds must be
poverty area residents and one-third must have been low-
income persons at the time they were hired.

Fourth, New Fund—A New Fund, to be directed by the
Secretary of Commerce in collaboration with the Director
of the Small Business Administration and the Secretary
of Labor will coordinate all long term lending policies.
Short term lending polices will be directed by the New
Fund in conjunction with the Secretary of the Treasury.

The proposed New Fund will start with an initial appropriation of $400 million the first year—an appropriation
which will increase by $150 million per year so that at
the end of five years the fund will have reached its maximum authorization of $1 billion.

Fifth, Direct and Guaranteed Loans—The primary purpose of the New Fund will be to guarantee and, in some
cases, to make long term loans to poverty area businesses.

In providing financing, the specified preference will be
for the New Fund to guarantee private loans rather than
to provide direct loans. In short, the New Fund will operate as a lender of last resort—making direct loans only

when there exists a reasonable assurance of repayment and when comparable financing cannot be obtained by the borrower from private sources, even with the type of guarantees which could be made by the Fund. As a general rule, all private loans will be subject to a guarantee against loss up to 50% of the amount of the loan, except that when the borrower is one of our major public companies, only a 10% guarantee will be provided.

Sixth, Interest Subsidies and Loan Periods—In order to raise the rates of return which can be derived from poverty area investments—thereby compensating for the unusual risks and difficulties involved in opening a business facility in these areas—direct and guaranteed loans will bear a subsidized interest rate. Long-term loans made directly or guaranteed by the New Fund will carry an effective interest rate 1% below federal borrowing costs. The only limitations on these subsidies will be that the federal payment cannot exceed 5% on any private loan, and, if the business is receiving tax incentives it cannot also receive subsidies. In order to take account of the economic realities of opening poverty area businesses, the New Fund will be authorized to guarantee and provide direct loans for terms up to 35 years. It will also provide loans for up to 80% of project cost. Both in terms of the repayment period and interest charges, these provisions offer great advantages over current federal loan programs.

Seventh, Approval of Guaranteed Loans—In order to avoid red tape and the bureaucratic delays that have invariably occurred in guaranteed loan programs, this proposal rejects the idea of specific government approval for each loan. Rather, the New Fund will be permitted to enter into two year agreements with private lending institutions under which these institutions will be authorized to make guaranteed loans and investments up to a specified quota. Periodic assessments of the performance by lenders will be made and unused quotas will then be reallocated.

Eighth, Short Term Capital—In regard to the development of short term working capital for poverty area businesses, we must establish a further mechanism beyond that of government loans and guarantees.

For years it has been the policy of the federal government in its capacity as a purchaser of goods to promote the development of distressed areas and to assist small businesses. In my judgment, the federal government should now adopt a similar economic development policy by utilizing deposits of public funds as a mechanism for encouraging private banks to provide short term bank credit for poverty area businesses.

Most funds which flow to the federal government in the form of taxes and bond purchase payments remain in the commercial banks through which they are paid in the form of deposits of the federal government. These deposits—which in recent years have normally amounted to about $4 billion—are called Treasury Tax and Loan Accounts and any bank may become eligible to hold such an account. The monies deposited of course earn income for the bank when they are invested, but, as in the case of any demand deposit, the bank pays no interest or other fee to the depositor.

In my judgment, the Secretary of the Treasury would be authorized to establish certain minimum requirements for loans to poverty area businesses, which must be met by special depositaries located in or near these poverty areas. The requirements would be tied to the average balance in the bank's Tax and Loan Account, so that the performance level that a bank would be expected to meet would relate to the benefit which the federal government gives the bank in the form of interest free deposits. The requirements might start as low as 3% of the bank's Tax and Loan Account during the first year and rise in subsequent years to as much as 15%.

This proposal would not simply constitute an additional burden for each depository bank. Any bank which met its percentage requirement would be eligible to receive further deposits of the federal government equal to a significant percentage of its qualified loans. These deposits—which would be in the range of 20 to 50% of the funds put into qualified loans—would not be kept in the bank's regular Tax and Loan Account where they would be subject to withdrawal. In an effort to give a greater incentive to the bank, these new compensating deposits would be maintained in separate accounts which would be kept open by the federal government for at least a calendar quarter.

The funds to meet these additional balances for the banks which do not meet their percentage requirement would be derived in the first instance from withdrawals from the banks which do meet their percentage requirement. If most banks meet them so that there is insufficient money available for non-complying banks to provide extra deposits to complying banks, the New Fund would deposit some of its reserve underlying the loan guarantee in complying banks.

Short term loans made by these depository banks would be subject to the same guarantees by the New Fund that will apply to long term loans. Moreover, an interest rate subsidy up to a maximum of 3% will be paid by the federal government. This subsidy will be utilized to reduce the short term costs of capital to qualified poverty area businesses.

Special Loan and Technical Assistance to Members of Disadvantaged Minority Groups and Poverty Area Residents

While the above program, providing credit to business operating in or near poverty areas will, of course, apply to businesses owned by members of disadvantaged minority groups and by low and moderate income residents of poverty areas, its primary benefit will be in inducing outside, established business to enter poverty areas. Special assistance should, in addition, be made available to members of disadvantaged minority groups—Negroes, Spanish, and Mexican-American, Puerto Ricans and Indians—and to poverty area residents. These are the people who have the greatest stake in the future of their own communities. They must be assisted to enter the mainstream of American economic life.

Special Loan Assistance:

I therefore propose that for enterprises, at least 30% of which are owned by members of minority groups and low and moderate income residents of poverty areas, the provisions of the above-described capital loan program be modified so that:

1. If there is a shortage of federal funds for direct loans or for loan guarantees, priority will be given to such businesses.
2. Retail businesses, as well as commercial and industrial enterprises, will receive both short and long term loans.
3. Federal guarantees will be for up to 90% of the total project cost, instead of 50%.
4. Eligible businesses need employ only 6 employees, instead of 9.
5. Loans will be for up to 90% of the total project cost, instead of 50%.
6. The federal government will provide guarantees of up to 50% of equity investments of institutions such as small business development corporations in order to create new sources of equity capital. No existing federal program provides guarantees for equity investments which are generally subject to rigid repayment requirements.
7. Community groups within poverty areas will be authorized to obtain loans for purchasing and building facilities for lease back to any businesses qualifying for long or short term loans.

Technical Assistance:

Capital, while vital, is not enough to establish viable businesses owned and managed by members of disadvantaged minority groups and low and moderate income residents of poverty areas. These groups have been so long excluded from business activities that they also need technical management assistance.

Present federal technical assistance efforts are underfinanced and suffer from serious deficiencies.

First, there has been significant lack of coordination. Some cities have several programs, others have none. Programs rarely work closely with each other, either nationally or locally. As a result, tools which are available to one group are often not used by others. Neither successes nor failures are known so that newer efforts frequently do not learn from earlier experience.

Second, most of the businesses created or helped by existing programs are marginal and many are sole-proprietorships. It is important to help existing small establishments even if they are not competitive. But it is a mistake to make such enterprises the major focus of a government effort. Instead, if indigenous persons are to play a significant role in American economic life, they must own and operate automobile dealerships, shopping centers, small and medium-sized manufacturing companies, and the like, and mechanisms must be established which will start a continuing process to create and maintain significant numbers of larger enterprises.

Third, existing programs have generally lacked expertise. They have rarely had the full-time participation of trained staffs with business experience. Minority and poverty area citizens must know when and how to get assistance, both from the government and private industry. They must be able to understand and put together complicated financial arrangements, and be able to communicate with other businessmen.

I therefore propose that a minimum of $10 million a year be appropriated to provide federal grants for local technical assistance programs. These programs should enlist the combined efforts of business leaders, local government, and other important elements in the community, with substantial participation and control by the leaders of minority groups and poverty-area residents they are to serve.

At the same time, these programs must have on their staffs full-time business experts. As our large corporations become increasingly interested in meeting the problems of poverty, they may be willing to lend some of their best talent. All programs should include at least these elements:

　　—*They must reach out* to members of minority groups
　　and residents of poverty areas to motivate them to

enter business or to expand and improve existing businesses.

—*They must help open up* new business opportunities—for example, by creating a committee of large corporations committed to providing sub-contracts; by helping businessmen obtain contracts from the federal and local governments; by obtaining franchises to be operated by minority and poverty-area businessmen; by starting shopping centers in urban renewal and model cities areas; and by persuading urban renewal and other government agencies to contract with poverty area contractors to build and rehabilitate housing.

—*They must provide sources of capital*—for example, by starting Small Business Investment Companies to provide equity and working capital, perhaps by seeking funds in the community; by starting Local Development Companies to provide the physical facilities and land needed by new businesses; by persuading private financial institutions to ease credit criteria for business or to provide loan pools; by assisting minority or poverty-area businessmen to obtain loans from private financial institutions, SBA, or EDA and through the new program which I have proposed today.

—*They must provide continuing training, counseling and assistance*—for example, by persuading established corporations to offer internships in their own marketing, accounting, cost control or other departments prior to receiving subcontracts from assisted companies; by persuading established corporations to give continued technical assistance through having their own staffs on call by minority or poverty-area businessmen; by asking local colleges or other institutions to give special business courses; by giving individual counseling to existing and potential businessmen; by providing contracts to management consulting companies to assist minority and poverty-area businessmen.

The federal government should also be making other efforts to provide management and ownership assistance to members of minority groups and residents of poverty areas. Plans to aid small business should be required in all model city plans. The Department of Labor can pay private corporations to provide training and technical assistance to existing and potential minority and poverty-area businessmen as it now provides funds to corporations to train the unemployed. The Office of Education can develop special programs to provide high-quality management training through scholarships to business schools and through special business school courses. Federal funds can pay for research into new techniques for assisting minority and poverty-area businessmen. And the federal government can coordinate and assist the efforts of local programs.

It is of vital importance that the federal government involve our national corporations in this effort. They can provide training, subcontracts and franchises, loans or equity capital, and technical assistance. They can, as the Fairchild-Hillyer Corporation has in the District of Columbia, start manufacturing plants, jointly owned with a neighborhood organization in a poverty area, with the objective of completely turning it over to the community in just a few years. National corporations can, as they have agreed to do in Baltimore, provide financial support for a small business investment company controlled by Negroes. All this can occur throughout the country by joining the dedicated efforts of business and government.

These proposals will require appropriations of only $43 million the first year and $337 million over five years for interest subsidies and technical assistance. In addition, $1 billion will be required for the New Fund over five years to provide direct federal loans and as a reserve for guaranteeing private loans, but these funds will be recoverable by the federal government. It is a reasonable estimate that these measures will result in the loan of about $3 billion dollars by private lenders and the federal government to all kinds of businesses in or near poverty areas and for the establishment of many successful businesses owned by members of minority groups and residents of poverty areas.

These loan and technical assistance proposals and my tax incentive program proposed last July will not, of course, solve all the problems of poverty. They are important steps. They will offer a mechanism for bringing new business and jobs into our poorest areas.

But they are but one part of the job we must begin. They must be joined with other equally important efforts.

They must be combined and coordinated with present federal education and manpower training programs. They must also be used in conjunction with other new programs which I have proposed and sponsored in the Senate—an emergency employment program to provide 2.4 million new jobs in public service and private enterprise and the housing program which I sponsored in 1967 to give tax incentives to private industry to build and rehabilitate housing for low income families.

For Release
Friday, May 31, 1968

A Program for the Urban Crisis

Statement of Senator Robert F. Kennedy

The next administration will face no problem more serious than the crisis in America's cities.

Rioting and violence have scarred our cities for four consecutive summers. Centuries of deprivation and discrimination have ripened into frustration and bitterness, which have in turn exploded into violence and looting. Men and women and children have died. Hundreds of millions of dollars' worth of property have been destroyed. Innocent people have suffered—families left homeless, policemen and firemen injured, businessmen burned out. Countless Americans now live in fear that it will happen again, in their communities, this time affecting them.

At the moment, with few exceptions, our cities are quiet. Many who expressed concern—even a commitment to act—seem to have resumed their daily routine.

But the slums are still there, now scarred a little more by the burning. Joblessness, rat-infested, over-crowded housing, schools which nurture drop-outs, a welfare system which forces fathers to leave home, the eight-hour wait in the hospital emergency room, the litter and the garbage—these are all still there.

And there can be no doubt of the seriousness of these conditions:

—In the typical big city ghetto, barely three adult men out of five have any work at all. Only two out of five earn $60 a week or more.

—In our urban slums as few as 30 percent finish high school—and those that do, stand no better than a 50-50 chance of having the equivalent of an 8th-grade education.

—An infant born to a Negro ghetto family is three times as likely to die in his first year of life. He has as much chance to live to age 20 as a white man has of living to 40. He and his parents and brothers and sisters, along with 40 per cent of those whose skin is black live in dilapidated, deteriorated housing, often without plumbing, more often than not infested with rats that bit as many as a quarter of a million people last year.

—When he is old enough to walk in the streets, he will be among the 1/3 of all Americans who now fear to walk alone at night in the streets of their own neighborhood, for he will be 3½ times more likely to be robbed and his sister 3¼ times more likely to be raped as the average person.

—And he may be among the 14 to 15 million Americans who go to school without breakfast or to bed hungry every night.

These are cold, hard facts. But they are merely statistics. They do not reflect the feeling of the hopelessness, the resentment, the distant look on a hungry face.

These conditions are still there.

And they will be there next summer and the summers after that unless we admit to ourselves that we can no longer afford to do business as usual—unless we have the will to make the sacrifices and commit the resources to do what is necessary.

But what shall we do? How are we to commit our resources?

Clearly, we must contain the violence whenever and wherever it breaks out. A violent few cannot be permitted to threaten the well-being of the many, and the hopes of their neighbors for progress. Those who lead others to burn and loot must feel the full force of the law. But the full force of the law means just that: the swift apprehension and punishment of lawbreakers. It does not mean senseless and unnecessary killing by those who act in the name of government.

But what are we to do before the violence begins? If business as usual will not do, what new direction are we to take? One possibility: we can pass repressive laws and provide a constant show of force, an occupying army which keeps the peace. That, however, would be a curious America indeed—a fortress America divided into armed camps, with harassment and denial of fundamental liberties a way of life for millions, an America where freedom and justice for all had become empty words, discarded slogans, things of the past.

I do not believe that is what the citizens of this nation want.

But, we must face the facts. If we reject repression as abhorrent to our most fundamental values, there is only one other path to take, only one other way to build an America that is safe and secure and full of opportunity. That is to act, with imagination and dedication, with wisdom and courage, to root out and eradicate the real agitators, the real causes of the violence: the festering conditions which have become synonymous with life itself for too many Americans.

Despair and sorrow and resentment can no longer be attacked with thoughts and words. We have already made too many empty promises. We are long overdue for action—swift action—just action—specific and comprehensive action.

The action we take must be based upon the following general propositions:

First, we must be willing to work together—black and white, government and private enterprise, clergy and concerned citizens—with all the energy and commitment that it is humanly possible to muster. Government alone cannot--and in a responsible society, should not—carry the sole responsibility. Not only would the cost be great, but the achievement of communication and dialogue between black and white demands the participation and involvement of concerned citizens, community organizations, foundations, and the business community.

Second, action on any one front alone will not succeed. Providing a man a job, while in my judgment the most important step we can take, will not improve the schools his children attend or assure that medical care will be available even though he can afford it. Building new housing without providing social services or transportation to get to work or accessible health services will result in one slum replacing another. Improving the quality of education or job training without any promise of a job at the end will not ease the drop-out rate. But action on all these matters in concert will build a community.

Third, residents themselves must participate in the development and implementation of local projects. The community itself must take the leadership, through resident-controlled institutions, in its own building process.

Fourth, as I have stated on many occasions in the past, no program to attack the problems of the inner city can be conducted in the isolation of the ghetto. Our efforts in urban America must be combined with programs to create opportunity for the poor on the farms and in small towns and suburban communities. Jobs, education, health care, housing—all must be provided for the poor wherever they live or want to live. Only through this kind of effort in all areas can we make it possible for both urban and rural disadvantaged Americans to live and work where they and their families wish.

At the same time, however, it must be understood that the building of a truly integrated society depends on the development of economic self-sufficiency and security in the communities of poverty, for only then will the residents of these areas have the wherewithal to move freely within the society. Those who speak of ending the colonialism of the ghetto must therefore recognize that the economic and social development of that community is at the heart of any policy of creating full mobility.

With these principles in mind, we must have a program —a program for rebuilding human lives.

The proposals outlined in this statement are specific and concrete. They are proposals which I have made before and in detail both in the United States Senate and during my campaign for the Presidency.

They are not general propositions or slogans or vague goals or new civil rights. They are part of a strategy for performance and for fulfilling the promises which we have made, but which, tragically, we have not kept.

I. *Employment*

Our first priority for action is to provide jobs for the unemployed and underemployed.

The Kerner Commission estimated that 1,034,000 non-white Americans in the poverty areas of our 50 largest cities are either unemployed or work at less than a living wage. The President's Manpower Report reveals that 750,000 men and women who want to work are not even counted on our unemployment rolls. They have given up looking for jobs that simply do not exist. Other analyses show that we have a job gap of 2½ million—the difference between the number of people (4½ million) who want to work and the number of existing job vacancies across the country.

Our goal must be to guarantee a job and guarantee training for every American who wants to work and for every American who is able to work at a better job.

We must achieve this goal through:

1. *An Emergency Employment Program*

I have co-sponsored in the Senate a program which would provide 2.4 million jobs in public and private employment in the next four years. It will help close the job gap by creating 1.2 million jobs in public service occupations—building and staffing our schools, hospitals, libraries, neighborhood health clinics, and municipal service agencies. It will employ people in community rehabilitation projects, rebuilding their own and their neighborhood homes, parks, and playgrounds and engaging in other tasks necessary to make our cities better places to live. At the same time this program will train people while they work so they can move up career ladders and into related private employment.

2. A Special Impact Program

This program, which I sponsored and which was enacted as part of the Economic Opportunity Act in 1966, channels direct federal aid into areas of especially high poverty concentration, focusing upon economic and community development projects coupled with manpower training activities. Although it has been authorized and funded by Congress for two years, the Administration has opposed the program and has spent most of the funds appropriated on other manpower activities. This program should be fully funded and implemented for the purposes envisioned by Congress. Its success has already been demonstrated in New York City's Bedford-Stuyvesant project, the only place where special-impact funds have been spent for the purposes envisioned.

In this project, which *Newsweek* Magazine has called "the most sweeping and comprehensive rehabilitation effort ever brought to bear on a single American community," community residents have worked out their own programs for jobs, housing rehabilitation and educational and cultural advancement, with financial and technical assistance furnished by government and by leading private citizens and business corporations.

3. A Business Development Program

This program was set forth last week in my detailed policy statement: "A Business Development Program for Our Poverty Areas." This three-part program is designed to create an economic climate in which businesses, especially those owned by members of disadvantaged minority groups and residents of poverty areas, will be able to establish new facilities and expand existing facilities in the centers of our cities, creating new jobs for the unemployed and underemployed.

First, it would, under legislation which I introduced last July, provide tax incentives, in the form of credits and deductions, for businesses located in poverty areas which employ and train at least 20 new persons, ⅔ of whom are low-income and unemployed persons.

Second, it would make long and short term credit available to any industrial or commercial enterprise including those owned by members of minority groups and poverty-area residents, opening a new business or expanding an existing facility having nine or more employees, ⅔ of whom are poverty area residents. Loans would be made available from private lenders and the federal government, with federal interest subsidies and repayment guarantees.

These proposals offer a mechanism for bringing new business and jobs into our poorest areas.

4. *Adult Education and Training Programs*

New jobs for the unemployed must be created, but at the same time we must upgrade our present work force. Current federal manpower programs are virtually closed to those already employed—even though their skills and energies may be far from fully used.

To upgrade our present work force and open up new opportunities for those already employed:

—New programs must be established to make it possible for those now in the labor force to return to school, continuing through college and beyond. The vast resources of this nation—in government, in union pension funds, in insurance companies—are sufficient to support a loan program to provide full maintenance for workers and their families while they return to school. Their further education would help to fill great needs in the technical and most highly-skilled occupations. It would also open opportunities for others to move up the ladder into the places vacated by those who go on to higher education.

—Other workers now employed must be given wider opportunities to participate in training and education programs. Special programs should be developed to enable workers to retain their present jobs while preparing for better ones.

—We must expand adult education opportunities for

all. Basic education is the key to life for millions of adults who are functionally illiterate—but present programs reach only 3 percent of those who need them. And for those now employed, intensive remedial education may be necessary if they are to have real opportunities for better jobs and higher education.

5. *The Mobility of Our Labor Force*

Workers should be encouraged to seek employment wherever the most promising opportunities occur. Yet, it is in the ghetto where jobs are needed most, while it is in the suburbs where most new employment opportunities are now opening up. We must develop new jobs in the city but, at the same time, enable city dwellers to fill jobs in industrial parks and commercial centers in the suburbs. This will require that special transportation be made available. We must help employers and municipal transportation systems design and furnish commuter services in reverse.

But labor mobility must be statewide and nationwide as well as citywide. We should enable workers to establish themselves in new communities where better jobs are available by gradually eliminating the penalties they now suffer when they change jobs by making pension rights more flexible, so that a worker does not lose the benefits of his labor when he seeks a new chance elsewhere; and by assisting in the problems a family encounters in moving to and getting established in a new community.

6. *Consolidating Federal, State and Local Manpower Activities*

Responsibility for present job-training and vocational education programs is spread among a multitude of federal departments and bureaus and in turn channeled through so many state and local agencies that it is impossible for those whom the programs are supposed to benefit and at best difficult for local administrators to know what funds are available in which programs or determine what is best for the individual.

We should work toward the consolidation of vocational educational and rehabilitation programs, manpower and development programs, and the programs for youth and adults under the Economic Opportunity Act. Eventually, these programs should be administered under one roof in Washington so that states and local communities will not have to deal with a bewildering and complex bureaucracy, itself so scattered among dozens of departments, agencies and bureaus that they themselves are often unaware of what their government competitors are doing.

At the same time, state and local manpower authorities should be encouraged to consolidate their efforts so that one-stop manpower services centers are available in every urban neighborhood and rural town. These centers should have trained counselors and placement officers, and access to a national network of computer technology, able to give a job seeker information on job openings anywhere in the United States.

7. Reform of the Welfare System

There are now over 5.2 million people receiving federal aid to dependent children, an increase of 700,000 in the last ten months. In 1967, the national bill for public assistance was nearly $5.5 billion: over $3 billion from the federal government and nearly $2.5 billion from state and local governments and the bill has risen since. Of the nation's total welfare budget, $1 billion is spent in New York and an equal amount in California. And these totals will rise again as more and more poor people leave farms and dying small towns all over the country.

The proposals I have outlined will create new jobs and open up existing job opportunities for the unemployed and underemployed generally. But specifically, they will provide the answer to the welfare crisis. That answer, as I stated in a policy statement on May 19, is work, jobs, self-sufficiency and family integrity; not a massive new extension of welfare; not a great new outpouring of guidance counselors to give the poor more advice. We need jobs, dignified employment at a decent pay.

Having moved toward real employment, we must also move toward an adequate system of assistance for those who cannot work. That system must, as I have proposed, be automatic, be based solely on need, have national minimum standards, and contain incentives to work for those who become able to work.

II. *Housing*

According to the Kerner Commission, housing is one of the three most intense grievances of Negroes and a major cause of discontent in cities which have had disturbances. Two thirds of nonwhite families in our large cities "live in neighborhoods marked by substandard housing and urban blight." In these neighborhoods often half the housing is dilapidated and without adequate plumbing. And conditions have not improved in recent years. In fact, surveys in New York and Watts show an increase in occupied housing units.

The Senate last week passed a housing bill which is a first step but which fails to include a system of tax incentives for private industry which I believe to be the most promising method for providing low-cost housing in our ghettos. The bill which I introduced last year should be enacted: It would provide that in return for a low-interest, long term loan, an investor would agree to build or rehabilitate a certain number of units, to be rented to low-income families. The investor would gain a 3 percent return on his base equity—but he would also receive a tax credit and accelerated depreciation, both geared to the size of his initial investment, and thus he would have a return of 12-15 percent on his initial investment. Such a program—with federal standards, local approval, and participation and power in the hands of residents themselves—would produce great multiple benefits—taking the burden off the shoulders of the federal government, providing industry with a new source of profit, and housing the poor in a way which strengthens, not weakens, their own stake in society.

The aim of any housing program must be home ownership. My tax incentive bill provides extra benefits to encourage private developers to turn apartment ownership over to the tenants after an appropriate period. Further, I suggest that our public housing which now expels those whose incomes rise, begin to permit purchase of these units—thus rewarding tenants who achieve success instead of punishing them. Moreover, this home ownership feature should also be extended to moderate income families—those who earn between $4000 and $9000 a year—who now receive help in renting apartments, but not in achieving genuine home ownership.

We must also make good on our promises to cut down the enormous red tape and delay which has repeatedly slowed the construction of federal housing. Until a few months ago, it took up to two years to process moderate income housing projects—often long enough to render original cost estimates wholly inaccurate. This delay has in large part discouraged construction firms and architects from participation—and instead of the 60,000 units we were promised, we have built only 12,000 a year. There are promising alternatives to this obstruction, particularly in the "turnkey" projects—where private industry builds the housing with a minimum of pre-construction delay and turns it over for public use.

Most important, federal programs must promote maximum local participation and control. We must end the sense of frustration and impotence so many of these projects spawn, and replace it with a sense of community pride, as we have done in Bedford-Stuyvesant. We can, for example, channel federal funds into community-wide non-profit corporations, so that residents of neighborhoods themselves can plan and develop not just where they shall live, but how—and plan for the schools, parks and facilities that our programs in the past have too often ignored.

Finally, we should actively work to encourage job training and employment in the construction industry. Nothing would link the jobless more closely with their own community than the chance to enjoy productive labor in the rebuilding of their own neighborhoods.

III. *Education*

At a time when there are 2 million disadvantaged children between the ages of three and five, we reach only one out of ten with full-time headstart programs. Of the

600,000 high school students who could benefit from counseling and special training to go on to higher education, we reach only one of twenty with the Upward Bound program. And of those who gained little or nothing from our schools in the past—the 163 million adult Americans without an eighth grade education—we are reaching only one in forty. We must act to improve the quality of American education.

The federal government must fulfill its own promise to help states and local communities with the special expenses and problems in educating the disadvantaged. Over the last three years, a major and welcome effort has been made to meet our most critical educational needs. But now, in the wake of a $50 billion war, that effort is faltering; in our Title I Elementary and Secondary Education program—our most fundamental effort to help the children of poverty help themselves—we are spending less money for each child than we did two years ago.

—We must understand that federal funds cannot merely subsidize inefficient, ineffective education. Federal aid should be accompanied by more effective measurement, through testing and otherwise, of what our educational programs are accomplishing—measurement like that required in my amendment to the Elementary and Secondary Education Act of 1965.

—We must build new education systems, that genuinely reach and stimulate students. We need increased emphasis on educational research and development—which now represents less than ½ of 1 percent of all our national education spending. This kind of assistance which has won so many important breakthroughs in defense and space projects—can now begin to encourage new kinds of teaching methods, with new kinds of techniques, personnel and equipment.

—We must create experimental elementary and secondary schools not run by traditional administrative methods—competitive schools—both as a means of encouraging innovation and as a yardstick for measuring the effectiveness of our schools.

—We must begin to involve the community in our educational efforts. Too often—and particularly in poverty areas—the schools have become divorced from the needs and wishes of the parents and residents of communities. I think we can remedy this by bringing the school back to the community, and by bringing the community into the school. We can, for example, expand our efforts in adult education, developing after-class facilities for the parents of school children to increase their own education. We can use local neighborhood residents as classroom and playground aides. We can link job-training and health facilities to the school—so that education becomes a continuing process, and a help to the entire community. And we can help the schools become full-time centers of community activity—not just educational activities, but health care, employment, cultural, social and recreational activity as well.

—We must involve students in the important and relevant work of their communities—for example, by expanding the Work-Study programs, so that a student might alternate between classroom study and private employment—and thus earn for his higher education, learn a job skill, and continue to attend college, all at the same time. This kind of effort perhaps extended to high school students, would make a natural alliance between school and community—and improve both at the same time.

Finally, we must recognize the vital and changing role of the teacher in this process. We must understand—at long last—that teachers are professionals, who deserve the status and earnings of professionals. Moreover, we must honor this professionalism by permitting the teachers themselves to play an authentic role in determining educational policy. This right, however, is a two-way street. For it also imposes a great responsibility on the teacher: to reach across barriers of generations and background, to understand the world of the child, and to make what is taught relevant to what the child has already learned—in his home, among his friends, in his community.

IV. *Health Care*

Thirty percent of all American families with less than $2,000 income suffer from chronic health deficiencies. Life expectancy at birth is nearly seven years lower for the non-white than for the white child. Maternal mortality rates for the non-white mothers are four times as high as those for white mothers.

These conditions are aggravated by environmental factors which create a particularly low level of sanitation in our poverty areas: poor garbage collection, rats, lack of proper food storage facilities, lack of plumbing.

We have provided health care for our elderly through Medicare and Medicaid. But we have failed in our commitment to health care for the poor. To fulfill that commitment:

—First, we must put medical resources we now have to work more effectively within the community—and that means, in part, decentralizing health care with federal assistance under the poverty program, pioneering efforts by medical schools and community organizations which have already begun establishing neighborhood health centers staffed by health aides as well as doctors—which provide comprehensive family care in a dignified setting, close to areas of great need. Now we should further encourage this kind of effort by aiding the construction of neighborhood centers and "satellite clinics" with federal funds. For we may well find that such operations help not just the poor—but provide a model for development within affluent suburbs, where effective nearby health care is becoming increasingly difficult to find.

—Second, we must tap new sources of recruitment into the medical field, and develop new health careers for those we do recruit. The shortage of medical personnel is too clear to need lengthy discussion. We are graduating 8,000 doctors a year—2,000 less than we need just to keep up with the already inadequate standards. We have doubled the number of graduating nurses—yet we are still 150,000 short and that shortage is going to worsen. The answer, in my judgment, is to recognize what army and civilian experience has taught us: that sub-professionals can dispense a wide variety of simple medical care. We should begin to channel federal funds into programs which hire and train sub-professional health aides—putting them to work particularly in those urban and rural communities where health care is now most lacking. And we may well find that these aides can be trained for more demanding and rewarding jobs—including eventual training as physicians and nurses—thus helping themselves as they help all of us.

—Third, we must assist in the construction of hundreds of new hospitals and clinics, and medical schools to help all the people of America. Increased assistance for medical schools must involve incentives for those institutions to expand, recruit more minority group students, and involve themselves more extensively in the community.

—Fourth, while we improve health care, we must also improve the conditions which lead to poor health. All of our efforts to combat cancer may be—as one noted doctor has put it—less important than the single step of reducing the number of children who become cigarette smokers. All our programs to train new doctors may not mean as much to the health of our city as forceful action to eliminate the pollution of our air. All our emergency rooms will not ease the pain of auto accident victims as much as effective controls on unsafe drivers and unsafe cars.

V. *The Protection of Our Citizens*

There are those who call the poverty areas in our cities "jungles" and refer to them as "brutal societies" which may "annex the affluent suburbs." But the serious and accelerating problem of crime will not be reduced by preying on the legitimate fears of those who are justifiably afraid to walk the streets at night. Over the long run it will be reduced by the building of a society in which people do not want to and do not feel the need to violate the law—a society where equal opportunity for all is a reality, a society where self-respect and self-esteem are not commodities reserved for the economically advantaged.

But effective law enforcement is also critical.

We need a serious program to deal with the problems of crime through effective law enforcement—not a program of trial by confession which presumes guilt from the mere fact of arrest.

First, we must treat our police like the professionals they are. We place our lives and our homes in their hands, yet we pay them disgracefully low salaries and force them to moonlight. We expect them to expose their lives to danger in our behalf, yet we leave their families without adequate life insurance protection. We require them to make split second judgments on legal, social and moral questions, yet we do not provide them with enough up to date education and training opportunities. All this must be remedied. We must provide salary increases, life insurance, education and training for our police—and we can do so through the combination of state and local initiative with federal encouragement and support.

Second, we must bring law enforcement techniques out of the era of the whistle and the nightstick and into the 20th century. Through local experimentation and testing, and through the work of a National Institute of Criminal Justice, we can determine how modern science and technology can best be applied to law enforcement problems, and we can help local police forces apply this knowledge to their activities.

Third, we must apply modern technology especially to find effective force which does not maim or kill. There are too many situations—whether in the midst of mass disturbances or on a lonely street on a dark night—in which police are now faced with the choice between the use of deadly force, which may be out of all proportion to the offense committed, and doing nothing at all. Surely advance research, properly supported by the federal government can develop incapacitating agents which bring more offenders to trial—and assure that all offenders do have a trial.

Fourth, we must focus our efforts on reducing the single biggest source of crime—recidivism. A convicted offender is a prime candidate for future crimes; but by the same token he is a prime candidate for the prevention of future crimes. In most parts of the country the average parole and probation officer has more offenders to handle than he can possibly keep track of, let alone help to rehabilitate. The answer lies not just in more money—it lies in training more correctional and parole and probation officers; it lies in fitting the rehabilitation program to the offender; it lies in a criminal justice system which has the time and the capacity to do the job right.

Fifth, we must take major new steps to prevent crime before it happens—by keeping young people from turning into criminal offenders. Half the serious offenses in the United States—ranging from murder to auto theft—are committed by young men and women aged 17 or less. Many, perhaps the great majority of these young people, commit relatively minor offenses before they engage in serious criminal activity. I propose that the states with federal assistance create half-way houses in which non-serious young offenders could receive supervision, training, and education, in their own communities before they are caught up in the vicious atmosphere of adult prisons.

Sixth, we have to make new and vigorous efforts against organized crime. The techniques for dealing with organized crime are no longer novel. They require only greater application and effort. We can make that effort at the federal level and I urge all state and local governments to make a similar effort.

Finally, in each of these areas, and over all the country, is the need for citizen support for local law enforcement. This means voting for the funds to pay our police the salaries they deserve. It means reporting crimes, taking the witness stand, serving on juries. It means participating in anti-delinquency programs, giving jobs to released offenders, and volunteering to act as probation advisers. It means ending citizen participation in the activities which nourish organized crime—in gambling, prostitution, and petty corruption. We also need real efforts to create two-way communications and understanding between the police and the community, especially poor and minority neighborhoods. For the people of these neighborhoods suffer most from the curse of crime—they need protection most, and they can least afford the burden of crime. They want to cooperate with the police, and this cooperation can be strengthened if our police forces are integrated, if they have sub-stations in the ghetto, if they listen to what the communities have to say.

* * * * * * * * * *

This is not a program to reward burning and looting. It is not a program to buy off further violence. It is a program to rebuild, maintain and protect human lives. It is a program to save our nation from a mounting and ever more demanding cycle of hate and fear, and ultimately to make our nation fulfill the promise of its founders. It is a program which will provide the best means to assure that America does not, as some suggest it will, become "an armed camp of 200 million Americans living in fear."

Bibliography

Kennedy, Robert F., *The Enemy Within*. New York, Harper & Row, Publishers, 1960.

―――――, *Just Friends and Brave Enemies*. New York, Harper & Row, Publishers, 1962.

―――――, *The Pursuit of Justice*. New York, Harper & Row, Publishers, 1964.

Shannon, William, *The Heir Apparent*. New York, The Macmillan Company, 1967.

Thommesch, Nick and Johnson, William, *Robert Kennedy at 40*. New York, W.W. Norton & Company, Inc., 1965.

Thompson & Meyers, *Robert F. Kennedy: The Brother Within*. New York, The Macmillan Company, 1962.

White, Theodore H., *The Making of The President 1960*. New York, Atheneum Publishers, 1961.

Index